THE TRANS GENERATION

The Trans Generation

How Trans Kids (and Their Parents)
Are Creating a Gender Revolution

Ann Travers

NEW YORK UNIVERSITY PRESS

New York

NEW YORK UNIVERSITY PRESS
New York
www.nyupress.org

© 2018 by New York University
All rights reserved

Library of Congress Cataloging-in-Publication Data
Names: Travers, Ann, author.
Title: The trans generation : how trans kids (and their parents) are creating a gender revolution / Ann Travers.
Description: New York : New York University Press, [2018] | Includes bibliographical references and index.
Identifiers: LCCN 2017054995 | ISBN 9781479885794 (cl : alk. paper)
Subjects: LCSH: Transgender children. | Parents of transgender children. | Transgender people—Identity. | Gender identity—Law and legislation.
Classification: LCC HQ77.9 .T71525 2018 | DDC 306.76/8—dc23
LC record available at https://lccn.loc.gov/2017054995

To every kid and every parent that I interviewed:
Thank you. You are the beating heart of this book.

CONTENTS

Introduction

People know what they do; frequently they know why they
do what they do; but what they don't know is what what they
do does.
—Michel Foucault

February 17, 1962: Toronto, Ontario. In the hospital, the doctor, in the
usual way, tells my unwed mother, "It's a girl." Fifty-five years later, I
bear both the psychological scars of the effects of the branding of me as
a girl and eventual woman and the wrenching separation from my birth
mother. In the story I tell about myself, I am unable to separate the sex
assignment imposed on me from the sexism and misogyny that were my
due as a girl or from the gender policing and homo-hatred I received for
not being very good at it. Nor, for that matter, can I untangle the privilege of my whiteness and relative wealth from the patriarchal burden of
shame imposed on unwed mothers and their offspring and my own bad
luck in the adoption game. I come from all these things. These social
forces are real; they shape opportunities unequally. I am all these things
and more.

My daughter and I recently discussed the lack of agency that children
typically experience: most kids do not have much say in many things,
and all have absolutely no control over how they come into this world
(out of whose body, in what place and time) or typically who raises them
and how. We are all born into systems of power and privilege, and this
concept of the "sociological imagination," as C. Wright Mills famously
coined it, has a significant impact on our life chances and choices. Our
biographies are shaped by our lived experience in specific geopolitical and historical moments. Context is not everything, but it certainly
counts for a lot.

Being called a "boy" or a "girl" and assigned correspondingly gendered names and pronouns are two of the many dimensions of power

that adults exercise over children and that shape how they experience the world. For the most part, this power is taken for granted—so much so that in 2011, a Toronto couple's decision to keep the specifics of their child's genitals private, coupled with a gender-neutral name, Storm, generated heated media and online commentary that signaled a deeply rooted belief in the appropriateness of adults imposing sex categories on children.[1] Parents are expected to do gender work with their children properly. Some, such as Storm's parents, Rogue Witterick and David Stocker, make efforts to resist sex stereotyping by choosing gender-neutral names and resisting the efforts of others to assign gendered clothing, characteristics, and activities to their children on the basis of their assigned birth sex; but the binary sex system is so pervasive that most children succumb, and those who do not typically struggle for support.

I define "transgender" in a broad and historical sense to include people who "defy societal expectations regarding gender." Trans activist Julia Serano notes that "not everyone who falls under this umbrella will self identify as 'transgender,' but all are viewed by society as defying gender norms in some significant way."[2] While Serano and others distinguish between those who are transsexual—individuals who transition from their assigned sex to their affirmed sex—and those who are transgender, the issue of terminology is complicated because individuals understandably have very strong feelings about how they identify. I use the term "transgender" and its shorthand, "trans," interchangeably to speak in very general terms about kids who defy gender norms, but I choose each person's own language to describe them specifically.

I have been traveling in ethnographically rich circles, both socially and as a researcher, offline and online, formal and informal, with transgender kids and their families for over seven years. This book is fairly unique in that I rely on the direct reports of trans kids and their parents to map in time and space the ways in which they are disabled[3] by environments that rely on naturalized binary gender systems. Relying on parents to report the experiences of children and young people is inherently problematic,[4] and I address this limitation by including the voices of a number of trans kids themselves, who describe their experiences in their own words. Doing this is particularly important because, as critical childhood studies scholar James Marten observes, "children may be among the least articulate of all members of society. By the time they are fully literate and aware of the possibilities and challenges posed by their surroundings, they are hardly children at all. And they are, it goes without saying, literally without political power. As a result, it is very difficult to get at their point of view, and most treatments examine institutions, ideas, or policies that shape the lives of children rather than flesh-and-blood youngsters."[5]

Children do have strong feelings about their gender identities, so I draw on the embodied experience—"the suffering"[6]—of my participants in navigating the gendered spaces that disable them as well as the pleasure and empowerment they experience in resisting the dominant narratives that restrict their sex/gender identities and expression. But the perspectives of parents, while not synonymous with those of their children, are very important because they are typically their children's primary adult attachment, and it is parents who most often advocate on their behalf.

For the purposes of this book, "childhood" is defined as an institutionalized stage of life from birth to the "age of majority" (which varies from jurisdiction to jurisdiction across Canada and the United States from 18 to 21 years of age). In discussing the experiences of specific young people, this text uses the term "children" to refer to those 15 years of age and younger, "youth" to refer to those between the ages of 16 and 21, and "kids" to speak more generally about people 18 and under.

My research confirms that trans kids resist the very names and pronouns associated with the sex category that has been assigned to them at birth, which puts them in potential conflict with families, peers, school and sports/recreational institutions and programs, healthcare systems, juvenile justice systems, organizations that provide social support, and work environments. All children do gender work, but the gender work that trans kids do to resist the sex/gender identity assigned to them is particularly powerful in its ability to make the social construction and imposition of binary sex and gender systems more visible. The experiences of trans kids also throw into sharp relief the extensive labor that the people in their environments engage in to impose and naturalize cisgender binary categorization.

Many of the trans kids in my study regularly experience crisis as a result of the restrictive ways in which sex categories regulate their daily lives and put pressure on them to deny their internal sense of who they are in gendered terms. Critical trans activist and legal scholar Dean Spade identifies government identity documents, bathrooms, and sex-segregated facilities as key points of vulnerability and insecurity for trans people,[7] but relationships with sex-defined peers, sex-segregated/sex-differentiated activities and spaces, gender-coded clothing and hairstyles, pronouns and names, access to healthcare, and gender policing by adults and peers also play a significant role. This perspective is reflected in the experiences of many of the kids and parents I spoke with.

In my own life, when I have called sexist assumptions about fundamental male-female difference into question or attempted to interrupt them, as my three children and I navigate the everyday spaces of the daycare, the birthday party, the playground, the classroom, sports and recreation, and so on, I have often been made to feel like a deluded heretic. Parents and caregivers routinely present me with "evidence" that their children's cisgender conformity is fundamental to their nature rather than environmentally mediated. My efforts to provide more, rather than less, gender-neutral space for all kids is intended to redistribute power: to open up options for kids' own gender self-determination, to reverse the privilege that masculinity and male bodies enjoy over femininity and female bodies, and to influence the circulation of cultural and material resources in more equitable ways.

As educational scholar Mark Hellen observes, the majority of transgender children and youth are "non-apparent";[8] the lack of acceptance of gender diversity in their environments leads many to keep themselves hidden. Most trans kids who lack parental acceptance and support and/or appropriate healthcare either adapt to pressure or are driven underground. This is the self-perpetuating logic of "the Thomas Theorem,"[9] whereby "situations that are defined as real become real in their consequences."[10] On the other hand, however, visible trans kids are at higher risk of discrimination and violence. Ultimately, both those who are visible and those who are invisible are vulnerable to high-risk behavior, self-harm, and suicide.

There have always been children who refuse their gender designation—and, truth be told, I was one of them—although most do so in silence. Since the mid-1990s, however, an increasing number of kids are finding it possible to openly resist the sex category assigned to them at birth and to identify themselves in unexpected ways. This agency has become possible as a result of adult transgender activism, the availability of information about LGBT people and identities via the Internet, and emerging social movements on behalf of transgender kids consisting of parents, therapeutic/medical providers, and trans people of all ages.[11] We now see trans kids circulating on TV talk shows, in social media posts, and in mainstream news headlines. This visibility both reflects and contributes to a cultural shift toward advocacy for greater gender openness in Canada and the United States. But cultural spaces of acceptance and support remain few and hard to come by. Trans kids need us to fight for them and along with them, whether they make themselves known to us or not.

In the past five years, some positive changes have come about in law and policy in various jurisdictions in Canada and the United States. In 2014, the province of British Columbia was the first in Canada to allow transgender people, including children, to change the gender marker on their birth certificates without having to undergo sex reassignment surgery. This development was a result of a case brought to the British Columbia Human Rights Tribunal on behalf of Harriette Cunningham, who was 11 years old at the time. "In 2013, with the help of her grandmother and human rights lawyer barbara findlay,[12] Harriette began petitioning local representatives to overturn legislation that required trans people to undergo reassignment surgery before changing the gender on their birth certificates. When Bill 17 passed in 2014, Harriette was the youngest of 30 British Columbians to receive their newly accurate identification."[13] Harriette subsequently appeared before the tribunal to argue for the elimination of gender markers on birth certificates altogether. This goal has yet to be achieved, although as of 2017, BC Care cards for provincial health insurance can now be obtained without a gender marker. In 2014, transgender 11-year-old Tru Wilson's parents launched a human rights complaint on her behalf against the Vancouver Area Catholic Diocese and achieved, via an out-of-court settlement, the desired policy change to recognize transgender girls and boys as their affirmed sex.[14] In March 2016, a human rights complaint between the parents of eight-year-old Bella Burgos and the River East Transcona School Division in Manitoba was resolved in favor of affirming transgender students, including access to washrooms and changing facilities according to their affirmed sex.[15] Similarly, Maine's highest court ruled in 2014 that a transgender student's rights were violated when her school forced her to use a staff bathroom rather than the girl's bathroom.[16] The passage of AB 1266 into law in California, signed by the governor on August 12, 2013, allows children "to participate in sex-segregated programs, activities and facilities," including on the basis of their affirmed gender rather than their birth sex.[17] Since 2004, many school boards on both sides of the border have adopted trans-inclusive policies.[18]

Other potential watershed cases were until recently before the courts, the most high profile being the American Civil Liberties Union's legal challenge on behalf of transgender boy Gavin Grimm's right to use the boys' washroom at his high school. When a lower court upheld Grimm's right to use the boys' washroom, the school district appealed to the U.S. Supreme Court. Many trans people and supporters hoped that this judicial body would establish a federal precedent in support of transgender rights. But a change in the political landscape from an Obama White House that voiced its intention to support transgender students to a Trump administration that included transgender students among its vulnerable targets sent the case back to the lower court, which, in light of the new administration in Washington, subsequently overturned its original decision and ruled against Grimm. A subsequent appeal of that decision appears to have been stalled by Grimm's June 2017 graduation from high school and, hence, his legal standing in the matter before the courts. Trans-oppressive attitudes are persistent in U.S. and Canadian culture and policy, and the increasingly sinister efforts by the Trump administration and many U.S. state governments to resist or roll back legal and policy gains on behalf of trans people indicate the extent to which trans kids remain marginalized and at risk.

As trans kids are a very vulnerable population, I have taken great pains to ensure their anonymity. For this reason, I locate them nationally only and provide very general markers related to their racialization. While this forecloses more nuanced analysis of individual cases with regard to the impact of specific forms of racialization and specific geographical contexts, it is a necessary measure. The threshold of anonymity I provide is such that individual transgender kids and/or their parents are not identifiable. However, communities consisting of transgender children and youth and/or their parents are often closely knit, and some of the stories I report on may be familiar to members of these networks.

Every region of the mainland United States and all regions of Canada with the exception of the Yukon and Nunavut are represented in my research. A greater number of voices participated in this study than are represented here. In two cases, as children aged from the time of the initial interview to a publication date three years later, parents withdrew their participation in order to let their children decide if and when to tell their own stories and out of the increased concern about their children's safety following the election of Donald Trump.

I interviewed 19 transgender kids and 23 parents of transgender kids in Canada and the United States between 2012 and 2017. My overall sample consists of the experiences (some told to me directly and some by their parents) of 36 kids. These kids live in various regions across Canada and the United States and range in age from four to 20. Most of the kids in my study come from middle-class families, but at least five are working class or living in poverty. Of these kids, 15 are Euro-Canadian or Euro-American, meaning they are racialized as white, while the remainder are racialized to some degree as nonwhite, 13 of them visibly so. Of the kids in my study who are racialized as nonwhite, five identify as Asian Canadian or Asian American, six as Black Canadian or Black American, six as Indigenous or Native American[19] to varying degrees, and one as Latinx.[20] I know of four of the kids who are adopted. Three kids live in nonurban areas. The gender identities that these kids affirm put them at odds with traditional notions of binary gender. These identities include gender nonconforming, transgender, trans nonbinary, male, female, boy, girl, trans boy, trans girl, gender neutral, and agender, and several kids require more than a few words to sum up their identities.[21] Wren (11, Black Canadian), for example, described herself this way: "I was born a boy, but I like being a girl."

Most of the trans kids and parents of trans kids whom I interviewed for this book were met through family gender conferences, Facebook networks for parents of transgender kids who are active in supporting their children, and chain referral sampling. Of the parents I interviewed, 19 were mothers (two of whom were partnered with women and five of whom were single parents), and four were fathers (one of whom was partnered with a man). In spite of active support by many of the fathers of trans children, emotional and support work on behalf of trans kids, like other familial emotional and support labor, remains highly feminized. Fathers are often deeply engaged with their kids in general and around their difficulties with trans oppression, but more often mothers negotiate daily challenges and are the spokespeople for the family. In many cases, in two-parent families, queer or straight, both parents attended meetings with school officials to seek accommodation for their kids. Because most of the parents interviewed were located via networks or organizations that support trans kids, the dominant narrative was one of revelation, adjustment, acceptance, and support through advocacy or activism.

I identify my participants by pseudonyms, age, racialization, and nation of residence. After serious deliberation, I decided not to indicate whether a particular participant was "designated male at birth" or "designated female at birth." Identifying my participants by the sex they were assigned at birth is an important way to render visible the power relations at play as sex/gender categories are imposed and the consequences for kids who resist. This analysis does emerge in many of the stories I share, but in describing my participants, I honor their self-definitions. I do so for two reasons: first, because of the way sex markers have been imposed on the kids in my study and how hard they, and often their parents, have had to work to resist this imposed marker; and second, because information about assigned sex satisfies a cis-sexist need to "know" who everyone "really is." In many ways, I think it is valuable to exclude this information entirely. The social disruption I am advocating for in this book can therefore be more fully experienced in the reading.

One of the experiences I have enjoyed the most in the work of this book has been the extent to which I often "forget" the sex category to which my participants were originally assigned: indeed, I rarely think of them in terms of genital variation at all. I find myself unable to remember who anyone "really is," in that trans-oppressive cultural way of needing to know the nature of a person's genitals in order to take them seriously as the gender they affirm. Far from experiencing this "forgetting" as problematic, I find it incredibly freeing, and it actually reflects my vision of a more gender-just future based on the trans-positive perspective that "gender is not genitals."[22] In writing this way, I have endeavored to model a much more open and less biologically deterministic way of enabling and respecting each person's right to determine their own gender. This is a transformative experience that I would like to see generalized. I acknowledge that the reader may find my failure to identify the assigned sex of my participants frustrating at times, and I hope it comes to be appreciated as a valuable aspect of the experience of reading the book.

An important dimension of gender self-determination involves the creation of new language to allow for a greater range of identities. The English language is less thoroughly gendered than are French and Spanish, for example, whereby objects and not just people have a gender, but English features explicitly gendered pronouns. In addition to emerging terminology to describe gender identities beyond the binary, new gender-neutral pronouns are being used by trans people of all ages, perhaps the most common being the replacement of "he/him/his" and "she/her/hers" with "they/them/theirs."[23] This is a challenging adjustment for adults, although, as some of my research indicates, young children not only seem to be more adaptable in this regard but often invent new language for themselves as needed. Stacey, mother of four-year-old Cassandra (Euro-Canadian), for example, described how children in one of her older daughter's classes asked after Cassandra by saying, "Where's your brother/sister?" In spite of my own increasing preference to be addressed using "they/them/their" pronouns, I struggle to get this right on behalf of others. Gendered pronouns are such an ingrained habit. To avoid misgendering[24] people as much as possible, I do a lot of background work: there are signs up in my office that say "they/them/theirs," and I have asked my family to refer to me with these pronouns, partly to explore adopting them myself but also to aid me in internalizing them.

I have been deeply affected by my interviews with trans kids and their parents. I intentionally conducted each interview as an act of emotionally invested social action research[25] in support of gender self-determination and reduced vulnerability for trans kids. My heart needed to be open, and I needed to be fully present to do this. As Stef (17, Euro-Asian Canadian) talked about what they had experienced in school (as a transgender girl starting at age five and as a gender-neutral person starting at age 14), for example, I responded by saying, "You have put up with a lot of shit!" To this, I received an emphatic "Yes!" Feeling deeply understood by a compassionate adult is important to children and youth and feeds their resilience. I remain aware of this need in all my interactions with the trans kids with whom I work. Supporting the authority of my participants with regard to their own gender identities is as important to me as it is to learn about who they are and how they are navigating their lives. Unlike traditional, and inaccurate, portrayals of science and academic research as being characterized by so-called objectivity and lack of invested interest, the social action model of research is explicitly designed to develop knowledge that can be used to fight oppression.

There are difficulties involved in writing about vulnerable populations for diverse audiences, and I have encountered these at several stages. There are considerable tensions and debates within trans communities about what is necessary for recognition, equality, and safety. It is a challenge to generate space for this critical analysis while keeping in mind the potential consequences for transgender kids.

The overall purpose of *The Trans Generation* is to make life better for transgender kids in particular and for all kids in general. My general argument in the book is that trans kids are incredibly vulnerable because of the way in which gender identities are imposed on children in general, with particularly negative consequences for trans kids. I document the ways in which unsupportive families, schools, healthcare programs and delivery mechanisms, bathroom facilities, and sports and physical recreation programs harm trans kids and the positive results that come with acceptance and support. A central piece of the book, a chapter titled "Parenting," documents the incredible time, energy, love, intelligence, and courage that supportive parents of trans kids devote to making it possible for their children—and trans kids in general—to show up as who they really are. A key argument of the book relates to how resources for this kind of support are unevenly distributed, particularly with regard to race and class. The theoretical framework I draw on for the book is based on the activism and scholarship of queer and trans scholars of color as it enables a more critical discussion of the lives of transgender kids.

I end the book by applying debates within queer and trans communities about reformist versus more radical social change programs and strategies to the matter of how best to empower transgender kids. I center the most precarious trans kids to argue against an either/or approach to these debates, insisting on the power and value of carefully leveraging rights discourse to achieve measures of immediate harm reduction within the context of a broader anti-oppression framework. The book concludes with the outline of a more comprehensive program for social change. As this book is intended for a mixed audience of academics, students, trans people of all ages, family members and friends of trans kids, and those who care for and work with kids, I provide a brief list of recommendations in Appendix A.

C. Wright Mills once said, "Neither the life of an individual nor the history of society can be understood without understanding both."[26] I hope that this book will contribute to an understanding of how oppressive contexts shape the lives of trans kids and how we can work together both to foster individual resilience and to generate widespread social change.

1

Transgender Kids

Whenever we are crossing the Canadian-U.S. border, my instructions to Wren—and her response—are always the same: "I will be calling you 'he.'" She always asks me why. We have had many discussions about this, and none of them have been satisfactory for either of us. But before we leave home each time, I insist that she refrain from wearing a skirt or a dress until we are across the border. (If we are driving, it's not unusual for us to pull into the nearest shopping-mall parking lot to enable her to "change back" into herself.) Most of the time, she and I are in solidarity in the face of the failure of others to understand who she is or to realize that the categories they impose upon her are contrived and oppressive; but the erasure of her identity is real, and it hurts every time. The last time we flew to the United States, I watched as she came through the security sensor gate behind me. I didn't even notice that one of her fists was clenched until the guard who was waiting to wand her asked her to open her hand. When she did, she revealed a delicate, iridescent pink hair scrunchie. I realized that she was trying to find a way to hang onto herself in the face of this denial of her person. I was stunned by her ingenuity and torn up by the way she was left empty-handed. I don't tell her that security personnel might react intrusively and even aggressively, if they notice she is "really" a boy but presenting as a girl. We might be separated and questioned about the nature of our relationship—I am her adoptive mother—and the standard of care I am providing for her. These things have happened to families that I know. As she grows up, Wren will increasingly engage with gendered and racialized systems that put her at risk. She is only nine years old, and I fear that the truth about the extent of the potential danger lying ahead would harm her development.

—Jordan, parent

On an August afternoon in 2011, I found myself at a AAA baseball game in the U.S. Southwest, standing in a long line at the concession stand because I had promised my daughter a slushy. I was surrounded by kids of all ages. When the one in front of me turned around, she caught the involuntary look of surprise in my eyes and cheerfully called me on it, saying, "You thought I was a boy, didn't you?" "I thought you looked like me," I replied. She looked like I did when I was 11—an unmistakably queer kid. She went on to tell me that people think she is a boy all the time and that she doesn't mind but her mom hates her short haircut. We chatted for a bit, but when we got close to the front of the line, I switched gears and got serious, saying, "I want you to remember me. Remember that I told you that someday, probably when you go to college, you'll meet lots of other people like us, and they will love you. And your life will be great." We stood there for a moment, eyes locked, saying nothing. I felt like I had reached across time to do for her what nobody did for me, and I found doing it empowering and portentous—until later that day, when I realized how elitist it was to assume a college escape plan was in her future.

The light at the end of the tunnel I attempted to provide to the presumably Euro-American kid at the ballgame came from *my* story, which is based on a combination of race and class privilege and good timing; but most transgender kids will never attend postsecondary school, and even most of those who do will be unable to remain in what for me has come to constitute a relatively queer- and trans-positive bubble. The world of the university did and does provide me with a favorable habitat. From what this kid told me about her parents, however, her family may not have the resources to send her to college: her dad ran the concession stand at the ballpark. Her gender nonconformity and her age—just on the cusp of puberty and the greater pressure that "tomboys" experience to conform to feminine norms as they grow into teenagers[1]—triggered my concerns about her vulnerability, and I wanted to throw her a lifeline. In my effort to speak to her, I spoke mostly to myself. She was full of resilience: she was unfazed by the responses of others to her gender nonconformity and really seemed to enjoy engaging with complete strangers about it. This was an important lesson about the tendency to project our own experiences and desires onto the children we feel affinity with. This theme drives the book: how to decenter my own whiteness, class privilege, and professional status to present a more nuanced analysis of transgender kids in North America.

Nine years ago, in 2008, gender educators Stefanie Brill and Rachel Pepper published *The Transgender Child*, a groundbreaking book that provided adult caregivers of and service providers for children who affirm a sex/gender identity other than the one assigned to them practical guidance and a supportive framework for navigating the process of social and/or medical transition. The emergence of affirmative (as opposed to punishing, "corrective," or "reparative") resources such as this one,[2] for networks of parents and professionals focused on supporting transgender children,[3] was in response to critical need. A recent report released by the Williams Institute at the UCLA School of Law concluded that one in every 137 teens between the ages of 13 and 17 identifies as transgender.[4] In *Being Safe, Being Me*, the authors of the Canadian Trans Youth Health Survey noted that nearly two-thirds of the respondents reported self-harm over the previous year, and one in three had attempted suicide.[5] Equally troubling are the figures relating to poverty: one in five younger trans youth (14–18 years) and more than one in three older trans youth (19–25 years) went without food at some point in the previous year because they could not afford it.

In a study investigating school climate, the Egale Canada Human Rights Trust reported that 95% of transgender students felt unsafe in schools, 90% reported being verbally harassed because of their gender variance, and 50% said that their teachers and other adults in positions of authority failed to intervene when anti-queer or trans-oppressive comments were made.[6] Other studies have reported that doctors, teachers, and classmates often misunderstand gender-nonconforming kids,[7] which can result in damaging feelings of social isolation. Many are diagnosed with learning disabilities and/or psychological problems because of stress, depression, and suicidal tendencies.[8] Recent data suggest that a disproportionate number of LGBT youth are homeless. Another study reports, "Most transgender children still live in the shadows, hiding from a world that sees them as freaks of nature. Rejected by their families, many grow up hating their bodies, and fall victim to high rates of depression, drug abuse, violence and suicide."[9] If this is where it can end, where does it begin?

The Two-Sex System

The seemingly "natural" basis of binary sex/gender systems assumes that "sex" is a biological term to describe a binary system of anatomy and that "gender" is a cultural term that describes social expectations of sexed bodies, yet these definitions have been challenged by queer, feminist, trans, and intersex theory. As queer theorist Judith Butler insists, sex "has been gender all along";[10] the very "fact" of the two-sex system is an *ideological* rather than a *naturally occurring* phenomenon.[11] With few exceptions, however, the "realness" of binary sex, and what are assumed to be naturally corresponding gender differences, is received wisdom so absolute that feminist scientific and cross-cultural evidence that establishes sex and gender variation beyond dyadic systems is dismissed.[12] In short, this system continues to operate as a powerful and inflexible social and cultural foundational force. In fact, Canadian and U.S. sex/gender systems appear to be resilient enough to adapt to some transgender disruptions by restabilizing around binary categories, which may lessen the relative precarity of transgender kids who undergo affirmative medical intervention early enough to avoid puberty. In contrast to the view of transgender adults, dominant biomedical models view the prepubescent bodies of children as blank slates that may be subject to the kind of intervention that restabilizes binary gender systems.[13] Transgender scholars Susan Stryker and Paisley Currah pointedly define gender "as a biopolitical apparatus that operates on all bodies to produce unequally distributed life chances; gender privileges not just men over women, but also the legibly or functionally gendered over those who become inhuman waste due to their incoherent, messy, resistant, or ambiguous relationship to biopolitical utility."[14]

Research and anecdotal evidence indicates that children have a strong sense of their own gender identity by the age of three or four and some earlier than that. Indeed, one of the parents I interviewed described how her daughter, Cassandra insisted, "I is a girl," at two and a half years of age. But the circumstances under which children experience gender—both the gender that is imposed on them and the gender they feel themselves to be—are complex and difficult to unpack. Anyone who has spent any time around babies and small children has to have observed how distinct their personalities are and how they bring something uniquely of themselves to every interaction and context. Children are not blank slates, as early approaches to child development and education insisted,[15] but rather are fundamentally social beings who strive for the agency to construct themselves as much as they are constructed by interactions with people and institutions around them. Children engage with their environments in mutual developmental interaction between personal and social systems. Psychoanalyst Adrienne Harris captures this complex relationship in her description of gender as "soft assembly," as "personal and social, personal and political, private and public. Any individual experience of gender is rooted in personal history, collective histories, and the slowly but also rapidly evolving, historically shifting world of bodies, words, and material life."[16] Much as Karl Marx asserted that "men [sic] make their own history, but they do not make it as they please; they do not make it under self-selected circumstances, but under circumstances existing already, given and transmitted from the past,"[17] gender necessarily emerges in context. Children make gender their own, but they are limited by the tools they are given. Transgender kids shine a light on the ways that children do gender and the creativity and determination they bring to this task.

The increasingly visible social movements of trans kids and their parents and caregivers insist that children do know their own gender identities and that they both are and should be the authorities when it comes to any claims about their gender. Yet prevailing attitudes about children and teenagers allow adults to dismiss the statements that young people make about themselves and the world around them. Nonbinary trans kids, or those who do not stick with one transition but retreat, move sideways, or go ahead in a different direction, are cited as examples to reinforce cultural norms and prescriptions that infantilize teenagers and preteens.

While some headway is being made to recognize the capacity of children to determine their own gender, this acknowledgment is extended much less to sexuality. Gender scholar Kathryn Bond Stockton observes that the circulation of transgender children in mainstream media depends on their being constructed as both sexually innocent and fundamentally heterosexual.[18] This is a central contradiction that informs mainstream discourse about children, gender, and sexuality in general. In a groundbreaking study of kindergarten children and gender, critical childhood studies scholar Annika Stafford observes that "discourses of children's innocence and discourses of difference work together to normalize rigidly gendered heterosexuality, compelling children to conform to such norms or face social othering in the form of isolation and persecution for their characteristics that do not fit within the strict boundaries of normalcy."[19] A considerable volume of research tells us that children develop physically and mentally in keeping with access to resources and opportunities.[20] Drawing on new research findings relating to the "plasticity" of the brain, sociologist Raewyn Connell observes that there is strong evidence that social context/interaction drives brain development.[21]

Another factor to consider is what sociologist Barrie Thorne has observed in children and their peer cultures: they are not just passive recipients of society's gender system but rather active interpreters and co-constructors of meaning.[22] Similarly, Connell remarks, "Children deal with the same institutions and with overlapping groups of adults. One of the key competencies children learn is to recognize the prevailing masculinities and femininities in the adult world. Whatever ideology prevails in the gender order, children grow up under its shadow."[23]

Coping Strategies

The kids in this book developed a range of coping strategies to deal with the shadow of the gender order. These include invisibility; trying to make the assigned category work; living a double life; engaging in self-harm; gender and/or sexual nonconformity; socially and/or medically transitioning; branching out beyond the binary; and engaging in education and activism to bring about social change.

Invisibility

All the kids in the book experience dissonance, if not a powerful dis-identification, with and resistance to the binary sex/gender identity imposed on them. The fact that I was able to identify and interview them speaks to the degree of privilege that most of their families (birth, adoptive, or chosen) have been able to rally around their children's gender self-determination. It does not mean that all participants come from relative wealth, however, although many would qualify as middle class. But these trans kids are known to me, and their experiences shed light on the many others who lack the safe environments required to show themselves. Speaking of the relationship between privilege and visibility, Kai, an LGBT youth worker, told me, "Young people are saying directly to me, 'Like I already am so teased and bugged and bullied for these other aspects of my identity that there is no way I'm going to start outing myself on invisible identities.' Like, 'I'll just restrict myself and conform and do whatever I need to do to not have to deal with that aspect of difference because these ones that everyone sees, no matter what I do, are taking up so much of the plate of my energy that I can't even get to that.'"

Sucking It Up

Most trans kids probably try very hard to make a go of being the girl or boy that people around them expect them to be, either because they are not aware of any options or because rejecting one's assigned identity can be overwhelming and difficult to undertake. For some, this process is short-lived, but even those who go on to adopt a more visible strategy often give it a shot. Cameron (18, Euro-Canadian) explained about his experience early on, "I was very passive in some ways, and if my parents told me I was something, then that's what I was. But I never really totally felt like I fit in with girls or like with girls' qualities." Now identifying as a trans guy, Cameron described his experience this way: "I tried really hard to fit in when I was 12 because I still had no idea what was going on; I didn't know that being transgender was even a thing. I never doubted that I was a girl because, you know, I was basically being trained to be a housewife; there were no other options." Michael (17, Asian Canadian) described himself as having tried in his early teens to banish his discomfort about his body and assigned female gender role by putting his heart and soul into an exaggerated performance of femininity. Michael described himself as having been "rather extreme about it," wearing makeup, feminine clothing, high heels, and the like. But, he laughed, "It didn't work." Michael began living as a man at age 16.

Living a Double Life

It is not unusual for trans kids with supportive families to begin the process of transition by presenting and expressing themselves according to their affirmed gender at home before taking on other social spaces. Several kids in the study have safe space for their gender self-determination at home but conform to their assigned category, more or less, everywhere else. Lennox (11, Indigenous/Canada), for example, is currently living a double life that she finds painful. At home, she is a girl, while at school, she is a boy. She explained, "It's difficult because I don't like switching back and forth. It's just hard just because I don't know what to be. I really want to be a girl, but at school, I'm used to being a boy." Lennox feels safe with her family and can absolutely count on their support (her mother is a trans parent activist) but is afraid she would lose her friends and be all alone at school if she showed up as herself. At present, she's not willing to risk doing this, but the stress she experiences around her sex/gender is significant. Like Lennox, Tru Wilson[24] (12, Black/Euro-Canadian/Indigenous) lived a double life for several years, being a girl at home and a boy at school. Tru experienced this situation as torture: "The pain was just too unbearable. People talk about torture and how like in horror movies and how you're hung up by your wrists and like all that stuff, but they don't know torture. They don't know the pain that you go through where it just feels like you're—where it just feels like something's tugging and tugging and tugging at you and pushing down on your body until you feel like you're going to collapse." Other kids who lack safety at home do the opposite: they present as their affirmed gender in social spaces other than their home while conforming at home.

Most of the trans kids in my study have strong parental support, but those with fewer resources (family and financial support for transition or gender self-determination) have still found a way to build community and experience at least some gender authenticity in (often online) peer networks. For this latter population, having to conform to their assigned sex/gender at least some of the time—with regard to clothing, presentation, names, and pronouns—is really painful and consistently results in negative mental health consequences.

Engaging in Self-Harm or Attempting Suicide

Trans kids are disproportionately at risk for self-harm and suicide.[25] Many of the kids I spoke to struggle with depression and self-harm, and their sex/gender identity issues appear to be a factor in these feelings. Trans kids are particularly vulnerable to coercive pressure to conform to societal gender norms, which often results in bullying and gendered harassment by peers and often debilitating social stigmatization.[26]

Many of the kids in the book have struggled, or are struggling, with anxiety and depression related to gender dysphoria (see glossary) or because the gender-restrictive contexts of most of their surroundings contribute to their struggles with mental health. Five kids have attempted suicide, and at least twice that many have engaged in self-harm (primarily cutting). Dylan (15, Euro-American), for example, was living with his working-poor family in a trailer park in a small community in the U.S. when I interviewed him. He reported experiencing extreme "gender dysphoria" and mental anguish at the onset of puberty and continues to be mostly unable to live as the young man he really is. His gender dysphoria is so intense that, he said, "If I don't have a chest binder, I won't leave my house." The compromises that Dylan is regularly forced to make cause him extreme mental anguish: "It's not like I wear dresses and skirts. I thought about it, and it just makes me uncomfortable and really angry, and I'm like 'No.' I usually cry if I have to wear something like that. I hate it so much. But I don't know, like, I usually wear skinny jeans. It's more of a gender-nonconforming thing." Dylan emphasized, "Me coming out as trans was not only self-acceptance, but it was asking others to accept the person that I wanted to be and who I realized that I was." He was looking forward to being able to legally change his name from the feminized one on his birth certificate to "Dylan" when he turns 16, saying, "That will be pretty exciting. Even if they're not using the right pronouns yet, I'll still have my name. My name's important to me."

Dylan reported struggling with depression, self-harm, and multiple suicide attempts, for which he was receiving therapy. The day of the interview, Dylan was off work because he had cut himself badly the night before. Although he knew the wound needed stitches, his terror of hospitals was keeping him away from the emergency room. He assured me that he planned no immediate further self-harm:

I got rid of everything I could have used or would have used, so there's nothing that I'm planning on doing. It's not as bad as it used to be. It is pretty bad still, but I used to cut daily, multiple times a day, two or three times a day. I'd wake up and cut, and before bed I'd cut. And so it got to the point where I didn't see it as such a big deal. They aren't deep or anything—never needed stitches—and then a while ago, I started cutting deeper, where I would need stitches. I actually—when I cut really bad, I have to call my mom, count how many days I can go without.

I found this admission alarming and handled the situation as skillfully as I could—via Skype. I know that all the kids in my study are vulnerable to self-harm and/or suicide, and I try to communicate to them that I believe they are who they tell me they are and that they matter. And I mean it every time. I made several attempts after the interview to reach Dylan to see how he is doing, but I have not been successful. I know there is a good chance that he's busy or he's changed his email address or something like that, but I do worry about him.

Gender and Sexual Nonconformity

Some of the kids in the book are more or less comfortable with the sex identity assigned to them but resist conforming to the sexist gender expectations they encounter. Ray-Ray (16, Euro-Canadian) has always found gender norms confining, both socially and with regard to his self-expression. Ray-Ray identifies as a boy and doesn't think that is going to change, but he has always been gender nonconforming and is often read by others as "different," saying, "I definitely don't fit the stereotype." When he was younger, he wore dresses for special occasions and "would always go to the girl's section with all the colors and sparkles" when shopping for clothes. Ray-Ray's mother, Nadine, herself experienced censure from people in their rural, conservative community for letting her son be "weird." This was why Ray-Ray's family relocated to another part of the country to a "rather hippy," rural environment when he was still quite little. Ray-Ray thinks that because of this relocation, he has "never felt really harshly judged": "which was really good, and I'm glad about that." While Ray-Ray feels fairly sexually fluid, he described the pressure he feels to "identify as something": "because with people partnering up around me, I want to too. And my mom just keeps telling me, 'Well, you've got to try something to see what you like, right?' And I kind of have a really big problem with decisions. I'm kind of scared of making decisions. It takes me a long time. So I think that's part of my problem, like why I haven't been with anybody yet. And also because people really don't know which way I swing probably. So they're not able to approach me." But this makes Ray-Ray uncomfortable too: "If you partner up with somebody who identifies as a woman or a girl for the first time, does that make you straight? I don't feel that way. I feel like I'm still open. That's not a deciding factor." Ray-Ray noted that others assume he is gay because of their investment in gay stereotypes: "People who know me, who have known me since I was little, sometimes mention how it's funny how the first thing I did when I got my dollhouse with all the things for Christmas from my dad was vacuum the whole thing and how I wore dresses and all that. I feel like I *should* be gay, but I don't really know."

All the kids in the book have encountered society's conflation of gender and sexuality, so it was not unusual for some of them to think of themselves as potentially gay, lesbian, or queer before coming to understand that it is their gender identity that is nontraditional. Several of my participants who were designated female at birth began their gender journey by identifying as lesbians or bisexual because they "didn't even know that transgender was a thing," but when their online activity and/or engagement with the LGBT community exposed them to a range of gender identities, binary and nonbinary, they shifted their attention from their sexuality to their gender and found themselves more "at home." Helen (16, Euro-Canadian), for example, wishes they had known about the existence of nonbinary genders much earlier in their life. They have trouble even naming their gender identity! The first nonnormative identity Helen embraced concerned sexuality: "Yeah, I am a lesbian. . . . But . . . once I found out there were nonbinary genders, I was . . . I think I am one, and I think I like them." Helen described themselves as "one of those people who really needs experience in order to understand things," so it was not until they went to an LGBT camp and met nonbinary people that they understood themselves fully. After all, they observed, "in my town, I am the only nonbinary person I know of." Several of my participants reported having a parent ask them, "Aren't you just gay?" or even "Could you not just live as a gay person?"—imagining that being gay would somehow be easier than being transgender.

Alternative sexual identities are a source of pleasure and self-realization for some and a way station on the way to gender self-determination for others. Quinn (18, Indigenous/Euro-Canadian) said they came out "initially as bisexual": "right before I got into this relationship with a girl, and I started identifying as a lesbian part way through it, and when we broke up about half a year later, I said, 'Well, if I'm attracted to girls, what makes a girl?'" Issues around sexual orientation, at least in conventional terms, stop making sense when people let go of the sex/gender binary. As Quinn explained, "If you're like, 'Oh, I'm attracted to girls,' but a lot of girls don't have vaginas, and when you take into account that there's a huge percentage of the population that's intersex[27] and not as many people are dyadic as most people tend to think, then like what makes a girl or a boy? Nothing really. . . . You're just like, 'Oh no, nothing makes sense anymore.'" Quinn began the process of resisting their assigned gender category by first identifying as "gender queer": "Because it's a term I'd heard used around before and because I was at the time identifying as queer because I wasn't as comfortable with my orientation. Not that I wasn't comfortable, but I didn't really know how to identify: 'Oh no, like I used to think I liked girls, and now I'm having some trouble with this; so I'm queer, and I'm also gender queer, super queer.' I identified myself as 'super queer,' to be honest, a lot of the time."

While sex education in public schools may emphasize consent, safety, consideration, and self-care, at best, as opposed to abstinence and an explicitly anti-LGBT curriculum, at worst, it doesn't always leave open the question about what kinds of sexual/romantic and nonromantic attachments kids ultimately want to establish. This is because the internalization of the model of monogamy forecloses a lot of self-discovery and self-knowledge. Polyamorous and kink communities emphasize consent and communication and model other ways to relate sexually to people that, for some, bring more pleasure and build more community. Some of the kids in this study feel empowered by and are contributing to new language around a range of gender and sexual identities. Quinn said, for example, "If you want to get really, really specific, I am a demi-polyromantic, polysexual, gender-queer individual." Quinn defines themselves as "polyamorous and polysexual and polyromantic": "but I usually just describe myself as queer because that's so much easier, in addition to being a demi-romantic, which is on the aromantic spectrum." Quinn took visible pleasure in providing me with a crash course in newly emerging language around gender and sexual identities:

> This is a fun thing! In addition to having different romantic or sexual orientations like bi, poly, homo, hetero, etcetera, pan, there's also those four romantic orientations, and then you have different degrees sort of. So you have asexual, which I'm sure you know what that is, someone who doesn't experience sexual attraction, and then you have alosexual, which is the opposite. And the same is true for romanticism, and then you have all these different degrees within that. So "demi" is one of those, and "demi" means partial, of course, but specifically in this case, it means after you have a really strong emotional bond with the person. So it takes me like months and months and months of knowing someone in order to develop romantic feelings for them. I don't really get crushes, which is great because none of my friends seem to benefit from them.

Hunter (13, Indigenous/Canada), identifies as a "gay, demi-sexual male who is also polyamorous." He explained, "Demi-sexual means if you start to get to know a person, then you start feeling sexual attraction to them. So the more you know them, the more sexual attraction you feel for them, and like, it's something that you can't actually choose. It basically chooses you, I guess." The way that gender- and sexual-minority people of all ages produce language beyond the limits of binary gender, heterosexuality, and monogamy is an exciting thing to chronicle. This living dictionary of identity and practice is constantly being updated and revised. It reflects grassroots knowledge and community formation/ negotiation rather than top-down diagnosis and categorization by scientific and medical communities (or moral mandates stemming from conservative religious traditions). Trans teens in particular are actively engaging in these processes of knowledge generation and exchange.

In the absence of visible transgender people and people with nonbinary identities in the lives of the trans kids in the book, many have developed their own language to explain their dissonance/dysphoria, while others have experienced a "eureka" moment when they learned of the existence of other transgender people. Accessing or developing new language is a key aspect of empowerment for trans kids. For example, Tru described having feelings about not being a boy in first grade that solidified by fourth grade into the knowledge that "I am a girl." With the help of a supportive friendship group, Tru developed her own language to describe a sense of self that was at odds with what was being imposed on her. Tru explained,

> I said that I was "half boy and half girl." And the term "he/she" came to me a little later when I started talking about it with my friends, and they said, "You could—just to like be more simple—you could also call yourself a 'he/she.'" I thought that I was a boy that liked dolls and boys. I didn't know that I could actually change. Then I thought, "What if I could turn into a girl?" And then it started to become a feeling of me being a girl. And then as it grew and got more stronger, it just became a fact, and I knew that I was a girl. I just didn't know how to explain it.

A key facet of Tru's empowerment was finding a way to explain to adults in her family and at her school that they had her gender wrong. As soon as Tru socially transitioned, "everything changed": "It felt so good when we got rid of my boy clothes. It felt so good when I got my very first dolls for Christmas. And it felt so good to hear the first time someone called me Tru and didn't ask if that was right."

Several participants experienced unease with their gender identities and their bodies, an experience that was painfully heightened at puberty, but they lacked the language to make sense of it. Michael started to feel "really different" and depressed around puberty: "Like I didn't feel how I thought a girl should feel like." Michael experienced a sense of dissonance with his assigned sex/gender identity and social standing as a girl, but, he said, "I just thought maybe I'm just a tomboy, right? But that didn't work either [*laughs*]. Because as a tomboy, guys still treated me as a girl, and you know they're all—they have to be all gentleman-like towards me, and that made me feel kind of like, what's the word? Undignified? I feel like I should be on the same level as them. They shouldn't be treating me differently." It was not a matter of feeling that he was treated unfairly, he said, but rather, "they were just treating me like they would treat any other girl, [softer] like how they were treating other girls." Michael did not have words for his experience until he met a transgender person for the first time, and then everything fell into place for him. He described a chance meeting with a female-to-male (FTM) transgender person through a friend as being "like a spark" (he punctuated this statement by snapping his fingers). Prior to this meeting, Michael had never heard of trans people: "But after I met him, I'm like 'I think this is what all these feelings, all these experiences are.'" He then turned to the Internet for more information.

Transitioning

When a person undergoes *social transition*, the process typically involves announcing a change in gender identity along with new pronouns and often, but not always, adopting a new first name. One begins to "live" as the affirmed gender. Where legally possible, obtaining new government identification featuring the affirmed rather than assigned sex marker is an important part of this process.

Government identification often presents trans people with an insurmountable barrier to social transition. "M" or "F" sex markers on government identification play a fundamental role in imposing a binary-based sex category on kids and in enabling or preventing freedom of movement. Birth certificates include assigned sex markers and are necessary to register for school and many recreational programs and to obtain a healthcare card and passport. Identity documents that contain a sex marker that does not match the way in which one's gender is "read at a glance" or a person's affirmed sex are a source of precarity for transgender people of all ages. Cameron explained why he wanted to legally change his name and sex marker, for example: "I would like to not have the 'F' on the top of my health card and my licenses and my whatever, but I'm not in a position where I can get that changed legally right now." The province he lived in at the time required sex reassignment surgery to change the gender marker on government ID. When I interviewed Levon, parent of Caroline (six, Black American), in 2013, he explained that they would not visit Canada or any other country until their daughter was old enough to have the sex-reassignment surgery that was a requirement for a U.S. passport (the policy was changed in 2014). Levon said it was out of the question for his daughter to have to present as a boy even for a few hours because it would be so damaging to her mental health: "I could never ask her to do that."

Fortunately, some of the restrictive requirements for obtaining government-issued identity documents congruent with affirmed, rather than assigned, sex have been removed. According to the National Center for Transgender Equality, as of 2014, trans people who are U.S. citizens can "obtain a full ten-year passport with an updated gender marker if you have had clinical treatment determined by your doctor to be appropriate in your case to facilitate gender transition. No specific details are required about what type of treatment is appropriate for you."[28] Starting in 2014, trans Canadians became able to obtain passports reflecting affirmed gender without undergoing sex reassignment surgery. As noted earlier, a legal case on behalf of a trans child in British Columbia— Harriette Cunningham—resulted in a change to that province's Vital Statistics Act.[29] Many other provinces have similarly changed requirements.[30] In 2011, Australia introduced a three-gender marker system on its passports, allowing transgender citizens to switch from "M" to "F" or vice versa and intersex citizens to list their gender as "X." As of August 31, 2017, the government of Canada made it possible for citizens to obtain a Canadian passport with "X" as a third option for a gender marker. In March 2017, the province of Ontario introduced the option of "X" "in the sex field of its driver's licence, to ensure the fair, ethical and equitable treatment of people with trans and non-binary gender identity."[31] In the same year, Oregon became the first U.S. state to add the new gender option of "X" to its driver's licenses.[32] While adding "X" as a third option reflects a significant cultural shift toward greater gender inclusion, "X" still marks gender, and it might actually put people traveling with such documents at risk at international borders.

While the ability to obtain government identification congruent with one's gender identity is an extremely significant step with regard to recognition and harm reduction for trans people, many trans people suggest that even *requiring* a gender marker is fundamentally oppressive. Trans activists and allies are fighting for an end to the inclusion of sex markers on government identification entirely.[33] For example, in 2017, a British Columbia parent applied for a judicial review in order to procure a birth certificate for their child without a sex marker.[34] In the same year, three Saskatchewan families of trans kids took their fight for a gender-neutral birth certificate to the province's human rights commission.[35] At the time of this writing, these cases were unresolved.

When a person undergoes *medical transition*, the process includes any or all of the following: puberty-suppression therapy in the case of children to interrupt "natal" puberty; cross-sex hormone therapy; sex reassignment surgery (top and/or bottom); other cosmetic procedures. These medical treatments fall under the wider umbrella of *trans-affirming healthcare*. Puberty-suppression therapy via "hormone blockers" is referred to as the "Dutch protocol" because it originated in Amsterdam. Unlike in Holland, however, many North American clinics support early social transition for children. The term "transition" is most typically understood according to the logics of the sex/gender binary, but it need not be restricted to this. Some people who assert a nonbinary identity, for example, undergo a social and/or medical transition. Some trans people who access affirming healthcare may also socially transition, and some may not; trans people who socially transition may or may not access trans-affirming healthcare. In a number of regions, however, the ability to socially transition or change one's sex marker on government-issued identity documents may hinge on receiving specified medical treatment[36] under the supervision of a licensed professional.

Some of this study's participants volunteered that they were on hormone blockers and/or cross-sex hormones, while others intended or hoped to be. Some volunteered their plans for surgery, while others had no access to appropriate healthcare (because of lack of financial resources or parental support); and still others had no desire to medicalize their gender identities. Many voiced regret about not having been aware of transgender possibilities earlier in their development so that they could have taken hormone blockers to prevent undesired physical changes at puberty. Very few in the study grew up knowing that alternative gender identities were a possibility or that you could "switch."

Branching Out beyond the Binary

One of the accusations leveled at trans people in general and trans kids in particular is that our gender variance is "just a phase," and this attitude can operate by putting pressure on some of us to be more binary conforming, fixed, or fully transitioned than might be optimal. This pressure can have a profound effect on some trans people, making us feel that we must hold fast to a narrative that proclaims the permanence of transition, as if one has finally ended up where one belongs on a linear and binary-based gender-identity highway. Stef, however, has had multiple transitions and is bound to confound some trans people for whom the need to defend the authenticity and permanence of their identity is particularly acute. This feeling is because of the way their story may be taken up by anti-trans activists.

Stef transitioned to Stefanie at age five, legally changed their name and pronouns, and first took hormone blockers and then cross-sex hormones. But when they were 14, Stef said, "I started feeling that I really didn't like gender norms and how, even if I was a female, that I would not fit into certain categories." Stef resists both a binary-based trans narrative of permanence and the kind of criticism of that narrative that legitimates trans-oppressive refusals to acknowledge the "realness" of trans kids' gender identities. Of their time as a girl, Stef refuses to say "it was just a phase" or that it was a mistake: "[being a girl was] just something that I did really want back then, and now I want something different."

Stef learned about and got to know gender-fluid and agender trans people via the Internet, which helped them transition from being a transgender girl to a gender-neutral/agender identity. They decided, "Well, today I'm just going to be Stef." This process of resistance and discovery was aided by an online trans group in which Stef felt safe enough to try out gender-neutral pronouns. This transition was complicated, however, because Stef feared that the trans friends they had made at various camps, conferences, and online spaces—and who had served as a lifeline to keep "Stefanie" going while "she" struggled in trans-oppressive school settings—would turn their back on them if they ceased to be *her*. Much to their relief, Stef has not been abandoned by their friends, but they expressed regret about not being exposed to more options earlier in their life, specifically about gender-fluid and gender-queer identities. While Stef refuses to repudiate their time as a girl or to express regret about the affirming healthcare they received, they believe they may have opted for a less binary-based trans identity at an earlier time if they had known about these possibilities. Stef describes themselves now as "trans identified," saying, "I used to be female, but now I'm androgynous."

The lack of visible nonbinary options limits the embodiments that trans kids are able to explore, which had a significant impact on Kidd (18, Black/Native American). Kidd explained what this lack of information when they were younger denied them: "the chance to express myself and try to figure out who I was in that sense like a lot of other kids did." Although they mostly flew under the radar in high school, only presenting as a girl with close girlfriends, Kidd fully expected to transition to a woman after graduation. They explained, "Throughout my high school career, I actually thought I was completely a transgender girl." But Kidd changed their mind about transitioning when they had the opportunity to explore their gender more after high school.

Kidd moved to another city to live with their older sister, who is a lesbian, after high school. Here, they had the space and support to explore themselves "gender wise, sexuality wise all that good stuff." In this new environment, where Kidd was "more free with being Carmella [the name they give their female persona] all the time," their understanding of their gender identity changed and, so did their plans to transition. Kidd came to an understanding: "I am actually in this middle space that does not exist, and that is when I started doing my research and was like, 'Oh, you know, there is this nonbinary, and I am more like that than anything else.'" Kidd went on to say, "Even though quite a percentage of me was Carmella, there is a percentage of me that is Kidd [the name they give their male persona]. I realized that I am both and neither at the same time. I did not want to completely get rid of Kidd, as he is a part of who I am." As Kidd embraced a nonbinary identity, they abandoned their plans to transition to a woman, explaining, "This kind of rolling who I am feels right." Kidd now identifies as nonbinary, asks to be addressed using "they/them/their" pronouns, and only regrets not being made aware of all the possibilities regarding gender and sexual identity earlier in their life.

Most of the kids in this book view gender as a spectrum. Michael believes that children and young people should be able to "try stuff out, find what fits for you." Some have very politically nuanced understandings of gender-identity issues and resist the sex and gender binary entirely, at least for themselves. Quinn identifies as a "queer, nonbinary, trans person of color" and laments the invisibility of gender-diverse trans people. In their analysis of gender, Quinn emphasized relationships of power and oppression: "The *assigned* female at birth, *assigned* male at birth, it really renders the power dynamic clear, doesn't it?" According to Quinn, "I was sort of thinking maybe I'm bi some time in grade 7, but the gender thing, there wasn't really a lead-in to it; it was just sort of like a giant rock fell from the sky, and suddenly I had to pay attention to it. It was like that, and I started walking around being like, 'Look, there's a rock here,' to all my friends." Some trans kids affirm a binary identity but embrace gender nonconformity, which can be really confusing to people they encounter, adding to the feelings of pressure and stress that these trans kids experience. Cameron, for example, explained why he took some time to feel entitled to define himself as a guy: "every once in a while, I like to throw on a skirt."

Social Change

Many of the trans kids in my study are very open about being trans, partly for their own comfort but also for political reasons: their own difficult experiences lead them to want to create more space for other kids to determine their own genders and find acceptance. Knowing that they have done things that will make things better "for the next trans kid" is a source of great pride to a number of the kids in the book. They have done this in a variety of ways, from engaging in highly visible legal cases and participating in pride parades as openly trans to speaking publicly in support of transgender-inclusive policies (at school boards or in recreation districts, for example). Others are incredibly private and do not wish to be "out there" about anything at all, least of all about their trans status, but they have found quieter ways to make a difference. Some kids feel that participating anonymously in my research is a way for them to contribute to education around trans issues without risking a loss of privacy or putting themselves in harm's way. Not surprisingly, social change approaches among trans kids and their parents mirror tensions within broader queer and trans communities and other social justice struggles.

Significant debates in transgender studies and queer and trans communities include those between queer-identified proponents of transgender identities who model an antiessentialist gender future[37] and transsexual-rights authors and activists[38] who may or may not see themselves under the LGBT umbrella but are concerned about ending the mental distress, discrimination, and violence that transsexuals face.[39] Critics of this latter approach argue that the tendency to limit transgender issues to transsexuality fails to represent the range of visible and invisible individuals and identities and the disproportionate access to appropriate healthcare that is a function of race and class.[40] It is important to see transgender kids against the backdrop of these debates within and between queer and trans communities because these tensions are present in the social movements they and/or their parents interact with. Other tensions within queer and trans communities that are reflected among activist trans kids and their parents relate to a focus on trans identity as a single issue versus an analysis of discrimination against trans people within an overarching system of oppression.

It is true that some transgender kids are "gender conforming"[41] in that they conform to binary identities—though not the category to which they were assigned at birth—and this may be easier for many people to understand and accept and for mainstream institutions to adapt to and integrate; but they are a relatively privileged, albeit extremely vulnerable, minority. This subset often has both the desire for and access to gender-affirming healthcare, and their circumstances may be less insecure than those whose avowed identities are nonbinary or for whom gender-normative clothing, identity documents, hormone therapy, and/ or surgery is out of reach or undesirable. But it is also accurate to say that kids who affirm a binary-based trans identity are vulnerable, and those without significant resources and support are even more so. For those who are visible in the face of opposition, the discrimination and bullying they experience from adults and peers is very damaging and greatly increases the risk of mental health struggles, self-harm, and suicide. Those who are invisible often witness trans-negativity and struggle with feelings of isolation and self-hatred.

Trans Kids and Precarity

Given the range of complex experiences trans kids are vulnerable to, it is crucial to situate transgender kids within broader relations of power and oppression, yet existing resources for the public (versus academic critical theory)[42] tend to focus on relatively privileged, rather than socio-economically marginal, children. A more integrated anti-oppression approach to understanding and supporting transgender kids is required. In the remainder of this chapter, I focus on two trans kids, Wren and Finn (14, Euro-American), to draw together recent theorizing relating to precarity, children and childhood, critical disability, and queer and trans scholarship on the biopolitics of gender and race.

Wren socially transitioned to a female identity when she was seven but, at the age of 11, told me she wishes she had been left alone to be who she was without having to think of or explain herself as *any* gender. I have had the chance to interview her twice, and it is very interesting to track the consistency of her sense of gender identity and how she sees this playing out in the future. When I first interviewed her at age seven, right after she had switched her pronoun, she told me, "I was born a boy, but I like being a girl." At 11, she explained that she felt pressure to transition: "I would not say I wanted to *be* a girl. I just wanted to wear those kinds of clothes, so that people assumed that I'm a boy that likes being a girl. But I didn't. I was actually kind of fine with who I am—just wearing different clothes was what I kind of wanted and having my hair different, longer."

The "effeminaphobia," as gender theorist Eve Sedgwick called it,[43] directed at gender-nonconforming boys is keenly felt by kids such as Wren who are designated male at birth and are gender nonconforming. Wren told me that she thinks she probably would not have felt the need to transition as a girl if people had not made such a big deal about her gender nonconformity. But the microaggressions that Wren endured as a consequence of the gender confusion she provoked in other people—and their insistence on making it *her* problem—translated into too much anxiety for her. I am struck by Wren's tremendous courage to resist what was expected of her rather than conform. Trans activist Julia Serano lauds the courage of all trans kids given the "presence of systemic societal transphobia."[44] But conforming would have come at too great a cost for Wren. Wren told me how she would feel if she had been unable to express her femininity: "I would feel like my true self isn't really my true self, like I'm not in the same body as I used to be, like I'm not in the body I want to be—stuck." But when I asked Wren, at age seven, about her vision of herself in the future, she was very matter of fact in explaining that she did not see transgender womanhood as an option. She told me of her plan to "change back" into a boy when she turned

10. I was a bit surprised to hear this given how stereotypically feminine she is, although I never doubt anyone's assertions about their gender identity. When I interviewed her in 2015, she was 11, and the timeline for changing back had shifted for her; but the vision of her future had not: she was operating in stealth mode at a new school, and she hoped to pass as a girl until she turns 14 or 15, at which point she plans to "change back into a boy." Wren consistently refuses the possibility of trans adulthood for herself, explaining, "I am Black. I don't want to be trans too." Wren's life chances are shaped by the class privilege of her parents, but in seeing no future for herself—literally—she displays a sophisticated and heartbreaking political awareness about the disabling effects of being transgender and subject to anti-Black racism.

Finn[45] is another trans kid who saw no future for himself. In the course of my research, I learned, via his mother's heartbreaking announcement in an online parent group, that Finn had committed suicide at the age of 14. I obtained permission from his mother to share some of what she wrote in a later post to the group.

> It's been five weeks since my 14 year old transgender son Finn took his life. We had a discussion that night at dinner about his next Lupron[46] shot, and how we were going to pay for it since we'd just gotten a letter that day of our second denial of state insurance, and had been told by Lupron's owner company, Abbvie, that we were slightly over income and it was unlikely that we'd qualify for their patient assistance program. We couldn't afford the $1400 out of pocket payment. We talked about other options, but he was afraid of the side effect of weight gain. He begged me to do a GoFundMe for him, but I told him we couldn't do it for something ongoing. He left the table upset. Oh, how I wished I would have checked in on him. But he spent most of his time holed up in his room, and I was trying to be respectful of not intruding. Later that night, while I slept in the next room, he quietly left the house and walked to the railroad a few blocks away, and lay his body across the track. It was the 11:00 train.[47]

Finn and many other trans kids find puberty too difficult to bear and, faced with what they see as limited options for the future, choose death. Many of these kids are isolated, but many are also, like Finn, deeply loved and supported by their families and friends. As I picture this beautiful kid lying down on the tracks and remaining there while the train thundered toward him and over him, I am struck by the power of his will. This was no suicide attempt to signal a need for help but rather a grim and determined choice. I see Finn not as a victim of trans oppression but rather as a casualty, because of the obvious agency he displayed in choosing death. That he weighed his options and decided the best decision was to die speaks to the limited agency available to him and the hopelessness about the future he felt. I shared these thoughts with his mother, and she agreed, saying, "I was struck by that mere determination and courage it must've taken to stay on those rails as the train roared down towards him." His mom described Finn as gifted and wise but lacking the maturity to manage his considerable emotional sensitivity. She explained, "He had to lay down that load he was carrying somehow. The hopelessness he felt in the road ahead of him is what broke him that night. But even if he had no problem getting Lupron, he still had his internal demons." But, she said, "if the barriers to taking Lupron were not there, I don't think he would have died that night." For Wren and Finn, like many vulnerable trans kids, being trans is only one dimension of their precarity.

To be alive is to be precarious—it is an inevitable part of the human condition—but we are unequally so. Judith Butler defines precarity as an inevitable social condition in which "one's life is always in some sense in the hands of the other. . . . Survival is dependent on what we might call a social network of hands."[48] In *States of Insecurity*, political theorist Isabell Lorey defines precariousness as "insecurity and vulnerability, destabilization and endangerment," as opposed to "protection, political and social immunization against everything that is recognized as endangerment."[49] Lorey uses the term "precarity" specifically to refer to "naturalized relations of domination, through which belonging to a group is attributed or denied to individuals. Precarity involves social positionings of insecurity."[50] Moreover, Lorey and Butler both contend that modern practices of governing are precisely about this differential distribution of precariousness. The key tension for neoliberal states involves governing via imposing precarity on part of the population but not so much that it results in insurrection. Indeed, Lorey remarks, "Managing this threshold is what makes up the art of governing today."[51]

Lorey draws on the work of Michel Foucault with particular emphasis (for our purposes) on the historical emergence of biopolitical governance. In the West during the 18th and 19th centuries, liberal humanist doctrine combined with population-management strategies offered up by the emerging disciplines of psychology, criminology, and medicine to establish new mechanisms for state governance that marked the modern capitalist nation-state as distinct from former modes of ruling. According to Foucault, the emergence of this modern state necessitated a shift away from power as overt dominance/violence to "biopower."[52] The emergence of biopolitical governance reflected an overall shift from state violence that crudely dictated life or death to state population management that fostered life or disallowed it. In this reading, colonialism, neoliberal capitalism, racialized socioeconomic relations, and heteropatriarchy all can be cited as (closely related) forces that combine to produce a "differential distribution of precarity."[53]

The socioeconomic and cultural legacy of the Enlightenment, capitalist transformation, and colonial appropriation reveals power operating through naturalized categories of sex, gender, sexuality, race, citizenship, ability, and age that are mutually constitutive. White settler nations and neoliberal globalization have their roots in the imperial projects of the emergent modern capitalist nation states of western Europe. The central ideology of these (ongoing) colonial projects is liberal humanism. Liberal humanist philosophy maintains that only humans are capable of reason, and only some humans rise above biological disadvantages related to gender, racialization, social class, sexuality, age, and non-Christian status. Those who are deemed to lack this capacity to be fully human are understood to be "disabled" and are, accordingly, subjugated.[54]

Racialization

Canada and the U.S. occupy huge, varied, and contested geopolitical spaces. Both nations brand themselves as democracies, but each is more accurately understood as a "white settler society,"[55] albeit with different histories of displacing/committing genocide against Indigenous populations and subjugating racialized minorities. White settler societies required land, labor, and capital investment,[56] and these logics explain histories of genocide, slavery, white settlement, and forced migration. These histories provide a crucial genealogy of contemporary socioeconomic inequality wherein gender, race, class, sexuality, and immigration/citizenship status are key axes of inequality and oppression in both countries. Queer and trans scholars of color and antiracist allies, writing in the tradition of critical race and biopolitics, identify hierarchies relating to race, gender, sexuality, class, and disability as an "assemblage" of oppression.[57] Describing sexuality as a heavily racialized "organizing principle of social life" and "a form of power that exists regardless of an individual's sexual identity," for example, sociologist C. J. Pascoe establishes a clear link between children, gender, sexuality, and race in the United States.[58] In *Dude, You're a Fag: Masculinity and Sexuality in High School*, Pascoe speaks of "gender and sexuality regimes" and contends that "gendered power works through racialized selves."[59] In describing the racialized operation of "fag discourse" in a U.S. high school, Pascoe emphasizes that homophobia is not a racially neutral phenomenon: it is mostly white boys who call each other the abject "fag" in order to establish themselves as appropriately masculine. Black American boys in Pascoe's study, however, were less likely than white boys to be on the receiving end of the "fag" epithet, but their less suspect Black masculinity was bifurcated by racist notions of hypersexuality/hypermasculinity on the one hand and their relative impotence in the face of racialized national economic and political systems on the other.

Canadian critical race[60] and Indigenous scholars[61] have written extensively about the white patriarchal construction of citizenship in the national imagination and with regard to the distribution of status and resources. This scholarship emphasizes the role of whiteness and masculinity in colonial/genocidal relationships with respect to Indigenous peoples and racialized and oppressed groups. Black feminist scholars,[62] for their part, have made significant contributions to feminist, queer, and trans analyses of gender and sexuality by demonstrating how these are integrated with race, ethnicity, social class, immigration status, and dis/ability to create privileged and abject categories of people and legitimate, versus deviant, gender and sexual identities and practices. Transgender people of all ages are constituted by, and constitute themselves within, these particular sociohistorical contexts or assemblages.

Queer/trans necropolitics reflects an engagement between critical race and queer and trans scholarship that is uniquely positioned to situate transgender kids in Canada and the U.S. "Necropolitics" emerged as part of a tradition of radical critical race theory that builds on Foucault's analysis of biopower. It is a framework for analysis that identifies "assemblages"[63] of oppression that unevenly distribute resilience versus harm, life versus death, along axes of race, class, sexuality, and gender. Introduced by critical race scholar Achille Mbembe in 2003, necropolitics is consistent with Lorey's vision of the modern state as unevenly distributing precarity in that it defines sovereignty as the power of the state "to dictate who may live and who must die."[64] Some people are awarded life and life-sustaining resources, while others are killed outright, condemned to a "slow death" by virtue of being starved for resources, treated to "social death,"[65] and/or violated on a day-to-day basis. In a similar vein, geographer Ruth Wilson Gilmore defines racism as "the state-sanctioned or extralegal production and exploitation of group-differentiated vulnerability to premature death."[66]

A key feature of the biopolitics of the modern nation-state concerns necropolitics: the rationalization of inhumane treatment, violence, and oppression for the greater good. Subhabrata Bannerjee's introduction of the term "necrocapitalism" emphasizes the mutually constitutive relationships between state and capitalist "necropower" for distributing precarity (for example, in the increasing use of privatized military forces in the so-called war on terror).[67] While Mbembe focuses explicitly on state atrocities on a large scale,[68] queer and trans necropolitical theorizing focuses on systemic racism, classism, and institutionalized state violence (in the form of policing, urban planning, the prison industrial complex, borders, the war on terror, and lack of access to healthcare).[69]

Queer/trans necropolitical theorizing challenges the notion that LGBT organizations and individuals in the West have made gains resulting in changes to law and government policy. Trans and queer scholars of color and antiracist, antipoverty allies[70] have resisted white, middle-class, "homonormative"[71] and "transnormative"[72] milestones because they have failed to attend to issues beyond gender and sexuality. As such, critical queer and trans scholarship resists the assimilation agenda of mainstream LGBT politics.[73] Transgender scholars Riley Snorton and

Jin Haritaworn[74] draw on Mbembe's theory of necropolitics, Duggan's analysis of (white, middle-class) homonormativity, and assemblage theorist Jasbir Puar's concept of homonormative nationalism or "homonationalism,"[75] to formulate an explicitly trans necropolitics that focuses on the day-to-day experiences of racism and poverty for trans people of color.[76] Indeed, trans necropolitical theorizing resonates powerfully with the findings of the 2011 report *Injustice at Every Turn: A Look at Black Respondents in the National [U.S.] Transgender Discrimination Survey*, which concluded that trans people of color in the U.S. experience a relentless barrage of microaggressions. The report revealed that while "discrimination was pervasive" for all respondents who took the national transgender discrimination survey, "the combination of anti-transgender bias and persistent, structural, and individual racism was especially devastating" for black transgender people and other people of color.[77]

Childhood

Scholars in the field of critical childhood studies situate "children" as a socially constructed demographic category—like gender, sexuality, race, class, and disability—that acts as a lens through which we can see more clearly how power operates. These categories can be mobilized to maintain systems of oppression and affect different transgender kids in particular ways. Dean Spade proposes that instead of organizing efforts for change around notions of individual "rights," we identify and critically engage with race, gender, sexuality, class, and immigration status as "vectors of vulnerability and security that intersect to impact life chances," examining how "gender categories are enforced on all people in ways that cause particularly dangerous outcomes for trans people."[78] Critical childhood studies suggests that age is another such vector, with "childhood" generating particular interrelations of precarity that subject "minors" to varying degrees of subordination. Age categories, in concert with other ascribed variables, are used to organize populations with regard to access to care and resources. As critical childhood studies scholar Annette Appell observes, childhood is transitory but foretelling: "Unlike other subordinated groups, children will outgrow their subordination as children, but whether they will be subordinated as adults depends very much on their childhood, that is, their race, class, and gender, or perhaps more accurately the race, class, and gender of their parents."[79] Analyzing children as a socially constructed minority group subject to, and implicated in, relations of oppression is a central piece of the puzzle in order to understand trans kids in all their complexity.

The way we organize children as a disempowered demographic group, and childhood as a cultural system/ideology for imposing and justifying this disempowerment, also returns to the liberal humanist legacy, this time of an age-based binary: innocence/dependence versus rational knowledge/autonomy. The liberal humanist fantasy suggests that the apex of human development is to be antisocial: when you grow up, you rely on no one but yourself. It sees children as innocent and benevolently disempowered by purportedly responsible adults. This view has been sharply criticized by feminists for rendering invisible the extensive care work and interdependence that humans of all ages require to survive. Feminist critiques of liberalism's foundational view of the citizen as autonomous counter it with a fundamental belief in interdependence and group life in which we rely on the care received from others.[80] The ideology of individualism has adapted to neoliberal times and operates powerfully in discourses of governance today that normalize the gutting of social welfare provisions.

The relationship between "transgender" and "childhood" is a troubled one given that children are not typically credited with the ability to authenticate their own gender identities or to know themselves. The experiences of children, who are understood as not yet fully human, are rendered less real, their feelings and desires less important, and their capacity for agency limited at best. The line between childhood and adulthood is further blurred because children's dependence is largely imposed on them and because many of those who are no longer legally minors still lack meaningful autonomy/agency. Given that only adults are recognized as politically capable,[81] a transgender child is by definition disempowered and more precarious.

In contrast to liberal humanist definitions of children and childhood that view children as passive, a more critical definition of children sees them as capable of agency, although to varying degrees, depending on factors such as race, class, gender, and so on. Critical childhood studies scholar Natascha Klocker describes children's agency on a continuum from thinness to thickness, whereby "'thin' agency refers to decisions and everyday actions that are carried out within highly restrictive contexts, characterized by few viable alternatives. 'Thick' agency is having the latitude to act within a broad range of options. It is possible for a person's agency to be 'thickened' or 'thinned' over time and space, and across their various relationships. Structures, contexts, and relationships can act as 'thinners' or 'thickeners' of individual's agency, by constraining or expanding their range of viable choices."[82] Measuring children's agency involves an examination of the nature and frequency of structural barriers or entitlements and "microaggressions."[83] According to sociologist Sonny Nordmarken, "Microaggressions are routine in social interaction; all social actors deliver them. These often unconscious and unintentional messages manifest as brief, unthinking slights, snubs, insults, or other indignities, frequently embedded within a stream of communication. They are verbal, nonverbal, and environmental, and they can appear in facial expressions, body language, terminology, representation, or remarks."[84] Kids are exposed to, and dole out, a range of microaggressions, but the power of adults over children complicates most settings. These microaggressions wash over and through kids and include various forms of racism, state surveillance, criminalization, poverty, sexism/misogyny, coercive sex/gender assignment and policing, queer oppression, trans oppression, and invisibility. Viewing agency as a continuum draws attention to the complexities of inclusion as well as exclusion. I notice that there are often costs to the inclusion and privilege that some of the kids in my study are able to experience, such as the self-hatred and sense of isolation that can come with invisibility or the reluctant binary conformity with which one of my subjects felt he had to comply in order to participate in sport.[85]

Beyond simply limiting the agency, in varying ways, of actual children, however, the social construction of childhood as a disempowered state does much more than control and discipline children; it is mobilized more broadly to justify practices of neoliberal governance that punish other marginal populations. In an examination of sex-offender registries in the United States, for example, educational scholar and prison abolitionist Erica Meiners reported two key findings: first, that the imagined victim in state discourse about sex-offender registries is a (by definition, innocent) white female child; and second, that in practice, sex-offender registries actually disproportionately target and harm those who are some combination of young, LGBT, and visible minority rather than the (exceptional) sexually deviant adult stranger.[86] Meiners noted that a child's minor status, which precludes legal consent, is used to put LGBT and/or visible minority kids and young people engaging in consensual sex on sex-offender registries, with devastating lifelong consequences. Not only do sex-offender registries fail to protect children from far more routine sexual abuse at the hands of adult family members and trusted others, but they inflict harm on children who defy prescribed boundaries.

Western societies lean heavily on constructions of this imaginary innocence and on romanticized discourses of childhood. This "imagined" child, who must be sheltered from unseemly lifestyles and behaviors, lest the child become corrupted or scarred by the experience, turns out to be white, relatively wealthy, a citizen of a wealthy nation of the global north and heterosexual and yet sexually "innocent."[87] There is also a privatization of childhood—as children are defined as dwelling outside the public sphere ("for their own protection")—which masks the power relations at play. These critical perspectives emphasize the ways in which "the child" has generated "languages of contention"[88] with respect to various forms of deviance relating to gender and sexuality as well as class, race, and intelligence.[89] Puar observes, "Historically speaking, settler colonialism has a long history of articulating its violence through the protection of serviceable figures such as women and children, and now the homosexual"[90]—and now, I might add, via the sexually innocent transgender child. The legitimacy of adult authority over children counts on the subliminal link between childhood, innocence, and vulnerability. This innocence, queer scholar Sarah Chinn notes, is an impossible fantasy,[91] yet this imagined child invites normative understandings of sex, gender, race, social class, and citizenship.[92] To adequately empower trans kids, binary sex and gender systems need to be understood as part of a larger assemblage of power relations. I examine how these forces impact the precarity of trans kids via the lens of critical disability scholar Tobin Siebers's theory of complex embodiment: because of its promise in guiding our fight to make the lives of kids such as Wren and Finn literally, more livable.

Disability

Siebers characterizes Western culture as founded on "the ideology of ability,"[93] despite the fact that this flies in the face of the fragility of the human body—our fundamental precariousness. This ideology of ability is fundamental to liberal humanism's hierarchy of humanity and helps to generate an individual's status and qualification for inclusion and access, or exclusion and denial. Colonialism, racialization, patriarchy, class oppression, and "adultism"[94] are all organized around this notion of what it is to be fully human versus not-quite-human, nonhuman,[95] or disabled. Trans kids experience precarity because they are "other" in binary-based schemes of sex/gender differentiation, but the social forces of race, class, age, family, and community support produce variable vulnerability to interpersonal and state violence.

Identity and disability, for Siebers, are socially constructed and complexly embodied; they are "the theories that we use to fit into and travel through the social world."[96] Siebers exhorts scholars to go beyond making general statements about the social construction of identity categories, insisting that we must "map as many details about the construction as possible and . . . track its political, epistemological, and real effects in the world of human beings."[97] In contrast to medical models of disability that define disability "as a property of the individual body that requires medical intervention," the social model of disability defines disability "relative to the social and built environment, arguing that disabling environments produce disability in bodies and require interventions at the level of social justice."[98] Siebers draws our attention to "built environments" that normalize some physical capacities while associating others with disability, which has particular relevance for trans people, as sex-segregated bathrooms and the activities related to urination, defecation, and menstruation that people are unable to opt out of, for example, socially construct visible trans and gender-nonconforming people as deviant, that is, disabled.[99]

The disabling impact of built environments causes suffering for some people, but these shared experiences of suffering—the "dossier"—can be mobilized for resistance.[100] Sharing this dossier of disabling experiences renders power relations that socially construct categories of disability more visible; that is, they enable us to see the blueprint. And if we can see the blueprint, we are better able to modify or dismantle oppressive environments. In seeking resistance strategies to racist and anti-trans systems of oppression, Riley Snorton pointedly asks, "what stories do we need to surround ourselves with for the presents we currently inhabit?"[101]

The kids in the book demonstrated profound determination to realize and disclose their affirmed genders in often forbidding social contexts that disabled them along multiple axes. They engaged in self-directed identity construction despite incredible environmental pressure to go along with the sex/gender assigned to them. Conversations focused on vulnerability and the harms they experienced but also on the pleasure of self-definition and the possibilities inherent in resistance to coercive sex assignment. There is reason to resist the sentimentality of dominant narratives about transgender kids as either helpless victims or heroic resistance fighters, though the stories that follow show that at times these narratives are not misplaced.

Exposing the blueprint of the social construction of binary systems of sex and gender by documenting the experiences of transgender kids is an act of resistance. As Siebers suggests, precarity is embodied, mapped in time and space, in complex ways. Left unchecked, precarity can disable transgender children, but documenting and sharing it can confront, resist, and transform unjust environments. The stories of trans kids and their parents, as related in this book, are important.

In the next four chapters, I pay particular attention to four key questions:

1. Why do some trans kids have more agency and seem to thrive, while others have less resilience and suffer more?
2. How does poverty and gendered and racial violence impact the lives of trans kids?
3. How do we make the lives of trans kids more livable?
4. How might some social change efforts and achievements on behalf of trans kids who are visible and supported by mobilized parents unwittingly marginalize more precarious racialized and/or impoverished cisgender kids?

In chapter 2, I chronicle the many ways that my participants are disabled in school settings and the consequences of this disabling for their current and future precarity.

2

Schools

I think high school is always sort of stressful and big for anyone, but on top of that, I'm coming in as a different person from other people's perspective. So, in the first few weeks, I think it was super difficult for me. Lots of people were still getting my pronouns and name wrong because they were adjusting, the kids from my old school; I was getting questions. And then at this point, people started to gossip. So the kids from my elementary school were telling the kids from other schools that I was trans. And as a result, I started sort of getting hate from some of them.
—Greg, 13, Euro-Canadian

From 1967 to 1971, I attended an all-white elementary school in Toronto, Ontario, that served the western-European Canadian middle- and upper-middle-class families residing on the neighborhood's east side and the poorer western-European Canadian and southern- and eastern-European families living on its west side. I do not remember having a classmate who did not "pass" as white until fourth grade, when I moved out of the neighborhood. Girls and boys had separate entrances to the school building: we lined up at least 100 yards apart. The playground was sex divided: the boys had an area that was at least six times bigger than that allocated to the girls. Girls skipped rope and played jumpsie[1] next to the teachers' parking lot, while boys ran wild, in great swooping arcs on the larger part of the playground. By third grade, I remember crossing over to the boys' side on occasion, without censure, as long as I had a legitimate purpose: running laps because I had joined the cross-country team, for example. School activities were routinely organized by grouping girls and boys separately. Although it was a little unusual, I had friends who were boys and friends who were girls, but rarely did these two groups come together out of school. For the most part, I moved freely back and forth.

But at school, there was a dress code. Until I was in fourth grade, when the influence of second-wave feminism began to impact Canadian public school culture, girls in Ontario schools were required to wear skirts and dresses—no pants allowed. I hated this dress code, hated the leotards with the crotch that hung down to my knees no matter how often I pulled them up, hated freezing to death before school and at recess when frigid winter winds whipped up from the lake, and hated not being able to wear jeans or pants. Finally, in third grade, I received permission from my teacher to wear pants to school in the winter as long as I wore them under a skirt and took them off as soon as I arrived in the classroom. That this was a huge victory for me indicates how little agency I had around my choice of clothing.

I am a relatively privileged person with regard to key measures of whiteness, class position, and employment in a respected professional field, but as a gender-nonconforming adopted girl who lacked a secure attachment with either parent, one of whom was emotionally abusive, I was dogged by loneliness, depression, and self-hatred throughout my childhood and adolescence. I was occasionally lifted up, just enough, however, by teachers whose regard and warmth carried me along. It happened first in third grade, when my teacher distinguished herself from her predecessors and treated me with warmth and interest. I flourished in her care. Mrs. B. was young—and pretty hip, when I think back—and seemed to like all the things that other adults did not like about me—my smarts, assertiveness, natural confidence, roughness, and athleticism. She must have been a feminist. She liked me, odd girl that I was, and I could feel it; I was starved for it.

Yet not everyone in that classroom flourished—the kids in the bottom-tier reading group, for example, were disabled by a performance-oriented, "skill and drill" delivery model of education and had low status among their peers. There were probably children in that classroom whom I do not remember at all who had a miserable time while I flourished, perhaps had a miserable time, in part, *because* I flourished. There was always a pecking order, whether I had a good teacher who cared about me and the class in general or a teacher whose authoritarianism just reinforced existing hierarchies. In these early school years, I learned how awful it felt to be on the bottom of that pyramid, and I was forever fearful of being consigned there. I wish I could say that I responded less oppressively to this lesson, but I did not. For that to have happened, I would have needed coaching from an adult I trusted. Instead, I learned to hold my own and contributed to the toxic environment brewing around me.

How School Shapes Us

As my own experience indicates and as a number of studies have shown,[2] the 13 years children normally spend in school in Canada and the U.S. shapes personality and worldview and negatively or positively determines future opportunities. School success is a predictor of future economic success, and this outcome corresponds strongly to the socio-economic status of a child's family. For some students, school is a place of learning, opportunity, and social engagement; for others, it is a place where they fail and/or are targeted, defeated, and unsafe. Between these two extremes live a range of others, who do not attract attention, neither thriving nor visibly flailing. Some of these children *appear* to be fine, at least on the outside, but inwardly struggle with depression, anxiety, and shame and/or are living under the shadow of abuse. Some play a waiting game, biding their time until they can get out from under adult thumbs. Yet somehow there always seem to be a few particularly charismatic survivors who bristle with resilience and energy: the flamboyantly queer and incredibly talented; bold and unapologetic girls; racialized kids whose brilliance allows them to, at least partially, transcend the limits of the identities imposed on them. Some burn with a bright inner light and the strength to make the most of the tiniest opportunities. This latter group almost coheres with the promise of liberal individualism and a self-improvement mantra encouraging positive attitudes and hard work. However, relying on these examples is both too easy and naive, for even kids such as these can be crushed by oppressive forces. In C. J. Pascoe's book *Dude, You're a Fag*, for example, one of the kids she focuses on is a 15-year-old racialized, gender-nonconforming boy named Ricky, who is an incredibly talented dancer and choreographer. The failure of the school to protect him from anti-gay and anti-trans violence results in his being pushed out of school.

Schools are a central site where children bump up against an environment built around naturalized but falsely universal abilities: including but not limited to those related to gender and sexual conformity, English-language proficiency, neurotypical learning styles, the "able body," and white, middle-class standards of living and cultural norms. Kids must be enrolled in one form of government-certified school program or another until the age of 16, and so odds are school will be a difficult space for many kids at some point during this exposure, whether as a result of poverty, racialization, neurodiversity, inadequate support, physical confinement, adult authoritarianism, or sheer lack of relevance to the rest of their lives. Additional factors for LGBT kids, in general, and for most of the participants in this study include institutional reliance on binary sex organization, practices of sex segregation and differentiation, and anti-queer and trans-oppressive environments. Sex-segregated and sex-differentiated spaces and activities, both formal and informal, generate profound discomfort for transgender kids who assert their nonnormative gender identities, for those who are invisible, or for those who are just figuring themselves out. Schools are often spaces of psychological difficulty and physical danger for trans kids.

Canadian and U.S. studies clearly indicate that public schools are inhospitable to sexual-minority and transgender students. The 2011 *First National Climate Survey on Homophobia, Biphobia, and Transphobia in Canadian Schools* by the Egale Canada Human Rights Trust produced alarming findings that include the following:

- 79% of transgender students felt unsafe in their schools, particularly with respect to use of washrooms, change rooms, and corridors.
- 63% of transgender students reported having been verbally harassed about their sexual orientation.
- 74% of transgender students reported having been verbally harassed about their gender expression.
- 37% of transgender students reported having been physically harassed.
- 70% of all participating students reported hearing homophobic and transphobic remarks from peers.
- 10% of LGBTQ students and 17% of trans students reported hearing homophobic and transphobic remarks from teachers and school staff.[3]

These findings are echoed in a U.S. study authored by the Gay, Lesbian and Straight Education Network (GLSEN). The *2015 National School*

Climate Survey: The Experiences of Lesbian, Gay, Bisexual, Transgender, and Queer Youth in Our Nation's Schools reports the following:

- 58% of LGBTQ students felt unsafe in their schools because of their sexual orientation, while 43% felt unsafe because of their gender expression.
- 32% of LGBTQ students felt unsafe and/or uncomfortable enough to miss a day of school in the preceding months, while 10% missed four or more days.
- 49% reported experiencing electronic harassment/cyberbullying.
- 60% reported experiencing sexual harassment.
- 98% heard homophobic remarks, with 60% of these hearing this language frequently.
- 96% of LGBTQ students heard negative remarks about atypical gender expression, and of these, 70% heard these remarks frequently.
- 86% heard transphobic remarks, 40% of these frequently.
- 63% of LGBTQ students in this study reported hearing negative remarks about gender expression from teachers and school staff.[4]

The GLSEN report cites policies that specifically targeted transgender students, noting that 51% of trans students were unable to use their preferred name or pronoun, while 60% had been restricted to using a bathroom or change room according to their legal sex.[5] Tellingly, both studies identified sex-segregated spaces in schools, such as bathrooms and locker rooms, as particularly unsafe. Kids' experiences of homo-negativity and trans oppression are heavily influenced by adult authority, a hidden curriculum, and peer culture and tend to crystallize around bathroom and locker-room access and sex-segregated and sex-differentiated sporting practices.

The pressure on kids to act in "gender appropriate" ways, depending on their racial and class location, occurs because of the way that sex/gender is structured into existing institutions such as families and schools.[6] Gendered spaces, sex-segregated spaces, and sex-differentiated activities are often the first place of crisis for trans kids; where they are allowed to go, and who they are allowed to be when in those spaces, is typically restricted by the binary sex marker on their identity documents. Educational institutions use databases that require and perpetuate binary sex markers. Often this crisis can at best be resolved to allow for binary transition, for those who seek it, and tolerance for those who resist its categories altogether. At worst, it provides the basis of, and justification for, the systemic abuse and dehumanization of trans kids.

School-based peer groups—the artificial age-based segregation that characterizes modern schooling—are often challenging for trans kids to navigate. As Edgardo Menvielle observes, "The amount of rejection that children actually experience in the early school years varies significantly from severe to almost none. There is also great variation in children's social competence to secure a social position and to deal with rejection when it happens."[7] Nevertheless, in Menvielle's experience, trans kids "experienced more social difficulties and social anxiety, perhaps related to the enforcement of gender roles in real-time as well as the budding internalization of these rules by the child." Gender-variant kids "may experience significant social isolation" as a result of "a) pervasive girl-boy social segregation that develops in elementary school, b) the preference of many children to associate predominantly if not exclusively with same-sex peers, and c) children's enforcement of gender boundaries, often reinforced by adults."[8] Menvielle goes on to make an observation about the particular vulnerability of feminine boys in the punishing social context of the school, noting that "over time opportunities for friendship across sex groups become fewer. This is particularly marked for feminine boys who tend to receive the brunt of mocking and ridicule for not living up to the normative masculine expectations by other boys, and who also may lose friendships as girls' groups become more closed off."[9] It is important to emphasize that even those who are not personally targeted but who witness the routine homo-negativity and gender bullying that is particularly characteristic of interactions between boys and young men or who witness sexism and misogyny directed at girls and women shape and limit themselves in response.[10]

Hiding, Coping, and Surviving

Ray-Ray is troubled by the homo-negativity he regularly witnesses in high school: he hears other students saying things like "faggot" on a regular basis. Even this is not directed at him for his gender nonconformity, it bothers him because, he said, "my mom is gay" and because his own sexual orientation is up in the air. He finds it particularly disturbing that "people display these behaviors until you mention something, and they're all super apologetic. And it's kind of like, 'Well, you've got to stop doing it to actually mean your apology,' and they don't." From Ray-Ray's perspective, those who tend to make most of the homo-negative remarks are the jocks: "the guys who play basketball, they wear like athletic shorts all the time." Ray-Ray also observes a racial hierarchy at his high school. Although Euro-Canadians—and he is one of them—are a minority in his school, they are disproportionately represented among the "regulars," which is the term he and his friends use to refer to those at the top of the social pyramid. Ray-Ray observes that many of the homophobic jocks he referred to are well represented among the disproportionately white "regulars." Like Ray-Ray, Michael was not targeted himself but found the high school environment fairly anti-queer. According to Michael, the guys who make homo-negative comments are "kind of like not the well-educated group of people." Michael and Ray-Ray's accounts both situate "ignorant" white jocks at the epicenter of gender and sexuality policing.

Much to the dismay of Frank (13, Euro-Canadian), his official documents contain highly feminized first and middle names and the sex designation "F," which has caused serious difficulty, as his high school insists on using his birth name and birth sex on official school documents, including class attendance sheets. Frank explained why it is so important to him to have his gender identity publicly affirmed in school documents: "It's still hard because a lot of those kids are from downtown, not very accepting, so it's hard to have my entire personal information out there just from one little letter; it's my entire personal information in one little letter." While Frank is most afraid of "kids from downtown" who are racialized (Indigenous), impoverished, and really "rough," research suggests that anti-queer and anti-trans peer aggression is just as likely to come from high-status populations, making queer and trans kids a common target of verbal, social, and physical violence. Pascoe makes readers a witness to these events, underscoring the conflation of gender and sexuality: boys who perform masculinity inadequately are branded "fags" or described with female epithets.[11] Gender and sexuality put-downs tend to be used interchangeably.

Trans kids adopt various strategies in response to the sense of crisis they experience around sex-segregated and sex-differentiated spaces and activities in school settings. The freedom to socially transition is one variable key to their agency. There have been legal efforts to bar trans people from using facilities consistent with their affirmed identities in many U.S. states, but a number of schools *are* increasingly adapting to the presence of trans kids, some voluntarily and others because they are legally required to do so. Trans students are typically at the mercy of teachers and are extremely vulnerable; adults have a great deal of power over those who are deemed "minors," and this power is institutionalized in school settings where age-based subordination and binary gender systems combine to lessen the agency of trans kids. That said, there are many people working in school systems who care deeply and work tirelessly to empower trans kids, but commonly received knowledge about gender as a "natural" system can create blind spots and unwitting compliance in trans oppression.

The decisions adults in authority make about whether to respect a trans kid's gender identity have powerful consequences. Greg (13, Euro-Canadian) and Wren have had much better luck than Frank with their schools, where supportive administrators manually changed all their identity markers on class and attendance lists. School principals can override databases to replace assigned gender markers with affirmed ones, but stubborn technocrats and staff who do not understand how to support these students or are deliberately negligent and oppressive can make the situation worse. Hunter describes his experience coming out as trans when attending a special education program for children who are neurodiverse or learning disabled in his school district—he has been diagnosed with fetal alcohol syndrome. Hunter described arriving at school one morning and announcing to his class that he was transgender. His teachers responded by calling his mother to ask "if she was accepting this": "And, of course, she said, 'I wouldn't be sending my kid to the school dressed like this or saying a different name if I wasn't accepting it,' but they called her at least three or four times, like farther apart, and just kept asking the same question. But they would never say anything straight to my face." Hunter was understandably angry that they did not take his word for it. But the multiple calls to his mother speak to another dimension of oppression: Hunter's mother is poor, Indigenous, and a single parent—part of a demographic that is particularly vulnerable to state surveillance, oversight, and child apprehension. These repeated phone calls to her need to be understood within the context of ongoing colonialism.

Since coming out as trans, Hunter acknowledges that his teachers have had some adjusting to do as he has announced "at least three name changes in one class." Hunter has overheard his teachers misgendering him, referring to him by his "dead name" (see glossary) and dismissing the credibility of his transition. The assumption that children's and young people's identities are static and that their exploration of gendered identities, trying on of names, and so on are not to be taken seriously speaks to the disabling effects of binary gender and age subordination as key organizing principles of mainstream schools. That adults at Hunter's school responded to his transition by questioning his authority and that of his mother is consistent with the pervasive ageist assumption that children lack knowledge about, and authority over, themselves and the colonial assumption that Indigenous parents do not know what is best for their children. But socioeconomic privilege is not necessarily a mitigating factor.

Alicia (17, Euro-American) is a member of an upper-middle-class family living in a suburban U.S. community. Alicia experienced bullying and assault while attending a private school for boys. The religious orientation of Alicia's "super Catholic" school seems to have been a contributing factor. Alicia told me she "got bullied a lot": "Most of it was just, you know, people beating you up, throwing your stuff around, breaking your items, just a lot of getting called names and stuff. I got called a lot of [homophobic] names." One of the worst instances happened in a school bathroom when she found herself surrounded by all of the boys in her class: "As soon as I'd finished using the urinal, someone pulled me, threw me down on the ground, and everyone in the class started kicking me, and that was pretty bad. I got a lot of bruises. It happened to a lot of people; it wasn't just me. But it happened often to me." Alicia believes that if her peers had known she was transgender, "it would have been even worse," and this feeling contributed to her decision to remain hidden for years. Complaining to the administration about the assaults and indignities at the hands of peers proved fruitless for Alicia. Her school principal dismissed her complaints, telling her she was bringing it on herself, saying, "You look like a girl. You *should* put up with that stuff." This same message was delivered to Alicia's mother when she complained about the bullying her "son" was experiencing.

The administration's response to these complaints made Alicia feel she was on her own when she later experienced a sexual assault in a school bathroom. She succeeded in fighting off the assault by "stabbing the person a couple of times" with a pencil: "So it never happened again, but seeing as I'd already tried talking to the current principal about that stuff, I didn't really see that there was anybody to really go to about it." Alicia felt that there was no one to turn to, although she said, "Looking back on it, I could even have gone to the police or something, but when you're a kid you just think, 'Oh, no one's going to care and no one's going to listen, so why bother?'" It was only several years later that she shared these experiences with her parents when they were attending family counseling together and her mom and dad were struggling to understand why Alicia experienced so much stress about bathrooms. Left to her own devices, Alicia learned to stand up and fight back: "Before I was out of there, I managed to punch a couple people in the face, and that stopped a lot of the bullying." Leaving the all-boys school for a public high school improved Alicia's situation because she left her antagonists behind and was able to connect with some students who were either LGBT themselves or "less uptight about gender and sexuality."

There were no reliable adult allies that Alicia felt she could turn to as she experienced these harrowing ordeals and no one to whom she could truly show herself. She kept herself hidden until the last year of high school. Her parents became supportive as she transitioned, but she survived on her own for years. Although high school provided a better experience for Alicia, the trans-oppressive actions of the school administration and of one particular teacher created a forbidding environment in which to transition. Two years prior to transitioning, for example, she was pulled out of class and given an in-school suspension for wearing "women's" clothing, something that made no sense to her, as "it wasn't a dress-code violation." She had simply "started trying to expand [her] wardrobe": "You know, just trying to try out new clothing, . . . just a skirt and a top. It was just normal clothes." The gendered nature of the dress code was so taken for granted that no such stipulation was deemed to be necessary.

One of Alicia's high school teachers not only was explicitly anti-trans and racist but required students to perform in trans-oppressive class plays as part of their graded requirements. These plays contained homo-negative and trans-negative jokes. Alicia reported, for example, that her teacher would "have people cross-dressing on the stage, and then he'd make it really disgusting, you know, kiss the person and then have the person not realize it and then have the person get all angry." She described her "entire first two years" as "pretty darn uncomfortable in that class" because her teacher "continually cracked really offensive jokes. Most of his jokes were homophobic." Alicia found that her teacher began targeting transgender people in particular as transgender rights bills gained media attention in her state and around the region. Initially, Alicia stood up to him, telling him that his remarks and jokes were wrong and that he should stop, but the teacher responded by asking her if she was transgender. This question put her on the spot, and she backed down: "After he'd just finished saying all this gross stuff against transgender people, it's just really uncomfortable, especially since I hadn't come out to my teachers and stuff. It was just really stressful." Alicia's teacher was also crudely sexist and racist, making fun of Black students, for example, if "they walked into class wearing new shoes." Even though Alicia liked and excelled in the subject and would have earned a special diploma if she had stayed with it, she quit the class in senior year because she just could not take it anymore.

The majority of transgender kids, as Mark Hellen reminds us, are invisible,[12] and Alicia was one of them. This invisibility masks the harm that a binary and heteronormative social culture causes in school settings. In addition to harming visible queer and trans kids and invisible trans kids such as Alicia, it reinforces sexist and misogynist norms, and the harm that this does, to all of us, should be a call to arms.

A number of the trans kids in this book experienced verbal abuse, threats of violence, and physical violence at school that have made it impossible for them to continue attending, either temporarily or indefinitely. Such interruptions to school attendance have negative mental health consequences and significantly lessen the likelihood of academic success and therefore increase the likelihood of future precarity. Frank's experience is instructive and chilling with regard to the disabling environment of school contexts for (voluntarily or otherwise) visible transgender children.

There are significant differences between Alicia and Frank concerning access to wealth, gender-affirming healthcare, and opportunity.

Alicia was bullied in a wealthy, suburban private school. Frank is a member of a low-income family and lives in a conservative, rural Canadian community that is an eight-hour drive from the big city where his endocrinologist practices and his pro bono lawyer works. His mother, Catherine, is his family's primary breadwinner and has been unable to work for several years. Frank's experience in several schools has been characterized by anti-queer and trans-oppressive abuse by peers as well as teachers. The way the school administration and the school district handled violence furthered Frank's victimization. Frank has spent long stretches of time out of school—the longest period being a year and a half—because it has simply been unsafe for him to attend. He has been fortunate to have a few key allies, including his mother, his younger sister, and a big-city lawyer. They have not been able to keep Frank safe, but they have demonstrated to him that he is worth fighting for and have kept his very bright spark burning.

The disabling impact of coercive gendering began to impact Frank in preschool when, in contrast to the information on his birth certificate, he kept insisting that he was a boy. Preschool staff responded by contacting his mother to express concern and to recommend a behavior-modification program for him. Based on their knowledge of the family's history with domestic violence—Frank's father had assaulted his mother[13]—the preschool staff pathologized Frank's gender expression and assumed a position of authority over Catherine. The smallness of the community meant that this explanation for his gender expression followed Frank to elementary school, where it was adopted by most of the staff. Catherine experienced considerable pressure from both preschool and elementary school staff to put a stop to Frank's determination to live as a boy. Their certainty about the need for Frank to stop was troubling enough that she did try, at times, to get Frank to stop, but she saw the harm this was doing to him and started fighting to have Frank accepted as a boy at school. This battle has been mostly a losing one for both of them.

Frank experienced gender policing and anti-trans bullying from peers, teachers, and school personnel in elementary school. He was systematically misgendered at school and reproached and humiliated for insisting on identifying as a boy. Frank has resisted his assigned sex against fierce opposition for years. The extent of abuse that Frank has experienced in school contexts, without giving in or conforming, is an indication of how strongly he feels himself to be a boy and how incredibly courageous he is. Neither Frank nor his family had any knowledge of transgender people or possibilities until he was 11, when a knowledgeable and compassionate camp counselor he encountered introduced the term "transgender" to him. Catherine has long been lesbian and gay positive, but she had never heard of transgender people either, so they fought this fight on their own, in isolation from trans communities and LGBT resources, for nearly seven years.

Literature on resilience in children demonstrates the value of even a little adult respect and warmth for children who are deeply at risk; somewhere in their social network, someone acknowledges the child or young person and cares about them.[14] This acknowledgment does not remediate their structural oppression, but it does foster resilience in the face of it. Beyond Frank's immediate family, there have been a few adults in positions of authority who went to bat for him. According to Catherine, Frank has had a supportive social worker and a "great kindergarten teacher." As she describes it, the only way Frank would go to school in kindergarten was if his teacher picked him up and walked him to school herself. So she did this, every day, in spite of being a parent herself with children who needed to be dropped off at a different school beforehand. When Frank moved on to first grade, his new teacher was so abusive that he repeatedly ran away from school, frequently showing up at his mother's place of work on the other side of town. It was this pattern of truancy that resulted in Frank being assigned to a social worker, who turned out to be a key support. Frank's former kindergarten teacher noticed what was happening to him in first grade and went so far as to report her colleague to the provincial teachers' association—a huge step for her to take in a small town—and arranged to have Frank transferred back to kindergarten as "her helper" for the remainder of the year.

Sadly, the kindergarten teacher was an exception, as elementary school was an intolerant place filled with misery for Frank. Frank described both the teachers and his peers in elementary school as "brutal," explaining, "When I would tell the teachers that the kids were making fun of me, they didn't get told it's not right to discriminate against other people." In Frank's experience, if he reported it when kids would call him a "fag" or a "girl dyke," it just made the situation worse. Teachers regularly punished and shamed him for insisting he was a boy and would force him to "confess" to "really being a girl" in front of other students. Most of his teachers and the school administrators viewed him as either mentally ill or abhorrently deviant or both and saw it as their legitimate role to correct him and to ignore his mother's instructions to acknowledge him as a boy. The way they went about doing this speaks to the overall harshness of the school environment and the negative impact it would have on all the children in attendance. For example, as Frank's was an inner-city school, local corporations contributed Christmas gifts each year that were sex typed. Although Catherine repeatedly asked that Frank be placed on the "boy list," he would be given a toy stereotypically associated with girls, such as a Barbie, in front of the whole school. In one such instance, when given a doll, Frank ran away sobbing and was then given a detention for refusing to apologize to the corporate donor.

Frank was regularly bullied by a group of boys at school, and the staff condoned this behavior via their inaction. The bullying culminated in a violent sexual assault—off school property—by two of his classmates when Frank was 10 years old. According to Catherine, "Two boys ended up really brutally sexually and physically assaulting Frank. They damaged his septum and some vertebrae and penetrated him with objects. It was really brutal." Frank was hospitalized for five days after the attack. There were two particularly shocking outcomes related to this attack. First, a new social worker assigned to Frank when he was admitted to the hospital failed to make a formal report of the incident. And second, the school failed to implement a viable safety plan to enable Frank to return to school and instead went on to suspend him for refusing to be silent about the assault once he returned.

In the immediate aftermath of the assault, Catherine agreed with the school administration that it was in Frank's best interest to keep him out of school while a safety plan for his return was developed. But when a month went by without a word from the school, Catherine phoned the principal to tell him that Frank would be returning to school and that she expected him to be kept safe. The "safety plan" the school put in place consisted of keeping Frank's assailants in the same class with him and restricting Frank, who loved playing basketball at recess, to the area at the back of the school used by younger children, while the boys who had assaulted him enjoyed their regular access to the larger playground and the basketball hoops. The school seemed to be more concerned about protecting Frank's assailants than it was about protecting him. This attitude was evident when, upon his return to school, Frank was warned not to talk about the assault, or he would be suspended. Frank complied with this order, but when his assailants complained to his teacher that Frank had told friends of his who attended another school about the assault, the principal suspended Frank. Frank attempted suicide the day he was suspended.

Many victims of sexual assault feel their treatment by police and courts constitutes a "second rape."[15] Frank had a similar experience at the hands of school and school district personnel. The harm that authorities at Frank's elementary school have done to him is consistent with the acts of state "abandonment" and "letting die" highlighted by queer/trans necropolitics. That Frank has survived at all speaks to his incredible resilience and the support of his family. Catherine, focused on keeping her son alive, kept Frank at home after his suicide attempt and began a long, difficult, and ultimately unsuccessful fight to get the school to address issues relating to his safety in a meaningful way. Frank was out of school for a year and a half while this fight was going on. Catherine was quick to say that she did not want the kids who assaulted Frank to be criminalized for their actions. She sees their behavior as evidence of their own neglect and mistreatment, as Indigenous children living in poverty and with the damaging effects of ongoing colonialism. As she explains, "I'm not big on punishment; I don't even really support the whole punishment model, but I'm sorry, if it was race, we'd be doing something. But you shouldn't go around making homophobic, transphobic slurs either. When you know damn well that kid knows, and they've been told, and you're still calling my kid a fucking "he/she/it," time to up the discipline maybe." As a self-identified anti-racist ally and a working-class person with a strong labor background, Catherine had no desire to see these children harshly punished or further damaged. She just wanted to see measures taken to protect Frank (and other potential victims) from further harm.

After a year-and-a-half battle that went nowhere, Catherine gave up and enrolled Frank in another school in their district. He attempted to pass as a boy there; but the smallness of the community meant his status of being designated female at birth became widely known, and Frank once again experienced trans-oppressive abuse at the hands of teachers and peers. Fortunately for Frank (and Catherine), a lawyer who specializes in LGBT rights cases learned of Frank's case via word of mouth. This lawyer has worked pro bono on Frank's behalf for several years. This lawyer, Catherine explained, "saved Frank, saved us. She's fought with the school district. They're assholes. They just do what they want. I mean, we're treated better now, because we're lawyered up, right." But even with this legal support, Catherine feels relatively powerless in dealing with the school district: "I don't feel any safer to go up against the district. I know if I went up against the district, they're a little bit nervous about me, because I'm lawyered up, but when push comes to shove, if I had to get into a full-on battle with them, yeah—I wouldn't." The small town that Frank lives in and his family's lack of mobility due to poverty preclude the possibility of Frank reinventing himself in a new environment. But Frank is courageous and determined to stay, as much to fight to make things better for other trans kids as to maintain connections with the people he loves and who love him.

When I interviewed Frank in 2015, he was about to start high school and was excited about it. As stressful as he finds it all, Frank's resilience is evident in that he remains hopeful that each new environment will be better. Sadly, this optimism is often misplaced. I learned in a subsequent conversation with his mother that the principal of the high school was reneging on his earlier promise to remove Frank's dead names and female sex marker from attendance lists (which are posted on the door of each classroom). The principal claimed to be unable to accommodate this request because class lists have to correspond with the provincial database. Catherine responded by telling the principal, "I don't give a shit about any of that. I don't care if you have to manually go around and put 'M' on the class list. That's all I'm asking." This request was not unreasonable—a number of other trans kids I interviewed received this kind of confidentiality about their assigned sex from their schools. Although Frank was unaware of the principal's plans when I spoke with him, he was justifiably afraid that he would be harmed if others at his high school found out that he is trans. Soon after school began that fall, Frank experienced anti-trans bullying that made him afraid for his life, and he was forced to leave school once again.

Under the circumstances, Frank is an astonishingly courageous and resilient kid, but his life chances have been severely compromised by the hostile environments of the various public schools he has endeavored to attend. The assumption that binary sex categories must be determined by professional adults at the time of birth is clearly operating to harm Frank in the school environment and to contribute to his own and his family's precarity.

Tru Wilson's (12, Black/Euro-Canadian/Indigenous) very public story is another compelling example of the way religious schools often provide an added dimension of difficulty for trans kids. Tru's desire to transition in her religiously conservative private school in fifth grade placed her and her family in great conflict with the Roman Catholic Archdiocese of Vancouver, which administered both her school and her family's church. Tru's school provided a particularly difficult context for her transition because of its religious conservatism in general and the requirement to wear gendered uniforms, and, as her mother, Michelle, explained, "there were things where they would separate them by gender too, the girls on this side and boys on that side." Tru had been living as a girl at home and a boy at school for two months at this point, and this double life was causing her severe distress. As she described it, "It was basically torture for me to have to be forced to say that 'I'm Trey.' I wanted so badly to say my name is Tru, but I couldn't. Because at home I'm so used to being Tru, and I love being Tru, and it's just so amazing. But at school, I had to be Trey, and sometimes I couldn't deal with that. When someone called me Trey, I just wanted to shout out and correct them: 'My name is Tru, and you're going to call me that.' I couldn't take it anymore. The pain was just too unbearable." Without clearing it with her parents, Tru took the bold step of informing first her teacher and then the school principal, "I'd really like to wear the girl's uniform. You're infringing on my ability to express myself by making me wear pants." Michelle characterized this action as "incredibly brave," noting that prior to transitioning, Tru was a really shy kid, "not confident in her abilities or her skills. But she had these moments where she would just put herself out there."

The impact on Tru's mental health while she was forced to continue attending school as a boy alarmed her parents: it became clear to them that doing so was no longer viable. On the first day of the new school year, Michelle and Tru's father, Garfield, provided the school with a letter stating that Tru would be attending as a girl from then on, but the school refused to allow her to transition. According to Michelle, "The first time we sat down with the principal, he handed us a letter from their lawyer and said, you know, 'Even though we acknowledge that we need to respect based on the human rights charter [in British Columbia], we need to respect and support, we just want to be sure because this is a big thing to ask of your *son* and shouldn't be anything that's rushed into, and we'd like you to get a second assessment done.' And they gave us a list of doctors, one of which was Dr. Kenneth Zucker[16] in Toronto" (my emphasis). Michelle and Garfield were surprised by the opposition of the school administration and the school board, so, as a family, they weighed their options. Michelle got to work gathering resources by contacting the local LGBT center, where she was given the name of barbara findlay, a lawyer who specializes in advocating for transgender rights. findlay was initially optimistic that the school was open to Tru transitioning, but when the school sent a second letter refusing to allow Tru to transition on the grounds of religious freedom, it was clear they had a fight on their hands. As Tru told it, "I could stay at school and fight for it or go back to my old school, and I wanted to stay at my school so bad, because of all my friends, so I tried to fight. I tried to fight. I tried to stay, but I just couldn't." Tru had a very close group of friends at the school who lovingly supported her transition all the way, and it was extremely hard for her to leave them: "By the time I had almost finished transitioning, it felt like they were a part of me because they were so supportive, and if I left them, then that part of me would have been gone." But after two months of negotiating with the school and the school board, Michelle realized, "They weren't budging. They weren't going to move," and she and Garfield made the difficult decision to remove all three of their kids from the school (and the related religious community) and enroll them at a school where Tru's transition would be supported. As important as it is to focus on the vulnerability of the particular trans kid, this case provides a poignant example of the impact of trans oppression on the child's entire family—especially siblings who are attending the same school.[17]

Michelle and Garfield took time to settle their children into their new school and then had their lawyer file a human rights complaint against the Roman Catholic Arch Diocese of Vancouver.[18] This complaint was settled out of court in Tru's favor to enable future transgender kids to transition.[19] The terms of the settlement included a financial payment, the adoption of a gender inclusive policy in the school district, and a personal apology to Tru from the head of the regional Catholic diocese and its lawyers. Michelle describes taking strength from her Indigenous heritage throughout this process: as a granddaughter of a survivor of Canada's residential school system, she feels strongly that "there's something about people taking ownership for the damage that they've caused. An apology's huge." When Tru learned the terms of the settlement she said, "I felt so good, and for a second, I thought that I'd be able to go back. But then I told myself, 'No.' What they did was almost unforgiveable, and I was trying to be as generous as I could, and I gave them so much time. It was just torture, and I was breaking down, and I was paying less and less attention to my schoolwork, and it felt like my grades were dropping, and I just couldn't do it." Tru and her family have the satisfaction of knowing their efforts have produced social change. The next child who wants to transition at Tru's old school or at any school in the province will have to be formally accommodated.

A number of the kids in this book encountered considerably less difficulty in transitioning at their schools, which had a positive impact on their overall well-being. Socially transitioning at school typically, but not necessarily, depending on the school, requires a formal diagnosis of gender dysphoria and/or a letter from a doctor or clinician stipulating the necessity, from a health standpoint, of allowing the child to live in their affirmed gender. Wren's transition from gender-nonconforming boy to gender-conforming girl may have been the most seamless—it required no documentation or formal process, which was largely a result of the background work her parents had done to ensure that their (at the time) gender-nonconforming "son" started school in a welcoming environment. When Wren was four and approaching school age, her parents were worried that "he" would be targeted for gender policing if they enrolled "him" in public school, so they looked around for a more gender-inclusive alternative. Jordan, one of Wren's parents, explained, "At the time, we understood Wren as a gender-nonconforming boy. We didn't want 'him' to stop wearing dresses and skirts unless 'he' wanted to stop wearing dresses and skirts, not because 'he' was being teased or pressured."

There was no perfect school for Wren, but a "good enough," not very expensive private school in a completely inconvenient location vis-à-vis Wren's parents' places of employment ("but we did it anyway") was chosen because of the openness and willingness of the staff to work to create a safe space for Wren's gender nonconformity. In spite of the staff's lack of experience with transgender students or kids who were as gender nonconforming as Wren, they recognized that antibinary/antisexist work would benefit not only Wren but everyone in the school. Wren attended this "kind of hippy," as Jordan described it, Canadian private school from kindergarten through fourth grade, and it was during this time that she transitioned. The summer before she was to start second grade, Wren let her parents know that she wanted to be referred to with female pronouns. Her social transition at school, such as it was, was accomplished when Jordan sent an email to all the parents seeking carpool participants, referring to Wren as "my daughter" rather than "my son"—with no explanation. Jordan described this moment as "a beautiful nonevent."

While gender categories still played a role in the school, there was a lot of mixed, as opposed to divided, gender play through all grade levels, and Wren's teachers—and sometimes her classmates—often interrupted general incidents of sexism and specific queries about Wren's gender. As luck would have it, when Wren was in third grade, her new-to-the-school teacher was gender-nonconforming themselves with a gender-nonconforming child of their own. This teacher worked consciously to break down gender divisions in the social dynamics of the class. Wren told me that she felt that every teacher at her school "has done something about the boy/girl thing." The school proved to be a "good enough" environment for Wren to transition from boy to girl.

While Wren's transition was a "nonevent," Esme's was a carefully planned and scripted one. Esme (10, Euro-Canadian) transitioned as a six-year-old in first grade in the middle of the school term. In a process carefully managed by her parents—primarily her mother—and the school administration, an information session was held for parents of children in Esme's grade, and a local trans-positive expert delivered an in-class workshop to Esme's class to prepare them to welcome her as a girl. Esme hung out in another part of the school while this workshop happened. She revealed that she had a hard time reentering the classroom because though she very much wanted this transition, it came with a lot of anxiety for her: "The first day that they talked to the kids I got really kind of freaked out. I was in first grade, right? So I started crying. No one was teasing me or anything; it was just—if you tell someone something, it just feels a bit new to you." Esme went on to say, however, that although she was "crying in the morning, the rest of the day passed like normal; no one said anything about it." Things have gone relatively smoothly since. Occasionally Esme will be asked *the* question: "Are you a boy or a girl?" And although this microaggression makes her feel "kind of weird," she just says "girl" and gets on with it.

Switching Schools to Transition

Some trans kids move from school to school to escape trans oppression or to facilitate transition: some kids leave one school as their designated gender and arrive at another in their affirmed gender. When Canaan (18, Euro-Canadian) was 14, he switched high schools in order to transition to male at the beginning of ninth grade, but his desire for anonymity was completely negated by the actions of an ignorant but well-meaning teacher. His mother, Shari, reported learning that on the first day of classes, Canaan's teacher—who had just recently received LGBT sensitivity training—announced to the entire class that Canaan was transgender, thinking that publicly identifying and welcoming him constituted sensitivity and support. Canaan was devastated by this announcement. It defeated the entire purpose of changing schools and exposed him to gossip and harassment for the next four years of high school. It also misrepresented his identity. According to Shari, Canaan does not identify as transgender. He identifies as male. This difference is very important to him. What is so troubling about this incident is that the teacher thought he was being supportive: it reveals how much care needs to go into teacher training about trans issues and the importance of allowing kids to control the sharing of information about their gender identities.

Prior to Nina's understanding her child, Martine (12, Euro-Asian Canadian) as a transgender girl, she worked to get the school to be more gender and sexuality inclusive and to intervene in the gender bullying that Martin, whom she understood to be her "son" at the time, was experiencing. She recalled asking the principal if the school "could talk about things like homosexuality, like years back, and the school wasn't comfortable with that": "Then I asked one of the teachers, 'Can you read maybe one book on diverse families?' She said, 'No.' That was it. So I was alone dealing with that. I'd say, 'Well, we had a situation of bullying on the bus: they called Martin a girl, and she downplayed it. She said, 'Well, that's not really bullying.' I said, 'Well, if it makes "him" cry, and they're doing it again.'" Nina was similarly unsuccessful later when she asked the school to allow her daughter to transition. "I had meetings. I had the hospital come to the school. I met with the principal a lot, and basically she had almost never heard of this. I would come in and say, 'I need to talk about this issue.' 'Oh, okay. Well, all right,' and downplay my observation. And they'll say, 'But Martin looks so much like a boy here.'" Nina felt strongly that the school was pathologizing her as a parent rather than taking her concerns seriously, especially when a school board psychologist attended one of the meetings Nina had with the principal. During this meeting, the psychologist "did not say a word": "I was there for an hour and a half, and he just listened to me. Again, I felt like a hysterical mother." What really upsets Nina is that "while this is happening, the principal won 'Principal of the Year.'"

Martine transitioned as soon as she finished elementary school, and her mother reported, "We were able to breathe." Nina was relieved no longer to have to keep the secret. She explained, "We were hiding it. She was a girl at home, a boy at school, a boy outside. We were mixed up with the pronouns. It was a gray zone. I couldn't stand it. You know, 'Hide the dress! Don't be yourself, hide it,' just ugh. So now we are all breathing easier." As one of the benefits of living in a major urban center, Martine was able to enroll in a high school in another zone of the city where she could begin as a girl. Her mother explained that there, "Nobody knows her. She just started off as a girl, and that's it." This is an example of how complex the tension between secrecy and privacy can be. As this story illustrates, for transgender students such as Martine, gender policing and harassment affect mental health, school attendance, and achievement.

Stef transitioned from designated male at birth to a transgender girl at age five and then to a gender-neutral identity at age 14. When I interviewed them at age 17, Stef described experiencing a frequent lack of safety while attending various schools as a transgender girl and having to switch schools a lot. Stef explained, "Some schools were too hard for me [because of peers] bullying me a lot," and school personnel failed to protect them or were part of the problem. Stef ended up attending four high schools before ultimately switching to an adult education program in their school district. Stef's mother, Kazuko, explained that in one case, "Stef went to a new school, everything was cool. They were like, 'Just tell us which washrooms you want to use, and everything's fine.' They were very, very open. And then they lost the director that was the contact person for us, and he moved to another school. Then it started getting complicated. And then Stef decided, you know what, . . . so we just switched to adult ed." That Stef found it difficult, but not impossible, to attend school as a transgender girl but not as a nonbinary person speaks to the overwhelming binary organization of school institutions and settings. This is one of the ways in which there are limits to the transitions that are possible in school settings.

Greg planned his transition to coincide with the beginning of high school and started taking hormone blockers the year before. He walked out of his elementary school on the last day of the school year and immediately got his hair cut, came out to his friends via Facebook, and became a boy named Greg from then on. Prior to this carefully managed transition, he got himself organized emotionally and psychologically to deal with negative responses: "I set this rule for myself, which I still go by today, is if anyone was not accepting or not nice about it, I would simply cut them out of my life." Most of his friends have stuck by him.

Greg and his parents worked with his high school over the summer to make sure he could enroll as a boy. In this regard, he feels lucky to have been the second rather than the first openly transgender student to attend his high school. Greg described the school as "incredible" because the administration alerted all of his teachers in advance to ensure that they were prepared to act supportively if Greg encountered difficulties with his peers. Some trans students feel safer when their teachers are aware of their status because they can be on top of any class dynamics that emerge, while others—Canaan, for example—consider their status to be confidential medical information.[20] Even though Greg's legal documents had yet to be changed, the school worked around this by manually putting an "M" beside Greg's name on the attendance sheet. At first, the school wanted him to use a staff bathroom, but Greg refused and went on to use the boys' bathroom without incident. However, because some of the kids at his high school knew Greg from before his transition, word got out that he was transgender. Reactions ranged from confusion to "hate," but Greg had enough resilience and support to cope with the negative reactions.

Similarly, Michael purposefully transitioned between high school and university: "I had already planned it out, right, once I leave and I go to university, and I'm just going to change my name. And I was just like, 'I'm not going to interact with you guys' [*laughs*]." While still in high school, Michael kept a low profile, making sure to fly under the radar by keeping his head down and dressing in unisex style, but he "didn't bind back then": "So you could tell I was a girl." As he described it, he was "kind of a lonerish." Being disconnected from his surroundings in high school seems to have been what Michael needed at the time.

After graduating, Michael learned that another trans guy had attended his high school at the same time. Michael said that probably, like everyone else, he "thought she was a tomboy . . . or he [Michael corrected himself]." It speaks to the extent of their efforts to blend in that they were unable to see each other. They have since been in touch, and though it might have been helpful to know each other while in high school, not every trans person experiences the value of trans solidarity. There are trans people of all ages who avoid other trans and gender-nonconforming people, particularly visible ones, at least in certain spaces, because they are not ready for, or are uninterested in, being visible themselves.

As these stories indicate, the ability to change schools is an option for some trans kids but is impossible for many others. Moving kids out of hostile school environments is obviously not an option for everyone, especially in rural areas where either there are no alternatives or the community is too small to allow for anonymity. Changing schools requires parental consent and access to other resources, such as transportation, money for school fees, parental advocacy and know-how, and is further mediated by variables including racialization, class position, and language spoken in the home. For kids with multiple "special needs," a safe place to transition may come into conflict with other aspects of their precarity.

Homeschooling is an option for some trans kids who either do not want to attend or lack the safety they would need to participate in formal school settings, but it too involves interaction with administrative bodies committed to the binary model and extensive parental resources. One of the mothers in the study, Luna, homeschools her four children, and therefore she has to work with a homeschooling "base school" in her region. Of Luna's four children (Euro-Canadian), one is comfortable enough with their assigned sex, one is a 16-year-old trans girl, another is a seven-year-old nonbinary trans person, and the youngest "has yet to declare." Luna described how their family "put the school really on the spot around how they were going to manage having an out trans student": "And the interesting part of this is that actually, in the end, the most difficult facilitation was around my kid Otter, who is seven, because Otter is a borderlands person, a both/neither person around gender, and this is proving to be radically more challenging." Registering Otter for school turned out to be "massively difficult" because in the province the family lives in, "they have this computer system where there is this one box, and in that box there has to be an 'M' or an 'F.' And the eldest child was like, 'As long as I can control what goes in the box, I can make a choice, and I'm going to be happy with it.' Otter is like, 'You may not put an 'M' or an 'F' in that box because I am a both/neither person, and I refuse to have that letter associated with me.'" This experience speaks to the challenges that trans kids who defy binary intelligibility face in navigating school systems and school environments. Only Luna's tenacity and experience dealing with administrative systems enabled her to contest this limitation.

Many of the book's participants deeply resent the power and authority that adults in school have over them. Quinn identifies as nonbinary and was waiting until the end of the year—when they graduated from high school—to report two teachers for anti-trans behavior. Some of Quinn's teachers use correct pronouns and insist that their classmates do so as well, but, Quinn said, others "would sooner laugh at me than use my pronouns and frequently do." Quinn has two teachers, in particular, who refuse to use correct pronouns, even though they have asked them to do so repeatedly. One of these teachers accuses Quinn of changing their pronouns just to seek attention. According to Quinn, this teacher "throws her hands up in the air and says, 'Quinn, you don't have to make it so hard for me all the time. I'm an old woman. I can't just conform just to make one person happy. You're just going to have to deal with it,'" on occasion leaving the room in a huff in the middle of class. Sometimes when this happens, Quinn hears it from frustrated classmates, who say things like, "Why don't you just get over it? It's not that bad." These microaggressions hurt and disempower Quinn, and they have responded with the overlapping strategies of doing what they had to do to survive/resist and engaging in activism to achieve change (as part of their school's gay-straight alliance).

On occasion, Quinn's classmates are supportive. For example, in their last two years of high school, Quinn frequently wore a T-shirt with their pronouns on it—"they them their." One day when they were wearing it, one of their teachers "just kept on misgendering" Quinn: "He was using me as an example, and he kept on going, 'she, she, she.' So I actually turned my shirt around, and I was like, 'Here, you obviously can't get it, so here are my pronouns. They're on my shirt. If you forget, look at me while you are talking about me and read my shirt.' And he just started laughing and used 'she.'" But this time, first one then more of their classmates backed them up: "This one kid in my class slammed his hands down on the desk and started screaming at my teacher: 'Mr. X, you're being such a jerk. Can't you see that you're hurting Quinn. You don't have to be so mean to them. Why are you doing this?' And then he got up and left, and my entire class was like, 'Yeah, Mr. X, you don't have to be such a rude jerk. We know you're old and angry.'" Quinn felt both empowered by this support and fearful that it might lead to retaliation from the teacher. Peer support has the potential, in such a context, both to empower and to disempower, both to decrease and to increase the precarity of trans kids by upsetting the adults who have power over them. As far as Quinn knows, they are the only person at the school who uses "they/them/their" pronouns and are therefore readily identifiable. Quinn is understandably concerned that reporting these teachers before the end of the year could affect their grades: "It's sort of a horrible thing that I have to think about. How can I make sure that these adults, who have a lot of power over me— especially because they control my marks in a grade 12 year, and they're already really into weird power-trippy dynamics—how can I make sure that they don't hurt me?"

Trans kids adopt various strategies to survive or even thrive within the disabling environments and systems of formal schooling, including remaining invisible, avoidance via absenteeism or dropping out, transitioning—often switching schools to do so—and surviving, resisting, and fighting back. Their experiences bring the blueprint of the binary gender system into sharp relief and have the ability to suggest appropriate ways for transforming schools away from the ideology of heteronormativity and cisgender ability that is so damaging for trans kids.

Transitioning *in* School versus Transitioning *the* School

When schools have "allowed" the trans students in this study to transition, they have not transitioned the school *away* from binary sex differentiation. But to lessen the precarity of all kids, and trans kids in particular, we should be working toward a gender-inclusive school that forgoes—and explicitly counters—the disabling force of binary gender systems. The students whose stories are told here use qualifying language to describe even "successful" transitions in school settings.

For example, in spite of describing a supportive high school administration as "incredible," Greg had some misgivings. Although he acknowledged the administration did take some action whenever he reported experiences of trans oppression, "it never feels like they are taking enough action. It sort of feels like they are not taking it as seriously as they should be." While Greg felt fairly comfortable at his high school, he was still dealing with frequent microaggressions, which took a toll. His remarks speak to the limited extent to which this binary-based climate was targeted for change. Greg's school was still organized, formally and informally, by the binary sex/gender system of heteropatriarchy; he was supported in switching his identity from one to the other, but the fraught *system itself* was not examined as a subject for transition. Instead, how he was treated as an individual by other individuals—while a crucial dimension—became the principal focus and obscured the larger picture. Enabling and supporting transitions for binary-conforming trans kids *is* a crucial dimension of harm reduction, as Greg's, Esme's, and Tru's cases highlight in a positive sense and Frank's and Stef's underscore so negatively. Yet this focus fails to address the impact of binary gender systems on invisible trans kids, such as Alicia and Lennox, and on all those whose identities and behaviors are marginalized in other ways.

To illustrate this issue, Wren's transition is illuminating. When she was known as a gender-nonconforming boy, Wren's first school was one of her safer places, yet while Wren's transition at school was fully supported and relatively seamless, it raises questions about the role the school could have played in *transitioning the environment* around her. Jin (13, Euro-Canadian) is a gender-nonconforming kid who enrolled at Wren's school after leaving an unsafe public elementary school environment. One of Wren's parents, Jordan, and Jin's mother, Mickey, articulated a common assessment of the private school their children attended together as a "kind of hippy" place. More meaningful work to destabilize gender systems, however, had yet to be undertaken. For example, although pleased that all the kindergarten children used the girls' washroom, they noted there were still sex-segregated bathrooms for everybody else, although these were not, to their knowledge, policed. Wren and Jin used the girls' bathroom without incident. Both Jordan and Mickey, however, felt that the elimination of sex-segregated bathrooms, with regard to signage if not more extensive structural change, *could* have happened but that they would have had to initiate it and lead the social justice and educational work to motivate and execute it.

Like many of the parents of trans kids who become advocates and activists, both Jordan and Mickey are academic researchers whose work includes a focus on gender. As a result, they were able to share resources and expertise with school staff. For example, during the years that Jin attended the school, Mickey and her partner, Ry, shared resources, donated gender-inclusive and trans-inclusive children's books, initiated numerous meetings with the teachers about gender-inclusive education across the ages (including about the school's physical-education program, change rooms for swimming classes, and the older grade's year-end sleepover camp). Jordan provided the school principal with a copy of Gender Spectrum's "Gender Inclusive Schools" and, along with Mickey, met with the principal and another teacher to talk about undertaking some related projects for change.

While there was enthusiasm from all involved about undertaking the work of fully transitioning the school, after the first meeting with Jordan, Mickey, and school personnel, the difficulties in scheduling a second meeting, given the external obligations of everyone involved, stalled the conversation. This result speaks to the extraordinary demands already placed on the time and energy of people who *are* invested in the well-being of children—parents and teachers alike. Without budgetary resources to implement school district policies that target school systems and culture for change, action is dependent on donated labor. Under these circumstances, often the best outcome one can hope for, it seems, is that individual trans kids will be accommodated.

Transitioning School Board Policy

As an example of structural change at the school board level, in 2014, the Vancouver School Board (VSB), which is also my home district, updated its (2004) A: Foundations and Basic Commitments (ACB) "Lesbian, Gay, Bisexual, Transgender, Transsexual, Two-Spirit, Questioning Policy" to more effectively address inclusion issues relating to lesbian, gay, bisexual, trans, two-spirit,[21] and questioning (LGBT2Q) youth, a policy later referred to as the "sexual orientation and gender identities" policy (ACB-R-1). The role of a staff person, the part-time "Anti-homophobia and Diversity Teacher Mentor," was central in this process, as she provided support to staff and LGBT2Q kids and their parents in the district and worked with the Pride Advisory Committee, consisting of LGBT2Q community members, to draw the school board's attention to aspects of the policy that needed improvement. The VSB committed the district and all its schools to addressing anti-harassment in particular: "The board will strive to prevent, and to provide effective procedures to respond to any language or behaviour that degrades, denigrates, labels, or stereotypes students on the basis of their real or perceived sexual and/or gender identities and/or gender expression, or that incites hatred, prejudice, discrimination, or harassment on such bases." The new policy stipulates that the VSB will

- provide bathroom access according to affirmed gender category;
- use affirmed names and pronouns as requested;
- use affirmed names in all school correspondence when requested by the student and/or the student's parents (with the exception that information relating to a child's gender transition would not be shared with parents or guardians without the child's permission);

- invite participation by trans students in physical education and sex-segregated recreational and competitive athletic activities in accordance with their gender identity;
- resist directing students to reparative therapy programs or services;
- use professional development funds to deliver workshops for teachers and administrators on LGBT2Q+ inclusive curricula;
- provide learning resources in languages and formats easily accessible to ESL students and their families, where possible.

The policy update addressed bathroom and change-room access specifically with requirements about access to these spaces:

- "[They will be] assessed on a case-by-case basis with the goals of maximizing the student's social integration, ensuring the student's safety and comfort, minimizing stigmatization, and providing equal opportunity to participate in physical education classes and sports." This assessment prioritizes the comfort and safety of transgender students.
- "Trans students shall have access to the washroom and change room that corresponds to their gender identity. Students who desire increased privacy will be provided with a reasonable alternative washroom and/or changing area."
- "The decision with regard to washroom and change room use shall be made in consultation with the trans student."

Finally, the policy addressed the institutional framework of sex-segregated activities with the directive that "schools will reduce or eliminate the practice of segregating students by sex. In situations where students are segregated by sex, trans students will have the option to be included in the group that best corresponds to their gender identity."[22]

While this policy was a significant step forward to support transgender students, I know that anecdotally little has changed on the ground in schools and classrooms, and the policy is often only accidentally or voluntarily applied in the classroom. Sasha (six, Euro-Canadian) regularly bumps up against the binary organization of her VSB classroom, for example. According to her mom, Sonja, Sasha's classroom teacher regularly organizes the children as "boys" and "girls," which means that Sasha has to choose which gender to be when neither of the categories speaks to her. She experiences this situation as incredibly stressful and difficult. The overarching culture of binary normativity remains substantially unchallenged, and yet getting an update passed by the VSB was an important achievement. Gestures of acceptance and tolerance and public statements of support for queer and trans kids do make a difference; otherwise the Christian Right would not mount such fierce opposition to them.[23] But while measures such as these are meaningful—and difficult to achieve—they do not go nearly far enough. And policies without sufficient budgetary resources for staff training do little to change school cultures.

Furthermore, schools typically do not adopt measures for trans inclusion until a visible transgender kid shows up. This reluctance reflects a superficial rather than a substantive approach and means that issues relating to binary gender culture and gender policing typically receive little attention otherwise. This attitude is inadequate for the well-being of all of the kids at the school and is limiting for the trans kids who feel safe enough to become visible and in the identities they feel comfortable exploring and asserting. In Pascoe's recommendations for change as a result of her research at "River High," she identifies the need for legal protections for girls from sexual harassment and queer and gender-nonconforming youth from homophobia and transphobia.[24] But without teachers and administrators who are specifically trained and required to enforce policies, legal and policy change alone are insufficient. There is a dire need for proactive change to create more inclusive learning environments for all students. These include supporting gay-straight alliances, altering gendered school practices, and providing pro-LGBT2Q resources and education for all students.

* * *

Any analysis of the experiences of trans kids in schools needs to start from the premise that many school environments are unsafe for many kids and that issues of trans inclusion, or lack thereof, take place within a context of neoliberal restructuring.[25] Thus, teachers and school administrators are constantly being asked to do more with less, which relegates much of what they accomplish in their non-face-to-face teaching time to volunteer effort. Without a key person willing and able to drive the work of change, "good enough" environments for trans kids seem like a lottery win. This situation will not change until substantially increasing school budgets becomes a societal priority.

How many of the kids in our school systems are at risk of losing that inner spark not only because of trans oppression and homo-negativity but also because of the overlapping violence of misogyny and sexism, racism, poverty, ableism, authoritarianism, intolerance for neurodiversity, or ignorance and neglect? How many come to school hungry for food, safety, affection, or regard and yet fail to receive these and struggle accordingly? It is challenging to provide kids with safe and affirming environments and connections with others, but it is crucial to their development and the resilience and vitality of our communities. A key aspect of this safety is enabling their agency to name and claim preferred gender identities that they negotiate for themselves.

Efforts to specifically reduce the precarity of transgender students in school settings cannot be isolated from general measures for promoting child welfare (such as universal school breakfast and lunch programs, incidental fee-free learning, and adequate resources to support varied learning styles). Support for trans kids, therefore, needs to be grounded in a broader anti-oppression perspective.[26]

Changing school contexts to decrease the precarity of transgender kids requires a systemic approach to eliminating formally sex-segregated and sex-differentiated spaces and activities. This approach can combine with school-community-based initiatives to transform school culture within a broad-based movement to oppose neoliberal restructuring of social welfare, public school, and municipal systems. Schools that do allow kids to transition often fail to confront head-on the problems of sexism and misogyny associated with the binary gender system of heteropatriarchy but, rather, allow it to remain largely undisturbed. The appropriate focus for schools should be on *transitioning the school community away from the binary system of gender* and finding ways to interrupt and change other oppressive dynamics.

3

Spaces

When [Wren] was five, still so small really, she told me that
the bathrooms at the church we attend made her sad. She
stood before me as she said this, a small and anguished
child, frozen between two doors. She literally did not know
where to go—but she knew that loss would be the result of
either choice she made.
—Jordan, parent

As evidence of the change in the air today, the church that Wren and
her family attend recently designated all the bathrooms in the building
as "welcoming bathrooms," meaning that they are for everyone to use
regardless of gender identity.[1] It is too late to spare Wren the traumatic
experience referred to in the epigraph, but it will make a difference
for all the trans kids—whether visible or invisible—who follow in her
footsteps.

Issues relating to transgender inclusion in schools, as well as in public
spaces more broadly, tend to crystallize around bathroom and locker
room access because these spaces are central to the maintenance of the
binary gender order. Canadian and U.S. institutional and public culture
relies on binary sex difference as foundational. But extensive scholarship
has revealed the two-sex system to be a social construct rather than a
natural system.[2]

A socially constructed binary system is perhaps most obviously built
into the lived environment via sex-segregated facilities (bathrooms and
locker rooms) and sex-differentiated activities. Sex-segregated and sex-
differentiated environments are, unsurprisingly, sites of crisis for most
trans kids. In this chapter, the disabling impact of the institutionalization
of the binary sex system is made manifest in spatial terms, particularly
in the public/private spaces of bathrooms and locker rooms that certify
and regulate membership in gendered social groups and participation

in public life. As a requirement of public spaces, bathrooms are central to citizenship, and to use them, one must be readable at a glance or be, to use Judith Butler's term, "intelligible."[3] It is in the regulation of such spaces that binary gender is produced and becomes embodied. It is no surprise, therefore, that the "bathroom problem" is a pervasive theme in much queer and trans literature and scholarship. As queer scholar Jack Halberstam[4] emphasizes, "the bathroom problem . . . severely limits [the ability of gender-nonconforming people] to circulate in public spaces and actually brings them into contact with physical violence as a result of having violated a cardinal rule of gender: one must be readable at a glance."[5] The difficulties that trans and gender-nonconforming people of all ages confront in public spaces when needing to urinate, defecate, empty a colostomy bag, deal with menstruation, or other immediate and urgent acts of bodily maintenance that require privacy reveal a "blueprint" for the social construction of sex difference.

In a study of the disempowering experiences that gender-nonconforming women have with sex-segregated bathroom facilities in the United Kingdom, geographer Kath Browne introduces the term "genderism" to articulate the process whereby "those who transgress the accepted dichotomy of sex are policed." The bathroom is where "sites and bodies are mutually constituted within sexed power regimes." Browne emphasizes that "gendered spaces are *disabling* environments; it is the normative constructions of sex that are both built into, and interact in, everyday spaces that (re)produce the 'abnormal.'"[6]

The bathroom problem is not solely about gender nonconformity, however. As basic requirements of public spaces, bathrooms are central to access and therefore citizenship,[7] but this access is unevenly embodied. One need only think of the ways in which homeless, impoverished, racialized, and disabled people and survival sex workers are dehumanized and at times criminalized for performing urgent bodily functions in the street, denied privacy due to lack of sufficient public facilities and the prerogative of private enterprises to restrict access to their bathrooms. When out in public and badly needing a bathroom, the privileged among us are able to purchase something in order to gain access to the bathroom in a store or coffee shop. Indeed, white, middle-class privilege often enables people to access bathrooms without having to buy anything at all: our humanity is intelligible, and we are correspondingly treated with respect and/or kindness. In contrast, lack of bathroom access produces disabling consequences that further acts to exclude the marginalized from public space and civic participation.

Sex-segregated bathrooms reinforce sex difference and are a crucial part of the pervasively gendered environments in which children circulate. One of the ways kids know that they are not performing their assigned gender adequately is by how people react to them when they enter sex-segregated spaces or participate in sex-differentiated activities. The bathroom is one of the most urgent of these spaces. As Browne observes, the "moments where boundaries of gender difference are overtly (en)forced can illustrate how sites and bodies are mutually constituted within sexed power regimes."[8] Sociologist Judith Lorber views sex-segregated bathrooms as an intrinsic part of "the bureaucratic structure and the process of control of public space" that "replicates the supposed biological base of the gendered social order and the symbolic separation of men's and women's social worlds."[9] If privilege is defined as freedom from injustice, then bathroom privilege goes unnoticed by the majority of people who conform to gender norms and/or other aspects of socioeconomic privilege, yet it is a site of injustice for many, including the majority of trans people of all ages.

Gender Policing in Bathrooms

The experiences of the trans kids in this study underscore the damaging consequences of sex-segregated bathroom facilities in general and the denial of access on the basis of gender self-determination in particular. The trans kids in this study had troubling stories related to bathroom access, from gender policing to feeling trapped in or forced to use the wrong bathroom. Trans kids do experience acts of extreme violence (as happened to Alicia and Frank), but more often they are the victims of microaggressions from peers and adult authority figures who say, "You don't belong here," which minimizes their authority over themselves, negatively impacts their physical, social, and emotional well-being, and highlights the ways in which barriers to bathroom access produce social and/or physical disability. Peers typically play a central role in gender policing in school contexts. Often in school bathrooms, kids are unsupervised, and safety is lacking. Alicia's experience with violence in the bathroom at her private boys' school is telling in this regard. Many kids in the book avoided going to the bathroom, at school and in public, by purposely dehydrating themselves or by holding it, to the point that they risked permanent health consequences.

Several kids had to change schools because the administration in the former school refused to support an acceptable bathroom solution. For example, Sean (9, Euro-Canadian) is a gender-nonconforming girl. Starting in kindergarten and continuing throughout the time she attended that particular public school, a group of boys terrorized her and other gender-nonconforming girls by preventing them from using the girls' bathroom. According to her father, Hal,

> When she would try and go down to the washroom, there would be a group of boys—sometimes from her class sometimes from another class—who would see her in the hall, and she would try to go into the girls' room, and they would block her and say, "No, you are a boy. You can't go in the girls' room." I think one time she even went down towards the boys' room, and then the boys said, "No, you can't come in here," and these boys just gathered around her. They were bigger than her, and they would do this.

Sean's parents took this issue up with the school administration, expecting them to be equally concerned and to take effective action on Sean's behalf, but that is not what happened. Instead, the situation was dismissed, and they were given vague promises about an anti-bullying program being introduced in the future. While the administration failed to act, Hal reported

> Sean ended up doing this over and over again and holding it and being so scared to go that by the next year, she developed a whole series of bladder problems, and it was incredibly painful for her to pee. She often couldn't pee. She would be crying and screaming sometimes for an hour, and it would be like this every day. We finally took her to the hospital. . . . We went to a urologist, and they took a scan of her, and they basically said that she had so embodied that fear and through her actions of holding it in, it had actually changed the shape inside, like with her organs and her ability to control her bladder.

Sean's parents eventually learned that the same thing was happening to four or five other girls who had short hair whom these boys judged to be inadequately feminine. Powerless to protect her in this context, Sean's parents moved her to a different public school. For her part, Sean vowed she would never cut her hair short or wear pants again. This gender policing is a chilling example of the misogyny and gender terrorism many girls experience that more broadly includes slut shaming, sexual harassment, sexual violence, and rape culture and how early on in life some boys begin to participate in these oppressive dynamics.

Silver's mother, Sherene, had a similar story to tell, but Silver (six, Indigenous/Euro-Canadian) ultimately faced the harshest treatment from *adults* at her school. According to Sherene, Silver is consistently read by people who do not know her as a boy; Silver is okay with this in general, but it presents problems with regard to bathroom access. For example, when Silver was in first grade, she was "mistaken" for a boy by another girl in the bathroom and, in spite of her insistence that she was a girl, was told to leave. Unlike Sean, who experienced gender policing as an expression of dominance, the gender policing that Silver experienced in this instance seems to have reflected fear more than malice; girls are taught to fear boys and often have reason to. "Silver left the bathroom, and she went to the boys' bathroom. And then a teacher found her, so she still hasn't gone pee by this time, and she's probably six years old in grade 1. So the teacher sent her to the principal's office because she was in the boys' bathroom, which isn't allowed. And so she peed her pants." What Silver learned from these encounters was that she had nowhere to go to pee. For two weeks after this incident, "she peed her pants every day. She started bringing an extra shirt so she could tie it around her waist to cover up the pee." Sherene was deeply concerned for her daughter's well-being: "I started leaving work, taking my lunch. I'm driving across town at lunch time and taking her to pee and then leaving work so I could be there at the end of the day. Obviously it wasn't sustainable, but she was scared to go into the bathroom even with me."

Sherene's familiarity with the public school system in the district, and with educational systems more generally, made her a strong advocate for her daughter. She started by calling in the school district's part-time anti-homophobia staff person to address issues of school culture. When this failed to resolve the bathroom crisis for Silver, Sherene asked the principal to let Silver use the staff bathroom. According to Sherene, the principal responded by saying, "No. If we do that for her, we have to do it for everyone": "And I said, 'Look, they're doing it at universities all over the place. I've looked around a bit, and this isn't a big request, this isn't a strange request, and you actually have a kid in your school who requires some safety.' And she said, 'No. If we do it for her, we have to do it for everyone else.' I said, 'Well, do it for everyone then.' And she said, 'We can't do it,' and I said, 'Fine,' and I moved her." Moving to a different school in the district that immediately accommodated Silver's need for a gender-neutral bathroom without question solved the problem at school. But bathrooms in public spaces continue to be unsafe for Silver, and she needs an adult to accompany her. Sometimes this is a problem, particularly when Silver is with her dad (Silver's parents are separated). Once when Silver was with her dad at a park near his house, for example, she had to go to the bathroom. She asked her dad to take her back to his house a block away, but he refused, telling her to use the bathroom at the park. Feeling unsafe to do so, Silver wet her pants and ended up calling her mother to come and get her.

This fear of sex-segregated public bathrooms is widespread among trans kids. Dara, the mother of Davis (11, Asian American), described "a whole world of anxiety and managing" that Davis explained to her that "'she' had to do, with people perceiving 'her' as a boy in the wrong bathroom if 'she's' in the girls' bathroom." Although Davis was pretransition, Dara suspected her child would actually feel more comfortable in the boys' bathroom but was not willing to endure the process of coming out to peers and teachers that that would entail. Dara went on to tell me that Davis's class "had to make hopes, wishes, and dreams for fourth grade, and 'her' hope for fourth grade is that 'her' school would create a bathroom for both boys and girls, but then 'she' decided not to reveal that." Davis's teacher found a way to be on Davis's side by introducing a support structure and coaching Davis's peers to be bathroom buddies to mitigate their classmate's disabling experience of the bathroom. This gave Davis a feeling of safety while at school, but public bathrooms in other places continued to be terrifying. In a subsequent interview, Dara said that her son had transitioned, in part by switching schools, and was a much happier, less anxious child as a result.

Quinn told me, "I never really let on how much shit I have to deal with in bathrooms. I've been attacked in bathrooms in a way that I got out unscathed, but because I'm agile and a fast runner." They think this happens because "someone thinks that you don't fit in in a bathroom well enough": "Like, I guess I send out super trans vibes, because I can be wearing a dress in a women's washroom and be wearing a ton of makeup and people will walk in, give me double looks, look at the sign on the bathroom door, and then keep staring at me the whole time, which is super uncomfortable. And this happens whichever washroom I use, and bathrooms are essentially—like the signs on them as long as they're gendered, it might as well say, 'Get yelled at and get beat up.'" Quinn reports being spat at and shoved in public washrooms but "not so much in school bathrooms." They say that most of the difficulty they experience in using public bathrooms comes from adults. On occasions when they are challenged about being in the "wrong" bathroom, Quinn explained, "Sometimes I have to claim to be a gender I'm not in order to stay safe, mostly in bathrooms in public, not so much at school." They have had the most frightening experiences in public men's bathrooms when "wearing something that wasn't like 'super masculine'": "You can get some very negative feedback because people either think you're a 'tranny,' as they would put it and as I've been called multiple times, or that you're a boy in a dress, which is always confusing to them. It's mostly been when people walk in, see you washing your hands at a sink, and no matter how much you hunch over and try to hide yourself, they can see you in the mirrors, and they see your face, and they decide that you're not acceptable to be in this washroom, and then they might corner you." Quinn finds that women can be unpleasant but not as threatening as some of the men they have encountered: "Women just usually whisper about you and like give you very passive-aggressive looks because I guess that's how society trains us to be, which is horrible in its own right, but I've been screamed at by women in women's bathrooms before."

Quinn takes deliberate measures to minimize risks to their safety when using public bathrooms, including sizing up public washrooms for ease of exit should the need arise and appearing confident. Quinn noted, "The biggest safeguard, honestly, for washrooms is to just ooze confidence and swagger, but that's so hard because if you're attacked in some situations, then, like, you're going to be terrified going to washrooms in a similar location or if it looks similar or if you see someone who looks like the person who tried to hurt you." In contrast, at school, Quinn feels empowered to resist gender policing in the bathroom. When kids at school look at them weirdly in the bathroom, Quinn takes some pleasure in educating them: "It's mostly the new kids every year who look really, really concerned and confused, and then we have a conversation—I'm not using 'conversation' as a euphemism; we literally have a conversation. It's usually pretty one-sided, but they either are totally okay with it afterwards or they avoid me like the plague, which is fun." Being a member of their school's gay-straight alliance means that Quinn feels more empowered in school environments because they know they are not alone and have the advantage of being able to call on a collective voice.

Frank's devastating experiences in elementary school at the hands of teachers included experiencing psychological torture around bathroom access. Frank described feeling consistently humiliated by teachers around issues of bathroom use: it was one of the principal ways they imposed a female identity on him. One of the ways teachers repudiated his male identity on a daily basis was by forcing him to use the girls' bathroom and punishing and humiliating him when he used the boys'. They instilled in Frank such a sense of shame and self-surveillance that he reported to his teachers when he did use the boys' bathroom. On these occasions, he was given detentions. Frank is deeply offended by every aspect of this experience when he thinks about it now. He explained why being forced to use the wrong bathroom is so traumatic for him: "It is really simple things like using the bathroom that you don't want to use that can really hurt people: it embarrassed me so much. I cried, and I hid in the bathroom every single time. Every time I had to use the bathroom, I would hide in there until I made sure no one was in the hallway and nobody was in the bathroom, which was hard because it was in the main hallway. I hid in there for over half an hour sometimes."

Some kids experience gender dysphoria and *feel* like they are in the wrong bathroom, even though no one is physically preventing them from using the one they would prefer. Tru Wilson, for example, grew up feeling out of place in the boys' bathroom and longed to use the girls'. Lennox initially vocalized a desire for "bathrooms to be bathrooms" rather than sex-segregated spaces, saying that she wished for "a bathroom for everyone to use, like it's a boy-and-girls' bathroom; that's what I wish they had at school." But it soon became clear in our conversation that Lennox was most drawn to the girls' bathroom. When asked what she would do if she was able to choose between a gender-neutral bathroom and the girls' bathroom, her eyes lit up, and she said unequivocally, "The girls.'" As a trans child who is invisible outside her home, Lennox keeps her desire to use the girls' bathroom secret and finds having to use the boys' bathroom painful. For her, being able to use the girls' bathroom is crucial to living fully as a girl but is not something she is prepared to do at the moment.

Gender-Neutral or No-Gender Bathrooms

For some kids, neither sex-segregated bathroom is the right one. Stef, for example, identifies as gender neutral and describes using washrooms this way: "horrible for me because a lot of people kind of look at me, and they're kind of like, what the f——? What's going on here?" Stef regularly experiences a dilemma around which bathroom to use. They experience greater safety in girls' washrooms, find girls' washrooms to be cleaner, more likely to have mirrors and to be stocked with toilet paper, and because privacy is really important to them, more likely to have stalls with doors that close and lock. But when they use them, they said, "then everyone thinks I'm a girl, so then, well, shit, but I'd rather be safe and not get asked too many questions like, 'You're in the wrong washroom. Please get out of here.'" One of the worst experiences Stef has had to deal with around bathroom access occurred on a school trip to another country: "[Local men] wouldn't allow me to go into the washrooms, so I had to be escorted into the washroom by my teacher, which really sucks, and then escorted out of the washroom." For the sake of independence and comfort, Stef started using the girls' washroom on this trip but then encountered resistance from their teacher, who stopped them from going into the girls' washroom, saying, "I understand why you're going into the girls' washroom, but didn't you say that you were a boy?" Stef responded, "No, I'm not a boy. I already told you what my situation was, and I told you that if anyone is offended or anything, please talk to me. But expect that I will be doing what I need to do to *survive*" (my emphasis). The relationship between bathroom access and empowerment is clear: bathroom access is a survival issue. Like other kids I talked to, Stef found so-called gender-neutral public washrooms often to be inadequate:

> What schools and a lot of public places try to pass off as a gender-neutral washroom are often, like, one-stall rooms, which also don't make me feel terribly safe because when someone tries like knocking on the door 20 times or something like that, and where they have a child and they want to pee or something, and then they're really angry that someone is inside the washroom that they think is for like moms and stuff like that or dads who have babies and stuff like that or teenagers. And I don't really like the little, small, shitty little washrooms that they try to pass off as gender-neutral washrooms, which is really just like a family washroom that you just put "gender neutral" on.

Quinn experiences a similar dilemma: they use the girls' washroom most of the time because "the boys' washrooms are disgusting": "Like the boys pee everywhere, and there's toilet paper everywhere, and there's usually not toilet paper or soap. So I use the girls' just for cleanliness, generally speaking. However, being in the girls' washroom, generally speaking, I'm perceived as a girl being in the girls' washroom, and that makes me very uncomfortable. So I use the boys' whenever it's hygienic." The stall doors in either bathroom have no locks (which Quinn attributes to budget shortfalls), so they have to be held closed. And menstrual pad and tampon disposal bins are not provided in the stalls, which poses a particular risk for trans boys. When I asked Quinn if they are able to find gender-neutral washrooms when out in public, they spat back, "There's never a gender-neutral washroom." Where they do exist, the vast majority of bathrooms that are not gender designated are marked for the physically disabled or adult-led family groupings.

Stacey, Cassandra's mother, reported that, upon seeing a washroom with a sign indicating that it is a washroom for the "handicapped/men/ women," her daughter said, "I wish all bathrooms were like that. Then you could just go to the bathroom." Frank is in full agreement, saying, "I don't think anyone should be assigned to a strict gendered bathroom. I think bathrooms should be gender neutral." Frank cited the example of the open, gender-neutral washroom facilities provided at an annual conference for transgender adults and children and their families: "They even put signs over top of the little 'guy' and 'girl' signs, and it says, 'gender-neutral bathroom.' I think that's the best situation—the best thing to do." Political scientist Heath Fogg Davis suggests that the most meaningful challenge to sex-segregated bathrooms is to convert all bathrooms into "unisex or no-gender bathrooms" by "removing urinals and building additional private stalls in their place."[10] Bathroom access is foundational for well-being, and the trauma trans kids experience when denied it has serious social and mental and physical health consequences.

The trans kids in the book applied various, often situational, strategies to navigate bathroom access: remaining invisible, avoidance, making situational choices to survive, pursuing medical transition, and resisting/fighting back. Trans kids weigh the often-conflicting needs of gender self-determination, physical urgency, and self-protection in employing these strategies. The need for safety, by means of invisibility, for example, often comes with negative mental health consequences of its own. Social acceptance for gender-affirming, or nonbinary, bathroom access empowers trans kids.

Political Conflict around Transgender Bathroom Access

The space available for girls with penises, boys with vulvas, and children who identify outside the gender binary entirely is fearfully contracted in North American culture, as evinced by the recent rise of "bathroom bills" in the U.S. that stipulate that trans people must use public bathrooms in accordance with the sex they were assigned at birth. Recent legislation and policy debates regulating the access that transgender people have to these spaces in the United States and Canada expose trans oppression at its vilest and most disabling.

United States

HB2. In the United States, many states have considered trans-oppressive state "bathroom bills," driven by moral panics about men masquerading as women in order to sexually attack women and girls, with special hyperbole devoted to the specter of an innocent (white) female child being victimized in the bathroom by a man masquerading as a woman.[11] These bills are designed to prevent trans people from using bathrooms and locker rooms and other sex-segregated facilities according to their affirmed gender identities.[12] Anti-trans bathroom bills reinforce a cisgender binary sex system by restricting people to using bathrooms congruent with their "sex at birth." Only one state, North Carolina, however, has been successful in passing such a bill—House Bill 2 (HB2)—although a number are still pending.[13] The state legislature of North Carolina passed HB2 in March 2016 to negate a Charlotte city ordinance prohibiting discrimination against LGBTQ people. According to journalist Mark Stern, "HB2 nullified this ordinance, and any other municipal law that provided greater protections than state law. Since state law doesn't protect LGBTQ people, HB2 nullified all local LGBTQ nondiscrimination ordinances. More controversially, it also regulated the use of government bathrooms, including those in public schools and universities. Under HB2, individuals had to use the bathroom that corresponded to their 'biological sex,' as listed on their birth certificate. In many states, it is difficult or impossible for trans people to alter their birth certificate. So this provision effectively bars countless trans people from using government bathrooms."[14]

The immediate fallout from the passage of HB2 led to its partial repeal. After HB2 was passed, the state lost millions of dollars in business as the National Basketball Association (NBA), the National Collegiate Athletic Association (NCAA), and many headline performers, including Bruce Springsteen, canceled their events in the state. The subsequent electoral defeat of Pat McCrory, the North Carolina governor who championed HB2, was just the beginning of his employment woes. McCrory recently complained about his inability to find work, claiming, "Even after I left office people are reluctant to hire me, because, 'Oh my gosh, he's a bigot,' which is the last thing I am."[15] This pressure forced the partial repeal of HB2 by the state legislature on March 30, 2017. Its replacement, House Bill 142 (HB142), appears to be an equally damaging piece of legislation for LGBT rights in North Carolina, but it seems to have mollified the state legislature's more mainstream critics.[16] According to Stern, HB142 is "just as odious." The bill forbids "state agencies, boards, offices, departments, institutions," and "branches of government," including public universities, from regulating "access to multiple occupancy restrooms, showers, or changing facilities." It applies this same rule to "local boards of education," meaning these boards cannot pass trans-inclusive policies. Instead, local governments, public universities, and school boards would have to wait for permission from the General Assembly to protect trans people. . . . That's not the end of it. HB 142 would also impose a years-long moratorium on local LGBTQ nondiscrimination ordinances. The bill would bar any city from "regulating private employment practices or regulating public accommodations" until December 1, 2020. Stern goes on to note that "there is nothing to stop the General Assembly from extending this moratorium as its expiration date draws closer."[17]

GAVIN GRIMM: G.G. V. GLOUCESTER COUNTY SCHOOL BOARD. Other potential watershed cases have stalled before the courts, the most high profile being the legal challenge of the American Civil Liberties Union (ACLU) on behalf of transgender boy Gavin Grimm's right to use the boys' washroom at his high school. The ACLU and its Virginia affiliate took Grimm's school board to court in 2015 to fight the policy that restricted transgender students to gender-neutral washrooms. The policy in question was adopted in 2014, two months after Grimm had begun using the boys' washroom. According to the ACLU, the policy contravenes the provisions of Title IX of the U.S. Education Amendments of 1972, a federal law prohibiting sex discrimination by schools and that requires all institutions receiving federal government funding to implement gender equity. Grimm's case was dismissed by a U.S. district court, but he successfully appealed it to the U.S. Court of Appeals for the Fourth Circuit, which overturned the ruling. When a subsequent lower court upheld Grimm's right to use the boys' washroom, the school district appealed to the U.S. Supreme Court, which, in August 2016, temporarily stayed the Fourth Circuit ruling while it considered the case. This occurred within a changing political context, however: In 2016, the Obama White House voiced its intention to support transgender students. Many trans people and supporters hoped that the Supreme Court would therefore establish a federal precedent in support of transgender rights.[18] According to *Advocate* reporter Trudy Ring, a ruling by the Supreme Court in favor of Grimm would have set a precedent likely to produce rulings against North Carolina's HB2 and other state anti-trans bathroom bills.[19]

But the 2016 presidential election produced a change in the political landscape to a Trump administration that included transgender students among its vulnerable targets by officially withdrawing the Obama directive about supporting trans students. The new attorney general, Jeff Sessions, insists that federal protections under Title IX do not include gender identity.[20] The Supreme Court responded to this change by refusing to hear Grimm's case and returning it to the lower court, which, in light of the new administration in Washington, subsequently overturned its original decision and ruled against Grimm. Grimm graduated from high school in June 2017, and this change in his status was employed by the U.S. Court of Appeals for the Fourth Circuit to insist that a "lower court must sort out whether Grimm still has enough of an affiliation to his alma mater to pursue the case."[21]

Canada

BILL C-279 AND BILL C-16. At the federal level in Canada, Bill C-279, commonly referred to as "the bathroom bill," to "amend the Canadian Human Rights Act to include gender identity as a prohibited ground of discrimination" and to amend the Criminal Code to include "gender identity as a distinguishing characteristic," was introduced into the Canadian federal legislature in 2013.[22] The bill failed to pass through necessary levels of government at this time, however, but Bill C-16 was introduced and passed after the Trudeau government took power in 2016. Bill C-16 explicitly adds transgender rights to the *Canadian Charter of Rights and Freedoms*. As of June 2017, all provinces and territories in Canada include gender-identity protections in their human rights codes. These provisions can be leveraged by trans students and their parents to ensure access to bathrooms and change rooms in accordance with their affirmed gender. The case advanced by the mother of Bella Burgos provides a powerful example.

ELIZABETH BURGOS V. RIVER EAST TRANSCONA SCHOOL DIVISION. In the summer of 2014, Isabella (Bella) Burgos announced to her family that she was transgender—that she had "felt like a girl in a boy's body for four years."[23] With the full support of her parents, Bella returned to school that fall as a girl. In spite of the initial welcome from students and staff, Bella's safety and well-being were compromised when the parent of another child at the school complained about Bella using the girls' bathroom. This parent not only complained to the school principal but "yelled at the child and her older brother and lobbied other parents outside the school."[24] The school responded to this complaint by insisting that Bella use a gender-neutral bathroom rather than the girls' bathroom. Bella's parents were concerned about the negative impact this "segregation" would have on Bella's transition. According to Bella's father, Dale, "You want to make sure they feel welcome and happy at the decision they made. . . . Because this is probably the biggest decision she'll ever have in her whole life."[25]

Dale Burgos reported that Bella was harassed at the school by staff as well as by the aforementioned parent. "Our daughter was followed by staff to see which bathroom she used. She was approached by a janitor at one point. There were many instances like this in the school."[26] Insisting that access to the bathroom consistent with Bella's affirmed gender identity is a human right, Bella's mother, Elizabeth, filed a complaint with the Manitoba Human Rights Commission in October 2014, alleging that the school's insistence that Bella stay out of the girls' bathroom amounted to discrimination on the basis of gender identity. In this complaint, Bella's parents insisted that the school district needed to support transgender students with explicit and supportive policy provisions and provide students and school personnel with appropriate education and training.[27] They also contended that the school had failed to protect Bella from trans-oppressive bullying by the parent who yelled at her. In March 2016, the human rights complaint between Elizabeth Burgos and River East Transcona School Division was resolved in favor of Bella and her family. This constituted a significant win for transgender students in general. According to Kelly Barkman, superintendent and CEO of River East Transcona School Division, the agreement allows "for transgender students to have the right to use the washroom they identify with and the guidelines, if you look at it, do get into things such as resources, professional development, not only for the staff, but for the students."[28]

Successful human rights complaints such as this one and the out-of-court settlement guaranteeing transgender inclusion achieved by Tru Wilson and her family are clear indicators that transgender kids in Canada have legal rights to access bathrooms and change rooms according to their affirmed gender. But assumptions about fundamental differences between only two sexes and male athletic superiority create particular obstacles for trans kids who wish to participate in sport and physical recreation.

Challenges Associated with Sport and Physical Recreation

I turn here to the ways in which the regulation of gendered bodies accomplished by sex-segregated bathrooms is duplicated and amplified in the spaces of the change room and the sex divided and differentiated worlds of sport participation. Like bathrooms, sex-segregated and sex-differentiated sport and physical recreation spaces, facilities, and programs—including day and sleepaway camps, activities, and uniforms—place transgender kids in harm's way. These facilities and spaces are predicated on the taken-for-granted assumption that there are only two, fundamentally different sexes[29] and that boys and men have an across-the-board unfair athletic advantage over girls and women.[30]

For trans kids who transition to a binary identity, sport participation typically requires a switch from one gendered space to another, often but not always requiring medicalization for eligibility. I begin this discussion with the well-publicized case of Texas high school trans wrestler Mack Beggs. In 2017, Mack, then 17, was forced to wrestle in the girls' competition rather than the boys' in the Texas state championship—he went on to win. Beggs began undergoing testosterone therapy in October 2015, but his request to wrestle as a boy was turned down by the state's officiating body for school sports. The state requirement that student athletes participate in accordance with the assigned sex on their birth certificate (altering requires a court order) meant that Beggs had to decide whether to wrestle against girls or not at all. He chose to wrestle against girls rather than quit, in spite of feeling strongly that he should be competing against boys because, as he said, "I'm a guy." Reporter Christina Cauterucci described the "spectacle of an undefeated teenage boy demolishing his female opponents—or advancing after they forfeited—because officials won't validate his trans identity" as having "caused a confused uproar in the Texas high-school wrestling community. And, in the process, it has exposed the farcical conundrums that arise from trying to impose hard, abstract boundaries on the messy reality of gender."[31] Cauterucci noted that parents of female competitors, as well as the audience, booed Beggs as he participated and that parents and coaches claimed that he was cheating: "arguing that testosterone, often used as a steroid performance enhancer, gives Beggs an unfair advantage."[32] What is particularly interesting is that the assumptions that there are only two sexes and that testosterone provides an "unfair" athletic advantage are untroubled not only by anti-trans complaints about Beggs's participation while taking the hormone but by some trans-positive arguments in favor of allowing trans boys and trans men to participate in their affirmed sex category.

For example, when Dale Hansen, a Texas sportscaster, spoke out on behalf of Beggs's right to wrestle against boys, he argued that Beggs should not be penalized for a "genetic mix-up at birth."[33] This particular defense of Beggs's right to wrestle against boys takes both an ableist and a biological determinist approach grounded in a medical model of disability by making being transgender tantamount to having a "birth defect." Hansen also takes for granted the faulty logic of fundamental male athletic superiority. This is a clear indication that issues relating to transgender participation in sport cannot be understood independently from the historical role of sport in normalizing and reinforcing the ideology of the two-sex system and the widespread gender inequality (male superiority) that accompanies it.

Modern Sports' Role in Normalizing the Two-Sex System

Modern sport emerged in Europe and its colonies in the late 19th and early 20th centuries. From the outset, sport was a male-supremacist "civilizing"[34] and capitalist project[35] that represented, among other things, a backlash against the increasing power of middle- and upper-class white women[36] and the burgeoning working class. Sport was explicitly designed to emphasize sex difference, socialize boys and men into orthodox masculinity, enforce heterosexuality,[37] further the goal of white middle- and upper-class morality and leadership within Western imperialist projects,[38] and importantly, at least at the professional level, provide a return for capital investment. Any analysis of sport needs to have an intersectional footprint,[39] as race, class, sexuality, gender, and nation constitute relations of power and privilege[40] working in and through sport that are far from simplistic.

While sport at the international level (and much of the world) is organized around binary notions of biological difference between males and females,[41] queer feminist science[42] reveals the extent to which the taken-for-granted two-sex system is constituted by ideological assumptions about its existence.[43] It is no accident, for example, that queer feminist science scholar Anne Fausto-Sterling's *Sexing the Body* begins with a devastating critique of sex-verification testing at the highest levels of sport to establish the failure of science to demarcate boundaries between male and female bodies.[44] The measuring of bodily capacity that national and international sport is purportedly organized around underscores its significant cultural role in the hierarchical demarcation of sex boundaries. By virtue of sex-segregated sporting spaces and grossly unequal cultural and economic spaces, sport in Canada and the U.S. and much of the world is organized through taken-for-granted Eurocentric patriarchal models of binary sex difference. That these socially generated boundaries are culturally understood as natural and unmediated by social forces makes them all the more difficult to challenge.

The revelation that this two-sex system is ideological rather than natural underscores the role of sport in showcasing a vision of a stark biological divide between male and female bodies that is intricately bound up with gender injustice for women and gender transgressors throughout society. As sport sociologist Mary Jo Kane notes, the establishment of gender difference is a "product of patriarchal social construction."[45] "Male" and "female" bodies are produced, in corporeal terms, in social contexts that assume and privilege male athletic competence at the expense of female physical development.[46] Kane demonstrates that the gender binary paradigm in sport is grounded in biologically deterministic notions of gender polarity and features an emphasis on difference and the dismissal and deliberate invisibility of similarities between male and female athletes. This invisibility is essential for upholding male dominance and is achieved through the symbiotic relationship between mainstream sport and mainstream sport media.[47] Kane insists that a more accurate model for sport reporting would portray a gender continuum. Critical feminist sport scholars focus on the role of sport in contributing to gender inequality by reinforcing orthodox masculinity and perpetuating sexism.[48] As it stands, the institutionalization of the two-sex system *as natural* contributes to the cultural and economic marginalization of women, gays and lesbians, and transgender people in the world of sport and beyond.

For trans people of all ages, the sex segregation of sport is a key obstacle to participation. Within this field is an emergent subset of research that views the sex segregation of amateur and professional sport as deeply problematic.[49] In *Playing with the Boys: Why Separate Is Not Equal*, political scientist Eileen McDonagh and journalist Laura Pappano identify "coercive" as opposed to "voluntary" sex segregation for girls and women as the cornerstone of sports' contribution to gender inequality.[50] The predominant sex segregation of many sports and sex differentiation of activities within some less segregated sports (for example, gymnastics and figure skating) or different rules (for example, in basketball, golf, tennis, and volleyball) play an important role in normalizing gender inequality by packaging, showcasing, and emphasizing differences between male and female bodies to celebrate masculine superiority and justify extensive opportunity structures and disproportionate patterns of remuneration for male athletes.[51] The fact that the names of professional women's sport associations need to be specifically gendered while men's remain unmarked (for example, Ladies Professional Golf Association versus Professional Golf Association; Women's National Basketball Association versus National Basketball Association) is a powerful indicator of the cultural assumption that sport is a male realm. Sport is simply assumed to be a male prerogative unless an exception is marked. Understood in this light, privileged networks for resource distribution associated with and enabled by mainstream sport depend on fierce patrol of its borders. The regulation of the bodies of women and transgender people reflects the extent to which we, as interlopers, must be carefully policed.

Transgender athletes present a challenge to sex-segregated sporting institutions and programs whether they, as individuals, are interested in doing so or not. Concerns about transgender participation in sport tend to center on assumptions that a transgender woman has presumably been exposed to higher levels of testosterone prior to transitioning, and therefore this testosterone should be considered a "performance-enhancing drug." According to critical sport scholar Sarah Teetzel, however, comparisons between transgender women athletes and steroid use for the purpose of doping are misguided; past exposure to higher levels of testosterone produces no evidence-based comparative advantage.[52] Despite this fact, David McArdle notes that the United Kingdom's Gender Recognition Act of 2004 granted sport an exception to the requirements for legal recognition of transgender persons, fearing that transgender women, by virtue of their past lives as (presumably testosterone-saturated) "men," would dominate women in sport.[53] The underlying assumption of sex-segregated sporting spaces is that someone who is born male naturally has an "unfair advantage" when competing against women in sport.[54] In spite of documented overlaps between male and female athletic performance, these ideas continue to characterize and structure mainstream sporting policies and lean heavily on a Western trope of white, female frailty.[55]

The role of sport in normalizing and reinforcing binary sex ideologies and gender inequality is evident in the gender policing that occurs in change rooms and when people are participating in sport and physical recreation. As educational scholar Elizabeth Meyer observes, "Most traditional extracurricular activities have subtexts that subtly and overtly teach that certain forms of masculinity and femininity are valued over others. The clearest example of such an activity is that of elite amateur and professional athletic teams and the cheerleaders and dance squads that accompany them."[56] Sociologist of sport Michael Messner characterizes youth sports in the United States as reproducing "soft essentialist narratives that appropriate the liberal feminist language of choice for girls, but not for boys, thus serving to re-create and naturalize class-based gender asymmetries and inequalities."[57]

Barriers for Trans Kids

Sex-segregated sport and leisure facilities create a crisis for trans kids as a result of three different types of barriers: issues of access resulting from the sex-segregated structure of many sports, programs, and facilities; problems relating to participation in sex-differentiated activities within gender-integrated sports/activities; and difficulties relating to the climate of these environments. Because of these factors, many trans kids drop out or avoid physical activity altogether. Those for whom sport participation is a priority struggle to find ways to do so.

The assumption that male athletic superiority is a biological certainty is pervasive in Canadian and U.S. culture, and many of this study's participants and their parents echoed these sentiments. Dave (17, Euro-Canadian), for example, described himself as having participated in many sports when he was still presenting as a girl, but he stopped upon transition. As a man, Dave considers himself to be newly uncompetitive in the sports he previously played successfully as a girl. He feels he is too small to play hockey and overmatched in table tennis. Jenny, the mother of Nick (11, Asian Canadian), took for granted the athletic superiority of boys her son's age, attributing their superior skill level to male puberty. She observed that "their strength level [is much greater]" and therefore presents an obstacle to her son's participation.

Although many sport and physical recreation activities are formally sex segregated, some parents choose to enroll their gender-nonconforming and trans children in sex-*integrated* activities. Formal sex segregation in sport has received critical attention, but sex-integrated activities remain problematic. Gender-integrated environments provide a lower barrier in general because they do not force the issue in the same way, but they remain problematic and not just because of the extent to which sex-segregated changing/locker-room facilities are the norm. Within integrated sports and physical recreation programs, formal and informal rules often require different activities and uniforms for boys and girls. In gymnastics and dance, for example, boys and girls wear different uniforms and are required to train their bodies to perform in different ways that reflect, and reassert, widespread cultural beliefs in binary sex and male superiority. Given that 99% of the kids who participate in gymnastics will not reach the elite heights of the sport, non-gendered uniforms and instruction on all the equipment would benefit the majority, and transgender and gender-nonconforming kids could be spared sex segregation and differentiation in this arena. In Canada and the U.S., however, this is not the norm. As such, children's bodies are subjected to the gendered muscle development and physical differentiation that renders the resulting differences to appear as "natural."

Seeing the so-called sex differences in gymnastics produced through social practice and repetition gave Sean's father, Hal, a more critical perspective. Hal observed how sex-differentiated activities in gymnastics actually created gendered bodies. When Sean first enrolled in gymnastics, she was deeply disappointed to learn that she would not be able to work on the rings because they are designated as an apparatus for men and boys. According to Hal, "Sean had her heart set on doing the rings, but the rings are not allowed to her. But she started gymnastics with a Brazilian coach, who came and asked the girls, 'Can anybody do a chin-up?' But nobody could. And then Sean came and just ripped off nine chin-ups, and he was so excited he took her to all the other coaches. But she came back to me and said, 'I dunno what to do because I can't do the rings.'" Hal observed how this rule reinforced assumptions about sex differences: "The thing, too, that strikes me is that the boys that are struggling. They're not as strong as her, but they're doing it every day. And in a few years hence, they will become proficient, strong at this. And if Sean does not end up doing those exact muscle-building things, she will not. So then it will become this self-perpetuating dynamic that's going on." This is an example of the way that the "gender continuum" of overlapping sport performance is rendered invisible via social practices, with the result that the natural basis of sex segregation, sex differentia-tion, and male "unfair advantage" goes unquestioned.

Even in integrated community-center dance classes, it is often impos-sible to register kids without sharing information about their sex. Such information is assumed to be essential and is used to organize children's participation in gender-appropriate ways. Many feminist parents who ac-tively resist sex stereotyping are deeply troubled by the way sex markers are deployed to socialize children in distinctly gendered ways. Like many gender-nonconforming boys, Cody (five, Euro-American) routinely gets "mistaken" for a girl. According to Cody's mother, Zimm, Cody has long hair and a "mixed" wardrobe, likes superheroes, rough-and-tumble play, pretty things, and ballet. In his current ballet class, they "dress the boys and girls in different clothes." Zimm described the challenges that this differentiation poses for Cody and subsequently for her:

He is supposed to wear a uniform. He's supposed to wear black leggings and a white shirt. And the girls are supposed to wear a black leotard, and they can wear pink tights, and they have pink ballet shoes. And he has black ballet shoes, and I was so worried that he was going to flip his shit because he did not get to wear the pink ones [laughs] and the pink tights. It turned out not to be a problem, and he's willing to go along with it. I mean, it does visually distinguish him, as like clearly he is one of the boys in the dance class, with his really long, blond hair that several weeks ago he wanted me to put up in a bun.

Jordan described the difficulties they and their partner encountered in attempting to find a dance class for their (at the time) gender-nonconforming son:

> When Wren was four and still identifying as a boy, "he" took a ballet course through the community center, and because "he" wanted the leotard and the tutu that the girls had—there were no other boys in the class—I got them for "him." And "he" basically blended in until my use of the male pronoun in a conversation with "his" teacher outed "him" as a "boy." I asked the teacher to keep letting "him" dance as a girl, and it seemed to be going fine until the little performance at the end of the class. Wren was dancing in "his" pink leotard and tutu in the special performance, in front of all the parents and friends of the dancers. When it ended, the teacher called out to "him" in front of everyone and instructed "him" to bow, not curtsy, saying that "boys should bow, not curtsy." Everyone there looked very puzzled, and Wren was mortified.

Like many parents when they encounter overt discrimination against their children, Jordan marshaled their resources:

> I was angry about it and didn't sign Wren up there again. Instead, I went through a long and arduous process to find a dance class where my "son" could dance like the girls without censure. I was surprised at how difficult it was. I did find one of the really serious programs that allowed it. But when I chatted with other parents before, during, and after the dance class, I found myself avoiding using any pronouns to refer to Wren because I felt I had ruined things for "him" in the community-center class by outing him as a boy. But this avoidance felt really, really weird.

Gender essentialism is clearly "harder"[58] in some sports than others, as a result of the way certain sports are organized. Tight and revealing uniforms—such as swimsuits—present more of a challenge to transgender kids than do the bulkier uniforms that athletes wear in other sports.

Feminist sport scholars are increasingly challenging the appropriateness of sex-segregated teams and sex-differentiated activities.[59] My own research on gender and sport[60] is part of this tradition in part because the sex-segregated structure of many sport and physical recreation spaces make participation complicated for trans kids. The difficulties faced by kids who want to identify outside the binary are often extraordinary. Neither side of the binary is right for some, and this produces a sense of crisis because fully mixed spaces (gender integrated with unisex rules and uniforms) for sport and physical recreation are rare.

Jordan's account of finding a dance class where Wren, pretransition, could wear a pink outfit and dance "as a girl" exemplifies how parents must draw on socioeconomic privilege when negotiating so-called sex-integrated physical recreation spaces. Less privileged families would not have had the funds or access or time to travel to the "appropriate" dance class for Wren. Others may have had to settle for a local community-center class if they could afford one at all. If Jordan had not been able to devote the time, energy, and know-how to navigating these spaces, Wren would have had to either quit dancing, dance as a boy and wear the boys' outfit, or put up with the occasional misgendering, shaming, and censure from the teacher. The ability to support and advocate for trans kids is not evenly distributed. What about those whose parents are not able to leave work to attend their kids' sports events in order to run interference for them? What about families whose lack of economic resources leaves them with few or no options for sport participation?

Climate: Issues of Informal Inequality

Adding women as participants, tolerating gay teammates, and enabling trans participants who undergo medicalized binary transition do not, on their own, change the overall cultural role of an enterprise that normalizes binary sex systems via gender inequality, homophobia, and trans oppression. According to a University of British Columbia study, "Are We Leveling the Playing Field? Trends and Disparities in Sports Participation among Sexual Minority Youth in Canada," lesbian, gay, and bisexual teens are 50% less likely than their heterosexual counterparts to participate in sports.[61] While the study does not address transgender participation specifically, it is logical to assume that the binary normative nature of most sport programs combines with heteronorma-tivity to discourage participation by queer and trans kids. This is borne out in the research shared here and corroborated by data in the 2013 GLSEN report indicating that "11% were prevented or discouraged from participating in school sports because they were LGBTQ."[62]

Locker Rooms

Very much like bathrooms, locker rooms are spaces that impose binary gender structures and regulate access on the basis of intelligibility. Being included with same-gender peers is an important aspect of transition for many kids. But in group discussions at conferences or news interviews, I have witnessed a few parents of trans kids talking about the importance of their children being able to bond with their same-gender peers in the locker room without any acknowledgment of the extent to which male locker rooms in particular can be toxic environments with regard to misogyny and for gender and sexual minorities.[63] One of my partici-pants, Cory Oskam[64] (16, Euro-Canadian), emphasized how necessary it was to use the same locker room as everyone else in order to partici-pate in team bonding, but he also did his part to change the climate of the locker room. When Cory first transitioned, his school suggested he use a gender-neutral space, but he purposefully positioned himself as fundamentally male (rather than the trans, nonbinary identity he feels greater affinity for) to enable himself to dress with the team. At times, however, he found the locker room to be an uncomfortable space. Once while in a boys' hockey dressing room, Cory experienced discomfort as one of his teammates made homo-negative remarks to the group. Corey handled this incident by waiting until he was alone with the guy to ask him, "Dude, why do you say those things?" It takes courage to stand up to boys and men who are performing orthodox masculinity. On a num-ber of occasions since then, Cory has heard "faggot" and "pussy" used as pejoratives in the locker room, bringing to mind Pascoe's observation that "fag" is used as an abject category in the construction of adolescent masculinity.[65] Cory explained why hearing the guys in his locker room use these terms to "really put down women" was something he experi-enced as "really offensive": "I do identify as someone who was female at one point. And I do identify, like, as female once in a while. So it was not pleasant to hear." When this occurred on his hockey team, Cory complained to his coach: "'They're saying these words that make me feel uncomfortable,' and he's like, 'Yeah, those are words that shouldn't be said in the dressing room.' And then they were addressed in just a very anonymous fashion, by the coach saying like, 'I've heard that there's bad language in the dressing rooms, and that needs to go away.' And it really did stop." Dave, however, drew on the homophobic climate of the locker room to deflect attention away from his post-top surgery chest and to keep himself safe. When a boy asked him, "Why do your nipples look so weird?" Dave responded, "Dude, why are you looking at my nipples?"

Coping Strategies

Trans kids and their parents in my study applied four strategies to negotiate barriers to participation in sport and physical recreation: continuing to play as their assigned sex; avoiding or quitting sport; participating in recreational activities that are less sex divided/differentiated; and transitioning—with or without undergoing medical treatment.

Some trans kids remain invisible to enable them to fit in and so participate in sport on the same principle. For others who are visibly gender nonconforming, sport participation can be very challenging. Ray-Ray's mother, Nadine, shared an example of the ongoing labor she has had to engage in to enable her son to continue to participate in the sport of running:

> Ray-Ray took off one time in a race—this was probably about grade 5 or 6—and there was a guy standing on the edge of the field to tell the kids when they can cut in. He's one of the officials. He takes off running across the field yelling at the top of his lungs with the megaphone, "There's a girl on the track." And I was out there, and I jogged beside him, and I said, "That's a boy. He's my son. His name is Ray-Ray, and he'll probably win." And I walked away. That's how bad it was, and Ray-Ray just went—he just persisted, but other kids I know who are gender nonconforming would be horrified.

Ray-Ray has been competing in track since he was in third grade, and he is regularly marshaled away from the boys' competition and toward the girls. "His name is Ray-Ray Marvolo," Nadine explained, but "they would move his name to the girls' marshaling list when they saw his long hair, and then the guy marshaling the girls would stand there yelling his name until one of the other kids who knew who he was would say, 'He's not a girl; he's a boy.' And the guy still wouldn't get it. And I would often have to go to the marshaling tent. In fact, I almost always went to the marshaling tent to get him sorted and racing as a boy." Nadine shared this and other examples to emphasize how crucial it has been for her to run interference at every track-and-field event Ray-Ray attends. She regularly has to say, "This is my son; he is a boy." Without Nadine's advocacy at track meets, things would have been much harder for Ray-Ray.

In contrast to Ray-Ray's negative experience playing on a boys' soccer team, where his teammates treated him as an outsider because of his gender nonconformity, his experience with his high school's mixed-sex Ultimate Frisbee team has been positive. Some sex differentiation is built into the game—a certain number of girls or women are required to be on the field at all times—but the sport provides a more welcoming place for Ray-Ray. Even though he now stands six foot two, Ray-Ray is often read by opponents as a girl. This is actually an advantage for his team because they are often short of girl players. Ray-Ray told me that his coach asked him if he would be okay to continue "playing as a girl," and he happily agreed. He remarked that he finds this "kind of funny and fun!"

Several kids in this book stopped participating in particular sports or stopped playing sports altogether when they transitioned. While this represents a loss for some, such as Dave and Nick, others were happy to quit. According to Ingrid, the mother of Ziggy (15, Euro-American), when he was given the option of dropping out of physical education, he jumped at it. He experienced his school's reluctance to allow him to participate in physical education as a boy as a blessing. Ingrid explained, "Ziggy hated PE, and when the principal gave him the option of quitting [a course that was normally compulsory], he was thrilled." At the time of the interview, Ziggy was happily participating in his school's marching band, where gender has not been an issue for him.

Kids who defy cisgender binary categorization tend to experience frequent gender policing from children and adults alike. This comes in the form of the most common question: "Are you a boy or girl?" As a result, some trans kids who want to play sport present themselves as their affirmed rather than their birth sex. Going "stealth" works better for trans kids who embrace a binary identity and who are able to pass, either because they are younger or because they undergo medical treatment (as Dave and Cory did).

Jordan wonders how much Wren's decision to transition to female pronouns two years ago had to do with wanting to dance and dress the way she likes without having to constantly explain herself to children and adults. Jordan reported that Wren's participation in a day-camp program two years ago was the impetus for her transition from gender-nonconforming boy to a girl in every facet of her life: "During the sign-up process, Samantha [Jordan's partner] asked her, 'Do you want to go to camp as a boy or a girl?' Which I thought was really, like, neat. I was so focused on trying to make the overall environments more gender flexible that I never thought about asking Wren that. But Wren said, 'a girl,' without any hesitation, so that's how Samantha signed her up. She showed her how to change privately with her bathing suit in the change room. And Wren was totally successful, and I think it gave her a lot of confidence."

When Wren encounters bodily changes at puberty, her parents are prepared to provide their daughter with access to hormone blockers, but they will follow Wren's lead, even though sometimes "it's a tricky balancing act" to figure out what kind of support to provide. As a 10- and 11-year-old, Wren has participated as a girl on several sex-segregated teams without incident. This has not been complicated because the rules for transgender participation in her district do not require medical treatment until the age of 13. But Wren has just been selected for a competitive girls' hockey team outside of school, and policies in her region require transgender kids to provide documentation proving that they are under the treatment of a medical professional. Wren has been going back and forth about whether to take hormone blockers. She told me that she really does not want to, but she does not want to get outed or kicked off the team either. She is in a tough spot and does not know what to do about it.

Indeed, the sex-segregated structure of sport may be a deciding factor in driving some trans kids to undergo medical treatment or to transition along binary lines. According to Diane Ehrensaft, author of *Gender Born, Gender Made: Raising Healthy Gender-Nonconforming Children* and a psychologist with a clinical practice in the San Francisco Bay Area specializing in trans and gender-nonconforming children, the desire to participate in sport is a major factor driving gender-liminal youth to undergo binary transition.[66]

This dynamic was true for Cory, who is more comfortable with a non-binary identity and wanted to undergo testosterone therapy *and* continue to play on a girls' hockey team. In girls' hockey, he was an elite goalie with good prospects for college scholarships; but on the boys' team, there is a deeper pool of goalies and he felt he would be unexceptional. Taking testosterone was important for Cory because he did not want to develop breasts or have a period. He thus had to balance his desire to participate in girls' hockey with his need to shape his body in a manner consistent with his gender identity. Cory's former name was Anneke—and this is something he is very open about. Indeed, he had a very public gender-nonconforming identity of "just Anneke" from age eight to 13, but he found it necessary to affirm a male gender identity in order to access testosterone. Cory explained that his desire to take testosterone ultimately took precedence over his desire to continue to play girls' hockey. "Just Anneke" was just not working anymore.

Most, but not all, of the stories relating to bathroom access and sport participation come from, or concern, kids who have parental support for expressing their gender in whatever way they feel most comfortable. Most, but not all, of these parents are professionally educated and relatively economically privileged. Trans kids should not have to depend on luck or their family's cultural and economic capital to navigate public institutions or secure legal representation, nor should they have to depend on their parents' ability to move them to a different school or team—or, in some cases, another community—to experience safety and inclusion in the bathroom, in the change room, and on the playing field. More precarious transgender kids face extreme hardship in these environments.

Sport Policy Changes

The International Olympic Committee (IOC) arrived at a policy for the participation of transgender athletes in 2004. Colloquially known as the "Stockholm Consensus,"[67] it allowed fully (hormonally and surgically) transitioned athletes, with legally affirmed gender identities, to compete in their reassigned sex category.[68] This policy required transsexual athletes to undergo complete hormonal transition at least two years prior to competing in an Olympic event, to undergo genital-reassignment surgery, and to have documents proving legal recognition of their new sex by their home governments. In testament to the preeminence of the IOC in making sport policy, many international and national sporting bodies followed the IOC's lead in developing identical policies.

The Stockholm Consensus was widely criticized by sport scholars on the grounds that genitals are irrelevant to athletic performance, that the expense and/or invasiveness of surgery is a barrier for many athletes, and that many governments refuse to supply legal documents designating the appropriate legal sex identity.[69] In an influential 2010 report, *On the Team: Equal Opportunity for Transgender Student Athletes*, LGBT educator and sport scholar Pat Griffin and National Center for Lesbian Rights (NCLR) Sports Project director Helen Carroll deemed the Stockholm Consensus's requirement for hormonal and surgical treatment inappropriate for high school athletes aged 13–17. In this report, they refute the discourse of unfair male advantage by placing a higher priority on the benefits of participation over competition, arguing, "A transgender student athlete at the high school level shall be allowed to participate in a sports activity in accordance with his or her gender identity irrespective of the gender listed on the student's birth certificate or other student records, and regardless of whether the student has undergone any medical treatment."[70] Finding male and female adolescent athletic performance to be comparable, the report recommends that transgender high school students should be eligible to compete on whatever team they choose without undergoing a medicalized "sex change." At the college level, however, the report recommends that participation by transgender athletes require a formal diagnosis of "gender identity disorder" (now "gender dysphoria") by a licensed professional. Nevertheless, provisions are less invasive than in the Stockholm Consensus. The report urges that early-transitioning trans female athletes who used hormone blockers during adolescence and who currently take cross-sex hormones should be immediately eligible to participate in college sports, while those who transition after puberty should be required to undergo only one year of cross-hormone therapy prior to participation. Trans male athletes do not require any hormone therapy to be eligible to compete on men's teams but, once they have begun testosterone therapy, may no longer compete on women's teams. This protocol for participation in college-level athletics was adopted by the National Collegiate Athletics Association (NCAA) in 2011 and the Canadian University Athletics Association (CUAA) in 2012.

The 2011 IOC Regulations on Hyperandrogenism, known as the "Consensus Statement"[71] on sex reassignment and hyperandrogenism, responds to critics of the Stockholm Consensus by mirroring NCAA and CUAA policies. The Consensus Statement must be understood, however, within the context of controversy around sex testing for women athletes in elite amateur sport.

The IOC and its affiliates finally discontinued the long-reviled, scientifically unfounded practice of sex-verification testing for *all* women competitors prior to the 2000 Olympic Games,[72] but the IOC's hegemonic role in normalizing the two-sex system and male superiority continued via the provisions of the new Consensus Statement and ongoing but selective sex testing of women athletes. This was most dramatically evident in the recent case of the gender-troubling figure of South African runner Caster Semenya, whose "masculine" appearance became a subject of concern among competitors and sporting officials when she won the 800-meter World Championship in Berlin in 2009.[73] Semenya was forced to undergo invasive sex testing in order to continue competing. While the results of the tests have never been officially confirmed, the new Consensus Statement on hyperandrogenism and women athletes was a response to the controversy surrounding Castor Semenya as well as Indian runner Santhi Soundarajan.[74] The policy allows for women whose testosterone levels are deemed higher than "normal" to undergo treatment to normalize their levels and continue to compete.[75]

The circumstances under which Semenya was permitted to compete in the 2012 Olympics in London, where she won a silver medal, are unknown. But what we do know is that four other female athletes were identified as having hyperandrogenism and barred from competing. As sport scholar Lindsay Pieper chronicles, these athletes were taken to "Nice and Montpellier, France, for treatment. . . . The doctors recommended that the athletes undergo a corrective measure to ensure their future participation in sport. . . . The specialist also performed 'feminizing vaginoplasty,' and aesthetic (re)construction of the vagina. Put simply, the doctors completed an unnecessary operation that did not alleviate a health issue and then executed plastic surgery to ensure that the women's genitals aligned with accepted anatomical compositions."[76] This incident produced protest that came to a head in 2014 when Indian sprinter Dutee Chand was targeted for testing by the Sports Authority of India (SAI). When her testosterone levels were deemed to be "too high" to be naturally occurring in a "woman," Chand was given the option of undergoing surgery and hormonal treatment or no longer being eligible to compete. The SAI's policies in this matter lined up with those of the International Association of Athletics Federation (IAAF), which had in turn followed the lead of the IOC in setting such policy. Chand took her case to the Court of Arbitration for Sport (CAS) which, in 2015, "suspended the International Association of Athletics Federations' hyperandrogenism rules for two years."[77] The ruling stipulated that new evidence had to be provided by the IAAF within that time frame if Chand and other women like her are to be barred from competing. That new evidence is still pending. This ruling by the CAS did something unprecedented in international and national sporting policy: it questioned the long-held conviction, in the sport world and beyond, that testosterone levels are a clear indicator of sex identity and that the relative lack of this hormone among women explains across-the-board so-called female athletic inferiority. While this ruling pleased feminist scientists and social justice scholars and activists, the prejudice and hostility from other competitors and sport media continued to surround Semenya and other female athletes deemed too muscular to be "normal" women.

Although the IOC disagrees with the CAS ruling in the Chand case, there were no regulations in place for the 2016 Olympic Games in Rio, and none are expected for the PyeongChang 2018 games either. According to the IOC, "we are still awaiting the resolution of the Dutee Chand case."[78] When Semenya won a gold medal in the 800-meter race at the Rio Olympics in 2016, one of her competitors, Lynsey Sharp from Great Britain, who came in sixth, gave a tearful interview on the track in which she complained about the suspension of the hyperandrogenism rule: "I have tried to avoid the issue all year. You can see how emotional it all was. We know how each other feels [*seemingly referring to her white competitors*]. It is out of our control and how much we rely on people at the top sorting it out. The public can see how difficult it is with the change of rule but all we can do is give it our best."[79] *Guardian* reporter Andy Bull put it this way: "The unpalatable but unavoidable fact is that while neither of the other two medalists, Burundi's Francine Niyonsaba and Kenya's Margaret Wambui, have identified as hyperandrogenic, both have been subjected to the kinds of innuendo that Semenya herself experienced in 2009."[80] As political scientist Heath Fogg Davis observes, allegations that athletes such as Semenya are "actually men" are "often intertwined with racism and homophobia. Black female athletes who are muscular, dark-skinned, and competitively dominant such as Semenya have historically been and continue to be stereotyped as masculine and ugly, and thus failing to measure up to hegemonic feminine standards of being the kind of woman that straight men sexually desire."[81]

The IOC has obviously been scrambling to produce research to prove that testosterone levels impact performance outcomes. On July 3, 2017, *Guardian* reporter Joanna Harper announced that a study, published by Stephane Bermon and Pierre-Yves Garnier in 2017, purports to link testosterone levels to performance outcomes in male and female elite athletes. In referencing this study, Harper speculates that we may see the "reinstatement of rules imposing a maximum level of *male* sex hormones in athletes competing as female" and that "Caster Semenya could be forced to undertake hormone therapy for future Olympics" (my emphasis).[82]

In 2016, the IOC announced a new policy specific to transgender athletes: transgender athletes are now eligible to compete in the Olympics without having undergone sex reassignment surgery. The IOC's new transgender policy mirrors the NCAA and CUAA policy on transgender sport participation. While it is an improvement over the prohibitive requirements of the Stockholm Consensus, it continues to reflect an ideological commitment to a two-sex system (albeit a more complicated one) and an unquestioning belief in male athletic superiority. Transgender women are required to follow a hormone regime that negates the "performance-enhancing" effects of testosterone, while transgender men are not required to submit to any hormonal regime in order to participate as men in men's sports. Speaking about the NCAA policy on which the new Consensus Statement is modeled, sociologist Adam Love observed that while such policies on transgender participation are less restrictive than the Stockholm Consensus, "they embrace, perhaps even more explicitly, . . . the language of female physical inferiority," as they allow "male-to-female transsexuals to continue their participation on men's teams" but do not "grant similar rights to female-to-male transsexuals to continue participating on women's teams."[83]

The new policy on transgender participation is based on the norms of the Consensus Statement and took effect at the 2016 Summer Games, but, to my knowledge, no transgender athletes competed. The limited nature of inclusion permitted by the IOC continues to reinforce binary-based understandings of sex difference and is consistent with *gender-conforming*, as opposed to *gender-transforming*, transgender inclusion.[84] Gender-conforming policies of inclusion tend to be conservative in that they reify, rather than challenge, the sex binary that is instrumental in gender inequality, homo-negative trans oppression. Transgender people of all ages who do not conform to binary understandings of sex difference and resist identities grounded in male or female categories, who do not successfully "pass" as boys or girls or men or women, or who are unable to access trans-affirming healthcare are typically left out when it comes to participation in amateur or elite sport.

Although *On the Team* has been the most influential report to inform intercollegiate policies in the U.S. and Canada, other reports have also developed measures for transgender inclusion. The U.S. Transgender Law and Policy Institute's *Guidelines for Creating Policies for Transgender Children in Recreational Sports* emphasizes the importance of students' ability to participate in sport on the basis of their affirmed gender. This report disputes assumptions of male athletic advantage among preadolescent children, stating that no "hormonally-based advantage or disadvantage between girls and boys exists" prior to adolescence, that "gender segregation in children's sports is purely social," and that "individual variation with respect to athletic ability *within* each gender is much more significant than any group differences between boys and girls."[85]

The U.S. LGBT Sports Foundation has developed a "model policy" for sport participation. The "All 50"[86] policy is "based on a single principle: transgender high school student-athletes will compete in the gender in which they identify and have a positive sport experience."[87] While stipulating that all students have the right to participate in a sex category other than that which they were assigned at birth, the policy recommends the formation of a Gender Identity Eligibility Committee, one member of which must be either a physician or a mental health professional. The single criterion for this committee's determination is listed as "sincerity." There is no mention of required medical treatment in the document. This model policy represents a step forward for binary-based transgender student athletes, but it falls short by lacking provisions for nonbinary trans kids and recommendations for overhauling the sex-segregated and sex-differentiated structure of much high school sport. In *Sport in Transition: Making Sport in Canada More Responsible for Gender Inclusivity*, the Canadian Centre for Ethics in Sport speaks out against sex-verification testing, acknowledging that the science of sex difference is flawed science and therefore not a basis for organizing sport. With regard to transinclusion, it states, "Where feasible, transitioning sport will aim for the widest and easiest possible inclusion by supporting integrated sport activities."[88]

In a report published by the Canadian Teachers Federation, *Supporting Transgender and Transsexual Students in K-12 schools: A Guide for Educators*, teachers and administrators are instructed to enable transgender and/or gender-nonconforming kids to participate fully in all activities, including physical education and sport, in a manner consistent with their affirmed and consistent gender identity, with no requirement for medical treatment. The report *is* explicit that this includes locker-room, change-room, and bathroom access for transgender students but, importantly, prescribes making private facilities available to *any* student who requires them for any reason.

In *Questions and Answers: Gender Identity in Schools*, the Public Health Agency of Canada states that "school policies that segregate students by gender ignore and stigmatize individuals who challenge the typical 'male' or 'female' notions and can cause emotional and psychological distress for students" and that "gender-variant youth should be allowed to join sports teams according to their self-identified gender as opposed to requiring them to join based on their biological sex."[89] Obstacles to implementing such policies and their impact require further research.

High school policies for transgender participation in sport are uneven in the United States. The site where the "model policy for transgender students on high school teams" document can be found—TransAthlete.

com—provides a color-coded map of the U.S., according to the nature of the high school policy for transgender student athletes in each state.[90] Green represents "inclusive—no medical hormones or surgery required" (California, Colorado, Connecticut, Florida, Maryland, Massachusetts, Minnesota, Nevada, New Hampshire, Rhode Island, South Dakota, Utah, Vermont, Virginia, Washington, Wyoming). Yellow is defined as "needs modification, case-by-case or individual review" (Alaska, Arizona, Delaware, Georgia, Illinois, Iowa, Kansas, Kentucky, Maine, Michigan, Missouri, New Jersey, New Mexico, New York, North Dakota, Ohio, Oklahoma, Oregon, Pennsylvania, Wisconsin). Red is defined as "discriminatory—requires birth certificate or surgery and hormone wait period" (Alabama, Idaho, Indiana, Louisiana, Nebraska, North Carolina, Texas). Blue represents states with no policy (Arkansas, Hawaii, Mississippi, Montana, South Carolina, Tennessee, and West Virginia). It speaks to the traction that transgender rights has generated in the past decade that 16 of the 50 U.S. states have such low-barrier policies for trans participation at the high school level. However, recommendations for transgender inclusion in high school sport at the national level, in either the United States or Canada, have yet to be adopted, and it is too soon to tell how recently introduced policies will work in practice. The decision by the Trump administration to retract the federal government support of transgender students promised by the Obama administration is an obvious source of concern. Many trans activists are optimistic about the role of the courts in using Title IX to defend the rights of trans students, but we have yet to see how this will play out.

In Canada, to date, there are four provinces that have adopted transgender policies for athletic participation at the high school level. These include the Manitoba High Schools Athletic Association, BC School Sports, the Alberta Schools' Athletic Association, and the Ontario Federation of School Athletic Associations.[91] If I apply the color-coded model from TransAthlete.com, Alberta, British Columbia, and Manitoba are green, while Ontario is yellow (for transgender females only). Various school boards, including Toronto, Edmonton, and Vancouver, include provisions for the participation of trans kids in physical education and sport. The language of the "gender and sexual diversity" policy of the Vancouver School Board includes the recommendation that sex-segregated activities be eliminated wherever possible, but, to my knowledge, there are no Canadian public school policies that focus on sex integration in athletics. The extent to which provincial and territorial human rights codes in the *Canadian Charter of Rights and Freedoms* may be invoked to enable the participation of trans kids in sport is something to keep an eye on. To date, however, there appear to be no public school policy provisions in either Canada or the U.S. for nonbinary trans athletes who resist participation in either of the traditional sex categories.

The implications of this policy evolution for trans kids are uncertain, but it is reasonable to predict that kids such as Mack Beggs who undergo medicalized binary-based transitions will be the easiest to accommodate. Trans kids and their parents/guardians navigate these social environments and barriers to participation, often placing them in a crisis that can only be resolved by deciding not to transition or by choosing medicalized binary transition. Most trans kids in Canada and the U.S. are still running into significant barriers to participation.

* * *

Targeting gender systems, and their intersections with other systems of oppression, is the most effective way to improve the quality of life and opportunities for transgender and gender-nonconforming adults, youth, and children, while granting everyone gender self-determination. But this action needs to take place within an appreciation of the wider socioeconomic context. In keeping with neoliberal restructuring, Canadian and U.S. sports at the local and participatory (versus competitive) level have lost government funding, while professional and elite amateur sport franchises and programs receive the bulk of government funding.[92] Reinvesting in more accessible community-based, gender-integrated physical recreation programs would extend greater access to trans kids and reverse trends toward profit-driven investment in elite amateur athletics in the service of nationalism.

Sport and physical recreation programs and spaces that normalize the gender binary and female inferiority in conjunction with systems of privilege based on race and class need to be targeted. Love urges us to shift "away from the sex segregated two-sex system as much as possible . . . not only for the inclusion of transgender athletes but also as a means of promoting gender equity more broadly."[93] Yet how do we increase transgender inclusion without eliminating spaces for girls and young women to develop skills and confidence? To avoid undoing much of the progress that has been made in increasing the participation of girls and women in sport, McDonagh and Pappano suggest we target "coercive" as opposed to "voluntary" sex segregation for girls and women, given that the former is largely responsible for gender inequality.[94] Gender integration of all sporting spaces may simply have the negative impact of exposing girls and women to more sexism and misogyny so must be accompanied by significant anti-sexist and pro-LGBT initiatives. Advocacy and activism should target the binary gender system and its intersection with other systems of oppression (sexism, racism, classism) within sport and extend gender self-determination to all.

The "green" standard, to borrow the color scheme provided by TransAthlete.com, for bathroom and change-room access and sport participation, whereby affirmed gender is respected no questions asked, is ideal for kids who are comfortable with binary categorization but fails to address the role of sex-segregated spaces and sex-segregated and sex-differentiated activities in general in normalizing the ideology of the two-sex system and disciplining most of us to comply with it. Trans kids signal the need to reconfigure space and social practice away from these gender-oppressive dynamics.

4

Parents

> We left everything. Everyone was like, "Well, are your other
> kids going to stay here?" I'm like, "No. We're leaving as fam-
> ily. We came in as a family. We're leaving as a family because
> we support every member of our family. How could we let
> our other kids be part of a community that rejects their sib-
> ling? Are you fucking kidding me? Like what are you think-
> ing? No."
> —Michelle, parent

There are some kids and parents of kids for whom there was no "coming-out" moment, because they either very obviously failed to conform to traditional gender norms or were "persistently and consistently insistent"[1] about being a boy or a girl in spite of their assignment to the so-called opposite category. Some kids, such as Cory, never needed to come out because they were never "in," meaning they were always read as gender nonconforming or, as in Ray-Ray's case, always took full advantage of the freedom they had to express themselves by wearing dresses and sparkly things and playing with "cross-gender" toys.

It might seem strange that I am positioning a chapter on parenting and families after ones that focus on schooling and then bathrooms and sport/physical education: the "family" is listed in every sociology textbook I have ever seen as the primary or first agent of socialization that a child encounters. And families are typically, after all, profoundly gendered spaces. Indeed, in spite of being far from the norm, the socially constructed heterosexual, cisgender nuclear family is a key ideological building block of white-supremacist and colonial-capitalist heteropatriarchal societies such as Canada and the United States. But one of the things I focus on in this chapter is the extensive (mostly) maternal labor that is required to reduce the precarity of transgender kids both within family and friendship networks and in gendered environments outside the home. I discuss the significance of parent-led activist networks in promoting the well-being of trans kids and the way in which unevenly distributed cultural capital and material resources tend to drive activism on behalf of more privileged rather than more precarious transgender kids.

This chapter tells the stories of the work that my parent participants engage in, with heart and soul, on behalf of their kids and that has often come at considerable cost to their own mental and physical health. I also explore the costs and benefits of transition and trans oppression to the family as a whole and the role siblings play in supporting trans kids.

Family Acceptance and Support

Family acceptance is known to be the most significant variable with regard to mental health outcomes for trans kids.[2] According to Edgardo Menvielle, "Resiliency in the child is best achieved through a supportive family environment that fosters the development of self-esteem and social competences. . . . Our assumption is that GID [gender identity disorder][3] in children represents normal developmental variation. Consistent with an affirmative goal, parents are encouraged to unconditionally value their child, acknowledge his or her difference, assist their child in navigating schools and society, and advocate for changes in the family and community to minimize social hazards."[4] Psychologists Augustus Klein and Sarit Golub report "family rejection as a predictor of suicide attempts and substance misuse among transgender and gender-nonconforming adults,"[5] and we can extrapolate from this data to confirm the importance of family support for trans kids. In general terms, parents have a great deal of power over their children, and their support or lack thereof plays a central determining role in the degree of agency trans kids have. One study shows high rates of violence by parents against gender-nonconforming children and youth.[6] Much of the resilience that transgender kids are able to marshal depends, to begin with, on the extent of their parents' or caregivers' resources—cultural and material—and then the degree to which these resources are available to them. Both significant degrees of social inequality and the collective power of adults over children create variations in precarity among trans kids.

All the parents who directly participated in my research approached their children's gender identities with openness and encouraged the kids themselves to explore what felt right for them in the context of at least a somewhat-open, versus a binary-restrictive, vision of the gender landscape. The kids in the book who affirm binary or nonbinary identities took the lead in claiming these identities themselves. My observations in forums for parents of trans kids, online and offline, reveal some significant differences in how supportive parents approach their kids' assertion of a nontraditional sex/gender identity, with a minority viewing being trans in a manner consistent with a medical model of disability and belief in a two-sex system. The most consistent principle that parents articulated about their children's gender, however, was that their kids should be the ones to determine it. Parents collectively presented me with a dossier of evidence about the damage we do when we fail to listen to kids' voices and the benefits that result, not just for the kid but for the people around them—in the family and beyond—from recognizing kids' authority to self-define their own gender identities.

Child-Centered Parenting

Starting in early childhood, some of the kids in my study insisted on being seen as a gender other than the one they had been assigned at birth, and their families took them seriously, providing acceptance, support, and advocacy on their behalf and often on behalf of trans kids more generally. Many of these families are led by parents who intentionally worked to establish their family as a space free of sexism and gender stereotypes. Cassandra's parents, for example, had determinedly established a gender-neutral tone to their household. As Cassandra's mother, Stacey, describes it, "in our house, toys are toys, hair is hair, clothes are clothes. We actually had only gender-neutral toys in our house for a very long time." Cassandra was asserting "'I is a girl' at two and a half." Her mom responded, "Well, boys have a penis, girls have a vulva," thinking that perhaps her child did not understand anatomy and that it was time to explain. After that, Cassandra settled on being "both" for a while. But Cassandra's distress and behavior around her assigned gender identity prompted Stacey to educate herself, going "on the hunt for research" and buying "every resource possible" about transgender people and issues.

When Cassandra was around four, Stacey introduced the possibility of transgender identity to her: "I kind of described transgender to her in terms of 'most girls have a vulva, some girls are born with a penis—not many, some—but just different, and that's okay, and vice versa.'" And since then, Cassandra has "identified mostly as a girl."

The wisdom of supporting Cassandra as a girl was reinforced for Stacey and her husband by the changes in Cassandra's personality once her self-identification as a girl was honored. Stacey reports that prior to Cassandra's transition, she had wondered if her daughter was "on the autism spectrum because she wasn't making eye contact with people." But the new level of confidence Cassandra displayed posttransition indicated to Stacey how much Cassandra's being unable to assert a gender identity that she felt authentic about was compromising her ability to socially interact and be at ease. Stacey noted that this drastic change in Cassandra's behavior is what helped her husband: "because he was still struggling a little bit, but I think that's what helped him start doing some of the reading, seeing that the change in her behavior was so drastic." Increased social confidence is one of the benefits that a number of parents of trans kids have identified as resulting from affirming their children's gender identity.[7]

Cassandra's particularly strong gender conformity as a girl has occasionally puzzled Stacey and her husband because of their determination to help their children go beyond stereotypical gender identities and behavior. Stacey said, "I've got four girls, and she is the most feminine of all of them." I wonder if some trans kids who affirm a binary identity, however well supported they are at home, feel pressure to do more gender work in the world than they otherwise might if they had never had to resist the imposition of an identity that felt so fundamentally wrong to them in the first place. But then again, some folks, whether cisgender or trans, experience a powerful affinity with binary-based femme identities or masculine identities. We have seen the damage that radical feminist denunciation and gender policing of butch-femme relationships among lesbians has done, for example, and I, like Stacey, firmly believe that questioning the authenticity of anyone's gender self-determination is oppressive.[8]

The parents of Simon (seven, Euro-Canadian), Hilary and Andrew, also built feminist resistance to gender stereotypes into their family culture and rather successfully at that, because Simon was not their first child to express a nonnormative gender identity. Hilary's oldest son was designated male at birth and often talked about wishing he was a girl when he was six or seven. But Hilary reported that he went on to settle into being a cisgender male and expressing comfort about having done so. Hilary described him as having "fallen into the script of manhood as most men do," explaining, "I do think he probably has an inherent wider range, but I think, like most men, he has given up quite a bit of it." But this experience with her older son "primed [her] to be open to that," with the assumption that "you grow out of it." But that is not what happened with Simon.

Simon began insisting that he was a boy from the time he was two and a half. Unlike his brother, Simon demonstrated no gender fluidity at all. He was "consistently expressive about being male, and he didn't want to be a girl, didn't want to have long hair, didn't want to wear girls' clothes." When he was young, Simon became obsessed with lions, wanting in particular "to be a boy lion." Hilary and Andrew, as "good feminists," kept telling Simon that "girls are cool, girls can have adventures, girls can do all these things and be as tough as you want to be, and a girl lioness is so fierce and does all the hunting," and his response was, "I don't care. I need a mane, and I need to be a boy lion." Hilary explained how she feels when she looks back: "That was one of his ways of telling us who he was, by looking outside the species." She sees Simon as trying to express that he was really a boy in a variety of ways before she and her husband were ready to hear it.

Hilary and Andrew initially viewed Simon as a tomboy, but, Hilary said, "it just progressed to this point where whenever I saw something about transgender kids in the news, I would just automatically send it to my husband, Andrew, 'just for your information, just because it seems like we might be headed towards needing to deal with this.'" Hilary undertook the labor of educating both herself and Andrew about transgender issues so that they could respond appropriately to Simon. Although they began to think of Simon as transgender, Hilary and Andrew tried to put it off by saying "things like, 'well, there's things you can do when you're an adult to deal with this, but kids don't get to make that decision.'" They did this because they wanted to wait, to be sure, in case Simon, like his older brother, changed his mind. But Simon never wavered. Instead, he kept coming to his mother and asking what he needed to do to make sure he did not become a girl: "Just a little tap, tap, tap, 'tell me what to do to make sure this doesn't happen.' It was that that made me see how much that meant to him."

While Simon accepted Hilary's explanation that only grown-ups get to transition, she knew she "was lying by saying that it wasn't available to him": "By that point, I knew about hormone blockers, and so I didn't understand why I was trying to put them off. I mean, obviously I was probably trying to put them off for my own comfort." When Hilary realized that it was she and not Simon who was not ready for his transition, she got out of the way. After all, she explained, "the amount of trust he was placing in me made it more heartbreaking to realize that I might be leading him astray." Hilary quickly became convinced that it was time for Simon to transition. She explained to her husband, "He has all these friends to whom he is just a boy even if they're using female pronouns. So why are we not jumping on this? Like, quick, while they're six years old, and if we say now, 'He's a boy,' they will be like, 'Okay.' Let's do it now before it turns *political*" (my emphasis). She reflected on the moment she asked Simon if he would like to live as a boy: "I knew that as soon as I said it, I would never be able to take it back. I knew that as soon as I opened that gate, he would be so far through it and gone that there would be no reboxing him up. So, I mean, instinctually I knew that we were keeping him in a box."

Hilary expressed a bit of uneasiness about the role she played in enabling Simon's transition, however, because he did not appear to be in "sufficient distress" to qualify for the more typical narrative of imminent self-harm and/or suicide that is often used to justify social transition for children. It seems clear to me, however, that Simon was, in Ehrensaft's words, "insistent, persistent and consistent"[9] about his gender identity and that his parents took him seriously. When not extreme, distress can be difficult to measure, but more to the point, we need to create environments for kids to determine their own gender identities without trauma being associated with it. Early acceptance without the necessity of severe distress has obvious and positive implications for trans kids' mental health. Such a path may occur more readily in some anti-sexist and queer-positive households,[10] but other parents who have never given much thought to gender have responded very supportively to their children simply because they are deeply oriented to respecting children's voices or because the child's distress is so worrying.

Quinn's family responded to Quinn's news about their nonbinary gender identity with acceptance and support. When I interviewed Quinn, their family was still going through some adjustments, particularly with regard to their dad remembering to use the right pronouns. But Quinn's family has been creative about this issue, with their mom coming up with the idea of a pronoun jar. Quinn explained that "it costs 50 cents for every wrong pronoun." Quinn's mom demonstrated real sensitivity to them by doing this. Quinn appreciates the pronoun jar, particularly because, they explained, "my mom suggested it too because I would be way too scared to suggest this on my own just because of—not because I'm scared of my parents or how they'd react but because so many people have taught me that my gender identity isn't important enough."

Hunter described himself as "the third generation of queer" in his family and found his mother immediately in support of his newly disclosed identity. Hunter felt particularly happy about his family's response "after hearing about so many other people not being accepted and thrown out of their houses." Although his mom has been really supportive of his transition, the family is struggling hard to make ends meet. Hunter's mom is the sole breadwinner, supporting Hunter and his grandparents. Hunter reported, "There is not much food in my house, so I basically eat maybe once a day." That his mother found $110 to pay for his first prescription of testosterone and assorted supplies because the paperwork for provincial support had yet to go through speaks to the commitment this family has to supporting Hunter.

Some families can point to a specific moment when their children let them or somebody else know about the dissonance they experienced about their assigned sex/gender. In some cases, this occurs within the context of a warm and secure relationship between parent and child that is undisturbed by the revelation. The first person whom Helen told about their nonbinary identity, for example, was their mom, and both Helen's expectations and their mother's response were positive. "I was just like, 'I think I am gender queer, and I want to change my name.' I think I was more scared about the name part than the gender part because my mom is pretty progressive." It took Helen's mom a little while to get used to their new name and pronouns, but "she was cool with it."

Nina described herself as having "noticed something early." As early as age two, Martine consistently played only with stereotypical "girl" toys (dolls, not trucks) and went on to fixate on princesses. "We'd all laugh and say, 'Oh, "he's" in touch with "his" feminine side, and ha ha ha, no wonder, "he" has three sisters, no wonder, no wonder.'" By the time Martine started kindergarten, however, Nina began to worry about how fixated she was on stereotypically feminine toys, interests, and clothing. Nina was puzzled by this but mostly just figured her "son" was gay, which did not particularly trouble her. But starting at age six, Martine started to assert that she was a girl. Nina was concerned enough to talk with her pediatrician about this issue several times, and this doctor ended up referring Martine to a gender clinic.

Since transitioning, Martine is happier and enjoying more success at school, but Nina is careful not to overplay the role of transition as addressing every difficult aspect of her daughter's life—unlike, as she has observed, some of the kids in their local support group for whom transition appears to be a "magic bullet." But everyone in their family is doing better since Martine's transition; they are relieved that the time for keeping secrets about her gender identity is over, now that she is living as a girl and attending a high school in a district outside their neighborhood. Nina reports that Martine has gone from being an unhappy, lonely kid with few interests to someone who has friends. But they've gone from keeping Martine's identity as a girl secret to keeping her identity as a trans girl secret. I am not sure how this will play out.

Some children watch and wait to see how their parents respond to other LGBT people and issues relating to transgender people in the news. Some of these children stay invisible to protect themselves when they observe family hostility to queer and trans people, while others see evidence of queer and trans-positive attitudes as a sign that they are safe to show themselves. The kids I interviewed engaged in a range of activities (including persistent, consistent insistence,[11] coming out, strategic action, self-harm, suicide attempts, and mental health struggles) and experienced a range of feelings (fear, appreciation, openness, forgiveness, consideration, self-hatred, resilience, desolation, and loss) with regard to or as a consequence of relaying their nontraditional gender identities to their families.

Managing Family Reactions

The outcome for Michael and his family has been quite positive, but Michael carefully planned for the immediate negative reaction he expected his mom to have. Michael anticipated some difficulty telling his mother and father, explaining that, although divorced themselves, they are very "traditional." Michael lives with his mother and stepfather and managed his coming-out moment very carefully by writing his mom a letter and going to stay at a friend's house for a few days to avoid dealing with her initial reaction. As expected, "she was quite shocked, and she just kind of freaked out." Her response was more confusion than judgment, however: "She just kind of like, 'Oh my God, what's going on?' It was scary for her." His mother went from shock to denial, even calling on a gay male friend to talk some sense into Michael by warning him that he might not have children or a family or that he could get hurt. According to Michael, "Those things that he said did kind of sadden me a little bit, you know, because those might happen." But Michael was not deterred. "I stood my ground. No matter what she said, I'm like, 'No, this is—I'm serious about this.'"

Things were difficult between Michael and his mom for a month or so until his mom sought out a psychologist to help them work through things together. She specifically looked for and found a Chinese Canadian psychologist who spoke her native language and who specialized in child and youth gender issues. Michael and I laughed when he told me the psychologist's name because he is well known in the Canadian trans community as a warm and caring gender-affirming mental health provider. Michael and his mom and then his dad, who was less unsettled by Michael's announcement, worked with the psychologist to assist everyone in adjusting and supporting Michael. Michael told me that his dad initially asked him, "Are you sure you are not just a lesbian?" Asking if a child or youth might not "just be gay" is not an uncharacteristic response for parents of a kid who comes out as trans. But Michael's family put in the effort to give him the support he needed and he described himself as having a "good" relationship with both his parents as well as his stepfather. As Michael's case exemplifies, a lot of emotional labor on the part of trans kids themselves is required, even in the best case scenarios, to manage their gender identities within family contexts.

Cameron's experience with his family is at the other end of the spectrum. He comes from a fundamentalist Christian family in which he was homeschooled and completely isolated—except for the Internet—until he left home at 17. In preparation for coming out to his family, Cameron found another place to live and carefully packed up his things the night before his high school graduation. His father responded to Cameron's announcement by calling him "an abomination." During our (Skype) interview when Cameron told me what his dad had said, I leaned in toward the computer monitor and said, "You are not an abomination." I could see so much pain on his face as he softly whispered, "Yeah, I figured that out. But yeah, that's probably one of the things that stuck with me the most." The experience of Enrique (17, Latinx) with his father was not quite as horrible, but his dad's resistance to his gender identity made it clear to Enrique that he needed to move out and cut financial ties. Fortunately for Enrique, he found a home with his boyfriend's more accepting family and was doing well at the time of the interview.

Coming Out via Self-Harm and/or Suicide

Unfortunately, it is not unusual for parents to learn about their kids' nonnormative gender identities via their self-destructive actions. Some kids struggling with their assigned sex/gender category express their gender dysphoria through mental health struggles, self-harm, and even suicide attempts. Young people in general have higher suicide rates than adults do, but those who are LGBT and/or racialized are particularly vulnerable.[12] Whether trans kids are visibly gender nonconforming or not, the anxiety and distress many feel is harmful to their mental and physical health. It is actually not unusual for family members to become aware that their child does not feel "like a girl" or "like a boy" because the kid manifests anxiety or depression, engages in self-harm, or attempts suicide. I have spoken with only one parent—Finn's mom— whose child succeeded in killing himself, but I have interviewed kids who have attempted suicide and/or their parents. Whether successful or not, suicide attempts by kids are sometimes evidence of extreme gender distress, in probably far more cases than we are aware of.

Nathan (17, Euro-Canadian/Indigenous) was 15 when he tried to kill himself. The aftermath of his suicide attempt created the necessary opening for him to tell his family that he is male and about the agony he experiences about being forced to live as a girl and in a female body. I first interviewed his mother, Nora, when Nathan was 16. Nathan had been pushed out of school by anti-trans bullying and death threats the previous year. At the time, Nora described her son as being in a deep depression and cutting himself on a regular basis. Nathan's desire to obtain male government identification and enroll in a different school as a boy was thwarted because, at the time, the province he lived in required top surgery to change the sex marker on his identity documents. Nathan had the love and acceptance of his family, but the cost of surgery was completely beyond their resources. Nora described herself as being very frightened that Nathan would kill himself: "I'm to the point now where when I go to bed every night, I knock on his door, I tell him, 'I'm going to bed,' and I say, 'I love you.' If Nathan falls asleep before I go to bed, and he doesn't answer me when I knock on that door, I fly into a panic, because he didn't answer. That's the point that my life has gotten to."

Dylan attempted suicide when he was 13. He was living with his (very religious) grandmother at the time, and she, along with an aunt and an uncle, responded to his announcement that he is trans by verbally disowning him. Dylan's family struggles with poverty. His father is dead, and he currently lives with his mom and her boyfriend in a trailer park. From his comments, it seems clear that Dylan's mother cares about him but lacks the emotional and financial resources to give him the support that he really needs. This scenario played out when he came out to her as trans after his suicide attempt:

> We were just standing in my bedroom, watching TV. I'm just folding the laundry, super casual. I said, "Mom, I think I'm trans." And she's like, "Why do you think that?" "Because I'm trans." That was pretty much as far as that went. There really wasn't a reaction. I had been in therapy, and my mom didn't react because my therapist was talking at that point in time about how I don't respond well to reaction—like instant reactions when they're negative. So I think that she just was trying to be what was going to upset me the least.

Dylan's mom struggles with his gender identity, however, and this comes out in her continual use of female pronouns and his dead name. This situation is painful for him, and he fears that she may not give permission for him to take testosterone; she has been very clear that he is going to have to find a way to pay for it himself.[13]

Dylan has had a really tough time with some members of his family around his gender transition, but there have been small but significant moments of acceptance and support. His stepfather, for example, has found a way to be on Dylan's side. Recently, when ordering fast food, Dylan's stepfather used male pronouns to refer to him for the first time: "I wasn't wearing my chest binder, I wasn't trying to pass, and the guy at the counter said, 'Can I take your order, gentlemen?' I was like, 'French fries.' He was like, 'I want a number six, and he wants a large fries.' 'He.' That was huge. I cried. And then he started apologizing for not using my pronouns and name, and I'm like, 'No, this is perfect.'" And Dylan's grandmother has recently started talking with him again.

Hilary and Andrew, in contrast, view unconditional acceptance as a core responsibility of parenting and are uncomfortable when people treat them as if they are being heroic. Simon's parents are Euro-Canadian and middle class and, judging from my conversation with Hilary, highly intelligent, thoughtful, and well-informed people. Hilary describes the neighborhood where her family lives as "really, really liberal": "Like all the professors and doctors all live in the neighborhood, and they're all very educated and liberal. So publicly, nobody is going to say anything negative about us." But the way her neighbors tend to praise Hilary and Andrew for supporting Simon makes her feel uncomfortable at times: "I do get the feeling, sometimes, that when people are saying positive things about our parenting, that what they're thinking is, 'Thank God it's you and not me,' like when they're too effusive: 'Oh, you're such good parents.' 'No, we're actually letting our kid be themselves.' I don't actually feel like this is a superhuman thing, but sometimes when they go on about it a little too much, it feels like only a superhuman parent could deal with it."

While I agree very much with Hilary that parenting to enable gender self-determination should be a given, it certainly is not. The ways in which binary gender organizes people, relationships, and spaces requires an incredible amount of labor to resist. This chapter brings to light the phenomenal amount of care, advocacy, and activism required by parents to push back against cisgendered environments that harm their children. The resources—time, energy, money, connections, and know-how—required to resist social forces that render one's children precarious is not unique to parents of trans kids but is characteristic of families of more precarious children in general. For many of the kids in my study, after a brief period of adjustment, their parents responded to their gender declaration by consciously creating more space for them to determine their own gender identities and working hard to marshal resources on their behalf.

Emotional Labor and Care Work

Most of the parent advocacy on behalf of transgender kids in North America is engaged in by white, middle-class, and well-educated mothers, many of whom appear to be heterosexual.[14] Political scientist Kimberley Manning explains this demographic limitation as occurring within a neoliberal context where "health, education, and social care are relegated to the private sphere" such that "publicly tackling transphobia is only possible for those who can afford the costs of time, labor, finances, and risk." Parents "relying on reduced incomes, new immigrants, and others living on the margins of a reduced state, may have little capacity to engage in visible advocacy work."[15] For more marginalized families, "the emotional labor necessary to protect one's family from the mutually constitutive violence of transphobia, racism, and/or poverty as it is enacted by society and the state" is ongoing: the oppression of their kids is not the exception that it often is for more privileged parents.[16]

White, middle-class parents of trans kids are disproportionately able to mobilize in defense of their vulnerable trans kids, whether the kids themselves are racialized as white or not. Kai, a parent and an LGBT2Q youth worker, addressed this demographic reality by asking, "How do we protect young people who don't have privileged activists as parents? What empowerment strategies do we offer?" Hilary, too, reflected on the politics of race and class privilege in movements involving parents of trans kids: "I sometimes look at the families that look like mine (Euro, middle class, with a young, passing trans child), and I think there is a trend towards using our entitlement and privilege as our primary weapon in our child's defense—and then in our own defense when we feel uncomfortable. Our society prioritizes the righteousness of white mothers defending their children in a way that we don't for Black mothers and Indigenous mothers." Indeed, Manning points out that "it can become easy to lose sight of the struggles of parents who may not teach at a university, for example, and of the racialized transgender kids who are at far greater risk of violence than are our own white children."[17]

Some parents *are* simply more equipped to engage in trans-affirming care work than others are, and socioeconomic privilege is a significant dimension of this differential ability. Race and class inequality does disproportionately enable relatively wealthy and/or white trans kids to circulate in mainstream and social media because the resources parents are able to leverage (time, know-how, money, contacts, training, "respectability," etc.) are racialized and classed. The capacity to engage in voluntary labor—in practical terms—is unevenly distributed along racial, class, and ethnic lines, but another dimension concerns the extent to which parents themselves endure oppression that impacts their overall well-being.

Like care work in general, the parenting of trans kids is gendered as women's work, and it is primarily, although by no means exclusively, mothers who provide the support and advocacy to enable their children to transition.[18] Sociologist Arlie Hochschild introduced the gendered nature of care work in 1983, and since that time, numerous scholars have attempted to document "the less easily measurable emotional and management practices associated with meeting others' needs, and in some ways, meeting one's own needs."[19] Sociologist Amanda Watson observes that women are disproportionately charged with ameliorating "the emotional burdens of neoliberal capitalism," and this "cultural expectation on women to juggle or balance—by becoming agile or flexible—is a form of affective labor that is disciplinary, and divides women into 'deserving' or 'undeserving' mothers based on this ability."[20]

Forms of Care Work

Affirming parents of trans kids work really hard to create safety in the social environments and spaces that their children circulate in. Although not exclusively and often with the support of the children's fathers, heterosexual mothers of trans kids dominate parent networks and social movements. Given the gendered nature of emotional and affective labor in general in Western societies, it is not surprising that the frontline fight has been led by women, most of whom, but not all, are able to call on a degree of race and class privilege and/or the cultural capital that comes from experience engaging in other social justice struggles. The kinds of care work mostly mothers perform decrease the precarity of trans kids and include the following: educating themselves and other family members and friends; affirming and emotionally supporting trans kids and supporting the family as a whole in the face of trans oppression/ blowback; running interference and protecting kids from anti-trans aggressions large and small; educating people in positions of authority; fighting to create safety in the spaces and institutions kids have to navigate; locating and accessing appropriate resources; helping their kids recover from trauma; coaching kids to enable them to handle the situations they encounter and to build resilience in the face of oppression; and working for social change on behalf of trans kids in general. Family support is a crucial factor for decreasing precarity, but it cannot substantially mitigate poverty, racism, and trans-oppressive violence. Although parental activism and advocacy on behalf of trans kids is not limited by race and class privilege, the cultural capital and the resources necessary to advocate effectively are available only to a minority of the families that are committed to supporting their trans kids.[21]

An often-significant dimension of emotional labor engaged in by parents of trans kids concerns educating themselves about what is going on with their children and managing their own process of adjustment, which require accessing resources and critically engaging with their own reactivity. Doing so is necessary either to respond constructively to their children's expression of a nontraditional gender identity or to create the space, and sometimes even the language, for kids to affirm such an identity—as some trans kids need their parents to figure out what is happening for them before they can know themselves. This is what Dara had to do to enable Davis, for example, to express who he is.

I first met Dara about six years ago, when we both attended a conference for transgender children and their families. Neither of us, as it happened, had children with us: I was attending as a researcher, and Dara came alone because her child was far too anxious in general to manage such an experience. Dara told me that she came to the conference because she sensed that there was a gender dimension to her child's discomfort in the social world. Dara is highly attentive to her child, which gave her the insight to know that she would need to learn more about children who experience dissonance with their assigned sex in order to support him. Her instincts were correct. Dara described the process of needing to get "informed enough to start talking with 'her' [at the time]." Once they started to talk and Dara introduced language about various gender options, Davis gained clarity about his identity and desire to live as a boy and became able to express this to her.

Victor, Greg's father, is one of several dads I interviewed who took the lead in undertaking the affective labor that made it possible for his son to open up about being a boy. It was Victor who created the safety that Greg needed and who helped support Greg's mom in her own process of adjustment. Greg had been really struggling with his mental health prior to his transition, and one particularly bad night led to a breakthrough. Greg was in such distress that Victor took him to the emergency room, but once there, they waited for five hours without seeing a psychiatrist and ended up deciding to head home. A conversation that Victor initiated in the car on the way home gave Greg the freedom he needed to speak his mind. Victor had begun to suspect that Greg might be trans and had done some online research to learn more about it. Greg told me that his father asked him, "Have you ever felt like you're someone else?": "And I said, 'Yes.' And he asked me if I felt like I was a boy. And I said, 'Yes.'" Greg remembers his dad telling him that "no matter what," Greg was "still his child." Greg found this "really, really good to hear." The process of self-education that Victor undertook gave Greg the affirmation and support he needed to then come out to his mother, who had a little more trouble accepting the news at first. Victor then went on to help convince Greg's mom that allowing their son to transition was the healthiest option.

In contrast to parents who had to help their children express their gender dissonance, Kazuko, Stef's mother, found herself confronted with a child who "just screamed out" at her, "in a very affirmative tone, saying that, 'No, I'm not a boy. I'm a girl.'" In response, Kazuko "started to research and check things out and started to realize that, yes, [her] child had more of a female identity than male." As a result of her research, Kazuko came to believe that accepting a child's affirmed gender identity was much more beneficial than trying to change it. This resonated with Kazuko's child-centered approach to parenting in general, so with great courage, she registered Stef in school as a girl and went about achieving a legal name change.

A key aspect of caring labor by parents involves providing their kids with the gender recognition they so badly need. Sociologist Jane Ward introduced the concept of "gender labor" to describe the dimension of care work enacted by queer femmes within intimate relationships with trans men.[22] Being seen/recognized and valued for who you are is a key dimension of mental health and social stability. Mothers of trans kids are typically, although not exclusively, the people in kids' lives who provide them with this affirmation and reassurance.

It is not hard for Hilary to imagine what would have happened to Simon if he had been born to a family that would not accept him: "I see him as so sensitive that I'm too scared to ponder how much he could've been broken." She remarked that when she meets adult transgender people, she has trouble understanding how they made it through their childhood "without anyone seeing that [they] are in distress." Hilary told me, "I think it's much more crushing to endure a hardship when you are also enduring putting your identity aside. Like, when you have a solid foundation of who you are and knowing that the people around you believe in who you actually are, it's a lot easier to take that adversity."

For some parents, the process of accepting and supporting their trans child is very fraught. It takes some time, as Manning observes, for some parents to shift out of shame and disbelief and into activism on behalf of trans kids, especially if exposed to adult "experts" who pathologize their children's gender nonconformity.[23] Some parents feel shame or regret about taking a bit of time to work through this process rather than immediately accepting their children's assertion of their gender identity. In Frank's case, for example, Catherine experienced intense pressure—first from preschool and then from elementary staff—to refuse to accept Frank as a boy. Because of this resistance, Catherine acknowledged that there were times when she forced Frank to wear girls' clothes: "I just feel sick about that now. I wish I would have known the word 'trans' and what that meant. I'm a really strong person, and had I had some literature, had I known, I could have not fucked up, right? Because those experiences—I mean, Frank was being bombarded outside the home and from extended family, and it makes me sick that I contributed to that. And I mean, I did the best I could with the information I had, but it's shitty to look back and know that that's damaging to that little person." But Catherine soon recognized the harm that misgendering Frank was doing to him and went on to resist the efforts of others to gender police him. She has been his strongest supporter ever since. And Frank speaks only positively about his mom, describing her as "very experienced and open-minded and accepting." He remembers telling her that he was a boy, and his mom "just kind of went along with it": "She thought that I would grow up to be a tomboy and a lesbian. Obviously that's not the case, but I think my mom would be the first person who actually listened to me from day one."

Nina feels considerable shame about the time it took for her to come around to be the supporter and advocate that Martine needed: "My biggest shame is that I said, 'No, you're not. Stop it. Stop it.' I'm ashamed of that, but I know it's a normal reaction. I wasn't like, evil, but I still feel that that was wrong. But I just didn't know. I would say, 'Stop giving me a headache.'" Nina was under extreme duress at the time as a result of an overwhelming burden of family responsibilities, which, along with the lack of information about transgender identities in her social context, played a significant role in her initial refusal to listen to Martine's assertions about being a girl. Nina knows she did the best she could with the information and resources she had at the time, but she wishes it had been different and that she could have acknowledged Martine as a girl much earlier. But Nina is a dedicated parent who has worked very hard to create safety for Martine.

One of the main reasons otherwise-LGBT-positive parents sometimes resist their children's trans identities is because they are afraid of what lies in store for them. Trans and gender-nonconforming people in North America, at least in dominant Eurocentric cultural spheres, have been an extremely marginalized and often criminalized population. In spite of shifting social contexts that provide some measure of recognition and tolerance, parents fear that their children will be subject to discrimination, hatred, and violence—in short, that their life chances will be profoundly compromised. It is not unusual for parents to hope that their children can find a balance between authenticity and conformity that will enable them to put together a livable life. But parents' coming face to face with the negative consequences of denial and the positive impact of affirming their kids' gender self-determination often shifts many into the role of advocacy and activism. In this role, they wrestle with various strategies for providing their kids with the best life chances. As Luna described it, however, the fear for the safety of her trans daughter, Taya (16, Euro-Canadian), never entirely goes away:

> My most raw fear is for her safety and well-being. I fear the intolerance that I am seeing in the world and I guess, even though I strongly believe— and all the research is coming out now to say affirmation is the best parenting path—there are always the people who call me late at night or drop emails in my box or hand-delivered letters in my mailbox that say, "You will be responsible if there is a terrible outcome," like "if somebody harms your kid or if your kid harms herself, it will be on your head because you didn't discourage them from this path." And I guess there's just always that little nagging feeling of, you know, is there a better way of supporting, am I missing anything, is this the best that I can do in terms of assuring her confidence, all my kids' confidence, that they absolutely have the right to be whatever they are and absolutely have the right to engage with the world in a fair or more equitable way? Sometimes there are days when the outside world feels like it has so much more power than I do.

This undercurrent of fear is one thing that all parents of vulnerable children have in common, however differently situated they are in being able to ameliorate it.

All of the parents I spoke with, often unprompted, remarked on the very obvious positive outcomes that acceptance, their own and others', had for their kid. Dara is a professor who has used all her resources to gather information and to develop supports for her highly precarious son. Davis experiences multiple dimensions of precarity that negatively impact his agency, and Dara has worked tirelessly both to change the environments that negatively impact him and to foster the resilience that he will require to navigate the world. Although not without friends, Davis experienced the social dynamics of school as an outsider. Dara explained that since he started elementary school, he experienced such high anxiety on the playground that he was unable to play at recess. That changed posttransition: "For the first time since he was in first grade, he is now playing at recess. He is either playing basketball, playing four squares, playing capture the flag. He was a wallflower for years. For years, I've been talking to them [the school]: 'How do we help him do recess?' 'How do we help him just be with somebody? Just to get on the playground.'" Davis's transition has not been a miracle cure, but it has helped. Dara sees it in this way: "The gender transition has really made it possible for—it's like he has more of himself to bring to situations that are going to be difficult anyway because he finds social situations difficult." Once he began to feel comfortable being a boy around his parents (trying out his new name and pronouns), Davis relied on Dara to communicate for him or to act as his representative in every social sphere he transitioned in, including facilitating a change in schools and running workshops for staff—free of charge—on gender-inclusive practices. Gender transition and the social acceptance Davis has experienced have empowered him to deal with his general social anxiety more effectively.

Andrew gives Hilary a lot of credit for leading Simon and their family through transition in the timely way that she did. She said, "He's so cute. He just wants to give me all these accolades for the transition because he says that he wouldn't have realized that we needed to do it." Andrew tells Hilary that she has "saved Simon a surgery, and he won't have to get top surgery, and thank God for that. Getting on top of it way before puberty was really helpful." In a follow-up interview two years later, when Simon was nine, Hilary noted how Simon's plans for his future embodiment have shifted, and he is considering going through puberty rather than taking blockers. She attributes this to her son's "broad community of vibrant nonpassing trans mentors [who have] removed his fear of 'being trans wrong' because he sees these real, lovable people with awkward, interesting, livable lives, and he knows that he can fall anywhere on the spectrum and still just resemble these wonderful people that he already knows." Hilary worked hard to build this trans-diverse community for Simon and observed that it has paid off in terms of his resilience: "[It has] removed my fear of his suicide risk, because I know that it will be much harder for him to feel isolated when he's seen so many people who are just like him. It's harder for him to feel helpless when he sees people just like him who are changing the world."

Some families take longer to accept and adjust to their children's gender revelation. As mentioned earlier, Greg's mother took a little longer than his dad to accept him as a boy. According to Greg, "She was asking me, you know, 'Maybe it's a phase. Maybe, you know, how could you know for sure, you're only 13?' And she was asking, 'Why can't you just live as a gay girl?'" Greg understands that his mother's questions and concerns stemmed from fear for what a trans identity meant for his future quality of life and concerns about the health impacts of potential medical procedures. It helped when the doctor told Greg's mother, "Yes, your child is indeed transgender; no, this is not a phase." The doctor reassured Greg's mother, although, Greg said, "Personally I don't think it should require his validation."

In Tru's case, her mom, Michelle, was initially much more accepting than was her dad, Garfield. I interviewed Tru and Michelle together in 2015, and at one point in the interview, Michelle directed her remarks to Tru: "We were unsure how to deal with it because it was making Daddy uncomfortable, and people were concerned about your safety and your well-being and whether or not you were going to be bullied and what was appropriate behavior." Garfield brought his experience of being subjected to racist bullying when he was a child to the matter of his "son's" gender presentation. Michelle explained, telling Tru, "He didn't want you to go through that too." And Tru added, "And Dad wasn't really used to coming home from work and seeing his little boy running toward him in a princess dress." Tru said that her dad's discomfort made her nervous about telling her parents what was really happening for her. Instead, she chose to be strategic. She said she was "worried that they would react badly, that [she] would get in trouble for thinking it," and she decided to just say she "was a boy and a girl." Michelle and Garfield both responded with acceptance and support to this announcement, taking Tru out to the store and buying her clothes from "across the aisle" for the first time. Tru's parents took efforts to educate themselves, at her mother's prompting, and have become not only accepting and supportive of her but very public activists on behalf of trans people of all ages.

Like many parents, Tru's parents took some time to become the advocates she needed. "She was waiting for us to catch up," Michelle explained. Michelle was initially uncertain about what they should be doing about Tru's gender nonconformity. She started doing a lot of research about it and came to an understanding: "For boys to persist past those gender norms, it says the more it continues, there's a higher chance of your child being gay. And that was one thing I latched onto and just thought, 'Oh well, "Trey's" probably gay,' like 'big whoop'—you know, good to know now. But there was a really small percentage of that who identified as trans." Michelle sought out support, seeing first a psychiatrist and then a psychologist specializing in gender issues in children because, she said, "I wanted Garfield to be able to hear that us supporting our child is not detrimental to our child's development. I needed us to be on the same page, and I needed reassurance for me too." As Michelle described it, "As a parent, you are wanting that validation that what you're doing is the best thing for your child, because it's scary. As parents, we don't necessarily know what we're doing. Like, every day you don't know what you're doing. No matter how many other kids you have, it's always different, right?" Michelle and Garfield came to understand that Tru's well-being was at stake and that they needed to support her and her desire to live as a girl, so they told her, "We're going to fight for you to be Tru full-time, like all the time. And from here on in, we want you to be Tru."

Educating the other parent can be much more difficult than it was for Michelle, however. One of the challenging things that Nina has had to do was educate her ex-husband about transgender issues so that he, too, can support Martine as a girl. This was difficult because part of the problem was that Martine did not feel safe presenting as a girl around her dad and his wife. Because Martine's dad was not seeing it, he took that as evidence that Martine was not really a girl. It took multiple conversations for Nina to make him understand that he and his wife needed to provide Martine with the safety she needed to show up as herself.

For some parents of trans kids, they are unable to get the other parent on board, which has terrible consequences both for the kid and for the affirming parent. It is very difficult for a trans kid to have even one parent who does not support them, and it also places immense stress on the affirming parent. In some cases, this leads to divorce. Indeed, the nonaffirming parent may object so much to their child's transition that they take legal action to try to block it. This happened in the province of British Columbia in April 2016 when a father pursued legal action to stop the hormone-blocker therapy his trans son was undergoing with the consent of his mother, who was the custodial parent.[24] Lou, Stef's "bio dad," as Kazuko refers to him, took Kazuko to court. Lou had been supportive of "Stephen's" first transition to "Stefanie" but "started to freak out" when he learned that "Stefanie" was not wanting to have sex reassignment in the future. When Stef transitioned to an androgynous identity, Lou's opposition became extreme. Kazuko described this as devastating: "He wouldn't even respect the name change. He wouldn't respect calling Stef 'Stef.' It was, you know, 'Your name is Stefanie unless you change it legally,' 'You're a girl.' So it became very disastrous for the relationship. And to the bio-dad, it was more of, 'if you are going to identify as a female, there's only one way, and you have to have the surgery.'" Kazuko described Lou as being very homophobic but able to understand transsexuality as long as it was binary conforming in every way. Lou took Kazuko to court to try to stop Stef from transitioning away from Stefanie, claiming "parental alienation as well as trying to get shared custody." It took two years in court, and the judge ruled in Kazuko's favor. But Kazuko described the difficulties of going through this ordeal without support: "I was kind of alone. I had message boards, but that doesn't help when you need someone to talk to." It was up to Kazuko to provide the love and support to keep first Stefanie and then Stef resilient and alive in body and soul through ongoing socially traumatic experiences, and Lou's opposition to Stef's gender-neutral transition was a major source of trauma in itself.

Many parents have more than one child, so they need to take into account the needs of their other kids and the impact of having a transgender sibling. As psychologists Laura Edwards-Leeper and Norman Spack observe, "The child's wishes are not the only factor: the impact of the social transition on the child's siblings should be taken into consideration. Often, we find that siblings are the most supportive members of the family of the gender dysphoric child, often coming to accept the social transition quickly and becoming a primary ally when their gender dysphoric sibling is teased by peers. However, in other cases, the social implications of having a severely gender dysphoric brother or sister can be devastating."[25] Michelle, Garfield, and Tru and her two siblings had to make difficult decisions about how to proceed around Tru's transition because it affected everybody in the family. As Michelle explained,

> It was so scary because we went through the whole discussion as a family. Like are we going to have to leave town? Are we going to be able to talk to

our family anymore? Are we going to have support? Are we going to have to have really shitty conversations where we have to kick people out of our lives because they're assholes and can't deal with this? What's the best thing? Do we go stealth for her? Do we live open? Do we completely start our lives over just for her, you know, and how fair is that to the other kids?

Many of the siblings of the trans kids in my study have easily adjusted to their sibling's gender transition, often becoming their earliest and greatest defenders. Frank's younger sister, Marina, for example, regularly gets right in there to protect him from bullies. And Stacey described Cassandra's older sister, Brenda, as having only a little difficulty with Cassandra's transition initially because "she was concerned for her dad because he'd be the only boy in the family. So she was worried about daddy. Once Dan reassured her that he was okay, Brenda has been very accepting and easy going." Stacey recalled picking Brenda up from school one day: "I had all the kids with me, and a little boy in her class was like, 'Brenda, which one's your brother-sister? Which one's your brother-sister?' Right? And Brenda says, 'I just—I have a sister.'" Stacey supported Brenda around Cassandra's transition with great care and intention to ensure that "she had the tools and the language to deal with the kids at school." This support included doing role-play with Brenda to help her answer the kinds of questions other kids might ask her and asking the school counselor to check in on Brenda at recess to make sure she was doing okay.

Patrick, Wren's brother, was more resistant, however, to her transition, expressing sadness and frustration around feelings that he was losing his "brother." Patrick was almost four when Wren transitioned, and his initial response was sadness and resistance. Jordan, one of Wren's parents, recalled him saying, "I don't want Wren to be my sister. I want *him* to be my brother." Patrick needed a lot of coaching about respecting Wren's decisions about her gender identity, including the importance of not disclosing that she was designated male at birth. Patrick has outed his sister as "having a penis" several times, as recently as when he was six and she was nine. Wren understandably refuses to be enrolled in the same summer camp as her brother for this reason. Jordan had to explain to Patrick, on multiple occasions, that he was making his sister unsafe and that she needs to be the one to decide if and when to disclose. As

Patrick's parent too, Jordan wrestled with this issue, saying that "he's just talking about his reality, his life," understanding how hard it is for Patrick to keep any of his thoughts to himself in general. Patrick understands the situation now, but that required both coaching and maturity. Jordan acknowledged that Wren has yet to entirely forgive Patrick for his previous behavior.

Managing and educating extended family and friends requires a great deal of time and energy as well as a lot of insight and patience. On Simon's behalf, for example, Hilary sent out an email to her and Andrew's extended families announcing Simon's transition. This email resulted in both support and some resistance. One very valuable source of support has been an older gay relative, adored by everyone in the family, who has spoken out in support of Simon. He performed a crucial role in encouraging the rest of his family to accept and support Simon. Nina described the support she received from her parents as pivotal in helping her be there for her daughter. She described the "great blessing" of support for Martine that she received from her father as he lay dying. "On his deathbed, he said, 'Just let it be,' and that was great for me."

Jordan, a trans nonbinary person themselves, found themselves blamed by members of their partner's extended family for Wren's gender nonconformity. According to Jordan, "Members of my extended family said something along the lines of, 'It figures Jordan would have a transgender child.'" Jordan explained what is ironic about this attitude, however: "Following Wren's lead has brought about my own more explicit trans emergence, not the other way round." But Jordan reported having worked hard, "on principle, from the outset to create space" for all their children "to experience and represent themselves away from the constraints of the gender binary": "It kills me how little space I have been able to create for them in spite of all my efforts."

Luna has been surprised by interactions with members of her extended family because they have had years to get on board about her children's affirmed gender identities and seemed to get it but then behave in really hurtful ways. Luna explained, "The latest really challenging dynamic is that on Stanley's side of the family, there are very few girls born in the last several generations. And right now Stanley's brother's partner is pregnant, and there's all this family flapping about 'it's the first girl,' like 'it's the only girl,' like 'oh, in this sea of boys, this is the first and only daughter,' right? And it's so painful, like for Taya to stand there." Luna described how she interrupts conversations such as these that render her daughter invisible. In this case, she intervened by saying, "'I have a daughter, you know.' And you should have seen the expressions on people's faces, like they were nonplussed and confused—and this is nine years into the journey. You would think nine years into the journey people would have sort of taken some responsibility to figure it out a little better than that. So how do we engage with that part of the family?" Luna finds this situation very challenging because she values extended family and building relationships with people who have diverse opinions but, she said, "I just don't want to expose Taya to that idea, which is actually quite prevalent, that somehow there is a hierarchy of women and where exactly she falls and it's not at the top anyway."

For many of the families I have come to know, accepting and supporting their child's affirmed gender identity has not been without its costs. I've heard reports about grandparents, best friends, aunts, uncles, and cousins who have been barred from the house for their refusal to use correct pronouns and names, for their refusal to stop asking "why?" or because of anti-trans ranting. Parents have struggled so hard to create more safety for their children at school, on the playground, and at the rec center and have often met with great resistance. But the one place most of them are able to exert control over is the threshold of the family home. Granted, doing so requires economic independence from family members, which is (obviously) not always the case. But many of the parents have drawn the line at the door. Catherine explained, "I'm at a place now where I'll have the conversation, I'll be supportive, and I'll be kind, and I'll remind you, but there comes a point where, 'get on board or get out of the house,' because I'm sick of this." She has had to tell her parents and her sister that "they can't come over anymore, because they kept saying 'she.'" Catherine has drawn this line because she recognizes how harmful it is to Frank. Nathan's mom, Nora, echoes the sentiment, describing how she kicked a friend out of her house for refusing to call Nathan by his name: "'Jane,' I said, 'if you don't get the fuck out of my house now,' I said, 'I will be arrested here tonight.'" Nora's brother-in-law is not allowed in the house either for the same reason.

Shielding Transgender Kids from Harm

Jordan has run interference for Wren with other children as well as adults and consciously tries to open up space around gender in children's worlds: "Some kids would say to me, 'Is she a boy or a girl?' And I would just say, 'That's a really interesting question, isn't it? How come it's so important for us to figure that out?' And then they would respond, 'Well is she?' And I would say, 'It's like there it is, isn't it? Like what does it feel like to not know?' And then they would not answer but look at me like I'm just out of my fucking tree."

Engaging in care work to shield a trans kid from harm requires a lot of time, knowledge, social skills, and foresight. Parent advocates have to anticipate problems before they happen if they are to spare their children even some of the damaging consequences of oppression. Doing this can mean speaking with adults in a variety of contexts (the eye doctor, day camps, the school, recreation activities) that your child will interact with—in advance. It involves a lot of educational and affective labor, which adds to parental overload and calls on a great deal of cultural capital.

Part of the typical work of supporting trans kids involves absorbing as many microaggressions on the kids' behalf as you can—to spare them the negative mental health consequences of ignorance and oppression. A number of parents reported doing behind-the-scenes work to prepare people and environments to be less damaging to their kids. Cory's mom, Nicole, for example, shielded him from all kinds of adult resistance to his playing hockey, first as a gender-nonconforming girl and then as a trans boy. It was only years later that Cory found out about the extent of work his mom had engaged in on his behalf because keeping it hidden was one of the ways she shielded him from anxiety. For the same reason, Catherine worked hard behind the scenes to try to get Frank's new high school to ensure that his correct gender marker and name were on all official school documents. She wanted Frank to be able to experience inclusion as a matter of course; her inability to accomplish this was traumatic for both of them.

Parents often do a lot of the work involved in explaining their trans children to others. Kazuko described the effort involved in "trying to explain to people": "People think that Stef has reverted 'back' to the male identity. And I keep saying that Stef is on a different level now. They are embracing the masculine and feminine sides of themselves, being an androgynous identity, or gender queer or gender fluid. I think it's just going beyond what the binary is." But ultimately, parents have to help their children develop the resilience and skills to handle things on their own. The necessity for doing this is something that parents of more precarious children often feel acutely.

Building Resilience

While some parents fear that their child's transgender identity may be exposed and result in negative repercussions, Hilary, instead, fears secrecy. She feels strongly that too much privacy "feels really dangerous," that if Simon "has to keep it a secret, then it could be used against him." Hilary has communicated to Simon that being trans does not have to be a secret because she "wanted him to grow up embracing that": "I didn't want to step on any of that. I want him to grow up with activism tools so that he never feels hopeless. I want him to grow up able to answer any questions without shame so that he never associates any of this with feelings of shame." Trans kids and their parents obviously make decisions about visibility and disclosure in vastly varying social contexts with access to considerably different information and resources.

Eva is both proud of her gender-nonconforming son, Peter (six, Euro-Canadian), and worried about the difficulties he may face in his future: "I'm very proud of him for having the self-confidence to wear what he wants to wear to school and to continue wearing it, regardless of what people are saying. I think that's pretty amazing. I guess I'm worried that that's going to change one day." Eva defines Peter's gender identity as "very much a boy," reporting that he "has no difficulties with calling himself a boy, with going to the boys' washroom; he's very centered on being a boy. He very rarely has said he wished he was a girl, and he hasn't said that in quite a long time. So he's a very confident child. He seems quite happy to be who he is." At times, however, Eva worries that supporting Peter and his gender nonconformity may actually be increasing his precarity, explaining, "As a parent, you wonder, am I putting him in a situation where he's going to come home crying because somebody teased him?" As many parents of trans and gender-nonconforming kids do, Eva wonders where her son's gender nonconformity comes from, saying, "I think it would be pretty interesting just to know if he would be interested in wearing dresses if most of his friends at school were boys and how much of this has to do with his interests, because a lot of the girls are wearing dresses, or how much of it has to do with how much he loves *Frozen* and identifies with Elsa?" Concerns such as these relate to ongoing debates about nature versus nurture with regard to sex/gender, and I cannot help but wonder what it would look like if we puzzled as much about the source of gender conformity in cisgender girls and boys rather than naturalizing their gendered presentation and behavior to the extent that we do as a culture. Feminists do this work, but it often seems we have lost the battle for the mainstream since the 1970s, if we ever really had it: the critique of sex typing kids seems to have become more and more esoteric as the social worlds in which children circulate become bluer and pinker all the time.[26]

One of the things that many parents of trans kids do is coach their kids to stand up for themselves. Eva admires Peter's confidence in general and his resistance to sexist gender norms in particular. Because she observes how frustrating it is for Peter when other adults restrict his gender options, Eva invests time and energy in helping him learn to stand up for himself and coaching him about how to respond to various scenarios. She shared a particularly frustrating example: "We went to a shop with sun hats, because we needed to buy him a sun hat. And he picked out a pink one, and I was going to buy it for him. I was actually at the register, and the woman at the counter said to me, 'We have another store just across the street, and we have some hats in blue.' And he left the store—just walked out of the store." Eva felt it was important to her son's resilience to restore his confidence in his original choice:

> I went out after him and said, "Oh, it's fine. Why don't you get this hat?" And he said, "No, I don't want it," and I said, "Because of what she said?" And he said, "Yes," and I said, "You know what she is?" I think I might've said, "She's stupid," or something like that, you know, and I said, "If you want to wear this hat, you should wear this hat, and you shouldn't let this get in the way. If you really like the hat, let's go get it." And I went back and said, "Did you know he was perfectly happy about getting the hat before you said that?" She said, "Oh, well, I didn't mean anything by it." I

said, "Well, we were perfectly happy with the hat." So anyway, I managed to persuade him to come back to the store and buy the hat, and he did. And he wore it quite happily for the rest of the summer.

This kind of intervention is labor-intensive for Eva, but she undertakes it to build Peter's resilience, to push back against people and environments that constrain him and to enable him to develop the ability to do this for himself. But this is demanding work, and Eva herself finds "educating people all the time" tiring.

Hilary, too, sees fostering resilience in her children as a central part of her role as a parent. Speaking of Simon, she said, "I have to remember that it's on him to develop the skills to deal with this, that I cannot fix it so it will be smooth forever. All I can do is raise a resilient kid." Kazuko's educational and employment background helped her figure out how to build Stef's resiliency in the face of trans oppression. "[After] reading everything that I read, one of the most important conclusions that I came out with was that Stef has to see other people like them and be part of something bigger." Kazuko's own gender and sexual noncon-formity had taught her "the importance of building community, to not feel alone." She shared this sense of purpose on her child's behalf: "I wanted my child to build resiliency. I didn't want the thought of suicide, the violence. . . . I wanted just to build the kid's self-confidence and do everything to create a child whose adaptation techniques are ready for whatever's out there and then just try and protect them as best as I can while they were younger, hoping for the best."

Kazuko worked hard to connect her then-trans daughter with LGBTQ and trans communities and resources from the get-go. "We went to the United States when Stef was six to make sure that they met other kids like them. We went everywhere." She regularly traveled with Stef to camps and conferences in the U.S. and Canada and drove into the nearest major city to provide Stef with a trans-affirming peer and adult environment several times a month. When Stef was old enough to go to LGBTQ youth camps, Kazuko sent them. Kazuko explained, "That was one of my goals, that it would be beneficial for Stef to be around like-minded and similar-living kind of people in their community so that they know they're not alone, that they know that there's an openness out there that exists, because the school year can be really tough because of the ignorance and whatnot of people—so to build that strength and the bonds that friendship can have." Kazuko also facilitated Stef's use of Skype to connect with trans kids all over North America. The importance of the Internet and social media for enabling access to information and community was a recurrent theme in my interviews with trans kids and their parents.[27]

Sometimes cultivating resilience meets resistance from the kid, however. Jordan, for example, described a sticky situation: Wren holds what Jordan considers to be a fairly unrealistic belief that nobody remembers that she "used to be a boy." Believing it necessary to foster resilience in Wren, Jordan has spoken rather matter-of-factly to her about the likelihood that she will encounter someone who knows her from before, that she will be outed, and that her transgender identity is nothing to be ashamed of. Jordan is very careful to frame this very real possibility as an accidental rather than an aggressive act. Like other parents of trans kids, Jordan employs role-play to help Wren prepare for a scenario in which her trans identity is revealed by a kid or adult who means her no harm or by someone who asks her if she is a boy or girl. Jordan reported that Wren "hates this": "But I feel that leaving her unprepared for the likelihood of such an occurrence would be a failure on my part." Jordan told me, though, that there are damaging things that happen that they or Samantha never share with Wren. A friend of Jordan's got in touch on one occasion to say that they had happened to cross paths—in a bar—with a parent of a child from Wren's former school. Upon discovering that Jordan was a mutual acquaintance, the parent exclaimed—with great excitement—"Jordan's daughter has a penis!" Jordan was furious and "phoned this guy up and read him the riot act. He apologized and sounded really sincere, but Goddamn!" Jordan is convinced that telling Wren about incidents such as this would negatively impact her mental health.

Many of the parents of trans kids in this book devoted significant time and energy to trying to make their children's schools safe and welcoming places for trans kids to navigate: by laying the groundwork, educating staff, other parents, and children; facilitating transition; and advocating for their child. Several mothers went so far as to deliver gender-inclusive training workshops for teachers and other school personnel—free of charge—while many others did this work less formally via countless meetings with teachers and school staff. Still others provided schools with trans-inclusive resources and made connections with appropriate organizations on the school's behalf. It is not unusual at all for parents of trans kids to do this work gladly: they do it free of charge because they are just so happy to be able to do it, given how damaging things are to their children if business as usual continues. Some of these parents started out having expertise around gender issues, while others became experts through their efforts to educate themselves and others in support of their children.

Dara, for example, has engaged in serious gender work with all the schools Davis has attended. Davis has multiple bases of precarity that are not mitigated by the relative wealth of his family alone. The amount of labor that Dara engages in to empower her son is staggering—she has the cultural capital and financial resources to do this, and it is still so intensive. In addition to the time she has spent supporting her highly anxious son, coaching him to become more resilient, obtaining professional support, and driving to a city three hours away once a month to see his endocrinologist, Dara regularly spends huge amounts of time and energy working with school staff—voluntarily providing numerous workshops about creating gender-inclusive practices.

Stacey too has been hard at work educating herself, her children, her husband, her extended family, her school community, and the school staff. In her first discussion with the principal about Cassandra being a girl in spite of the male gender marker on her birth certificate, Stacey reported, "The principal kind of looked at me like I had my head on backwards." But as a result of Stacey's efforts, the principal ultimately agreed to accept Cassandra as a girl at the school. But Stacey considers this to be just the starting point for trans inclusion: she wants to ensure that Cassandra has the space and support to continue to explore her gender as she is going through school. With that goal in mind, Stacey took care to be proactive in instructing school staff about appropriate responses. In order to do so, she had to be able to anticipate situations that would come up. Stacey gave an example: "[I] asked that they don't correct, if they say things like—I would prefer that they don't even say, 'Boys line up here, girls line up there'—but if they do that and she picks the girls' lineup, I ask them not to correct her. Or if she picks the boys' lineup, I ask them not to correct—like shove her over to the other line."

It would clearly be beneficial to all children if gender were not used to organize kids at school.

When Hilary came to terms with the fact that Simon was a boy, she started organizing herself to work with the school to enable him to transition. That involved locating LGBT resources in her local community that helped her work with the school. She described the process of finding appropriate support as challenging: "Now that I think about it, I went through so many phone calls figuring out how to approach it." She finally found the right person to talk to when she made contact with a woman who ran a safe-schools program for her local school board. The LGBT resource person she found via the school district was a huge help, but Hilary had to be prepared for legal action, particularly around bathroom access. The school initially responded to news of Simon's impending transition by designating a gender-neutral bathroom and, "fairly predictably," wanting Simon to use it. But because of her research, Hilary said she "knew where this was going" and came prepared. "I went in prepared to do battle. I went in with lists, prepared to be like, 'If you take this position that he has to use the gender-neutral bathroom, you're going to lose and you're going to be on the wrong side of history.' I don't know if I would've had what it takes to go to the media and start a lawsuit over it, but I was prepared to threaten it for sure. I knew that in terms of a human rights challenge, it wouldn't stand to isolate a child like that." I am convinced that the gender work that these parents do benefits all of the children—cis and trans—with whom the adults they train come in contact.

Sometimes creating safer space for one's trans child necessitates a move from one school to another or even one part of the country to another. One of the reasons Ray-Ray's family moved across the country, for example, was to provide him with a more conducive environment for his gender nonconformity. The ability to move schools or locations to decrease the precarity of a trans kid requires a constellation of material and social resources that are very unevenly distributed.

The support of family cannot mitigate poverty, but it does contribute to resilience. I checked in with Nora a year after my initial interview and learned with great relief that Nathan was doing much better. A few months after our first conversation, Nora reported that Nathan somehow found a sense of resolve and decided to get a job to pay for his top surgery. His family helped him find employment in the fast-food industry and supported him in saving up enough money. He had the surgery in June 2016, and I saw a subsequent picture of him, standing proud, in a family photo. Nathan still struggles with depression but is doing much better. While his is a story of individual and family resilience, his financial inability to obtain the bottom surgery that he needs to feel whole is a significant factor that continues to compromise his well-being.

Parents of trans kids often become accidental activists, becoming radicalized around trans issues only because of the difficulties their kids experience. But as a result of advocating for their own children, many parents become well educated and serve as valuable no-cost resource providers for other parents of trans kids and older trans kids themselves. Kazuko, who had been damaged by her own experience of isolation in advocating for Stef, for example, took it upon herself to create more resources for parents of trans kids, believing that connecting parents with each other is really important. As an activist, she is involved in an organization that does training in the schools relating to supporting transitioning kids. Kazuko takes great pride in her ability to help parents of other trans kids: "I brag about that I can find anything, anywhere, any time, you know. Like, just tell me what you need, and I'll get it." The enjoyment of at least some dimension of privilege (wealth, education, experience as an activist) is typically necessary to enable parents to play these kinds of leadership roles. But this voluntary labor contributes to reducing the precarity of transgender kids more generally. Many parents of trans kids apply their volunteer labor to fill the gap in available services and care for trans kids and their families.

As I documented earlier in the book, some families have been able to access the legal support necessary to make human rights complaints on behalf of their children. This was the case for Tru Wilson and Bella Burgos, whose cases achieved real change that will benefit trans kids in each of their provinces. The option for families to pursue legal action in an effort to prevent their children from experiencing discrimination and trans oppression is disproportionately available to relatively privileged families. However, Frank and Catherine have been fortunate to receive extensive pro bono support from a lawyer who specializes in trans rights, while in the U.S., organizations such as the National Center for Lesbian Rights (NCLR) and the American Civil Liberties Union (ACLU) have taken a leading role in advocating for trans kids and footing the bill for many legal challenges.

Parents of Trans Kids as a Social Movement

A social movement of parents of transgender kids has been one of the driving forces behind the emergence of visible trans kids, support networks for families, legal and policy changes, and the burgeoning sector of affirming professional healthcare targeted to children. A minority of these parents are trans themselves and/or visibly racialized and/or male identifying, but much of the cultural power of movements of parents of trans kids lies in female cisgender conformity, presumed or actual heterosexuality, dominant narratives of motherhood, and middle-class whiteness.

However radical the more mainstream-appearing mothers of trans kids among this movement may actually be, their ability to project as nonthreatening and motherly enables them to intervene on behalf of queer and trans kids in ways that are less available to those of us who are some combination of queer, trans, racialized, or male presenting. These moms are particularly effective at engaging in social change efforts in kids' spaces, addressing issues of children, gender, and sexuality that have previously been mostly forbidden or are more risky when queer, and/or trans adults or men undertake this labor. Queer and trans adults have played a role in addressing queer and trans oppression in educational content and contexts, but the power of mostly white, middle-class, heterosexual cisgender moms to challenge schools and other institutions to change the way they do gender cannot be overstated.

Collateral Precarity

Trans oppression not only harms the trans kids themselves but has a ripple effect on all who love and care for them. In this sense, having a trans kid can result in a family experiencing what I refer to as *collateral precarity*. All of the parents I interviewed deeply regret the difficulty that their children experience and the trauma to the whole family that often accompanies this difficulty, but none of them regret their children's non-traditional gender identities.

Negative mental and physical health consequences often accrue to parents as they try to protect their kids from microaggressions, partly because of the effort involved but also because being unable to keep our children safe is a devastating experience for most parents. Seeing Stef mistreated and struggling to protect them, for example, has taken a toll on Kazuko. Stef explained the single most important reason that they did not commit suicide: "the reaction my mom would have. That terrified me, and I didn't want my mom to go through anything else, because she already had two big depressions. So that's pretty much the reason why I didn't kill myself." Supporting Stef has also cost Kazuko professionally. She described her current white-collar employment this way: "a really nice cushy, quiet job which is way below my intelligence and way below my qualifications, but it's quiet/nonstressful." Kazuko has prioritized the taxing work of supporting Stef and other parents of trans kids over career advancement and recognition.

In Frank's case, the violence and trans oppression he experienced sent shockwaves through his entire family. The stress resulting from the sexual assault on Frank and its aftermath required Catherine to go on long-term disability; as her family's sole breadwinner, this put them in poverty: "We lost our car, and we had to move to a cheaper place in a worse neighborhood." Catherine described the severity of the poverty they endured in the aftermath of the assault, saying, "We were chopping up furniture!" When I first interviewed her, Catherine had been off work for two and a half years. As she explained, "Since this has happened to Frank and since some of the community's response, I couldn't hold my shit together." Catherine dreams of moving to a big city and leaving their small town behind, but the monumental tasks of finding a new job and securing housing are more than she can handle at the moment. She explained, "When you've been kicked down, it's hard to—I don't believe in myself anymore. Like, I always felt pretty strong and pretty confident, and that's gone right now. I don't feel like, 'Fuck this, we can move and I'll find work, and we'll be good.' I don't feel that way anymore." Catherine described herself as having been fundamentally changed by the traumatic ordeal of trying to get the school to take appropriate action to protect Frank: "It killed me, it killed me. I will never be the same person. I've been in therapy for—well, since it happened, it's been two and a half years." There are significant costs to parents and families, costs that include negative consequences for economic security, professional advancement, loss of family and friends, parental overload and (mostly maternal) mental and physical health, and loss of activities, spaces, community, feelings of safety, and privacy.

For trans kids who do not have family support, the risk of self-harm and suicide, as well as poverty and criminalization, are disproportionately high. But often families' own precarity is so extreme that their efforts to support their child fall far short of what they need. Hunter is marginalized in multiple ways: neurodiversity, indigeneity, poverty, and gender. He has been attending what appear to be a series of "special education"—although we no longer call them that—programs and receiving services from his province's child welfare department for a number of years. Fortunately, this contact with the government has not resulted in his removal into care, as is so common for Indigenous children in Canada, but rather has put him in touch with crucial resources, including his participation in a group for transgender children and teens facilitated by a psychologist who is well respected by the local trans community for his affirmative-care ethos and advocacy work. Since I interviewed Hunter, however, he and his family were driven by severe poverty to move across the country to be closer to family support. This had the result of isolating Hunter completely from any kind of LGBT support not available within his immediate family or via the Internet and cutting off his access to affirming healthcare.

Collateral Benefit

Without prompting, a number of the parents I interviewed talked about the benefits they and their families have gained as a result of having a transgender family member. These include a really meaningful sense of accomplishment about their abilities to advocate and engage in social change, opportunities for intellectual and social development relating to greater understanding of structures of oppression, more space for everyone in the family to explore their own gender identities, a newfound sense of community with LGBT people and other parents of trans kids and meaningful new connections to LGBT and other social justice movements, and more authentic relationships with family and friends. During my second interview with Dara, when I asked her if she had ever imagined that parenting was going to be this hard, she burst out laughing and said, "No, not in a million years. This is taking me on a journey that I never imagined. I wouldn't change it for anything. It's, like, not even just about gender, the whole gender and race and developmental issues and where he's about to be tested for learning disabilities and just the whole early trauma and then, later, the rest of his life are just—it's incredible."

Limits to Radical Social Change

There are gender-essentialist and binary-normative narratives at play within some transgender networks and communities, and parent networks are no exception. For some, being transgender *is* "being trapped in the wrong body," which is equated with a medicalized disorder. Some transgender people and supporters look to the scientifically discredited "science of sex difference"[28] to ground the certainty they feel that transgender men are born with male brains and female bodies while transgender women are born with female brains and male bodies.

None of the parents of transgender kids whom I interviewed expressed their understanding of their children's gender nonnormativity in this way. Most of the parents in the book have a relatively nuanced understanding of diverse gender-identity possibilities. A few parents hung on to fairly stereotypical understandings of gender difference (referencing their children as having always preferred to play with trucks versus dolls, for example, as evidence of gender nonnormativity), but all followed their children's lead with an attitude of general openness about gender as a spectrum. While none of the parents I interviewed narrowly understood being transgender as a necessarily medicalized identity, in my travels to various conferences and in online spaces, I have encountered parents of trans kids who play a part in reconstituting transgender children within a stabilized gender binary: by taking for granted the inevitability and universal appropriateness of hormone therapy and surgical treatment options and/or by leaving homophobia, patriarchy, and misogyny unacknowledged. I heard one parent at a family conference, for example, say that he sees his transgender child as having a "birth defect" that needs to be medically repaired. Kazuko has come across this attitude as well. Not only did Stef's biological father, Lou, feel this way, but, Kazuko recalled, "There was a parent on one of the parent sites that we navigate. She was like, 'Oh, my God, my kid wants to stop the blockers. It's the end of the world.' I'm like, 'Whoa, wait a second. [*Laughs*] You know, this is still the child's body, and maybe the child wants to have the fertility to be able to save the eggs or save the sperm or whatnot. And maybe the body changes. They don't want to have that blocking anything. They want to go with the natural process and let whatever is be.'" Indeed, the radicalization that some parents of trans kids experience as a result of their children's resistance to traditional gender expectations is limited to gender and, even then, often fails to be critical of heteropatriarchy as an oppressive system. Troublingly, at least before the election of Donald Trump and the increased visibility of anti-LGBTQ white supremacists, not an insignificant number of white parents take it for granted that the main threat to the safety of trans kids comes from nonwhite (ignorant/conservative) communities. This assumption defies reality and plays into racist and xenophobic social practices and trans-/homonationalist agendas. As Manning points out, "The relatively few numbers of parents of color publicly advocating for their transgender children is . . . not due to cultural mores more conservative than those found in religiously conservative white families and communities, as is sometimes suggested, but rather a direct outcome of racist structures that exhaust and exclude."[29]

But the employment of gender-essentialist explanations for affirmed male and female identities among trans kids should not seem surprising at all given that pervasive gender essentialism is so culturally dominant, especially in the spaces where children circulate.[30] I suspect that some parents of trans kids adopt this perspective early on in the process as they struggle to make sense of the way their children's gender identity is turning their world upside down but that this perspective shifts over time as they engage in community building and activism with trans and queer adults.

Radical Potential

There are possibilities for greater radicalization of the mostly relatively privileged parent activists who make up these social movements, as a result of their engagement with diverse trans communities. I attended the "Gender Odyssey" adult and family conference in Seattle several years ago, for example, and found myself listening to a powerful key-note by an Asian American transgender woman, a former president of San Francisco Pride, who talked openly about her experiences of family rejection, discrimination, racism, and survival sex work. As I listened to this powerful speaker, I found myself looking around at the 200 or so people who filled the room. The audience was equal parts white, middle-class, heterosexual couples and a somewhat racially diverse group of (presumably) trans and queer adults. I watched the mostly straight, mostly white parents earnestly nodding with recognition and seeming personal connection to the activist moments in LGBT history that the speaker referenced, such as the Stonewall riot and the cen-tral role that trans women played in leading that fight against police violence. This really got me thinking about the extent to which some previously "unwoke" parents of trans kids are being radicalized. I know that many parents of trans kids made space for their transgender kids because they already had queer or feminist sensibilities and attachments to social justice issues more broadly. But I am certain that some came late to the party, which fills me with hope: that knowledge of the ways environments and institutions harm their otherwise privileged children will translate to engagement with anti-oppression social change move-ments more broadly.

Hilary came to parenting with a strong social justice orientation to begin with, but she described how having a transgender child opened her eyes to the struggles that more precarious families face in raising their children: "It was the first time I really had to confront that idea. I got it that other people had to raise their children in these much more visceral, under threat kind of ways. I got it and I mourned for it, but I get it at a different level now." Hilary also described how a friend helped her understand that the kind of social change work necessary to re-sist the precarity imposed on disenfranchised children is at odds with white, middle-class notions of appropriate behavior. Hilary referred to the "number-one criticism people have about parents who have trans-gender children" as "being the way of putting their children out there; politically as an activist, as a parent, you're using your children for activ-ist purposes, and people find this quite unforgivable." Hilary described how her friend identified the privilege underneath this judgment: "She said, 'As white, middle-class parents, we have this expectation that we would never, ever use our children politically, but nobody ever raises those same questions about a Black family that might choose to send their child to the first nonsegregated school. . . . When your child is marginalized, sometimes you have to put your child in the line of fire to ensure a better future for them.'" This statement resonated powerfully for Hilary, but she acknowledged, "It's just really hard for us to have that conversation when it's privileged parents and marginalized children because we don't have a script. I mean, parents expect to be able to pass their privilege on to their children. That is something I've really struggled with: having to make peace with the fact that my son will never get to be as safe as I get to be."

* * *

The extent to which the social movement of parents of trans kids is able to harness its power to really make a difference in reducing the precarity of trans kids will depend, in large part, I am convinced, on the extent to which trans oppression is understood to be part of larger systems of inequality and oppression and resisted accordingly. The most precarious trans kids are caught up in the necropolitics of racism, colonialism, enforced poverty, sexism, misogyny, and so on that shape their lives as or more profoundly than—but always in combination with—the imposition of a cisgender identity on them.

In the awful year that followed Trump's election and inauguration, with disturbing attacks on the gender self-determination of transgender kids and adults and on racialized, undocumented, and religious minorities, I have wondered about the extent to which social movements made up of parents of trans kids will be willing and able to form coalitions with other vulnerable groups. One of my purposes in writing this book is to encourage relatively privileged parent activists to think of transgender kids in all their diversity and to work in coalition with other marginalized communities to generate safety for kids who are even more unsafe than their own, to use their relative privilege to create more space at the table for everyone.

I view the care work of mothering as mitigating precariousness by definition, but for whom? To use a metaphor I loathe for a moment, that of the lifeboat, I ask, how do we get all the children in the boat—and, by necessity, in order to accomplish that, all their families in the boat? I have never felt a greater sense of purpose than I do as a parent, and I honestly fear how I might respond to a situation in which only a few children could be saved. It is highly likely that I would do anything to make sure that my children get in the boat, that I would do whatever I could to divert scarce resources to my own kids, not because they are of my blood (they are not) but because they are of my heart. But this metaphor of too few boats for too many people is what neoliberalism is all about: an illusion of a zero-sum game in which losers must exist in order for winners to be crowned.

5

Supportive Healthcare

> As a nonbinary trans person specifically who is not inter-
> ested in surgeries or any type of medical procedures, I don't
> feel like I'm trapped in the wrong body. It's more that I'm
> trapped in other people's perceptions of my body.
> —Quinn, 18, Indigenous/Euro-Canadian

In December 2015, the Centre for Addictions and Mental Health (CAMH) in Toronto, Ontario, closed its Child, Youth and Family Gender Identity Clinic and terminated the employment of its director, Dr. Kenneth Zucker. This was a move that many critics feel was long overdue, both reflecting and signaling a sea change in the clinical landscape vis-à-vis the treatment of transgender and gender-nonconforming children in North America. Zucker is a prominent psychiatrist specializing in the treatment of gender-nonconforming and transgender children who has become a person of controversy over the years because of his profoundly influential advocacy of a harmful "reparative" or "corrective" model of treatment. Zucker's influence on the medicalization and psychiatric management of gender nonconformity in children in Canada and the U.S. has been profound: he recently chaired the Working Group for the Sexual and Gender Identity Disorder Section for the 2013 fifth edition of the *Diagnostic and Statistical Manual* (*DSM*) that replaced the diagnosis of gender identity disorder in children (GIDC) with gender dysphoria (GD).

As an indication that debates about appropriate healthcare for transgender kids are far from over, however, a January 11, 2016, petition was circulated in opposition to Zucker's firing and the closing of CAMH. It was signed by some 508 "professional clinicians and academics" who expressed concern about the impact of trans activism on academic freedom. Along with several other scholars and activists, I responded by developing and circulating a counterpetition in support of the closing of

CAMH and emphasizing the need for accessible affirmative healthcare for trans people of all ages. This petition had more than 1,500 signatures when we submitted it.

In spite of this petition battle, the issues involved are multiple and very complex. I was surprised and deeply troubled, for example, to find queer feminist science scholar Anne Fausto-Sterling's signature on the original petition in support of Zucker, as her work has been a frequent touchstone in my own scholarship. I begin this chapter with a brief overview of the medicalization of gender nonconformity in children in North America. Bringing the hybrid assemblage–critical disability theoretical lens I introduced in chapter 1 into engagement with my interview data allows me to consider the transgender child in potentially new ways: as a particular expression of the multiple ways in which gender is experienced and assembled in North American contexts.

In keeping with critical disability scholar Tobin Siebers's instructions to go beyond merely identifying disability as a social construction to "look for the blueprint," to identify aspects of the built environment that produce disabled bodies/persons, I trace the recent history of the corrective medicalization of childhood gender nonconformity as one facet of the blueprint of the social construction of binary gender. A second facet I examine is the application of puberty-suppression therapy with the institutional—if not necessarily the recipients'—goal of enabling binary gender conformity and assimilation. I conclude that access to affirming medicalized transgender identities is limited by other dimensions of precarity, notably race, class, and binary gender conformity, such that much affirming medicalization inevitably tends to operate in a trans-normative way. I draw on the work of trans scholar Julian Gill-Peterson to observe how this context and these processes operate to position less precarious transgender children as (proto-)citizen-consumers and more precarious transgender children as have-nots in a racialized neoliberal biomedical market.[1]

Gender-nonconforming children have been identified as a clinical population and subject to increasing medicalization in North America since the 1960s, a process that added a clinical dimension to the gender policing that children experience in daily life.[2] Pioneers in this field capitalized on moral panics around homosexuality and transsexuality to develop diagnostic and treatment regimens that targeted mostly gender-nonconforming boys for gender-reparative therapy.[3] Like lesbian and gay "conversion therapy,"[4] these ongoing but increasingly illegitimate treatment programs use varying techniques aimed at "repairing" children's gender nonconformity, typically blaming parents in general and mothers in particular for having done a poor job of gender socialization in the first place. The work undertaken to formally pathologize gender nonconformity in children and establish a legitimate subfield of research in North America culminated in the inclusion of the gender identity diagnosis in children (GIDC) in the third edition of the *Diagnostic and Statistical Manual* in 1980.[5] GIDC persisted until 2013, when, under the leadership of the aforementioned Dr. Zucker, it was revised to the less pathological but still binary-gender-normative gender dysphoria (GD).

The achievement of a formal diagnosis in 1980 provided the researcher clinicians who were studying and treating gender-nonconforming children with legitimacy and contributed to the process of normalization regarding binary sex and gender logic in the United States and Canada. This subfield took as its foundation binary sex categories as naturally cohering with normalized gender identities and gendered behaviors. According to this logic, gender nonconformity was seen as pathological and in need of correction. Researcher and trans advocate Jake Pyne describes the medicalization of childhood gender nonconformity as a form of governance that enclosed gender-nonconforming children and their families in a web of surveillance and gender policing.[6] One of the most well-known programs that operated in the 1970s—the UCLA "feminine boy project"—made headlines in 2011 when a former patient committed suicide at the age of 38. The family of the boy, known as Kraig in the scientific literature, described him as having been totally broken by treatment to curb his gender nonconformity, including severe beatings that his father was instructed to administer.

There is considerable debate within trans and queer communities about the role that the GIDC diagnosis has played and that the revised diagnosis of gender dysphoria continues to play in regulating gender identities. Queer gender and sexuality scholars Eve Sedgwick and Phyllis Burke were among those who sharply criticized the initial GIDC diagnosis, seeing it as a replacement for the diagnosis of homosexuality as a mental illness that was jettisoned by the American Psychiatric Association in 1973 as a result of successful pressure from gay and lesbian clinicians and activists.[7] While treatment regimens targeting childhood gender nonconformity were initially oriented to preventing both adult homosexuality and transsexuality, the removal of homosexuality from the *DSM* in 1980 produced a shift away from concerns about sexual identity and toward preventing gender nonconformity. In this way, gender-reparative therapy nimbly adapted to the success of gay and lesbian activism against the pathologization of same-sex sexuality by focusing on eliminating gender-nonconforming behaviors in children, to the extent that, queer sociologist Karl Bryant argues, it *produced* homonormative (gender-conforming) homosexuals. Bryant observes that the "homophobia critique" of GIDC left transsexuality as well as other nonnormative expressions of neurodivergence as legitimate targets for prevention.[8] Trans and "mad pride"[9] activists have criticized lesbian and gay social movements for legitimating relations of power that operate via the construction of normal versus deviant subjectivities.

Many feminist, queer, and trans critics challenge the foundational assumption of binary gender norms that informs both the original and subsequent diagnosis. In 2004, queer feminist scholar Judith Butler characterized the GIDC diagnosis as contributing to the gender distress of gender-nonconforming children that its advocates purported to correct. She brought the concept of "intelligibility" to bear on GIDC, observing that power generates the range of possibilities for legible identities and expression. To be outside these parameters is to experience precarity: to risk abandonment, even death.[10] One study disputes the binary relationship between gender normality and gender deviance encoded in the *DSM*, claiming instead, "Our results clearly show that a non-unitary sense of gender identity, a wish to be the other gender and dissatisfaction with one's sexed body are not unique to trans people, but are also common, albeit to a lesser degree, in the 'normal' population."[11]

Bryant provides keen insight into these debates by observing that a formal diagnosis is far from being the first step in medicalization and may even produce opportunities to restrict medicalization. He points out that the significant research and treatment activity that began in the early 1960s was simply formalized with the publication of the third edition of the *DSM* in 1980; prior activity was already constitutive of medicalization in its own right but flew under the radar. The formal diagnosis of GIDC became a lightning rod for criticism and a mechanism for limiting the medicalization of gender-nonconforming children; it shone a spotlight on harmful reparative therapy practices that yielded criticism and activism. Feminist and lesbian and gay activists and critics played a significant role in making the all-encompassing corrective regimes (of psychiatry, social services, family, and school) visible in their employment of shame, manipulation, and brutality in the name of child welfare.[12]

Trans people and our allies face significant dilemmas around the diagnosis, relating to the role it plays in enabling access to healthcare, social transition, and legal rights on the one hand versus the oppressive role it plays in naturalizing cisgender binary normativity on the other. In spite of concurrence with the substance of critiques, many trans activists, scholars, and allies insist that eliminating the diagnosis will do more harm than good, arguing instead for harm reduction as the appropriate political strategy.[13] Psychologist Jemma Tosh, for example, insists that the elimination of the diagnosis would have terrible consequences for many trans people, including greater risk of mental distress, vulnerability to violence and discrimination, self-mutilation, and suicide.[14] She urges scholars and professionals to foresee the potential harm of our debates and recommendations for actual trans people.

Affirmative Transgender Healthcare

In recent years, there has been what Pyne refers to as "a paradigm shift" in the treatment of gender-nonconforming and transgender children toward affirmation and harm reduction.[15] An ever-expanding body of research shows that an affirmative approach and family support produce the best outcomes for transgender kids and young people. In 2011, the World Professional Association for Transgender Health (WPATH)[16] took a position against gender-reparative therapy, stating that any therapy that seeks to change the gender identity of a patient is unethical. This position has been reflected in legal change in certain jurisdictions as well. For example, in 2014, California passed the Student Success and Opportunity Act to ban reparative therapy and require schools to permit transgender children to participate in activities and to access spaces and facilities according to their affirmed gender categories; in 2015, the province of Ontario (home to CAMH) passed a law prohibiting gender-reparative therapy.

Trans activist Julia Serano notes the role of activism in bringing about a shift in the clinical treatment of transgender people of all ages toward an affirming approach. An affirming approach has been established as the best practice for increasing the life chances of transgender kids. This approach "challenges societal transphobia (rather than reinforcing it, as the gender-reparative therapy approach does)" and "favors an individual approach for each child, rather than pushing all children toward the same end goal (e.g., gender conformity)."[17]

As high-profile, government-funded gender-identity treatment programs that target gender nonconformity for correction lose legitimacy, publicly and privately funded gender clinics featuring affirming models of treatment for trans kids are springing up in many North American centers. Via these clinics, kids who affirm the "opposite" gender identity to the one they were assigned or who question their gender identities may be eligible for puberty-suppression therapy. Unlike in Holland, where the model of puberty-suppression therapy for trans kids originated, however, many North American clinics support early social transition for children. Social transition is a key way for transgender children to explore the extent to which a change in gender will bring about a lessening of the anxiety and distress they experience. Puberty suppression extends this period of exploration by delaying the development of secondary sex characteristics.

Affirming treatment focuses on enabling kids' families to accept and affirm their children's gender identity, supporting them in dealing with the mental health consequences of trans oppression and providing assistance and advocacy as the kids and their families navigate gendered environments. While the affirming treatment model does not steer patients toward any particular gender identity, when desired, hormone blockers and cross-sex hormones can be used to manipulate the body's growth patterns to correspond with prevailing Eurocentric binary sex norms.

Puberty-suppression therapy for transgender kids is designed to enable them to postpone puberty while they consider their options and to enable kids who choose to medically transition to visibly conform to binary sex norms, an ability that is associated with reduced precarity. In the clinical literature surrounding gender-affirming practice, the first goal of puberty-suppression therapy is to "buy time" for the child or young person before committing to irreversible development of second-ary sex characteristics. The second goal is a "more 'normal' and satisfac-tory appearance" after transition—a far more gender-normative capacity for passing and "realness" than has been available for adult transition.[18] In most cases, children who have been designated female at birth and who undergo puberty-suppression therapy will not need top surgery as part of gender confirmation surgery, and children who have been desig-nated male at birth will not need to manage the residues of voice change, facial hair, skeletal development, and a visible Adam's apple, for example.

Trans kids remain a highly contested population, however, as anti-trans critics are generating a moral panic around the access of some trans kids to affirming healthcare, with the accusation that "doctors and parents [are] turning children transgender." This panic, Serano notes, relates to the cis-sexist claim that trans people "have taken their pre-cious and perfect cisgender bodies, and transformed them into defective transsexual ones" while attempting to use constructions of childhood innocence to gain political traction.[19] Anti-trans authors of newspaper articles and opinion pieces express fear that some cisgender children are being pushed into the "wrong" puberty that will ultimately require expensive medical procedures to reverse.[20] The irony is that early transi-tion for trans kids who need it provides them with the opportunity to avoid future and expensive medical procedures to reverse the develop-ment of unwanted secondary sex characteristics.

Flawed as anti-trans arguments are, however, even trans and trans-positive scholars and activists who strongly support access to an affirm-ing model of trans healthcare for all who need it have concerns about how it operates within systems of power more broadly. The emergence of affirmative (as opposed to punishing and reparative) care resources and networks of parents and professionals focused on supporting trans kids *is* a response to a critical need, but I and others have observed that these resources are disproportionately available to relatively privileged (albeit vulnerable) rather than socioeconomically precarious trans kids.[21] I am also concerned about the way in which the deployment of these resources within social contexts that remain binary normative may impose limited transgender possibilities on children and young people and leave sexist and misogynist underpinnings of social, economic, and political life more generally untouched.

In the remainder of this chapter, I engage with a central dilemma: how can we protect and greatly expand existing access to affirming healthcare for all who need it while at the same time troubling the consequences of the privileging of an often-binary-conforming and inaccessible model of transgender embodiment/inclusion in society more broadly? I frame the topic of medicalization in this way because the varied experiences of trans kids in Canada and the United States are necessarily shaped by ongoing colonialism, neoliberal capitalism, racialized socioeconomic relations, and heteropatriarchy, conditions that produce a "differential distribution of precarity" that make some lives and not others *livable*.[22]

A key aspect of this dilemma relates to the risk involved in criticizing the way trans-affirming medical resources are being shaped and delivered when

1. these resources are literally life altering and life saving for many trans people;
2. many trans people of all ages lack these resources; and
3. transgender people in general are so vulnerable.

I fear that any criticism of affirming healthcare will have the unintended consequence of limiting access to it by feeding anti-trans agendas. But my knowledge of the history of social justice struggles in the West tells me one thing: when social justice movements construct themselves as "single issue" and foreclose critical discussion about the ways in which privilege operates within them, internal hierarchies such as those relating to race, class, gender, sexuality, (dis)ability, citizenship, and so on are reinforced.

What the Kids Want

The kids in my study have various plans for "transition." Some are already on hormone blockers or cross-sex hormones, while others intend to access this therapy in the near future. My participants experience varying degrees of dissonance between their assigned sex and how they define/name themselves and, for many but not all, gender dysphoria about their physical embodiment. Some kids take blockers because of gender dysphoria—to enable them to feel at home in their bodies—and are not trying to pass; some have various plans regarding surgery, while others reported having no access to affirmative health-care because they lack parental support and/or financial resources. And some have no desire to medicalize their gender identities. Several of my participants, in fact, voiced regret about not having been aware of non-binary transgender possibilities earlier in their own development. Three interrelated themes relating to medicalization and precarity emerged from my interviews with the kids and their parents: the trauma of the "wrong" puberty and the need for intervention, barriers to accessing affirmative care, and nonbinary troubles.

The Trauma of the "Wrong" Puberty and the Need for Intervention

Puberty is a pivotal time both for kids who have identified as transgender or resisted their assigned sex/gender for years and for kids whose transgender identities coalesce via a sense of crisis as secondary sex characteristics emerge. The trauma of the wrong puberty is a central theme that runs through my interview data. While hormone blockers can be understood to be an aspect of the blueprint of the social construction of binary gender, it would be a mistake for us to reduce them to this: many of the trans kids in my study experience puberty suppression not as a reconsolidation of binary gender but rather as a desperately needed source of liberation and relief from gender dysphoria and/or nonintelligibility. Gender dysphoria and trans oppression have a significant impact on trans kids' mental health and relationships to their bodies. According to Dara, Davis "started his period on his 11th birthday": "The place he was in the first 48 hours, I thought I was going to lose my kid. He was so, like—he just sunk so low. He could hardly talk. He just shut down, and it was awful. So it's good actually to live through that. Because I think certainly for me but for him too, it really clarified that this was not okay, that this was not how he wanted his life to be." Many of the trans kids in my study either do engage or have engaged in self-harm (primarily cutting and suicide attempts) that they explicitly relate to the gender dysphoria they experienced with the onset of puberty. Kazuko firmly believes that hormone blockers saved Stef's life, explaining, "It was something that was necessary at that point. There was already so much anxiety around everything else that the blockers, at the moment of time when they took it, freed them from a lot of the anxiety." Greg also experienced mental distress around puberty and started to cut himself. But he was able to disclose his self-harm to a caring and supportive school counselor who, as required by law, alerted Greg's parents. Greg's parents were deeply concerned for his well-being and used their resources to enable him to access appropriate mental health support and, subsequently, trans-affirming healthcare. Greg described going on blockers as "a huge relief." Fortunately for Greg, his parents came on board fast. In some such instances, however, parents respond with emotional abuse and/or physical violence or by forcing their children to undergo reparative therapy. The fact that trans kids are minors is a significant dimension of precarity, as parents or legal guardians play a central role in their ability to fashion for themselves a livable life, via acceptance, financial and practical resources that enable therapy and medical treatment, and, crucially, permission/consent.

Greg reported that his parents gave their consent for puberty suppression because they understood blockers to be fully reversible, in contrast to the cross-sex hormones or surgery that they found more worrisome. As Greg explained, "They liked the idea that blockers would give me another year or two to really sort of see if this is really what I want. So I think that it was just a win-win situation: for me, because I knew my parents were okay with it, and they would probably feel more at ease. And I was also more at ease knowing that I wouldn't have to continue through puberty." This intervention was crucial for Greg's well-being.

Some of my participants experienced painful unease with their bodies at puberty but did not have language to make sense of it, and this was a factor in their inability to access appropriate and timely affirming healthcare. Michael, for example, described himself as starting to feel "really different" and depressed around puberty but unaware that being trans was even an option until he met a transgender person. He is now on testosterone (T) and on the waiting list for top surgery in his province.

Like so many trans kids, the Internet was the starting point for Cameron in making sense of difficult feelings about his body. Cameron grew up homeschooled and isolated in a rural, fundamentalist Christian family. He "tried really hard to fit in" as a girl because he "didn't know that being transgender was even a thing." But, he said, "puberty freaked me out so much. I would scream and cry if my mom mentioned bra shopping or buying pads, and I just never knew why." Cameron was not exposed to LGBTQ people until he was 14 and got to meet some through an online writing site. They provided him with the space and the language to begin to make sense of his own experience of trauma around puberty.

I first interviewed Nathan's mother, Nora, when top surgery seemed completely out of reach. At the time, she told me that her son hated his postpubertal body so much that he engaged in more or less constant self-harm: "I think it was 10 when he started his period. When all that stuff started, that's when all the sports stopped. That's when anything to do with being outside and being seen stopped." Nathan hates his body, he "can't stand it," and because of this, Nora told me, "he continues to cut himself." Nathan has cut himself so much that "the tops of his legs and the tops of his arms are scarred up for life." Nora has "tried so many things to stop it": "It's actually gotten to the point where, like, me and my husband said, 'Well, if he's cutting himself, he's not trying to kill himself.' That's how bad it is. And I never thought I'd ever say that about one of my youngsters." Nora is not overstating the fear that many parents of trans kids have with regard to the possibility of their child committing suicide.

When Martine was seven, Nina made an appointment for her at a gender clinic. When Martine heard about it, she asked, "Does the doctor have the machine?" "What machine?" Nina responded. "The machine where you walk in as a boy and walk out as a girl." Parents and kids are vulnerable to doctors and psychologists who are culturally positioned as experts. Trans-oppressive professionals can do a lot of damage, and trans-positive professionals can be life saving. As Kazuko observed, "I think wherever you are, if you've got that one good doctor, because there's always that questionable one that can end up ruining your entire perception of stuff and make it hard on you. Because we've had doctors and psychologists that have told parents, like, the worst things ever, and the parent believes them because that's the doctor, right?" Esme's family was fortunate to find that "one good doctor" early on in the process. Esme has insisted that she is a girl since preschool and has been under the care of a trans-affirmative doctor since she was six. She told me, "I know I'm going to get the hormone blockers and the estrogen," explaining how she would feel if she were to grow a beard and have her voice get very deep: "I wouldn't feel like I was—that I was in the right body." Esme is really clear that growing up to be a man—"with a beard and everything"—is not what she wants. With the support of her parents, she will forgo "male" puberty and be one of the new generation of trans people who will be able to assimilate more effectively than were previous generations who were unable to prevent their bodies from developing in undesirable ways.[23] Esme may or may not wish to find a way to be visible as a transgender person, but it will likely be up to her. At present, she eagerly participates in pride celebrations and enjoys being visibly transgender. And unlike some trans girls, Esme does not regard her penis as a problem. Esme displays flexibility around her physical embodiment, explaining, "It doesn't really depend on what middle parts you have, you know? It doesn't really matter which one you have. It's just who you decide to be. Like, just say you have the same middle part as someone else: it doesn't mean you're the same as them, right? You can choose who you want to be." Because of her parental support and access to trans healthcare (family economic security and provincial and private health insurance), Esme *can* choose. The flexibility that some transgender kids experience around their bodies, however, is constrained by social contexts. Decisions to transition are also influenced, to varying degrees, by binary-normative contexts.

Children in general are socialized to internalize the sex/gender binary, and trans kids are no more or less than cisgender ones. Binary-conforming trans kids themselves are not reinscribing or reinforcing the gender binary; this is being done by environments that restrict legitimate gender identities, trans and cis, to binary-normative ones. But the solution is not to question the gender self-determination of or to deny affirming healthcare to binary-identifying trans kids any more than it is to prevent cisgender kids from identifying as girls or boys.

While I focus on trans kids, it would be interesting to learn how many cisgender girls become uncomfortable with their female identity once they hit adolescence. The state of grace for tomboys often runs out in this period.[24] Some of my female-to-male trans participants told me that when they hit adolescence and experienced this increased pressure to conform to feminine norms, they actually really tried to "go for it," meaning they went all out to conform to gender expectations for girls—

makeup, dresses and skirts, and high heels—but could not find the right fit. I wonder how many cisgender girls feel this way when they experience the weight of new expectations for appearance and behavior and are exposed to greater sexism and misogyny but, unlike trans boys, do not see transitioning away from a female identity to be desirable.

Most of the parents of trans kids I interviewed resisted binary-restrictive views of gender and sought to create as much space for their child to explore their gender identity as possible. Parents followed their children's lead and did not seek to impose any identity on them. But as feminist and masculinity scholars have demonstrated for decades, overarching binary-normative social contexts leave their mark on all children, even as some find ways to resist. This is as true for transgender as it is for cisgender children. Affirming trans health resources are deployed within social contexts that are organized on the basis of the sex/gender binary. As such, these contexts operate to limit transgender possibilities and reinforce the essentialist foundations of patriarchy and misogyny.

Several of the parents I interviewed talked about having mixed feelings about their children accessing affirming healthcare, but not because they resisted their kids' nonnormative gender identities but because medicalization poses a dilemma for some feminist parents. For parents who hold a critical perspective on the two-sex system and attendant gender binary, medicalization poses a dilemma. On the one hand, they resist both the naturalness and oppressive nature of the binary gender order and want their children to express themselves without these limits. On the other hand, their kids may clearly identify as a boy or girl and need to be recognized as such for the sake of their mental health and agency as a person. Dara, for example, initially struggled to reconcile her critical feminist perspective on the socially constructed nature of binary gender systems with Davis's severe crisis at the onset of puberty. But she could see that puberty was "profoundly traumatic to him" and "wasn't going to work," that medical intervention was necessary if he was to survive. In the end, this understanding made the decision to grant her consent an easy one.

Eva, parent of Peter, contextualized her concerns about the medicalization of transgender children within the increasing medicalization of children in general. Saying, "I think a lot of things are being medicalized," Eva articulated a critique of the for-profit pharmaceutical industry and the employment of medicalization as a tool of social control, citing the example of the diagnosis of attention-deficit/hyperactivity disorder (ADHD) and attendant pharmaceutical intervention that is being increasingly applied to children who struggle to adapt to relatively sedentary days in school classrooms.

Barriers to Accessing Affirming Healthcare

The politics of trans visibility versus the ability to assimilate or "pass" are complex. Trans scholar Tey Meadow observes that "the smallest gender outlaws" have "deeply different trajectories and life chances"[25] than did the adult trans people who have gone before them, owing to the ability of these youngsters to take hormone blockers. Forgoing natal puberty enables a subsequently less complicated medical transition and greater ability to pass as their affirmed sex in the future should they choose to do so. Different trajectories for trans kids, therefore, are considerably shaped by binary conformity and socioeconomic privilege. According to Siebers's logic, if we identify being transgender as a disability, one of the blueprints of the social construction of binary gender is puberty-suppression therapy. Critical perspectives on biomedicine as implicated in relations of oppression come into play.

It is not being transgender, per se, that increases the likelihood of self-harm and suicide among trans kids but rather cultural and social prejudice that does the damage. This is true whether one is visible or not, but visibility does correlate to a higher level of suicide risk and lower quality of life. According to Brynn Tannehill, board member of the Trans United Fund, "Being *seen* as transgender or gender non-conforming increases suicide risk."[26] This higher risk is mitigated by trans-affirmative healthcare that enables transgender people to pass. In a study comparing quality-of-life outcomes for trans women with and without access to facial feminization surgery, for example, surgeons Tiffany Ainsworth and Jeffrey Spiegel stated the following conclusion: "Transwomen have diminished mental health-related quality of life compared with the general female population. However, surgical treatments . . . are associated with improved mental health-related quality of life."[27] According to the U.S. Surgeon General and the National Action Alliance for Suicide Prevention,

Suicidal behaviors in LGBT populations appear to be related to "minority stress," which stems from the cultural and social prejudice attached to minority sexual orientation and gender identity. This stress includes individual experiences of prejudice or discrimination, such as family rejection, harassment, bullying, violence, and victimization. Increasingly recognized as an aspect of minority stress is "institutional discrimination" resulting from laws and public policies that create inequities or omit LGBT people from benefits and protections afforded others.

Individual and institutional discrimination have been found to be associated with social isolation, low self-esteem, negative sexual/gender identity, and depression, anxiety, and other mental disorders. These negative outcomes, rather than minority sexual orientation or gender identity per se, appear to be the key risk factors for LGBT suicidal ideation and behavior.[28]

While the decision by trans kids and their families to opt for hormone blockers may or may not be undertaken with the goal of passing in mind, it does play a role in enabling trans kids to assimilate as adults if they wish to, an ability strongly linked to reduced future precarity.

The framework of queer/trans necropolitics is a powerful lens for situating queer and trans lives within systems of oppression, focusing as it does on systemic racism, classism, and institutionalized state violence as axes of precarity that shape which categories of queer and transgender members of the social body live and which either die or are politically, socially, culturally, and economically abandoned. As this lens draws attention to "contemporary carceral and medical industries as key growth sectors in the Neoliberal era,"[29] it supports an exploration of the ways in which the life-affirming resources that enable transition for the trans kids who are able to access them have a necropolitical footprint for others without such access.

Socioeconomic dimensions of precarity are racialized in Canada and the United States and generate vulnerability to interpersonal and state violence. While I welcome (and celebrate) the harm reduction flowing from the "paradigm shift" from corrective to affirming medicalization of transgender kids in Canada and the U.S., I am concerned that the current neoliberal context means that access to this kind of healthcare is restricted to relatively resource-rich trans children. Julian Gill-Peterson emphasizes "the enforced precarity of the lives of many transgender children, particularly of color."[30] Indeed, aspects of precarity related to racialization and poverty receive little to no attention in scholarly literature, in resources for transgender kids and their families, or in mainstream or (trans-/homonormative) LGBT media.

In both Canada and the United States, there is a socioeconomic divide with regard to access to treatment. Dara reports, for example, that the annual cost of a hormone-blocking implant for Davis is US$25,000. His family has good health insurance, and Dara expected it to be covered; but she and Davis's dad are able to pay for it themselves if they have to. While doing so would place a strain on their finances, Dara acknowledged her family's relative privilege, knowing that for so many other families, this is completely out of reach. From being so in touch with her own child's precarity, Dara expressed a sense of desperation that other trans kids are unable to access such necessary resources and support.

In the United States, some private insurers cover hormone therapy and/or gender confirmation surgery, but many do not. In the U.S. gender-affirming clinical practice of Edwards-Leeper and Spack, the psychologists unsurprisingly observe, "We have witnessed a socioeconomic divide in regard to who is able to obtain treatment in our clinic."[31] While under the (now-jeopardized) provisions of the Affordable Care Act (ACA), discrimination against transgender people by insurance providers is prohibited, the remedy requires a legal challenge with attendant financial and/or cultural capital. It is too soon to tell what the implications of potential reform of the ACA may be for this issue, but there are obvious reasons to be fearful.

In contrast to the U.S., access to trans healthcare is partially mediated by the availability of public insurance in Canada, but race- and class-based and geographic factors that enable and obstruct access cut across national borders. Canadian provincial healthcare policies regarding treatment for transgender people vary from province to province, and there are always at least some upfront costs (such as paying a licensed professional for a diagnosis of gender dysphoria) and incidental costs such as travel, accommodation, and time off work for parents of kids in rural settings or provinces without transgender healthcare resources. Some provinces cover surgery only for adults, and in any case, wait times for publicly funded surgeries are long. Only some provinces cover the cost of blockers and hormones, while the costs of related medications, for depression and anxiety, for example, are unevenly funded. The quality of medical care in remote communities in general is poor, while Indigenous reservations in Canada and the U.S. are severely and systematically underresourced. This situation is complicated by the fact that the violent imposition of binary gender systems on Indigenous peoples has been part of the (ongoing) process of colonization.[32]

Some of my participants have supportive parents whose insurance policies and personal wealth have enabled access to affirming healthcare. There are some for whom cost is an occasional barrier and some for whom it is an insurmountable one. Many of my participants expressed significant frustration and anguish about lack of access to affirming treatment—whether because they could not afford it or because they were not old enough to access treatment without parental permission or both. For several trans kids in my study, lack of access to affirmative healthcare has had devastating consequences. Prior to Nathan's success in finding a job and raising enough money to pay for his top surgery, Nora reported being "terrified, constantly": "And it's all because of this damn top surgery. And I am literally terrified, because I know for a fact that once he gets this done, he's gonna be a completely different child. And it kills me that I can't do anything. I told him—I was like, 'Honey, if I owned my home, I would sell the fucking thing. I would do whatever it takes.'" The two years that Nathan spent out of high school because he could not get new government ID without top surgery cost him the opportunity to graduate with his peers. When last I spoke with his mother, he was still working on his high school diploma via adult education.

Enrique, for example, left home because of his father's unwillingness to accept his transition, and this interrupted his education. He moved in with his boyfriend's family and in this context is receiving emotional and financial support (his boyfriend's mother has been paying for his testosterone). But we know from numerous reports from social service organizations and research studies that many kids in Enrique's situation find themselves on the street. When I interviewed Dylan in 2015, he was living with his working-poor family in a trailer park in the U.S. He reported experiencing extreme gender dysphoria and mental anguish but was not at a place in his life where it was possible to live as a boy/man.

Dylan's economic and social vulnerability raises alarm as it affects his ability to obtain hormones and to live fully as a man, both things that seem profoundly necessary for his well-being. He reported struggling with depression, self-harm (cutting), and multiple suicide attempts, for which he was receiving therapy. According to Dylan, the catalyst for his first suicide attempt was a combination of "a pretty violent relationship" and "really bad gender dysphoria" at the onset of puberty.

Dylan has been told by his doctor that he has to wait until he is 16 to start testosterone, and even then his mother's consent will be required. He thinks she will give it, but he said, "She told me that she would not be paying for it." Dylan has started working at a minimum-wage service job and is hopeful that Medicaid will cover the necessary doctor appointments. But he knows that "all of the testosterone will be completely out of pocket because it's not covered." Dylan lives in a small community without any trans healthcare and will depend on someone else to take him into the city to see the transgender specialist he has been referred to. Like most young trans people, Dylan depends on the adults in his life for access to healthcare.

Economic security does not necessarily translate to access to affirming healthcare, however. As emphasized earlier, kids are limited by their social subordination to the adults who have immediate power over them. Alicia, for example, hails from an economically secure family but did not initially feel she could count on her parents for support. So at 16, she took matters into her own hands by making her own hormones in a high school science lab. Unbeknownst to her teacher or her parents, Alicia provided herself with hormone therapy for several months: "I'd taken a couple of chemistry classes, a genetics class, and some biology classes. And I had a bit of an ulterior motive. I think I did a pretty good job with that," Alicia said with pride. Once she told her parents and gained their support, their insurance and personal wealth ensured that she began to receive medically supervised cross-sex hormone therapy. But I have to hand it to her for her creativity and ingenuity in providing herself with affirming healthcare.

Speaking of two "classes" of transgender people emerging in Canada and the United States on the basis of access to and consumption of affirming healthcare is both instructive and simplistic. Barriers to accessing the affirming healthcare that aids the ability to pass include poverty, lack of health insurance, lack of family support, geographic inaccessibility, binary nonconformity, mental health issues/trauma, and coming to understand or being enabled to understand oneself as trans too late to redirect puberty. While transgender resilience is heavily influenced by multiple dimensions of privilege, other factors such as body type (the mutability of more androgynous versus stereotypically sex-typed physical features) and individual hardiness and resourcefulness also come into play. But for trans kids, their position as minors in the care of parents or state agencies and variations in their socioeconomic status are key elements of precarity.

Issues relating to racialization go beyond access, however. Gill-Peterson positions the medicalization of transgender children as always already steeped in sexism, racism, and ableism by exposing the field of endocrinology as a racialized project from the get-go, whereby the "discovery" of the body's hormone systems took place within a white, colonial, and heteropatriarchal context: "Biomedicine is at the forefront of the contemporary politics of sex, gender, sexuality, and race . . . , and the transgender child is emerging as one of its newest anchors."[33] Gill-Peterson describes the Tanner scale, the "five-point diagram of 'normal' puberty progression," as a eugenic device in that it is deployed racially to prescribe puberty-suppression therapy for Black and Latina girls, whose purported earlier puberty reflects "the much older colonial hypersexualization of and medical interest in the genitals of the black and brown female body."[34] The Tanner scale universalizes Eurocentric binary sex norms.

Nonbinary Troubles

In my interviews with Cameron, Helen, Quinn, Stef, and Kidd, they lamented the lack of childhood exposure to nonbinary people/identities, while Wren wishes that she had been left alone to be who she was without having to think of herself or explain herself in terms of any gender. Some of the kids and young people in my study have very nuanced understandings of gender-identity issues and see themselves as at odds with the gender binary. Quinn, for example, identifies as a "neurodivergent queer, nonbinary, trans person of color" and resists the imposition of power that allows anyone to assign gender to anyone else.

Many kids who identify as nonbinary, however, need trans-affirming healthcare. But in most contexts, the current process for accessing affirming healthcare depends on being diagnosed with gender dysphoria, and this frame sets limits on the embodiments available to transgender kids, at least officially: one is required to convince a licensed clinician that one *has* gender dysphoria in order to transition socially and/or medically. The script for such an encounter is readily learned via trans sites on the Internet, but not all nonbinary kids are sophisticated enough to adapt their story to fit with the binary narrative or comfortable with misrepresenting their gender identity. Their desperation for treatment or accommodation usually wins out, and there is considerable anecdotal evidence that some therapists collude in constructing a false binary narrative out of respect for their clients' right to gender self-determination and/or as a harm-reduction measure.

Cory Oskam, for example, took hormone blockers for four years to stop his body from undergoing "female" puberty. Cory wanted very much to take testosterone but was stalled because he was uncomfortable defining himself as male. The requirement that he claim a male identity as a condition for gaining access to testosterone was imposed on Cory, and he refused this condition for some time. The first time Cory met with a therapist for the necessary psychological assessment in the hope that he would be approved for testosterone met with failure. He was open about his nonbinary gender identity, and the therapist determined that he was not "trans" enough" and denied him the necessary paperwork. Cory was devastated by this determination and put things on hold for a few years. But his desire to go on T persisted, and he adopted a more sophisticated strategy with the next therapist he saw: "I answered the questions 'correctly' I guess. I was saying that, 'Yeah, I was born in the wrong body,' you know. 'I want testosterone.' . . . They asked me, 'Do you want breasts?' And I was like, 'No.' And 'Do you want to go through puberty now?' 'Male puberty? Yes. Not female puberty.' So I guess I just answered the questions correctly and got T." Now that he is on testosterone, Cory is assumed to be male, observing, "Testosterone does do its own thing, and I do look more male. And I am perceived as like a cis now in the world even though I don't identify as one."

While nonbinary trans people of all ages are becoming more culturally visible, most of the representation relating to trans kids continues to be binary conforming in nature and, as such, poses limited challenges to oppressive binary-normative cisgender environments. I am certainly not arguing that trans kids are pressured to take blockers and/or hormones against their will—I do not believe this to be the case. Rather, I am concerned that the social context of binary gender conformity that trans kids find themselves in is often so oppressive that hormone blockers and eventual cross-sex hormones may be essential for their very survival. My concern is that by altering their embodiment to conform to binary gender systems—in order to survive, thrive, and construct a livable life—some trans kids become the site of another individualized medical solution to a social problem that leaves structures of oppression untouched, including those of racialization and poverty that shape which kids are able to thrive in this way. As gender scholars Elizabeth Bucar and Finn Enke observe, "The vast majority of transsexual-identified individuals in the United States will not have a single surgery related to sex change, due to lack of access and/or lack of desire. Thus, any media coverage that focuses primarily on SRS [sex reassignment surgery; see "gender confirmation surgery" in the glossary] disproportionately excludes from its purview poor people, people of color, all gender variance that is not medically mediated, and the countless ways in which trans masculine and trans feminine people negotiate the sex/gender expectations of the culture around them."[35] At the same time, I need to emphasize that it is deeply problematic to be critical in *any* way of trans kids who conform to binary norms either because they self-define as boys or girls or as a means of reducing their precarity. After all, gender-conforming cisgender kids are rarely censored for doing just this. When trans-affirming children's physician Johanna Olson-Kennedy[36] gave a keynote address at "Gender Odyssey" a number of years ago, I asked her a question about the unintended potential of affirming healthcare for reinforcing the binary gender order. Her response was sharp and instructive, and I have never forgotten it: "Don't put the onus for the gender revolution on the shoulders of transgender children—they are just trying to survive." Singling out trans kids as a point of intervention against binary normativity would be especially cruel given their particular vulnerability; it would amount to another form of gender policing and run counter to the principle of gender self-determination for all, wherever one locates oneself on the gender spectrum, that I advocate in this book.

An Emergent Gender-Affirmative Industry

If someone had told me when I was 10 years old that I could take hormone blockers to avoid getting my period and growing breasts and be accepted as a "borderlands person," as one of my seven-year-old participants described themselves, I would have done it in a heartbeat. But the emergence of a "gender-affirmative industry" in which a great many people become invested for their livelihood and the entrenchment of a pharmaceutical industrial complex that sells chemical solutions to social problems to individual consumers and for-profit medicalization bears critical scrutiny. As Hilary remarked, there is tremendous potential in new technologies: "I feel like what's going to happen in the next 10 years, we could be 3-D printing stem cells into penises." But the interests of for-profit medical and pharmaceutical industries, as opposed to a more socially just public healthcare model, are a dynamic that trans scholars of color point to with concern.[37]

In the current neoliberal context, gender identity becomes something that is, to a degree, bought and sold. But instead of justifying opposition to trans-affirming healthcare that places the burden for resisting oppressive binary systems on the shoulders of transgender people, this critical scrutiny should encompass the multiple ways in which products and services aimed at binary gender conformity are marketed to and consumed by cisgender people as well.[38] Critical trans scholars and activists draw our attention to the ways in which the technologies of trans-affirming medicalization are unfairly singled out for critical scrutiny. In viewing the body as "an open technical system," Gill-Peterson resists a good/bad view of the medicalization of trans embodiment by demonstrating that such "technicity"—meaning the ability to use technology to modify the body, a capacity that is reflected in both taken-for-granted and novel practices, from clipping one's toenails to organ transplants—is widespread.[39] This perspective reveals the transphobia behind a singular focus on the body-modifying practices of hormone therapy and/or gender confirmation surgery "as a betrayal of the human's integrity."[40]

* * *

Binary gender systems provide an overarching framework of meaning that shapes and somewhat contains resistance as much as conformity.

As long as binary gender systems are in place, there are limits set on the scope of gender self-determination available to kids. Targeting binary gender systems for transition, rather than binary-conforming trans kids, is the appropriate strategy to widen the scope of gender self-determination available to all. This project is entirely compatible with the fight to expand access to trans-affirming healthcare.

Trans advocacy and activism by transgender people and our allies achieved at least a partial (and still highly contested) paradigm shift from gender-reparative to gender-affirming medicalization. I do not intend to minimize this accomplishment, but I do wish to subject this paradigm shift to critical scrutiny with regard to its unintended consequences. As a basis for my conclusion to this chapter, I return to the directive by Michel Foucault that I used to open the book: "People know what they do; frequently they know why they do what they do; but what they don't know is what what they do does."[41] Given the extent to which racialized, impoverished, and non-binary-conforming trans kids are denied recognition and care, transgender have-nots will continue to experience a heightened layer of precarity around gender nonconformity that complicates "the state-sanctioned or extralegal production and exploitation of group-differentiated vulnerability to premature death," to return to Ruth Gilmore's definition of racism.[42] By enabling some trans kids to reduce their precarity by accessing trans-affirming healthcare, disparities among transgender people are emerging in new and troubling ways. In spite of the increasing visibility of transgender people, we see binary gender normativity restabilizing itself as a basis for transgender inclusion. But access to such care is unevenly distributed to the extent that less precarious trans kids are being positioned as (proto-) citizen consumers in a racialized biomedical market that reflects and exacerbates existing socioeconomic divides. This is what what we have done is doing: we are enabling the survival of some trans kids and not others. Unless we engage meaningfully to challenge white supremacy, colonialism, and capitalist exploitation, it is what we will continue to do.

Conclusion

Beyond Hope

If I'm not vocally outraged at every injustice against trans people, I'm teaching Simon that some trans people are beyond hope and I'm leaving room for him to be beyond hope one day. I try to make the case that the vibrancy and health and inherent value of the entire trans spectrum is vital to our kids, no matter how much privilege they have, because it teaches them to value their transness, rather than only feeling valuable if they are overcoming transness. We can't free them from the box of their assigned gender just to put them in another box of "the right way to transition" or "the right way to be trans." And the truest way to build their self-esteem so that they can stand against bigotry and violence is to build pride that is without limits or qualifications.
—Hilary, parent

LGBT activism in Canada and the U.S. over the past decade in particular has been successful in achieving significant changes in legal and policy landscapes for LGBT people of all ages, although more uniformly in Canada than in the United States. LGBT social movements have used human rights or anti-discrimination legislation to resist discrimination on the basis of sexual and/or gender identity. There are now consequences for discriminating against lesbian, gay, bisexual, and transgender people in many jurisdictions and institutions.

Canada legalized same-sex marriage in 2005. In November 2015, newly elected Canadian prime minister Justin Trudeau announced that his government would "introduce legislation that will make gender identity a 'prohibited ground for discrimination under the Canadian Human Rights Act' and make the transgender community an 'identifiable group protected by the hate speech provisions of the *Criminal Code*."[1] Bill C-16, an act to amend the Canadian Human Rights Act and the Criminal Code, was introduced by member of Parliament and justice minister Jody Wilson-Raybould, passed in the House of Commons on October 18, 2016, and by the Senate to become law on February 14, 2017.

The Trudeau government engaged in unprecedented symbolic support of LGBT communities when, on June 1, 2016, the rainbow/pride flag was raised on Parliament Hill for the first time, and later that month Trudeau became the first prime minister to participate in a pride parade when he marched in Toronto. He was also front and center at the Vancouver pride parade later that summer. Many provincial governments and the government of the territory of Nunavut have protections for gender identity enshrined in their Human Rights Code. In July 2016, the British Columbia government explicitly added "gender identity and expression" to its Human Rights Code.

In 2011, Hillary Clinton, in her capacity as U.S. secretary of state, declared that "gay rights are human rights."[2] State bans on same-sex marriage were ruled unconstitutional by the U.S. Supreme Court in 2013. More recently, on May 9, 2016, U.S. attorney general Loretta Lynch announced that the federal government was taking the North Carolina state legislature to court over HB2—its controversial law requiring transgender people to use the bathroom corresponding to their birth sex. The Obama administration followed this statement on May 13, 2016, by sending a letter to every school district in the U.S. directing them to allow transgender students to use the bathroom appropriate to their *affirmed* gender identity. According to *New York Times* journalists Julie Davis and Matt Apuzzo, the letter lacked the force of law but contained "an implicit threat: schools that do not abide by the Obama administration's interpretation of the law could face lawsuits or a loss of federal aid."[3] The letter from the Obama administration clearly communicated the federal government's intention to include gender identity as a protected category under the gender-equity provisions of Title IX.

Too many LGBT people in Canada and the U.S. have been harmed by laws and social policies that are no longer on the books to dismiss the value of this pro-LGBT social and political change. Educational scholars Therese Quinn and Erica Meiners, for example, make a strong point when they state that "the gains of the LGBT movements in education—

including visibility, policy, curriculum, and climate—were almost un-imaginable a decade ago."[4] The successful employment of human rights discourse has effectively changed policies in a number of Canadian and U.S. school districts to stipulate that trans kids be treated according to their affirmed gender. Crucial institutional changes relating to access to new identity documents and sex-segregated spaces on the basis of af-firmed rather than assigned sex and access to trans-affirming healthcare are producing better outcomes for some trans kids. As a result of a series of legal challenges in many provinces and their spillover effects, people of all ages are now able to obtain new government identification with an affirmed gender marker without the requirement of surgery. Reparative therapy to correct sexual and/or gender "deviance" has been banned by law in the states of California (2012) and New Jersey (2013), the District of Columbia (2014), and the province of Ontario (2015).

I began writing this book in 2015, amid unprecedented, yet far from mainstream, support for lesbian, gay, and transgender rights in Canada and the United States. In addition to the statements of support from the high-level politicians in Canada and the United States just noted, in some cases, there have been financial consequences for governments that advocate blatant homo-negativity and trans-negativity.[5]

While LGBT rights have been enshrined at the federal level in Canada and at the provincial level in all but two provinces, the current conserva-tive shift in the political landscape of the United States and its chilling ef-fect north of the 49th parallel have increased the precarity of vulnerable trans children. The 2016 U.S. presidential election resulted in a dramati-cally different social and political landscape for vulnerable groups across the nation, LGBT people and trans kids among them. Though many Canadians appear to feel smugly superior about Canadian inclusive-ness, viewing racism and intolerance as a U.S. rather than a Canadian problem, ongoing patterns of oppression (colonial, racist, misogynist, and heteronormative) persist as foundational components of Canadian institutions and culture.[6]

In the first 100 days of the Trump presidency, executive orders radi-cally deepened forces of precarity for Muslim people, racialized im-migrants and undocumented people, people of color in general, Jews, refugees, the poor, Indigenous people, people with disabilities, women, and gay, lesbian, and trans people. Trump specifically targeted trans kids for persecution on February 22, 2017, when he announced that he was revoking the directive by the Obama administration to interpret gender-equity provisions in Title IX to allow trans students to use bathrooms and locker rooms consistent with their affirmed gender identities. Any hope that the Supreme Court would step in and issue a landmark ruling in support of transgender rights was dashed on March 6, 2017, when the court specifically referenced Trump's revocation of the Obama directive to refer the Gavin Grimm case back to the lower courts. The result there was no less discouraging.[7] The Trump administration reversed or attempted to reverse, as in the case of the right of transgender persons to serve openly in the military,[8] a number of pro-LGBT decisions of the Obama administration.

This climate has the potential to silence disagreement among various groups of LGBT people—about what strategies are appropriate and who benefits from so-called wins—with calls for unity. But calls for unity along any demographic line reflect the limitations associated with single-issue social movements in general: they center on the interests of the relatively privileged, so racialization, sexism, misogyny, and economic deprivation are either overlooked or tokenized. The experiences of working-class women and women of color, for example, have been overshadowed in the white, middle- and upper-class agendas of mainstream feminism, while wealthy, white, gay men have driven the agendas of LGBT organizations and social movements. Indeed, Dan Savage's "It Gets Better" campaign, initiated in response to the suicides of gay teens, has been criticized by anti-racist activists and scholars for speaking only to those lesbian and gay people who are not otherwise oppressed. It therefore fails to acknowledge that for many racialized and impoverished LGBT teens, it *does not* get better.[9] These teens do not leave oppression and tyranny behind as they grow to adulthood and move out into a more welcoming world; they remain dogged by discrimination and poverty, continue to be vulnerable to self-harm and suicide, and are disproportionately at risk for spending time in prison. The queer or the trans aspect of their oppression cannot be abstracted from the trauma of racialization and poverty that makes them disproportionately precarious. Many of the legal and policy gains for trans kids noted earlier are life enhancing at minimum and life saving in many cases, but they disproportionately benefit less precarious trans kids. As Catherine, Frank's mother, sees it,

There is this kind of little movement I've seen where people want to put this positive spin on life for trans folks. And I can't speak for trans adults, and I can't speak for trans kids, but as a parent of a trans kid, I can certainly tell you nothing has changed. What's changed is that we have some really amazing supports in our lives. In our community, the school district hasn't changed the way they do daily business. I get frustrated when it's, like, Caitlyn Jenner—good on her, that's awesome, but that is not the reality. They only focus all of the attention on all of the celebrities and everybody who's famous just to distract people from the real problems that are going on. They need to focus more attention on people who don't have money to get proper reassignment surgeries, who aren't able to be who they want to be because they're poor or they don't live in places that are accepting.

Advances in LGBT rights have taken place at the same time that we have seen widening social inequality, the expansion of a racialized prison industrial complex, ongoing colonial relationships with Indigenous peoples, and severe cutbacks to public education and social services. These contexts continue to disproportionately increase the precarity of LGBT people, including trans kids, who are impoverished, racialized, and undocumented residents of Canada and the United States.

LGBT scholars and activists of color and their allies draw attention to the ongoing violence of settler colonialism, the prison industrial complex, and neoliberal restructuring and trouble historically inaccurate narratives of Western progress and national myths of foundational social justice propagated by Canadian and U.S. (under Obama) political leaders when making pro-LGBT statements.[10] For example, when announcing that the federal government was filing a civil rights lawsuit against the state of North Carolina to declare its bathroom bill discriminatory, Loretta Lynch, the U.S. attorney general at the time, invoked the mythical narrative of the U.S. as a justice-seeking country, making reference to "the founding ideals that have led this country—haltingly but inexorably—in the direction of fairness, inclusion and equality for all Americans." Lynch identified similarities between North Carolina's bathroom bill and Jim Crow laws and opposition to same-sex marriage rights, acknowledging "a recognizably human fear of the unknown, and a discomfort with the uncertainty of change," while insisting that "this is not a time to act out of fear. This is a time to summon our national virtues of inclusivity, diversity, compassion and open-mindedness." Lynch stated that North Carolina's anti-trans bathroom legislation provides no benefit to society—and rather harms "innocent Americans." The implication is that harm remains the just deserts of the "noninnocent": racialized, impoverished, incarcerated, disabled, undocumented, street-drug-addicted, and suspected (brown) terrorists. In an unprecedented statement, toward the end of her announcement, Lynch spoke directly and movingly to the transgender community on behalf of the Obama administration: "No matter how isolated or scared you may feel today, the Department of Justice and the entire Obama Administration wants you to know that we see you; we stand with you; and we will do everything we can to protect you going forward. Please know that history is on your side. This country was founded on a promise of equal rights for all, and we have always managed to move closer to that promise, little by little, one day at a time. It may not be easy—but we'll get there together."[11] Although such homonationalist statements obscure structures of oppression, they have cultural power that lessens some of the precarity experienced by the trans kids in this book. Two things are true here: it was definitely better for some trans kids under Obama, but that administration was far from heroic. And things are definitely better for some trans kids under the Trudeau government in Canada than they were under Stephen Harper, but Trudeau's loyalty to big business and resource extraction and his government's refusal to equitably fund Indigenous children in Canada indicates little to no meaningful redistribution of wealth and power. This is because legal and policy reform often leaves structures of oppression untouched.

What's Wrong with Rights?

Movements that focus on achieving transgender rights and changing government policies rely on legal discourse as a strategic frame and view these initiatives as key mechanisms for improving the life chances of transgender people of all ages. These are part of broader LGBT campaigns and typically focus on achieving two key measures:

- The inclusion of gender identity and expression as protected categories in human rights statutes and public policies that recognize these rights by

enabling transgender people to access sex-segregated facilities and sex-differentiated activities according to their affirmed gender
- The enactment of hate crime legislation as protection from anti-queer and anti-trans violence

The basic rights that LGBT movements have achieved and that I benefit from include freedom from discrimination and police persecution, marriage rights/benefits for same-sex couples, and the right to adopt and retain custody of children. On a visceral level, when I stand in the dugout as a coach at a Little League game, although I experience feelings of otherness at times, I am still able to do so as an openly queer and gender-nonconforming person. That this was not possible in the past but is now is not a small thing, and frankly, it is not something I imagined possible when I was 16. Nevertheless, there is considerable debate among scholars and activists within trans communities about the appropriateness of prioritizing legal rights over working collectively to oppose state and corporate power. Much of this debate mirrors that within lesbian, gay, and queer communities and scholarship about the appropriateness of "marriage equality" as a primary goal of LGBT movements. According to this logic, gays and lesbians push for recognition as fully human, that is, respectable people, thereby qualifying them for the rights and responsibilities that go along with full citizenship. Critics argue, however, that this perspective only rehabilitates and reinforces oppressive liberal humanist hierarchies and systems of governance and expands the power of the state (especially through punitive measures) while normalizing private (familial) responsibility for social security.[12] In this sense, previously abject but comparatively privileged (white, middle- and upper-class, avowedly monogamous) lesbian and gay people are "folded into life" or welcomed into the nation and accorded citizenship.[13] Trans scholar Eric Stanley applies this analysis to trans movements, lamenting the "normalizing force of mainstream trans politics in the U.S."[14]

These debates necessarily relate to political strategy as well as endgame: are rights provisions, hate crime laws, and pro-LGBT statements by politicians the goals our social movements should pursue? What tactics are appropriate: legal challenges, political lobbying, or direct action? Radical critiques emphasize the failure of rights-oriented campaigns and measures to redistribute wealth and resources even as they expand legal and cultural recognition. These debates are paralleled within other social justice movements relating to women, racialized minorities, and children, among others.

Radical democratic theorist Nancy Fraser defines gender justice, and by extension democracy, in terms of "participatory parity," that is, economic and cultural equality for women.[15] For Fraser, gender justice is a foundational requirement of democracy and involves both recognition (legal and cultural inclusion) and the redistribution of material resources. While women, alongside other overlapping groups marked by mutually constitutive relations of sexism, colonialism, racialization, and class formation, were initially excluded from formal citizenship in self-proclaimed Western "democracies," this is no longer the case,[16] although this process of enfranchisement was geographically and racially staggered.[17] Yet in spite of the achievement of formal citizenship (for those who have documents), a great deal of evidence reveals that there are significant gaps between the legal status of women in these nations and full gender equality and that inclusion has particularly benefited women who are white, relatively well-off, and able to mobilize.[18]

In Canada, critical race scholar Sherene Razack observes that a gendered and racialized two-tier structure of citizenship was established through conquest and the Indian Act and subsequently by Canada's 2001 Anti-Terrorism Act.[19] Stephen Harper's Conservative government expanded the state's powers in Canada in 2015 when Bill C-51 allowed citizenship to be stripped from Canadian-born persons of foreign-born parents convicted of certain crimes. Feminist sociologist Sunera Thobani similarly positions citizenship in the Canadian context as a prize, as a tool for the domination and exclusion of others, rather than as a fundamentally emancipatory category.[20] Citizenship in Canada, from this perspective, is symbolically associated with whiteness, and whiteness acts as the unspoken norm against which racial difference is measured.[21] Furthermore, in jockeying for citizenship, white outsiders—women, workers, LGBT people—often trade on their race privilege at the expense of solidarity with other excluded groups. In this way, Thobani observes, "citizenship serves as a status that mobilizes national subjects, classed and gendered as they may be themselves, in defense of the institution against the claims of those designated as undeserving outsiders."[22] Various categories of exclusion, such as race, class, disability, and sexuality, intersect powerfully with the lack of legal and political recognition accorded children, who qualify as temporary *noncitizens*.

There are insider and outsider divisions within queer and trans communities. Mainstream LGBT movements narrowly focus on sexual and gender identity in pursuit of legal rights and recognition without complicating other subtexts of citizenship or seeking to redistribute wealth accordingly. Jasbir Puar observes that "any single-axis identity politics is invariably going to coagulate around the most conservative normative construction of that identity, foreclosing the complexities of class, citizenship status, gender, nation, and perhaps most importantly in the context of very recent events, religion."[23] In writing about queer movements, educational scholar Kevin Kumashiro observes that a single-issue focus on sexuality risks "complying with other oppressions and excluding their own margins," to the extent that "such movements become just like the mainstream except with different identities taking center stage."[24] This has the inevitable result of privileging queer and trans people who are disproportionately white, documented, middle and upper class, and gender conforming. If recognition can be measured in terms of rights and the formal privileges and responsibilities of citizenship, then what is necessary for redistribution? And to what extent do some relatively privileged trans-rights activists ignore or neglect these issues?

What Is Wrong with Punishment?

Over the past 30 years, a phenomenal expansion of the U.S. prison industrial complex has dovetailed with massive cuts to public institutions and programs of support for the most economically vulnerable. Understanding hate crimes legislation in this context links it to the ever-expanding punishment apparatus of the state, a state with a demonstrated record of disproportionately incarcerating people of color and poor people, in which groups the most vulnerable LGBT people are to be found. According to a 2017 report by the Williams Institute at the UCLA School of Law, incarceration of lesbian, gay, and bisexual people is three times that for the general population.[25] While not rivaling the United States and Russia, the two nations with the highest percentages of their populations in prison, Canada's prison population is expanding fast and is equally racialized: Indigenous and Black Canadian people are disproportionately subject to incarceration.[26] Hate crime legislation in Canada emerged in response to racism and religious persecution and is defined as "any criminal offense against a person, group or property that is motivated by hatred or prejudice towards an identifiable group." In addition to race and religion, sex or sexual orientation is included as an identifiable group.[27] A queer/trans necropolitics framework draws our attention to the fact that the employment of state repression against offenders as a measure for improving the lives of transgender people fails to provide justice, given the disproportionate policing and security measures that target and incarcerate people who are racialized, Indigenous, poor, migrants, LGBT, youth, and disabled. From this perspective, many trans people have more to fear from the state than they have to look forward to with regard to protection.

Queer/trans necropolitical scholars argue that LGBT support for hate crime legislation actually calls on the power of the state and state violence to protect LGBT people from violent "others." They note that this same state violence was only too recently used *against* LGBT people and continues to be used against Indigenous, racialized, impoverished, and undocumented people. By securing "human status" without questioning its foundation in liberal humanist ideas that are ultimately oppressive, privileged queer and trans people become complicit in that oppression. While many mainstream LGBT organizations celebrate the classification of anti-LGBT violence as a hate crime, a more critical analysis draws our attention to the disproportionate criminalization of racialized and impoverished persons for hate crimes against LGBT persons, thus perpetuating structural racism and classism and reinforcing state violence. Furthermore, punishment of this nature fails to protect *all* LGBT people from harm by instead *individualizing* anti-gay and anti-trans violence. The structural violence of heteronormativity and patriarchal sex/gender systems thus go unaddressed.[28] From this perspective, hate crime provisions represent elite LGBT interests and reinforce the security apparatuses of the carceral state, that is, the prison industrial complex. A carceral state inflicts great harm on vulnerable populations, queer and trans kids among them.

Privileged LGBT subjects often cite hate crimes against transgender women of color as justification for hate crime legislation and state recognition of transgender rights, but they do not adequately take up the central role of racialization and enforced poverty that generates this violence. Trans scholars of color Riley Snorton and Jin Haritaworn introduce the "traumatized citizenship model" to describe the way in which more privileged transgender subjects are able to leverage the violence waged against trans women of color to increase their legal standing.[29] From this perspective, the recognition of equal rights of citizenship (protection from discrimination) and access to state protection that the privileged "we" gain as a result of these strategies constitute collusion and perpetuate harms equally heinous.

In the U.S., President Obama signed the Matthew Shepard and James Byrd Junior Hate Crimes Prevention Act in 2009. On the surface, this recognition and repudiation of interpersonal violence against LGBT people and people of color was a watershed moment. After all, 40–50 years earlier, police were raiding gay and lesbian bars in the U.S. and Canada and beating and imprisoning patrons with impunity.[30] In a discussion of "queer investments in punishment," trans scholar Sarah Lamble notes that race- and class-privileged LGBT people's support for hate crimes legislation and harsh punishment for offenders means "many LGBT communities now partly measure their citizenship status on whether the state is willing to imprison other people on their behalf."[31] This issue is complicated by the lack of evidence that hate crime laws deter people from acts of violence.

Consider this case in point. A compelling example of the harm that hate crime legislation can deliver to already-marginalized people is the prosecution *as an adult* of Richard Thomas, a 16-year-old Black American boy, for his assault on a gender-nonconforming teen in the state of California. In "The Fire on the 57 Bus in Oakland," *New York Times Magazine* author Dashka Slater reports that, on November 4, 2013, an 18-year-old agender teenager named Sasha Fleischman was seriously injured when another teenager on the bus set their skirt on fire. At the time of the assault, Sasha, who is Euro-American and middle class, was attending an alternative private school in Berkeley. Richard, her assailant, was a resident of one of the city's poorer neighborhoods. He had experienced significant trauma-related losses over the course of his life. Richard was attending a high school with a graduation rate below 50% and was academically struggling. At the time of the assault, Slater states that Richard "was having trouble understanding his schoolwork and wanted to be tested for learning disabilities. He was worried about graduating. And the violence around him was pressing in. That fall, another friend, this one from Oakland High, was shot. At the end of October, while walking to the store in an unfamiliar neighborhood with his cousin Gerald, Richard was robbed at gunpoint by two teenage boys who took his money, his phone, his coat and his shoes."[32] Sasha was asleep on the bus when Richard and two of his friends began to ridicule them for their gender nonconformity. Richard and his friends decided to set Sasha's skirt on fire, expecting that the fabric would merely smolder and wake up its wearer and that this would somehow be "funny." Richard applied the lighter to Sasha's skirt, but the skirt went up in flames and seriously burned Sasha's legs. Surveillance footage from the bus was used to identify Richard, and he was arrested the next day. The county district attorney used her discretion to charge him with a hate crime and as an adult. Slater notes that hate crime legislation was introduced in the 1980s as a result of moral panics around skinhead attacks; offenders accused of a hate crime were subject to tougher sentences than if they had committed the same crime against a person who was not a member of a persecuted minority. Charging Richard as an adult denied him the anonymity legally provided to juveniles and increased the probability that he would do time in an adult facility.

When Richard was questioned by police about his motives for the attack, he stated, "I'm homophobic. I don't like gay people." His lawyer argued, however, that it made no sense to describe a child's nascent opinions as "hate." Even Sasha's parents objected to Richard being tried as an adult, while Sasha was uncertain about what kind of penalty was appropriate. "I know he hurt me," Sasha said. "He did something that's really dangerous and stupid. But then again, he's a 16-year-old kid, and 16-year-old kids are kind of dumb. It's really hard to know what I want for him." In a letter of apology to Sasha, Richard wrote, "I am not a thug, gangster, hoodlum, nor monster. I'm a young Black-American male who's made a terrible mistake. . . . I've also been hurt a lot for no reason, not like I hurt you, but I've been hurt physically and mentally so I know how it feels, the pain and confusion . . . of why me; I've felt it before plenty of times." Slater goes on to note that the National Center for Lesbian Rights, the Transgender Law Center, and the American Civil Liberties Union of Northern California wrote letters to District Attorney

O'Malley asking her to reconsider the charges, challenging the appropriateness of trying juvenile offenders as adults. The district attorney held fast, however, and Richard agreed to a plea bargain of seven years, the bulk of which would be served at an adult facility.[33]

Without dismissing for a moment the harm done to Sasha and the serious nature of the assault, is this what should have happened? Will this make LGBT kids safer? Is the criminalization of youth aggression a solution? The issues raised by critics of hate crime measures are also at play, albeit on a smaller scale, with regard to the adoption of punitive anti-bullying policies in many school districts.

The School-to-Prison Pipeline

Many school boards have passed anti-bullying and/or anti-homophobia policies that contest what has long been a normalized practice of targeting queer and gender-nonconforming children (as well as those who are racialized, visibly impoverished, physically and/or neurologically disabled, in care, fat,[34] or marginalized according to other markers of difference) for harassment and abuse. There is no question that official statements that this kind of behavior is inappropriate are an improvement over the long-standing normalization of such violence. In a 2012 report, titled *The Health of Canada's Young People: A Mental Health Focus*, the Public Health Agency of Canada defined bullying as "a form of repeated aggression where there is an imbalance of power between the young person who is bullying and the young person who is victimized. Power can be achieved through physical, psychological, social, or systemic advantage, or by knowing another's vulnerability (e.g., obesity, learning problem, sexual orientation, family background) and using that knowledge to cause distress." The report goes on to note that victims "tend to have high levels of emotional problems, while young people who bully tend to have the highest levels of behavioural problems. Young people who are involved in both bullying others and being victimized tend to have elevated levels of both emotional and behavioural problems, with this group of young people having the highest level of emotional problems and the second highest level of behavioural problems."[35]

As of July 2013, anti-bullying laws have been passed in all 50 U.S. states, and some Canadian provinces have anti-bullying legislation. Considerable research has demonstrated that punitive anti-bullying policies, rather than representing progress with regard to social justice, fail to protect vulnerable LGBT kids and instead contribute to a "school-to-prison pipeline" for racialized and disabled children and youth. This is true in both Canada and the United States. Educational researchers Therese Quinn and Erica Meiners echo social justice lawyer Andrea Ritchie's characterization of antibullying laws as "mini hate crime laws" in the way that they are "likely to both reflect and reinforce dominant sets of power arrangements."[36] In the past two decades, many public school districts in North America have passed "zero-tolerance" anti-bullying policies, often in an effort to protect themselves from legal action.[37] Child and youth studies scholars Monique Lacharite and Zopito Marini cite the 2005 case of *Jubran vs. North Vancouver School District #44* in Canada, in which a student took his school district to court because he was subjected to extreme bullying for years. The ruling assigned legal responsibility to the school district for failing to uphold its student code of conduct. While the case was a victory in the sense that it placed the responsibility for keeping students safe squarely on the school's shoulders, increasing the punishing capacity of schools has had very negative consequences for vulnerable students. Lacharite and Marini observe that Canadian courts and schools are "showing a new intolerance for bullying and establishing the need to classify bullying as a crime."[38]

Evidence suggests that anti-bullying school policies do not make LGBT kids safer because they individualize anti-gay and anti-trans aggression rather than attending to heteronormative structural factors and because they punish troubled kids rather than marshaling appropriate resources on their behalf.[39] In Lacharite and Marini's analysis of the zero-tolerance policy outlined as part of Ontario's Safe Schools Act, they observe that the policy "outlines specific punishments for inappropriate behaviors by using suspension and expulsion more often as well as police involvement and disciplinary measures." They go on to note, however, that the policy did not "include room for exception or unusual circumstance, and as it was employed more and more, expulsion and suspension rates rapidly increased, leading to another problem altogether, . . . an increase in dropout rates."[40]

Numerous scholars employ the metaphor of a racialized "school-to-prison pipeline" to describe the trajectory for kids rendered precarious by racialization and/or poverty or other dimensions of socially constructed marginality, noting that strong-armed anti-bullying policies actually reinforce institutional racism by exposing more kids to criminalization, family intervention, and systems of law enforcement. Research indicates that Indigenous, Black American and Black Canadian, immigrant youth of color, and disabled and LGBT kids are disproportionately targeted for discipline practices that push them out of school.[41] Such exclusion is a strong predictor of precarity, as many of these children in fact drop out, become poverty stricken, and are later incarcerated. A 2013 ACLU report titled "What Is the School to Prison Pipeline?" "concluded that students of color and disabled students are disproportionately suspended, expelled, and sent into the justice system, in comparison to white and nondisabled students."[42] Quinn and Meiners observe, "These gendered and racialized practices of removing students from their educational settings—the most dramatic educational sanction available—start in preschools, as indicated in a 2005 survey of 40 states' prekindergarten programs."[43] Yet this is business as usual. As critical childhood studies scholar Lucia Hodgson observes, "The criminalization of black children is a major component of their social oppression."[44] The school-to-prison pipeline contributes to precarity in that it is "a complex network of relations that naturalizes the movement of youth of color from schools and communities into under- or unemployment and permanent detention. . . . Because schools are sites of surveillance that are neither race nor gender-neutral, these laws entrench extant relationships to law enforcement. Criminalization in and outside of schools is a process of racialization, through which youth of color are normalized as those who are 'bad' and 'in trouble.'"[45] As desperate as Catherine was to protect Frank, she was cognizant of the need to avoid criminalizing the two Indigenous boys who sexually assaulted him, knowing that their behavior reflected their own trauma and marginalization. Her knowledge is consistent with research that indicates that bullying and interpersonal violence are often multidirectional. According to a recent study, "33% of the students who reported high involvement in bullying or victimization did so as dual participants, that is, they were involved in both."[46] Another study notes that students are often bullied because they are visibly impoverished and often resort to violence as a mechanism of defense.[47]

In the context of ongoing cuts to school budgets, policies that respond to student behavioral problems by allowing expulsion are attractive. Quinn and Meiners observe that if teaching staff are cut and those remaining are pressured to meet the needs of the same number of students, there is a greater likelihood that authoritarian systems of discipline and oppressive relationships will exist.[48] While queer critics of the school-to-prison pipeline emphasize that gender- and sexual-minority kids experience substantial and long-lasting harm in communities and schools, anti-bullying policies exemplify "how a carceral state can take up the harm and violence experienced, as well as the desires of communities for systemic change, to advance agendas that do little to make communities safer for those who are non-heterosexual and/or non-gender-conforming."[49] Quinn and Meiners observe that restorative or transformative justice practices are emerging in schools and communities in the United States in opposition to tactics of punishment and isolation.[50] These alternatives are severely underfunded, while more and more resources are being pumped into carceral facilities. Programs that address oppressive structures and cultures in schools that cause harm to students and teachers in a variety of ways are badly needed.

Reform versus Radical Change

If the rights framework has such clear limitations, to what extent, then, does it make sense to pursue "rights" for transgender kids? Does it inevitably serve only the interests of less precarious trans kids? After all, trans kids are striated by privilege with regard to their ability to exercise these rights. But while rights initiatives are limited, I am convinced that abandoning them would be a mistake. Rights *do* deliver important measures of harm reduction and can be strategically important in challenging oppressive cultures. Anti-homophobia and trans-inclusive policies that recognize and value gender and sexual diversity by focusing on changing school culture to be more inclusive do challenge oppressive aspects of heteropatriarchy and are not irrelevant, or the Christian Right would not mobilize so forcefully against them.

The discourse of rights can be a powerful tool for undermining oppressive constructions of human/not quite human/subhuman subjects. In Judith Butler's articulation of her "new gender politics," she argues that rights are foundational to social justice struggles and insists, "When we struggle for rights, we are not simply struggling for rights that attach to my person. . . . We are struggling to be conceived as persons. . . . If we are struggling not only to be conceived as persons, but to create a social transformation of the very meaning of personhood, then the assertion of rights becomes a way of intervening into the social and political process by which the human is articulated."[51] Siebers, too, links rights to the acknowledgment of human status and insists on the value of a social, rather than a medical, model of disability to challenge barriers to citizenship. Claiming citizenship via seeking rights, according to Siebers, has the potential to reveal the blueprint of social oppression, to show that disability is constructed rather than naturally occurring: "Disability seen from this point of view requires not individual medical treatment but changes in society. Social constructionism has changed the landscape of thinking about disability because it refuses to represent people with disabilities as defective citizens and because its focus on the built environment represents a common cause around which they may organize politically."[52]

Critical citizenship scholar Naila Kabeer articulates an "inclusive" or "horizontal" conceptualization of citizenship based on collective, as opposed to individualistic, criteria. This definition of citizenship focuses on relationships *between* citizens as much as it does on "the more traditional 'vertical' view of citizenship as the relationship between the state and the individual." Kabeer notes that "it is the collective struggles of excluded groups which have historically driven processes of social transformation."[53] This definition of citizenship echoes Fraser's concept of participatory parity as a measure of social justice. Indeed, critical citizenship scholar Ruth Lister makes this connection explicitly by invoking it to bestow "cultural citizenship."[54] Kabeer's definition of inclusive citizenship, like Siebers's vision of rights as a tool for social change, draws inspiration from political philosopher Hannah Arendt's definition of citizenship as "the right to have rights," that is, the right to be regarded as fully human.[55] An inclusive definition of citizenship focuses attention on the structural issues relating to resources for claiming and contesting citizenship and exclusion. Citizenship is as much a resource in itself as are the means (material and cultural) for embodying it and enacting social change. This link between rights and citizenship targets social structures, including state power, that privilege heteronormativity and cisgender binary normativity in concert with poverty and racism. Rights are an important tool for reducing the precarity of trans kids, but rights must be pursued within a broader anti-oppression strategy.

The value of obtaining trans rights in shaping cultural climate has been driven home very sharply by the damaging change in tone that emerged in the early days of the Trump administration. Rights do matter, as they shape cultural climates and legitimate student experiences of discrimination and provide avenues for recourse. According to the Canadian Civil Liberties Association, "Studies have shown that LGBTQ students feel safer and more accepted when they know their schools have policies and procedures that explicitly address homophobia." School board policies that entitle students to form gay-straight alliances are also crucial, as they "contribute to making school safer for LGBTQ students."[56] And a recent article in the *Guardian*, by Nicola Davis, announced a "drop in teenage suicide attempts linked to legalization of same-sex marriage." In this article, Davis reports that lesbian, gay, and bisexual students feel safer and report better mental health indicators in states where marriage equality has been achieved, as evidenced by a 14% drop in suicide attempts among lesbian, gay, and bisexual teenagers that is linked to states that have legalized same-sex marriage.[57] Rights- and policy-oriented changes do make improvements in aspects of the lives of some queer and trans students.

The federal enforcement of Title IX gender equity provisions in the U.S. to enable transgender students to use bathroom and change-room facilities consistent with their affirmed gender identities, promised by the Obama White House, signaled to trans people of all ages that we matter and that hatred and fearmongering should not guide policies that concern us. The subsequent change in tone from the White House emboldened anti-trans and anti-LGBT rhetoric and policy making. This shift speaks to the value of mobilizing rights as part of a broad-based anti-oppression strategy to empower transgender kids. In the final section of this chapter, I outline the general principles of a strategy that leverages rights within an anti-oppression model of transformational social change to reduce the precarity of *all* transgender kids.

Transforming Disabling/Oppressive Environments and Building Agency

The stories about the suffering and pleasure of trans kids that I have documented in this book reveal the importance of gender self-determination for all kids, the specific harms experienced by trans kids as a result of exposure to cisgender-normative environments and trans-oppressive policies and practices, and the ways in which multiple bases of oppression combine to render some trans kids more precarious.

Neither Wren, who is alive, nor Finn, who is no longer alive, could see a future for themselves as trans people. Their assessment of reality is chilling but instructive and guides me in making recommendations for empowering particularly precarious trans kids. Social movements dedicated to supporting trans kids need to focus on the needs of the most precarious by combining work to achieve specific measures to enable gender self-determination with a focus on transforming environments to meaningfully support all kids. In contrast to the more typical subtext of trans kids as relatively privileged, we need to keep the most precarious trans kids in mind in our social change efforts. What are the forces and structures that are currently disempowering *these* kids? How do forces of oppression relating to racism, poverty, colonialism, and sexism, for example, combine with imposed gender systems to place some transgender kids in particular at terrible risk. This work occurs within a context where even relatively privileged trans kids are incredibly vulnerable. But radical change will require social movements on behalf of trans kids to build powerful coalitions with other marginalized communities to protect the many vulnerable kids in our midst and the vulnerable adults they will grow up to be. As Kimberley Manning observes, "Under the glare of the media spotlight personal testimonials can contribute to the erasure of some trans* lives: it can become easy to lose sight of the struggles of parents who may not teach at a university, for example, and of the racialized transgender kids who are at far greater risk of violence than are our own white children."[58]

For the 1995 co-authored book *In School: Our Kids, Our Teachers, Our Classrooms,* former Canadian National Hockey League star Ken Dryden spent a year observing in a Canadian high school. Through this process, he determined that education was being delivered to those he called "the front-row kids" by teachers who, for the most part, had been front row kids themselves. Dryden saw "back-row kids" engaging via resistance and so worried the most about the "middle-row kids," whose educational needs were being neglected. He advocated restructuring public education to specifically target middle-row kids.[59] I see an important parallel for movements in support of trans kids. The visible kids are the ones with the most support, yet even with this support, they are very vulnerable. But centering social change efforts around these kids will not produce a sufficient increase in life chances for the most precarious trans kids. If instead we direct our social change efforts to increasing the agency of the most precarious trans kids, this will incorporate the gender self-determination needs of more privileged trans kids.

We must invest culturally and materially in the most vulnerable kids and their families, by establishing a baseline of security for all not only by reversing cuts to social services, school budgets, community centers, and healthcare services but by recommitting to and radically expanding a welfare state model. Components of this model include guaranteed housing and basic income for all, a public not-for-profit model of healthcare, and equitable nation-to-nation relationships with Indigenous peoples that include reparations for land theft.

Key points of contact between trans kids—apparent or nonapparent—and the public sector include education, the healthcare system, social services for children and families, the criminal justice system, and community centers. In general, we should advocate for the training of public-sector service providers to adopt gender- and sexual-diversity inclusion and affirming approaches and to be able to identify and intervene on behalf of kids who are experiencing gender coercion or anti-gay or anti-trans peer or adult aggression. Identifying basic needs and ensuring that they are available to all is a core component of a broad-based anti-oppression agenda.

As I see it, we have four key tasks. First, we must find ways to put pressure on social institutions and spaces to generate room for all kids to determine their own gender identities within a wider range of possibilities. Second, we must strive to ensure that gender-affirming healthcare becomes available to everyone. Third, we need to target gender systems for dismantlement while respecting and supporting people for whom binary gender identity has resonance. Finally, and most importantly, the most precarious trans kids need to be at the center of all our social change efforts: this can be accomplished only through a redistribution of cultural and material resources and the abolition of incarceration as a system of social control. It is beyond the scope of this book to engage in a discussion of how to radically reform criminal justice and prison systems, but I and other prison abolitionists emphasize that punishment regimes are the wrong end of the social stick to invest in: incarcerating nonviolent members of vulnerable communities reinforces the vulnerability of those communities and hence the precarity of trans kids. But the institutional and cultural shift necessary to decrease the precarity of trans kids directly addresses many of the primary factors that determine the likelihood that one will spend time in prison. Anti-racist and anti-poverty activists have long documented the role of oppression, poverty, and trauma in leading to the criminalization of already vulnerable people and the use of state violence and imprisonment as tools of containment and social control. A radical shift away from punishment and toward intense social and material investment in children to protect them from abuse, coercion, and violence is the most effective way to empower transgender kids.

Long-term goals for transforming harmful environments include removing gender as a mandatory identity category for government documentation, investing cultural and material resources heavily in the most vulnerable children, providing safety nets for all community members to ensure a baseline standard of living above the poverty level, transforming inequitable and colonial relationships with Indigenous peoples, ensuring access to gender-affirming healthcare within the context of a no-barrier public healthcare model more generally, abolishing prisons, and engineering a cultural shift away from practices that naturalize and reinscribe human hierarchies toward egalitarian patterns of interaction and decision making that by necessity include an open-ended gender spectrum. Thinking in terms of the most precarious transgender kids is a powerful orientation for a vision of a more just and equitable future for all of us.

*　*　*

When I traveled by car from Canada to the U.S. in 2016, a Euro-Canadian, visibly gender-nonconforming, middle-class, designated female at birth, nonbinary, trans masculine person, with my Black Canadian daughter in the car, I felt confident in my own power in the world—so confident that when I realized I had forgotten my passport, I didn't panic. I explained to my daughter that I was optimistic we would be let through, but I was careful to point out that this would be because of my whiteness and visible class privilege and that—unjust as it is—it would be unsafe for her to approach the border with the same sense of entitlement when she is old enough to travel on her own. As I expected, the border agent allowed me to enter the U.S. on the basis of my British Columbia driver's license alone. This is what entitlement *feels* like: confidence, positive expectation, legitimacy. I want this for all of us.

As I prepared to undertake a subsequent cross-border trip with my daughter in 2017, just after the election of Trump, I worried about my phone being searched, about my relationship with my daughter being questioned by border guards, about my "gender issues." I was anxious about the trip and anxious about the future. Nothing untoward happened that day, but the experience of anxiety was significant in itself. I realized I had gotten used to being seen as respectable.

The first Sunday after the election, the Black American preacher at Mount Zion Baptist Church in Seattle, Washington, delivered a powerful sermon about the necessity of principled action for social justice. Speaking to a primarily Black congregation that had experienced so much oppression, he acknowledged the temptation to give in to cynicism and hopelessness. Instead of giving up, however, he urged the congregation to go beyond hope to engage in the "politics of the broken-hearted: to stand in the tragic gap between cynicism and idealism." I believe that gap is where most parents of particularly precarious kids live.

I came to parenting with a keen commitment to make space for my children to resist the constraints of gender and racism and to let their hearts grow big with self-regard and kindness for others. The research and advocacy I do on behalf of trans kids comes from places of hurt, regret, and desire for redemption in my own history, and in this sense, it is extraordinarily selfish. I wish I had been allowed to be, and had the courage and support to be, a happier and kinder child and young person, but in parenting and interacting with kids to enable them to be authentic, happier, and kinder than I was, I find my own tragic gap and the core political and intellectual purpose of my mature years as a scholar.

I find it heartbreaking that Wren sees no future for herself as a black trans woman. But I see flashes of possibility and resilience in her. When we were talking about the difficulties involved in being different, Wren observed that these same difficulties can be gifts. So I asked her if she thinks being trans is a gift. This is what she said: "I've heard of gifted as in magical—like mutant. If you're transgender, you are basically kind of like a mutant. There are things that are harder for you, but there are things that you can really do and are really amazing. Like you're special in your own special way. Like you're an X-Man." I hope that Wren will someday find a way to claim all of herself. For all I know, she will do this by coming to see herself, literally, as some kind of an *ex-man*. But it is not enough for us to hope that she and other trans kids are able to find this space: we have to go beyond hope and build a big enough lifeboat for all of them—and, by extension, all of us.

ACKNOWLEDGMENTS

Over the past few years, I have noticed a change in my reading habits: I now begin each book or article with the acknowledgments. This is because they allow me to see the author both in context and as a person. Similarly, I wrote this book as a member of a number of overlapping kinship networks and communities, and I wish here to honor the people who hold me up, keep me grounded, educate and challenge me, and make space for my work.

My editor, Ilene Kalish, believed in this project from the outset and helped me in all phases of the work. She set high standards and was invested in my success. I am incredibly lucky to have had her stewardship and encouragement. Shari Dworkin and Jodi O'Brien offered early encouragement and ongoing support and directed me to Ilene Kalish and NYU Press. What a gift! I owe a huge debt of gratitude to Jane Ward and Georgiann Davis, who, as reviewers, were the absolute model of outstanding academic peer review: deeply engaged with the work and generous with constructive feedback that pushed me in all the right ways.

Delia Douglas, Michael Hathaway, Jenny Shaw, Wendy Chan, Gwen Bird, and Nadine Boulay read earlier versions of the work and gave me encouragement and valuable feedback. I am specifically grateful to Delia Douglas for generously pushing me to address racism and colonialism in more meaningful ways. This has profoundly shaped my scholarship. Kathleen Millar and Jenny Shaw were particularly helpful as I worked to theorize precarity. Amanda Watson helped me integrate theorizing relating to affective labor to describe the gendered nature of reproductive care work. Ken Clement and Jack Saddleback were generous with their time in sharing their insights about the particular challenges experienced by two-spirit and gender-nonconforming Indigenous kids. Wallace Wong shared important insights from his clinical practice with trans kids and encouraged me to write this book. Patti Bacchus helped me understand school board policies relating to LGBT kids. Andrea Fatona assisted me with appropriate terminology and provided a valuable sounding board for making sense of the complex relationships relating to racialization and transness. barbara findlay filled in gaps in my understanding of legal matters relating to trans issues in Canada, while Asaf Orr and Helen Carroll did so for the USA. Jennifer Marchbank, Lindsey Freeman, Jessi Jackson, Kari Lerum, Dara Culhane, Amie McLean, and Kathleen Millar assured me that my work was important and bolstered my resilience when challenges emerged. Marina Morrow, Brian Burtch, Sharalyn Jordan, Jennifer Marchbank, Rodney Hunt, Elizabeth Saewyc, Mary Ann Saunders, Brenda Jamer, Jennifer Thomas, and Megan Simon helped me get a research program on trans kids under way. Jennifer Marchbank, Sharalyn Jordan, and Nadine Boulay have been generous and inspiring colleagues in our shared project relating to supports for trans kids in the Greater Vancouver area. Bev Neufeld provided encouragement and expertise around grant writing, while Megan Simon was totally indispensable in our eventual success in securing a major grant. Suzanne Norman has been my go-to person for questions around publishing. Jennifer Breakspear, while executive director of Qmunity, worked with me to get a community-based research project under way that paved the way for this book. Tiffany Muller-Myrdahl provided peer support around developing a writing timeline. Nadine Boulay and Alex Werier assisted with the nuts and bolts of preparing the manuscript.

A number of scholars with particular expertise relating to transgender kids influenced my work and were valuable and generous sounding boards. They include Cindy Holmes, Kimberley Manning, Jake Pyne, Elizabeth Meyer, Annie Pullen Sansfacon, Jennifer Marchbank, Karl Bryant, Julie Temple Newhook, and Julian Gill-Peterson. In addition, four parents of trans kids thoughtfully shared feedback with me about some of the conclusions I came to in a talk I gave relating to the book.

The CRIRAFETS (Critical Race and Feminist Technoscience Reading Group), consisting of Kathleen Millar, Michael Hathaway, Stacy Pigg, Coleman Nye, Jessi Jackson, Lindsey Freeman, Amanda Watson, and Nick Scott, provided intellectual companionship during a pivotal year of writing.

The Canadian Institute for Health Research, the Social Sciences and Humanities Research Council of Canada, and Simon Fraser University's Faculty of Arts and Social Sciences provided funds in support of my research. SFU's Office of the Vice-President, Research provided funds to assist with preparing the manuscript for publication. The Department of Sociology & Anthropology at Simon Fraser University continues to provide an encouraging environment for critical teaching and scholarship. My own office perches on the end of the hallway of the Department of Gender, Sexuality and Women's Studies. In addition to providing my research project on trans kids with office space, they have welcomed me as their own for years now. I have benefited immeasurably from their warmth and goodwill.

Marilyn Gates, you fed my resilience first when supreme good fortune landed me in your undergraduate class in 1986 and then as a colleague, when you told me to write from the gut. Your fingerprints are all over this manuscript.

Kendry, you made me a mom. Your arrival was the beginning of the best part of my life, and your companionship at close to 20 academic conferences has been such a joy. You inspire me with your courage. Langston, I love how hard we can laugh at the same thing without ever having to say anything. Thank you for all the elephants, all the hugs, and all the baseball games. Hanna, you gave me enough time to get it right. Thank you so much for that. I love to love the dog with you. Charlie, Jack, and Thunder, you have made my office furry enough to feel like home over the years. And dog kisses are magic.

Gwen, my biggest thanks and appreciation are reserved for you: first, for all the practical labor you dedicated to enabling me, otherwise known as "the grumpy and demanding houseguest" that you put up with off and on for three years, to write this book; second, and most importantly, for the emotional labor you dedicate to me and to our children—to this quirky little family we built and hold together. This has been the real difference maker. Your steadfast love and belief in me allowed me to open a vein and let this book pour out. I can never thank you enough—but I will try. One vacation at a time . . . one retirement plan at a time . . .

APPENDIX A

Recommendations

Immediate and significant harm reduction for trans kids can be achieved via short-term goals/interventions with regard to key points of contact between kids, their parents, and the public sector. Many of them target kids as a whole for benefit; this is necessary given what we know about the invisibility of many transgender kids, race- and class-based differences among trans kids, and the harm that restrictive and sexist gender categories inflict on the many kids who would not categorize themselves as trans or gender nonconforming.

SCHOOLS
- Transition school spaces and practices away from sex/gender categories
- Integrate gender- and sexuality-inclusive sex and gender education curricula into the mainstream to support gender self-determination for all
- Address sexism, racism, and other bases of oppression by integrating an anti-oppression approach into the school curriculum
- Invest more resources into schools to enable them to be sites of individual and community empowerment

BATHROOMS, LOCKER ROOMS, AND SPORTS
- Provide low-barrier public bathroom access for everyone—all gender, all age, all color, all ability, all neighborhood, all income
- Provide all-gender multiuser and single-user bathroom and change-room facilities and educate people of all ages about bathroom and change-room etiquette
- Prioritize no-user-fee, sex-integrated sport and recreational opportunities for people of all ages and incorporate egalitarian values in the organization and culture of these activities

- Eliminate male-only sex-segregated sport at all levels of play while maintaining girl- and women-only sporting spaces with no-questions-asked trans-inclusive boundaries as an interim measure
- Invest public funds in community-based sport and recreation programs rather than elite athletics

PARENT ACTIVISM

In outlining recommendations for parent activism, I wish to acknowledge that much of this work is already being undertaken and that I am highlighting the importance of certain kinds of action rather than pretending to offer instructions.

- Embrace open-ended gender self-determination for everyone
- Engage in parent-to-parent peer support
- Have as a central goal the transitioning of environments away from binary gender systems and attendant systems and cultures of patriarchy and misogyny
- Form coalitions with other marginalized groups to decrease the precarity of all kids
- Fight for the expansion of public resources accessible to all kids and their families: shelter, food, education, recreation, child care, social welfare, citizenship
- Pool resources (cultural and material) and work very consciously to address socioeconomic barriers to parent participation

AFFIRMING HEALTHCARE
- Develop a public-health model of all-gender trans-affirming medicalization (low-barrier access) in the context of a public-health delivery model in general (one tier for everyone)
- Lower the age of consent to lessen the social subordination of children and young people
- Transition social spaces and institutions away from sex/gender categories

APPENDIX B

Resources

TEXTS

Young-Adult Fiction / Personal Memoir

Coyote, Ivan E. *One in Every Crowd*. Vancouver, BC: Arsenal Pulp, 2012.

Gino, Alex. *George*. New York: Scholastic, 2015.

Gold, Rachel. *Being Emily*. Vancouver, BC: Arsenal Pulp, 2012.

Kulkin, Susan. *Beyond Magenta: Transgender Teens Speak Out*. Somerville, MA: Candlewick, 2014.

Lowrey, Sassafras. *Lost Boi*. Vancouver, BC: Arsenal Pulp, 2015.

———. *Roving Pack*. Vancouver, BC: Arsenal Pulp, 2012.

Peters, Julie Anne. *Luna*. Vancouver, BC: Arsenal Pulp, 2006.

Spoon, Rae. *First Spring Grass Fire*. Vancouver, BC: Arsenal Pulp, 2012.

Wood, Jennie. *A Boy like Me*. United States: 215 Ink, 2014.

Children's Books

Beam, Cris. *I Am J*. Boston: Little, Brown, Books for Young Readers, 2011.

Bladacchino, Christine. *Morris Micklewhite and the Tangerine Dress*. Toronto: Groundwood Books, 2014.

Coyle, Carmela LaVigna, and Mike Gordon. *Do Princesses Wear Hiking Boots?* New York: Cooper Square, 2003.

Coyote, Ivan E. *Tomboy Survival Guide*. Vancouver, BC: Arsenal Pulp, 2016.

Garvin, Jeff. *Symptoms of Being Human*. New York: Balzer + Bray, 2016.

Girard, M.-E. *Girl Mans Up*. New York: HarperCollins, 2016.

Goto, Hiromi. *Half World*. Toronto: Razorbill Canada, 2009.

———. *The Water of Possibility*. Regina, SK: Coteau Books, 2001.

Hall, Michael. *Red: A Crayon's Story*. New York: Greenwillow Books, 2015.

Herthel, Jessica, and Jazz Jennings. *I Am Jazz*. New York: Dial Books, 2014.

Hoffman, Sarah, and Ian Hoffman. *Jacob's New Dress*. Park Ridge, IL: Albert Whitman, 2014.

Kilodavis, Cheryl, and Suzanne DeSimone. *My Princess Boy*. New York: Aladdin, 2010.

Thom, Kai Cheng. *A Place Called No Homeland*. Vancouver, BC: Arsenal Pulp, 2017.

Wittlinger, Ellen. *Parrotfish*. New York: Simon and Schuster Books for Young Readers, 2007.

Yolen, Jae, and Heidi E. Y. Stemple. *Not All Princesses Dress in Pink*. New York: Simon and Schuster Books for Young Readers, 2010.

Resources for Trans Kids

Andrews, Arin. *Some Assembly Required: The Not-So-Secret Life of a Transgender Teen*. New York: Simon and Schuster Books for Young Readers, 2014.

Bornstein, Kate. *My Gender Workbook: How to Become a Real Man, a Real Woman, the Real You, or Something Else Entirely*. New York: Routledge, 2013.

Bornstein, Kate, and Sara Quin. *Hello Cruel World: 101 Alternatives to Suicide for Teens, Freaks, and Other Outlaws*. New York: Seven Stories, 2006.

Egale Canada Human Rights Trust. "Two Spirits, One Voice." ("A community based initiative that seeks to bolster supports for persons that identify both as LGBTQ and Indigenous—Two Spirit people. Funded through the Ministry of Community Safety and Correctional Services, this program works with educators, healthcare workers, law enforcement and other community service providers.")

Jennings, Jazz. *Being Jazz: My Life as a (Transgender) Teen*. New York: Crown Books for Young Readers, 2016.

Pessin-Whedbee, Brook, and Naomi Bardoff. *Who Are You? The Kid's Guide to Gender Identity*. London: Jessica Kingsley, 2016.

Sharman, Zena, ed. *The Remedy: Queer and Trans Voices on Health and Health Care*. Vancouver, BC: Arsenal Pulp, 2016.

Stigma and Resilience among Vulnerable Youth Centre. *Canadian Transgender Youth Health Survey*. Vancouver, BC: Stigma and Resilience among Vulnerable Youth Centre, 2013. (National survey with Canadian youth who identify as transgender or gender-queer and are between the ages of 14 and 25, based on 900 responses from transgender youth from all provinces and territories except Nunavut and the Yukon.)

Taylor, Catherine G., and Tracey Peter. *Every Class in Every School: Final Report on the First National Climate Survey on Homophobia, Biphobia, and Transphobia in Canadian Schools*. Toronto: Egale Canada Human Rights Trust, 2012.

Testa, Rylan Jay, and Deborah Coolhart. *The Gender Quest Workbook: A Guide for Teens and Young Adults Exploring Gender Identity*. Oakland, CA: Instant Help, 2015.

For Parents/Family

Angello, Michele, and Ali Bowman. *Raising the Transgender Child: A Complete Guide for Parents, Families, and Caregivers*. Berkeley, CA: Seal, 2016.

Brill, Stephanie A., and Lisa Kenney. *The Transgender Teen: A Handbook for Parents and Professionals Supporting Transgender and Non-Binary Teens*. Jersey City, NJ: Cleis, 2016.

Brill, Stephanie A., and Rachel Pepper. *The Transgender Child*. San Francisco: Cleis, 2008.

Duron, Lori. *Raising My Rainbow: Adventures in Raising a Fabulous, Gender Creative Son*. New York: Broadway Books, 2013.

Ehrensaft, Diane, and Edgardo Menvielle. *Gender Born, Gender Made: Raising Health Gender-Nonconforming Children.* 3rd rev. ed. New York: The Experiment, 2011.

Ehrensaft, Diane, and Norman Spack. *The Gender Creative Child.* New York: The Experiment, 2016.

Erikson-Schroth, Laura, and Jennifer Finney Boylan, eds. *Trans Bodies, Trans Selves: A Resource for the Transgender Community.* New York: Oxford University Press, 2014.

Evans, Cheryl B. *I Promised Not to Tell: Raising a Transgender Child.* Self-published, available on Amazon, 2016.

Hubbard, Eleanor A., and Cameron T. Whitley. *Trans-Kin: A Guide for Family and Friends of Transgender People.* Boulder, CO: Bolder, 2012.

Kane, Emily W. *The Gender Trap: Parents and the Pitfalls of Raising Boys and Girls.* New York: NYU Press, 2012.

Kreiger, Irwin. *Helping Your Transgender Teen: A Guide for Parents.* Ashford, CT: Genderwise, 2011.

Nealy, Elijah C. *Transgender Children and Youth: Cultivating Pride and Joy with Families in Transition.* New York: Norton, 2017.

Pepper, Rachel. *Transitions of the Heart: Stories of Love, Struggle, and Acceptance by Mothers of Transgender and Gender Variant Children.* Berkeley, CA: Cleis, 2012.

Travers, Robb, Trans PULSE Project, and Canadian Electronic Library. *Impacts of Strong Parental Support for Trans Youth.* Toronto: Trans PULSE Project, 2012.

For Policy Makers/Educators

Balsam, Kimberly F., Yamile Molina, and Keren Lehavot. "Alcohol and Drug Use in Lesbian, Gay, Bisexual, and Transgender Youth and Youth Adults." In *Principles of Addiction: Comprehensive Addictive Behaviors and Disorders,* edited by Peter M. Miller et al., vol. 1, 563–574. San Diego, CA: Elsevier, 2013.

Bloomfield, Veronica E., and Marni E. Fisher, eds. *LGBTQ Voices in Education: Changing the Culture of Schooling.* New York: Routledge, 2016.

Cahill, Sean. "Black Sexual Citizenship: Understanding the Impact of Political Issues on Those at the Margins of Race, Sexuality, Gender, and Class." In *Black Sexualities: Probing Powers, Passions, Practices, and Policies,* edited by Juan Battle and Sandra L. Barnes, 190–212. New Brunswick, NJ: Rutgers University Press, 2010.

Canadian Rainbow Health Coalition, Transcend Transgender Support & Education Society, and Vancouver Coastal Health Authority. *Caring for Transgender Adolescents in B.C.: Suggested Guidelines.* Canadian Electronic Library. Saskatoon, SK: Transcent; Vancouver, BC: Vancouver Coastal Health, 2006.

Cianciotto, Jason, and Sean Cahill. "Lesbian, Gay, Bisexual, and Transgender Youth: A Critical Population." In *LGBT Youth in America's Schools,* edited by Jason Cianciotto and Sean Cahill, 9–35. Ann Arbor: University of Michigan Press, 2002.

Coupet, Sacha M. "Policing Gender on the Playground: Interests, Needs, and the Rights of Transgender and Gender Non-conforming Youth." In *Children, Sexuality, and the Law,* edited by Sacha M. Coupet and Ellen Marrus, 186–223. New York: NYU Press, 2015.

Fedders, Barbara. "Gender at the Crossroads: LGBT Youth in the Child Welfare and Juvenile Justice Systems." In *Children, Sexuality, and the Law,* edited by Sacha M. Coupet and Ellen Marrus, 224–254. New York: NYU Press, 2015.

Fisher, Emily S., and Karen Komosa-Hawkins, eds. *Creating Safe and Supportive Learning Environments: A Guide for Working with Lesbian, Gay, Bisexual, Transgender, and Questioning Youth and Families.* New York: Routledge, 2013.

Fisher, Sylvia K., Jeffery M. Poirier, and Gary M. Blau, eds. *Improving Emotional and Behavioral Outcomes for LGBT Youth: A Guide for Professionals.* Baltimore: Paul H. Brookes, 2012.

Mallon, Gerald P. *LGBTQ Youth Issues: A Practical Guide for Youth Workers Serving Lesbian, Gay, Bisexual, Transgender, and Questioning Youth.* Rev. ed. Arlington, VA: CWLA, 2010.

———, ed. *Social Work Practice with Transgender and Gender Variant Youth.* London: Routledge, 2009.

McDermott, Elizabeth, and Katrina Roen. "Troubling Gender Norms: Gender Non-Conforming Youth" and "Trans and Genderqueer Youth Online." Chapters 4 and 5 in *Queer Youth, Suicide, and Self-Harm: Troubled Subjects, Troubling Norms,* 62–102. London: Palgrave Macmillan, 2016.

Meyer, Elizabeth, and Annie Pullen Sansfaçon, eds. *Supporting Transgender and Gender Creative Youth: Schools, Families, and Communities in Action.* New York: Peter Lang, 2013.

Miller, S. J. *Teaching, Affirming, and Recognizing Trans and Gender Creative Youth: A Queer Literacy Framework.* Queer Studies and Education. London: Palgrave Macmillan, 2016.

Nova Scotia Department of Education and Early Childhood Development. *Guidelines for Supporting Transgender and Gender-Nonconforming Students / Student Services.* Halifax: Nova Scotia Department of Education and Early Childhood Development, 2014.

Orr, Asaf, and Joel Baum. *Schools in Transition: A Guide for Supporting Transgender Students in K–12 Schools.* American Civil Liberties Union, Gender Spectrum, Human Rights Campaign, National Center for Lesbian Rights, and National Educational Association, 2016.

Pullen, Christopher. *Queer Youth and Media Culture.* Basingstoke, UK: Palgrave Macmillan, 2014.

Russell, Stephen T., and Jennifer K. McGuire. "The School Climate for Lesbian, Gay, Bisexual, and Transgender (LGBT) Students." In *Toward Positive Youth Development: Transforming Schools and Community Programs,* edited by Marybeth Shinn and Hiorkazu Yoshikawa, 133–149. New York: Oxford University Press, 2008.

Russell, Stephen T., Amanda M. Pollitt, and Jennifer M. Elsevier. "School Environment for LGBTQ/Sexual Minority Youth." In *International Encyclopedia of the Social and Behavioral Sciences,* edited by James D. Wright, 86–90. London: Elsevier, 2015.

Sadowski, Michael. "Respecting the 'T' in LGBTQ." In *Safe Is Not Enough: Better Schools for LGBTQ Students.* Cambridge, MA: Harvard Education Press, 2013.

Simkins, Sandra. "The Special Needs of Lesbian, Gay, Bisexual, and Transgender Youth." In *When Kids Get Arrested: What Every Adult Should Know*, 175–178. New Brunswick, NJ: Rutgers University Press, 2009.

Taylor, Catherine G., and Tracey Peter. *Every Class in Every School: Final Report on the First National Climate Survey on Homophobia, Biphobia, and Transphobia in Canadian Schools*. Toronto: Egale Canada Human Rights Trust, 2012.

Vaccaro, Annemarie, Gerri August, and Megan S. Kennedy. *Safe Spaces: Making Schools and Communities Welcoming to LGBT Youth*. Santa Barbara, CA: Praeger, 2012.

WEBSITES

Egale Canada Human Rights Trust: http://egale.ca
Addresses LGBTQI2S human rights

Families in TRANSition: A Resource Guide for Parents of Trans Youth:
www.rainbowhealthontario.ca/resources/families-in-transition-a-resource-guide-for-parents-of-trans-youth/
The first comprehensive Canadian publication to address the needs of parents and families supporting their trans children; summarizes the experiences, strategies, and successes of a working group of community consultants—researchers, counselors, parents, and advocates, as well as trans youth themselves; provides the stories of parents and youth along with practical and sensitive parent-to-parent and professional therapeutic advice; written and published by CTYS (Central Toronto Youth Services) with the support and collaboration of many community members and organizations, especially P-FLAG Toronto (Parents Family and Friends of Lesbians and Gays) and Transceptance (a Toronto support group for parents of trans youth)

Gender Creative Kids: http://gendercreativekids.ca
Provides resources for supporting and affirming gender-creative kids within their families, schools, and communities, based in Canada

Gender Fork: http://genderfork.com
"A supportive community for the expression of identities across the gender spectrum"

Gender Odyssey: www.genderodyssey.org
Provides education and support of families raising gender-variant, gender-nonconforming, gender-fluid, cross-gender, and transgender children and adolescents; holds annual conferences

Gender Spectrum: www.genderspectrum.org
Provides education, training, and support to help create a gender sensitive and inclusive environment for all children and teens

LGBTQ Resources and College Affordability: www.affordablecolleges.com/resources/lgbtq-college-resources/
A guide to LGBTQ colleges that breaks down the individual components that make a campus LGBTQ friendly and is intended to help you navigate potential schools

NCLR: National Center for Lesbian Rights: www.nclrights.org/our-work/transgender-law/transgender-youth/
Provides resources for transgender youth
PFLAG Transgender Network: www.pflag.org/transgender
Trans Active: www.transactiveonline.org
An internationally recognized nonprofit focused on serving the diverse needs of transgender and gender-nonconforming youth, their families, and allies
TransAthlete.com
Transgender Equality: www.transequality.org
Trans Kids Purple Rainbow Foundation: www.transkidspurplerainbow.org
An organization supporting trans youth—in schools, in the media, and against homelessness
Trans Parenting: www.transparenting.com
Provides support and educational resources to parents and their advocates raising a gender-independent child
TransParents: http://transparentusa.org
"Provides support, information and resources to help parents confidently navigate their gender independent child's personal journey of self-discovery to authentic living"
Trans Student Educational Resources: www.transstudent.org
Trans Youth Equality Foundation: www.transyouthequality.org
Provides education, advocacy, and support for transgender and gender-nonconforming children and youth and their families; based in Portland, Maine; includes a podcast, TransWaves
TransYouth Family Allies (TYFA): www.imatyfa.org
"Empowers children and families by partnering with educators, service providers, and communities, to develop supportive environments where gender may be expressed and respected with a vision towards a society free of suicide and violence in which all children are respected and celebrated"

FILMS

Growing Up Trans. The Passionate Eye. Canadian Broadcasting Corporation, 2016.
Pink Boy. Documentary by Eric Rockey. 2016. http://pinkboyfilm.com
Transforming Gender. Doc Zone. Canadian Broadcasting Corporation, 2015. www.cbc.ca/doczone/episodes/transforming-gender
The Youth and Gender Media Project. New Day Films, 2011.
Four short films "that capture the diversity and complexity of gender nonconforming youth. These award-winning films provide students and educators with unique tools to explore critical questions about gender identity and family acceptance, and are ideal for discussions about bullying and inclusiveness."
- *Creating Gender Inclusive Schools*
- *I'm Just Anneke*
- *The Family Journey: Raising Gender Nonconforming Children*
- *Becoming Johanna*

APPENDIX C

The Kids

Name	Age	Ethnicity/racialization	Country
Alicia	17	Euro-Canadian	U.S.
Cameron	18	Euro-Canadian	Canada
Canaan	18	Euro-Canadian	Canada
Caroline	6	Black American	U.S.
Cassandra	4	Euro-Canadian	Canada
Cody	5	Euro-American	U.S.
Cory Oskam	16	Euro-Canadian	Canada
Dave	17	Euro-Canadian	Canada
Davis	8; 11	Asian American	U.S.
Dylan	15	Euro-American	U.S.
Enrique	17	Latinx	U.S.
Esme	10	Euro-Canadian	Canada
Finn	14	Euro-American	U.S.
Frank	13	Euro-Canadian	Canada
Greg	13	Euro-Canadian	Canada
Helen	16	Euro-Canadian	Canada
Hunter	13	Indigenous	Canada
Jin	13	Euro-Canadian	Canada
Kidd	18	Black/Native American	U.S.
Lennox	11	Indigenous	Canada
Martine	12	Euro-Asian Canadian	Canada
Michael	17	Asian Canadian	Canada
Nathan	15; 17	Euro-Canadian/Indigenous	Canada
Nick	11	Asian Canadian	Canada
Peter	6	Euro-Canadian	Canada
Quinn	18	Indigenous/Euro-Canadian	Canada
Ray-Ray	16	Euro-Canadian	Canada

Name	Age	Ethnicity/racialization	Country
Sasha	6	Euro-Canadian	Canada
Sean	9	Euro-American/Canadian	Canada
Silver	6; 8	Indigenous/Euro-Canadian	Canada
Simon	7; 9	Euro-Canadian	Canada
Stef	17	Euro-Asian Canadian	Canada
Taya	16	Euro-Canadian	Canada
Tru Wilson		Black Canadian/ Euro-Canadian/Indigenous	Canada
Wren	9; 11	Black Canadian	Canada
Ziggy	15	Euro-American	U.S.

GLOSSARY

AFFIRMED SEX/GENDER; SELF-AFFIRMED SEX/GENDER: the sex/gender one self-defines as

AFFIRMING HEALTHCARE; GENDER-AFFIRMING HEALTHCARE; TRANS-AFFIRMING HEALTHCARE: any combination of hormone blockers, cross-sex hormones, and surgery to achieve physical consistency with one's self-defined sex/gender, and/or mental health support to address the negative consequences of trans oppression

AGENDER: a descriptor for a person who does not identify according to sex/gender systems; includes nonbinary gender identities and not identifying with the gender system at all

ALOSEXUAL: people for whom sexual pleasure is a solitary pursuit, if indeed it is pursued at all

ASEXUAL: someone who does not experience sexual arousal/attraction

ASSEMBLAGE: a sociohistorical convergence of hierarchy and oppression

ASSIGNED SEX/GENDER AT BIRTH: a doctor's medical pronouncement that "it's a girl" or "it's a boy," which is the basis of legal sex identity, the binary-normative sex/gender category imposed on infants

ASSIMILATION: the ability of a trans person to be read in social situations as cisgender (also see STEALTH)

BINARY NORMATIVITY: the assumption that there are only two sexes and that these two sexes are markedly different

BINARY SEX/GENDER SYSTEMS: sociopolitical and economic systems based on a binary view of sex

BINDER/BINDING: the practice of using tensor bandages or customized compression garments to flatten breasts to create the impression of a more typically masculine chest structure

BIOPOLITICS: the integration of biology with political power

BIOPOWER: the employment of population management for political ends; the political control of bodies

BLACK: racialized members of the African diaspora

BOTTOM SURGERY: removal of uterus (hysterectomy) and ovaries (ovariectomy) and surgical construction of a penis (phalloplasty) to create more typically male genitals; surgical removal of the penis and construction of the vagina (vaginoplasty) to create more typically female genitals

CHILDHOOD: a socially constructed stage of life from birth to young adulthood

CHILDREN: the demographic group from birth to age 15

CISGENDER: the state of correspondence between assigned sex/gender at birth and self-identity; a normative category

CIS-SEXISM: the assumption that congruence between assigned sex/gender at birth and self-identity is the norm

CONVERSION THERAPY; CORRECTIVE/REPARATIVE THERAPY: psychological/psychiatric treatment designed to "cure" gay, lesbian, and trans and gender-nonconforming people

CROSS-SEX HORMONES: hormones associated with the "opposite" sex/gender category that are sometimes employed by trans people to achieve greater physical consistency with their self-defined sex/gender or to reduce vulnerability to discrimination and violence

DEAD NAME: the inappropriately gendered name imposed on and subsequently repudiated by a trans person

DEMI-ROMANTIC: romantic attachment based on the prior establishment of emotional intimacy

DEMI-SEXUAL: sexual attraction based on the prior establishment of emotional intimacy

DIAGNOSTIC AND STATISTICAL MANUAL (DSM): the "bible" of the American Psychiatric Association; the central diagnostic and treatment resource for the psychiatric and psychological professions

EURO-AMERICAN: a person living in the United States who is racialized as white/has European ancestors

EURO-CANADIAN: a person living in Canada who is racialized as white/has European ancestors

EUROCENTRIC: institutions and/or belief systems that place people of European heritage who are racialized as white at the center of leadership, knowledge production, and importance; typically associated with a view of whiteness as consistent with civilization and dominant notions of rational progress

FEMALE TO MALE (FTM): a trans person assigned female at birth who has medically and/or socially transitioned to a male identity

GAY-STRAIGHT ALLIANCE (GSA): clubs or student groups designed to reduce homo-negativity and support LGBT students, most typically at the high school level

GENDER CONFIRMATION SURGERY: surgical procedures that enable the body to conform to gender identity, including but not limited to chest reconstruction, genital reconstruction, and facial reconstruction; also referred to by the less preferred terminology of "sex reassignment surgery"

GENDER CONFORMING: consistent with normative binary sex/gender stereotypes or characteristics

GENDER DYSPHORIA (GD): the distress or dissonance that people of all ages may experience when their sex/gender identity is in conflict with the sex/gender identity they were assigned at birth or that their physical characteristics signal to others; a somewhat less pathologizing but still binary-oriented diagnosis that replaced GIDC (see below) in the fifth edition of the *DSM* in 2013

GENDER ESSENTIALISM: the assumption that biology plays a significant determining role in gender identity, which does not vary from one sociohistorical context to another

GENDER FLUID: a descriptor for someone for whom gender varies over time or an identity that resists binary categorization

GENDER IDENTITY DISORDER IN CHILDREN (GIDC): a diagnosis whose inclusion in the third edition of the *Diagnostic and Statistical Manual* in 1980 reflected the formal medicalization of gender nonconformity in children; a diagnosis whose focus is children who fail to conform to the sex/gender assigned to them at birth

GENDER LIMINAL: a descriptor for someone whose sex/gender identity is ambiguous (in the context of a sex/gender binary)

GENDER NEUTRAL: a descriptor for a person or place not organized according to sex/gender systems

GENDER NONCONFORMING: unwilling or unable to conform to binary sex/gender norms

GENDER QUEER; NONBINARY: someone who does not conform to binary sex/gender norms

GENDER SELF-DETERMINATION: the right of every person to know and be known according to an internal sense of gender identity

HETERONORMATIVE: people, spaces, and social practices organized on the basis of the centrality of the heterosexual couple

HOMONATIONALISM: homonormative nationalism; when privileged LGBT people express loyalty to the nation-state and/or when states position themselves as progressive on the basis of their inclusion of relatively privileged LGBT people

HOMONORMATIVITY: when more conservative/privileged LGBT people (white, wealthy, binary-gender conforming) experience social inclusion without troubling broader patterns of hierarchy and oppression

HOMOPHOBIA: fear and hatred of lesbian gay bisexual and queer people on the basis of an assumed norm of heterosexuality

HORMONE BLOCKERS: puberty-suppression therapy via medical intervention

HYPERANDROGENISM: a condition of women who are considered to have natural testosterone levels above the so-called normal female range

INDIGENOUS: the original inhabitants of a geographic territory; the preferred term for first peoples in general residing within the borders of the Canadian nation-state

INTERSEX: people whose genetic/reproductive traits defy simple binary sex categorization

LATINX: a gender-neutral ethnic descriptor for people of Latin heritage in the U.S. and Canada

MALE TO FEMALE (MTF): a trans person assigned male at birth who has medically and/or socially transitioned to a female identity

MICROAGGRESSIONS: "the death of 1,000 cuts"; daily and seemingly benign forms of oppression that, experienced collectively, produce trauma

MINORITY STRESS: the mental health consequences of oppression

MISGENDER: to apply a sex/gender descriptor or pronoun that is inconsistent with a person's self-defined sex/gender identity

NATIVE AMERICAN: the preferred term for Indigenous/first peoples in general residing within the borders of the U.S. nation-state

NECROCAPITALISM: the relationship between death and capitalist relations of production

NECROPOLITICS: the relationship between death and political power

NECROPOWER: the relationship between death and power

NEURODIVERSITY: the recognition that neurological variation among humans is normal, in opposition to a socially constructed mental state as the norm according to which variation is measured and pathologized

NONBINARY; TRANS NONBINARY: a descriptor for someone who identifies outside binary gender systems

PANSEXUAL: a descriptor for someone who is attracted to people regardless of sex/gender identity

PASSING: the ability to be intelligible to others in terms of one's self-defined gender identity

PHALLOPLASTY: surgical construction of a penis from the patient's own living tissue

POLYAMOROUS: being capable of or desiring intimate sexual relationships with more than one partner

POLYSEXUAL: typically refers to those who are attracted to trans, nonbinary, or genderqueer people but can also refer to people who are attracted to multiple genders

PRECARIOUSNESS; PRECARITY: the fundamental vulnerability that is characteristic of human life and the ways in which this fundamental vulnerability is striated

PRONOUNS: the gendered nouns used to refer to specific persons

RACIALIZATION: the social and historical process whereby a more powerful group imposes a framework of biological inferiority onto another

SEX REASSIGNMENT SURGERY: see GENITAL CONFIRMATION SURGERY

SOCIAL TRANSITION: the process of beginning to live as the sex/gender that one self-defines as

STEALTH: descriptor for a transgender person who passes or for whom information about their transgender status is kept private

TANNER SCALE: a normative scale for measuring physiological development according to a Eurocentric binary sex model

TITLE IX: the 1972 U.S. legislation that requires all institutions receiving federal funds to maintain gender equity

TOMBOY: a masculine, gender-nonconforming, or inadequately feminine girl

TOP SURGERY: a double mastectomy and nipple grafts for a male-contoured chest; breast implants and chest reconstruction for a female-contoured chest

TRANS: short form for "transgender"

TRANS BOY: a child or young person assigned female at birth who self-defines as a boy

TRANS-EXCLUSIVE RADICAL FEMINISTS (TERFS): a conservative/trans-oppressive strain of radical feminism that views gender in essentialist terms, or as inevitably linked to the genitals one is born with, and that sees transgender women as men masquerading as women

TRANSGENDER: an umbrella term for people who defy simplistic adherence to binary sex/gender categories

TRANS GIRL: a child or young person assigned male at birth who self-defines as a girl

TRANSINCLUSION: policies and practices related to transforming trans-oppressive/binary-normative environments to include people of all genders

TRANSNORMATIVE: a descriptor for relatively privileged transgender people who are willing and able to assimilate to binary gender systems and norms without calling into question broader relations of oppression

TRANS OPPRESSION: the discrimination and harm experienced by trans and gender-nonconforming people

TRANSPHOBIA: fear and hatred directed at those who do not conform to binary sex/gender systems and a mechanism for maintaining these systems

TRANSSEXUAL: a person who medically and socially transitions from their assigned sex at birth to their self-defined sex/gender

TWO-SPIRIT: A First Nations / Indigenous / Native American term to describe a person who has both a masculine and a feminine spirit; can relate to gender nonconformity or same-sex sexuality or both

VAGINOPLASTY: surgical construction of a vagina

NOTES

INTRODUCTION

1. Witterick, "Dancing in the Eye of the Storm," 21.
2. Serano, "Detransition, Desistance, and Disinformation."
3. I rely on the theorizing of critical disability scholar Tobin Siebers, in *Disability Theory*, to use the term "disabled" to refer to the way in which built environments confer privilege on some people and act to disable others. I elaborate on this topic at greater length in chapter 1.
4. Blum-Ross, "What Does It Mean for Children to Have a 'Voice' in Research?"
5. Marten, "Childhood Studies and History," 52–53.
6. Siebers, *Disability Theory*, 28.
7. Spade, *Normal Life*, 32.
8. Hellen, "Transgender Children in Schools," 92.
9. Thomas and Thomas, *Child in America*, 301.
10. Macionis and Gerber, *Sociology*, 132.
11. Meadow, "Child," 57–59.
12. barbara findlay deliberately spells her name without capitalization.
13. Underwood, "Ms. Chatelaine."
14. Canadian Press, "Human Rights Complaint."
15. Cloutier, "Transgender Girl's Human Rights Complaint."
16. Stout, "Transgender Teen Awarded $75,000 in School Restroom Lawsuit."
17. Queer Voices, "California's Assembly Bill 1266 for Transgender Student Rights Signed."
18. For example, the San Francisco Unified School District in 2004, the Toronto School Board in 2012, the Edmonton School Board in 2011, and the Vancouver School Board in 2014.
19. The preferred identity term for the peoples who, for over 10,000 years, have occupied the continent they refer to as "Turtle Island," on which the Canadian and U.S. white settler states were established, on the Canadian side of the border is "Indigenous," while south of the border, Indigenous peoples tend to self-identify as "Native American."
20. "Latinx" is a recently introduced gender-neutral term to describe persons of Latin American descent.
21. Most kids and parents use sex and gender terminology interchangeably; for example, it is not unusual for someone to define themselves as "male" in one

moment and a "boy" in another without implying different meanings. This is not something I feel it is necessary to investigate or trouble; rather, it reflects nonacademic common language.

22. Not to mention intersex individuals, whose genitals are ambiguous as far as binary categorization goes.

23. There is a literary and popular-culture history to troubling gendered pronouns, often in feminist science fiction. Think of the opening to science fiction writer Ursula K. Le Guin's 1969 book *The Left Hand of Darkness*, "The king was pregnant" (7) and the use of "Sir" to refer to Captain Janeway on *Star Trek* and Marge Piercy's use of "per" as a replacement for "him/her" in her 1976 novel *Woman on the Edge of Time*.

24. To misgender someone is to refer to them with gendered terms or pronouns that do not correspond to their affirmed identity.

25. Kapoor and Jordan, "Introduction," 4.

26. Mills, *Sociological Imagination*, 3.

CHAPTER 1. TRANSGENDER KIDS

1. Halberstam, *Female Masculinity*; Chinn, "I Was a Lesbian Child."

2. Pyne, "Gender Independent Kids."

3. Meadow, "Child."

4. Herman et al., "Age of Individuals Who Identify as Transgender."

5. Veale et al., *Being Safe, Being Me*.

6. Taylor and Peter, *Every Class in Every School*, 23.

7. See, for example, Hellen, "Transgender Children in Schools."

8. See, for example, Grossman and D'Augelli, "Transgender Youth and Life-Threatening Behaviors."

9. Goldberg and Adriano, "I'm a Girl"

10. Butler, *Gender Trouble*, 14.

11. Fausto-Sterling, *Sexing the Body*.

12. See, for example, Connell, *Gender*; Jordan-Young, *Brain Storm*; Karkazis et al., "Out of Bounds?"

13. Castañeda, "Childhood."

14. Stryker and Currah, "General Editors' Introduction," 303.

15. Matthews, "Window on the 'New' Sociology of Childhood."

16. Harris, *Gender as Soft Assembly*, 175.

17. Marx, "Eighteenth Brumaire of Louis Bonaparte," 595.

18. Stockton, *Queer Child*, 8.

19. Stafford, *Is It Still a Boy?*, 3–4.

20. See, for example, Dowling, *Frailty Myth*; Jordan-Young, *Brain Storm*.

21. Connell, *Gender*.

22. Thorne, *Gender Play*.

23. Connell, *Gender*, 103–104.

24. Her real name, as requested.

25. Crissman et al., "Transgender Demographics."
26. See, for example, Brill and Pepper, *Transgender Child*; Brill and Kenney, *Transgender Teen*; Ehrensaft, *Gender Born, Gender Made.*
27. There is considerable debate within scientific communities about the percentage of intersex people in the overall population. Feminist science scholar Anne Fausto-Sterling, in *Sexing the Body*, estimates that 1.7% of the population is intersex, while one critique of her research, by Leonard Sax ("How Common Is Intersex?") claims that the percentage is 100 times lower than that. The United States Affiliate of the Organization of Intersex International webpage claimed the 1.7% figure in 2015.
28. National Center for Transgender Equality, "Understanding the Passport Gender Change Policy."
29. Government of British Columbia, "Change of Gender Designation."
30. An intersex birth certificate was issued recently; see Levin, "First US Person to Have 'Intersex' on Birth Certificate."
31. Government of Ontario, Ministry of Transportation, "New 'X' Gender Option Now Available."
32. Wamsley, "Oregon Adds a New Gender Option."
33. See, for example, the Gender-Free I.D. Coalition: http://gender-freeidcoalition.ca.
34. Zeidler, "Parent Fights to Omit Gender."
35. S. Mills, "Gender-Neutral Birth Certificate Fight."
36. Ranging from hormone therapy to surgery depending on jurisdiction.
37. See, for example, Burke, *Gender Shock*; Butler, *Gender Trouble*; Halberstam, *Female Masculinity*; Halberstam, *In a Queer Time and Place*; Noble, *Sons of the Movement*; Travers, "Queering Sport"; Travers and Deri, "Transgender Inclusion."
38. For example, Namaste, *Invisible Lives*; Namaste, *Sex Change, Social Change.*
39. Elliot, *Debates in Transgender, Queer, and Feminist Theory.*
40. Holman and Goldberg, "Ethical, Legal, and Psychosocial Issues."
41. Travers, "Queering Sport."
42. See, for example, Gill-Peterson, "Technical Capacities of the Body"; and Saketopoulou, "Minding the Gap."
43. Hatred of the female and the feminine; Sedgwick, *Epistemology of the Closet.*
44. Serano, "Detransition, Desistance, and Disinformation."
45. His real name, as per his mother's wishes.
46. Hormone blockers.
47. Finn died in June 2017.
48. Butler, *Frames of War*, 14.
49. Lorey, *State of Insecurity*, 10.
50. Ibid., 12.
51. Ibid., 2.
52. Foucault, *Birth of Biopolitics.*
53. Butler, *Frames of War*, 25.
54. Siebers, *Disability Theory*, 12.

55. Thobani, *Exalted Subjects*.

56. Glenn, "Settler Colonialism as Structure," 57.

57. See, for example, Gill-Peterson, "Technical Capacities of the Body"; Gosset, "Silhouettes of Defiance"; Haritaworn, "Loyal Repetitions of the Nation"; Haritaworn, Kuntsman, and Posocco, *Queer Necropolitics*; Kumashiro, *Troubling Intersections of Race and Sexuality*; Kumashiro, *Troubling Education*; Puar, *Terrorist Assemblages*; Puar, "Homonationalism as Assemblage"; Puar, "Q&A with Jasbir Puar"; Snorton and Haritaworn, "Trans Necropolitics"; Weheliye, *Habeas Viscus*.

58. Pascoe, *Dude, You're a Fag*, 10.

59. Ibid., 55.

60. See, for example, the works of Sherene Razack, Sunera Thobani, Eva Mackey, and Delia Douglas.

61. See, for example, Coulthard, *Red Skin, White Masks*; and Simpson, *Dancing on Our Turtle's Back*.

62. Crenshaw, *Fighting the Post–Affirmative Action War*; Higginbotham, "African American Women's History"; P. Collins, *Black Feminist Thought*; P. Collins, *Black Sexual Politics*; hooks, *Feminist Theory from Margin to Center*; hooks, *Yearning*; hooks, *All about Love*; Lorde, *Sister Outsider*; McKittrick, *Sylvia Wynter*; and Williams, *Alchemy of Race and Rights*.

63. Assemblage refers to integrated systems of oppression: an intricate web of social history / social forces that surround us and impact experience in embodied ways. See, for example, Puar, *Terrorist Assemblages*.

64. Mbembe, "Necropolitics," 11.

65. Berlant, "Slow Death."

66. Gilmore, *Golden Gulag*, 28.

67. Bannerjee, "Necrocapitalism."

68. Such as colonialism, the Nazi concentration camps, apartheid, and the Israeli occupation of Gaza.

69. See, for example, Snorton and Haritaworn, "Trans Necropolitics"; Haritaworn, Kuntsman, and Posocco, *Queer Necropolitics*; Puar, *Terrorist Assemblages*.

70. Noble, *Sons of the Movement*; Noble, "My Own Set of Keys"; Noble, "Our Bodies Are Not Ourselves"; Spade, *Normal Life*; Stanley, "Gender Self-Determination"; Stanley and Smith, *Captive Genders*; Stryker, "Transgender History, Homonormativity, and Disciplinarity."

71. In *The Twilight of Equality: Neoliberalism, Cultural Politics, and the Attack on Democracy*, Lisa Duggan coined the term "homonormativity" to describe "a politics that does not contest dominant heteronormative assumptions and institutions, but upholds and sustains them, while promising the possibility of a demobilized gay constituency, and a gay culture anchored in domesticity and consumption" (50). Duggan purports that visible white and/or "respectable" (middle-class consumers) LGBT individuals who conform to binary sex and gender norms have achieved rights and experience a measure of inclusion, without having unsettled the foundations of oppression.

72. Susan Stryker proposed this terminology in correspondence with Jasbir Puar; Stryker, personal communication, 2016.
73. Jasbir Puar, for example, builds on Duggan's concept of homonormativity in *Terrorist Assemblages* to describe assimilationist, rights-oriented LGBT campaigns, coining the terms "homonationalism" (homonormative nationalism) and "queer necropolitics." In this sense, previously abject but comparatively privileged (white, middle- and upper-class) queer and trans people are being "folded into life," welcomed into the nation, accorded with citizenship. From this perspective, the newly welcomed among the transgender community are more likely to be transnormative at least to some extent (binary conforming, middle class, white). Similarly, in "Settler Homonationalism: Theorizing Settler Colonialism within Queer Modernities," Scott Morgensen describes the way in which privileged LGBT subjects buy into the community as "naturalizing settler colonialism" (121).
74. Snorton and Haritaworn, "Trans Necropolitics."
75. Homonormative nationalism: Puar, *Terrorist Assemblages*.
76. In the introduction to *Queer Necropolitics*, Jin Haritaworn, Adi Kuntsman, and Silvia Posocco emphasize that "social inclusion is realized through practices of 'letting die,' that is, through dying in abandonment. Letting die, abandonment, and differential belonging are directly connected to the operations of forms of governance in late liberalism that determine some subjects as morally deserving, while simultaneously justifying punitive measures for those deemed undeserving as necessary, just, and rational" (7–8).
77. Grant et al., *Injustice at Every Turn*, 2.
78. Ibid., 29.
79. Appell, "Pre-political Child of Child-Centred Jurisprudence," 20.
80. Butler, *Frames of War*.
81. The boundary between childhood and adulthood is linked to the "age of majority," which varies from 18 to 21 depending on jurisdiction in Canada and the U.S.
82. Klocker, "Example of 'Thin' Agency," 85.
83. Pierce, "Psychiatric Problems of the Black Minority."
84. Nordmarken, "Microaggressions," 130.
85. I return to this topic in more detail in chapter 3.
86. Meiners, "Offending Children, Registering Sex."
87. Stockton, *Queer Child*, 5.
88. Carter, *Quality of Home Runs*, 23.
89. Stockton, *Queer Child*.
90. Puar, "Rethinking Homonationalism," 338.
91. Chinn, "I Was a Lesbian Child," 158.
92. See, for example, Hodgson, "Childhood of the Race"; Meiners, "Trouble with the *Child* in the Carceral State."
93. Siebers, *Disability Theory*, 288.
94. Flasher, "Adultism," 521.

95. Weheliye, *Habeas Viscus*, 4.

96. Siebers, *Disability Theory*, 281.

97. Ibid., 289.

98. Ibid., 284.

99. I address the disabling role of bathrooms and other facets of sex segregation specifically in chapter 3.

100. Siebers, *Disability Theory*, 28.

101. Snorton, comments at "Trans-of-Color Roundtable Discussion," Trans* Studies Conference, Tucson, AZ, 2016.

CHAPTER 2. SCHOOLS

1. Rubber bands were linked together and held by one girl at each end to form a modified sort of high jump. The goal was to jump over the rope of rubber bands, and you were allowed to use a foot to pull it down to jump over. It was incredibly acrobatic, and the girls who were good at it were astonishing in their athleticism. I was pretty good at it, and I missed it when I moved on to middle school, where we are all too cool to play like that anymore.

2. For example, OECD, *Equity and Quality in Education*.

3. Taylor and Peter, *Every Class in Every School*, 15–18.

4. GLSEN, *2015 National School Climate Survey*, 4–6.

5. Ibid., 5.

6. Berkowitz and Ryan, "Bathrooms, Baseball, and Bra Shopping."

7. Menvielle, "Comprehensive Program," 359.

8. Ibid., 359–360.

9. Ibid., 360.

10. Pascoe, *Dude, You're a Fag*.

11. Ibid.

12. Hellen, "Transgender Children in Schools."

13. Frank's father is no longer on the scene, and a court order prohibits him from contact.

14. See, for example, Hoffman, "Risky Investments."

15. Madigan and Gamble, *The Second Rape*.

16. Dr. Kenneth Zucker is a prominent psychiatrist specializing in the corrective treatment of trans and gender-nonconforming children. I situate Dr. Zucker in the treatment field more thoroughly in chapter 5.

17. Menvielle, "Comprehensive Program."

18. Private schools in British Columbia receive government funding and are subject to the British Columbia Human Rights Code.

19. The family decided to settle out of court rather than spend years fighting the case. They did not want to put Tru through that.

20. Asaf Orr, attorney for the National Center for Lesbian Rights, insists that transgender status is confidential medical information and should be treated by all school personnel accordingly; person communication, 2015.

21. "Two spirit" is a term embraced by a number of Indigenous communities in Canada and the United States to refer to community members who are neither male nor female or whose sexuality cannot be described as heterosexual.
22. Vancouver School Board, "ACB-R-1."
23. As it did in Vancouver and typically throughout Canada and the U.S. for LGBT-positive measures in schools.
24. Pascoe, *Dude, You're a Fag*, 166–167.
25. Meiners, "Trouble with the *Child* in the Carceral State"; Quinn and Meiners, "From Anti-Bullying Laws and Gay Marriages."
26. Meyer, *Gender and Sexual Diversity in Schools*.

CHAPTER 3. SPACES

1. This chapter is partly based on a previous chapter published in *Child's Play*, edited by Michael Messner and Michela Musto: Ann Travers, "Transgender and Gender Nonconforming Kids and the Binary Requirements of Sport Participation in North America." Since that publication, policy analysis has been updated, and additional interviews have been conducted.
2. See, for example, Fausto-Sterling, *Sexing the Body*; Karkazis et al., "Out of Bounds?"
3. Butler, *Undoing Gender*, 34.
4. Some of the authors I cite in this manuscript published their work under first names they no longer attach to themselves, and I follow their current lead in identifying them. While this frustrates bibliographic systems and sometimes makes locating a source a little less straightforward, affirming their gender self-determination and self-naming is a crucial aspect of a trans-positive politics.
5. Halberstam, *Female Masculinity*, 23.
6. Browne, "Genderism and the Bathroom Problem," 335, 336, 339 (my emphasis).
7. Ibid.; Molotch and Nolen, *Toilet*.
8. Browne, "Genderism and the Bathroom Problem," 336.
9. Lorber, *Breaking the Bowls*, 35–36.
10. H. Davis, *Beyond Trans*, 80.
11. Cavanagh, *Queering Bathrooms*; Meiners, "Offending Children, Registering Sex."
12. T. Ring, "Supreme Court to Hear Gavin Graham Case."
13. For a comprehensive overview of state attempts to pass anti-trans bathroom legislation, see Kralik, "'Bathroom Bill' Legislative Tracking."
14. Stern, "HB2 'Repeal' Bill."
15. Abramson, "North Carolina Governor."
16. The NBA announced after the partial repeal that it will hold its 2019 All-Star Game in North Carolina.
17. Stern, "HB2 'Repeal' Bill."
18. Davis and Apuzzo, "US Directs Public Schools."
19. T. Ring, "Supreme Court to Hear Gavin Graham Case."
20. Lopez, "Trump's Justice Department Just Rescinded a Memo."

21. Marimow, "Case of Virginia Transgender Teen."
22. Open Parliament, Bill C-16.
23. Ricci, "Transgender Child Told You Can't Use Girls' Bathroom."
24. "Family of Bella Burgos."
25. Quoted in Ricci, "Transgender Child Told You Can't Use Girls' Bathroom."
26. "Family of Bella Burgos."
27. Cloutier, "Transgender Girl's Human Rights Complaint."
28. Ibid.
29. Karkazis et al., "Out of Bounds?"
30. The underlying assumption of sex-segregated sporting spaces is that someone who is born male naturally has an "unfair advantage" when competing against women in sport. Assumptions of unfair advantage lean heavily on a Western trope of white, female frailty (to justify a long-reviled and scientifically unfounded practice of sex-verification testing). Assumptions of female inferiority rest on the ideology of the two-sex system, and this ideology plays a significant cultural and economic role in the devaluation of women, gays and lesbians, and transgender people. See, for example, Cavanagh and Sykes, "Transsexual Bodies at the Olympics"; Dowling, *Frailty Myth*; Love, "Transgender Exclusion and Inclusion in Sport"; Sullivan, "Gender Verification and Gender Policies"; Sykes, "Transsexual and Transgender Policies in Sport."
31. Cauterucci, "Trans Boy Who Won the Texas Girls' Wrestling Title."
32. Ibid.
33. Wong, "Texas Sportscaster Shreds Trans Phobes."
34. Carter, *Quality of Home Runs*, 13.
35. T. Collins, *Sport in Capitalist Society*.
36. Bullough and Bullough, *Cross Dressing*.
37. Pronger, *Arena of Masculinity*.
38. Carrington and McDonald, "Marxism, Cultural Studies and Sport."
39. Ibid.; Banet-Weiser, *Most Beautiful Girl in the World*; Crenshaw, *Fighting the Post–Affirmative Action War*; Douglas and Jamieson, "Farewell to Remember"; Douglas, "Wages of Whiteness"; Dworkin and Wachs, *Body Panic*; Collins, *Black Sexual Politics*; Travers, "Thinking the Unthinkable"; Travers and Deri "Transgender Inclusion and the Changing Face."
40. Puar, *Terrorist Assemblages*.
41. Kirby and Huebner, "Talking about Sex"; Davis, *Beyond Trans*; Pieper, *Sex Testing*.
42. Butler, *Undoing Gender*; Butler, *Gender Trouble*; Fausto-Sterling, *Sexing the Body*; Halberstam, *Female Masculinity*; Haraway, *Modest_Witness*; Haraway, *Simians, Cyborgs and Women*; Jordan-Young, *Brain Storm*; Pieper, *Sex Testing*.
43. Jordan-Young, *Brain Storm*; Karkazis et al., "Out of Bounds?"
44. To justify a long-reviled and scientifically unfounded practice of sex-verification testing for women athletes only, the International Olympic Committee (IOC) and its affiliates finally discontinued the practice of sex-verification testing for all women competitors prior to the 2000 Olympic Games.

45. M. Kane, "Resistance/Transformation," 191.
46. See, for example, Dowling, *Frailty Myth*; Pronger, *Arena of Masculinity*; J. Ring, *Stolen Bases*.
47. See, for example, Birrell and McDonald, *Reading Sport*; Messner, *Power at Play*; Messner, Dunbar, and Hunt, "Televised Sports Manhood Formula"; van Sterkenburg and Knoppers, "Dominant Discourses about Race/Ethnicity."
48. See, for example, Broad, "Gendered Unapologetic"; Cahn, *Coming on Strong*; M. Hall, *Girl and the Game*; Heywood and Dworkin, *Built to Win*.
49. See, for example, Cohen, *No Girls in the Clubhouse*; Dowling, *Frailty Myth*.
50. McDonagh and Pappano, *Playing with the Boys*, 6.
51. Burstyn, *Rites of Men*.
52. Teetzel, "On Transgendered Athletes, Fairness and Doping."
53. McArdle, "Swallows and Amazons."
54. Sykes, "Transsexual and Transgender Policies in Sport."
55. Travers, "Thinking the Unthinkable."
56. Meyer, *Gender and Sexual Diversity in Schools*, 9.
57. Messner, "Gender Ideologies, Youth Sports," 151.
58. Ibid.
59. Travers, "Sport Nexus and Gender Injustice"; McDonagh and Pappano, *Playing with the Boys*; J. Ring, *Stolen Bases*; Cohen, *No Girls in the Clubhouse*.
60. Travers, "Sport Nexus and Gender Injustice"; Travers "Queering Sport"; Travers, "Women's Ski Jumping"; Travers, "Thinking the Unthinkable," Travers and Deri, "Transgender Inclusion."
61. Doull et al., "Are We Leveling the Playing Field?"
62. GLSEN, *2015 National School Climate Survey*, 5.
63. Sabo, "Myth of the Sexual Athlete."
64. His real name, by request: Cory is a very public trans activist, and being visible as a trans person is very important to him.
65. Pascoe, *Dude, You're a Fag*, 51.
66. Ehrensaft, personal communication, 2012.
67. IOC Medical Commission, "Statement of the Stockholm Consensus on Sex Reassignment in Sports."
68. Sykes, "Transsexual and Transgender Policies in Sport."
69. Cavanagh and Sykes, "Transsexual Bodies at the Olympics"; Love, "Transgender Exclusion and Inclusion in Sport."
70. Griffin and Carroll, *On the Team*, 25.
71. Pieper, *Sex Testing*, 182.
72. Cavanagh and Sykes, "Transsexual Bodies at the Olympics"; Pieper, *Sex Testing*.
73. Nyong'o, "Unforgiveable Transgression of Being Caster Semenya."
74. Pieper, *Sex Testing*.
75. In "On Transgendered Athletes, Fairness and Doping: An International Challenge," Sarah Teetzel successfully uncouples concerns about testosterone as a performance-enhancing substance from concerns about steroid use in sport by

establishing that the performance-enhancement effect resulting from doping is far greater than any advantage, if such advantage exists at all, from past or present levels of testosterone predating or resulting from gender transition. Indeed, Teetzel regards the latter as negligible.

76. Pieper, *Sex Testing*, 183.
77. BBC Sport, "Dutee Chand Cleared to Race."
78. Carr, "Here's What the 2018 Olympic Gender Regulations Look Like."
79. "Tearful Lynsey Sharp."
80. Bull, "Caster Semenya wins Olympic gold but faces more scrutiny."
81. H. Davis, *Beyond Trans*, 112.
82. Harper, "Using Testosterone to Categorise."
83. Love, "Transgender Exclusion and Inclusion in Sport," 380.
84. Travers, "Queering Sport."
85. U.S. Transgender Law and Policy Institute, *Guidelines for Creating Policies*, 2–3.
86. Referring to all 50 U.S. states.
87. LGBT Sports Foundation, "All 50."
88. Canadian Centre for Ethics in Sport, *Sport in Transition*, 29.
89. Public Health Agency of Canada, *Questions and Answers*, 9.
90. TransAthlete.com, "K–12 Policies."
91. The Alberta organization is a voluntary organization, while the other three have set policies that must be complied with.
92. Gruneau, "There Will Never Be Another Gordie Howe."
93. Love, "Transgender Exclusion and Inclusion in Sport," 382.
94. McDonagh and Pappano, *Playing with the Boys*, 6.

CHAPTER 4. PARENTS

1. Ehrensaft, *Gender Born, Gender Made*.
2. Pyne, "Gender Independent Kids."
3. GIDC was the diagnosis listed in the *Diagnostic and Statistical Manual* from 1980 to 2012.
4. Menvielle, "Comprehensive Program," 363.
5. Klein and Golub, "Family Rejection as a Predictor," 193.
6. Roberts et al., "Childhood Gender Nonconformity."
7. Meadow, "Child."
8. Nestle, *Persistent Desire*.
9. Ehrensaft, personal communication, 2012.
10. Certainly not those headed by trans-exclusive radical feminists!
11. Ehrensaft, personal communication, 2012.
12. Grossman and D'Augelli, "Transgender Youth and Life-Threatening Behaviors."
13. Dylan is not the first transgender person in his family. His older sister is a transgender woman whose own struggles with poverty (Dylan reported that she was homeless for some time) have been a barrier to her obtaining trans-affirming healthcare.

14. Manning, "Attached Advocacy and the Rights of the Trans Child."
15. Ibid., 584.
16. Ibid., 585.
17. Ibid., 590.
18. Ibid.
19. Watson, "Accumulating Cares," 27.
20. Ibid., 262–263.
21. Manning et al., "Fighting for Trans* Kids."
22. Ward, "Gender Labor."
23. Manning, "Attached Advocacy and the Rights of the Trans Child," 583–584.
24. Allen, "Court Ruling a Victory for Transgender Boy."
25. Edwards-Leeper and Spack, "Psychological Evaluation and Medical Treatment," 331.
26. E. Kane, Gender Trap.
27. Nora, however, worries about trans kids using the Internet to learn about themselves because "often the first thing you find when you Google something is the suicide stats."
28. Connell, Gender; Jordan-Young, Brain Storm; H. Davis, Beyond Trans.
29. Manning, "Attached Advocacy and the Rights of the Trans Child," 585.
30. E. Kane, Gender Trap.

CHAPTER 5. SUPPORTIVE HEALTHCARE

1. Gill-Peterson, "Technical Capacities of the Body."
2. E. Kane, Gender Trap; Serano, "Detransition, Desistance, and Disinformation."
3. Bryant, "Making Gender Identity Disorder of Childhood."
4. Psychological/psychiatric treatment designed to "cure" gay, lesbian, and trans and gender-nonconforming people.
5. American Psychiatric Association, Diagnostic and Statistical Manual, 3rd ed.
6. Pyne, "Governance of Gender Non-conforming Children," 79.
7. Sedgwick, "How to Bring Your Kids Up Gay"; Burke, Gender Shock.
8. Bryant, "In Defense of Gay Children?"
9. "Mad pride" activists resist the stigma associated with mental illness and challenge neuronormativity, insisting that neurodiversity is a feature of humanity; Fitzpatrick, "Trans Activists, Don't Throw Mad People under the Bus!"
10. Butler, Undoing Gender, 8.
11. Joel et al., "Queering Gender," 314.
12. Bryant, "Diagnosis and Medicalization."
13. Winters, "Proposed Gender Dysphoria Diagnosis in the DSM-5."
14. Tosh, Perverse Psychology, 14.
15. Pyne, "Gender Independent Kids," 3.
16. Formerly the Harry Benjamin International Gender Dysphoria Association.
17. Serano, "Detransition, Desistance, and Disinformation."
18. Giordano, "Lives in a Chiaroscuro," 580.

19. Serano, "Detransition, Desistance, and Disinformation."
20. Such as Wente, "Transgender Kids"; Singal, "How the Fight over Transgender Kids."
21. Gill-Peterson, "Technical Capacities of the Body"; Meadow, "Child."
22. Butler, *Frames of War*, 25.
23. Meadow, "Child."
24. Chinn, "I Was a Lesbian Child"; Halberstam, *Female Masculinity*.
25. Meadow, "Child," 58.
26. Tannehill, "Truth about Transgender Suicide" (my emphasis).
27. Ainsworth and Spiegel, "Quality of Life of Individuals," 1019.
28. U.S. Department of Health and Human Services, Office of the Surgeon General and National Action Alliance for Suicide Prevention, *2012 National Strategy for Suicide Prevention*, 122.
29. Haritaworn, Kuntsman, and Posocco, introduction to *Queer Necropolitics*, 16.
30. Gill-Peterson, "Technical Capacities of the Body," 414.
31. Edwards-Leeper and Spack, "Psychological Evaluation and Medical Treatment," 323.
32. Morgensen, "Settler Homonationalism."
33. Gill-Peterson, "Technical Capacities of the Body," 412.
34. Ibid., 413.
35. Bucar and Enke, "Unlikely Sex Change Capitals of the World," 323.
36. Johanna Olson-Kennedy is an adolescent-medicine physician specializing in the care of trans and gender-nonconforming children and youth. She is an assistant professor at the Children's Hospital of Los Angeles.
37. Haritaworn, Kuntsman, and Posocco, introduction to *Queer Necropolitics*, 16.
38. For example, plastic surgery, razors, and cosmetics.
39. Gill-Peterson, "Technical Capacities of the Body," 408.
40. Ibid., 407.
41. Quoted in Dreyfus and Rabinow, *Michel Foucault*, 187.
42. Gilmore, *Golden Gulag*, 28.

CONCLUSION

1. Government of Canada, "Bill C-16."
2. Capehart, "Clinton's Geneva Accord."
3. Davis and Apuzzo, "US Directs Public Schools."
4. Quinn and Meiners, "From Anti-Bullying Laws and Gay Marriages."
5. As noted in chapter 3, for example, the passage of HB2 had significant financial consequences for the state of North Carolina.
6. See, for example, Razack, "Gendered Racial Violence"; Mackey, *House of Difference*.
7. I have summarized this case in the introduction.
8. There is critical debate within queer and trans communities about the value of being able to serve openly in the military, given its role in spreading violence across

the globe; however, it is important to note that for many low-income Canadians and Americans, many of whom are members of visible minorities, the military is a much-needed source of employment and is often the only route available for postsecondary education.

9. Grzanka and Mann, "Queer Youth Suicide."

10. Puar, *Terrorist Assemblages*; Snorton and Haritaworn, "Trans Necropolitics"; Haritaworn, Kuntsman, and Posocco, *Queer Necropolitics*; Morgensen, "Settler Homonationalism"; Meiners, "Trouble with the *Child* in the Carceral State."

11. Lynch, "Attorney General Loretta E. Lynch."

12. For example, Duggan, *Twilight of Equality*; Puar, *Terrorist Assemblages*; Whitehead, *Nuptial Deal*.

13. Puar, *Terrorist Assemblages*, 10, xii.

14. Stanley, "Gender Self-Determination," 90.

15. Fraser, "Feminist Politics in the Age of Recognition," 27.

16. Lister, "Inclusive Citizenship."

17. Indigenous women were enfranchised in 1950 in Canada, although the lack of ballot boxes until 1962 made this legal capacity meaningless. In the United States, Native American women received the right to vote in 1924, and Black women received the right to vote along with white women in 1920; but until the 1965 Voting Rights Act, minority voting rights were largely symbolic.

18. Regarding the University of British Columbia's pursuit of diversity via the hiring of white women, see Thobani, "After UBC Ousted Arvind Gupta as President."

19. Razack, *Casting Out*, 4.

20. Thobani, *Exalted Subjects*.

21. See, for example, Krebs, "Hockey and the Reproduction of Colonialism in Canada"; and Denis, *We Are Not You*.

22. Thobani, *Exalted Subjects*, 76.

23. Puar, "Q&A with Jasbir Puar."

24. Kumashiro, *Troubling Intersections of Race and Sexuality*, 5.

25. Williams Institute, "Incarceration Rate of LGB People."

26. Correctional Investigator, *Annual Report*; Brosnahan, "Canada's Prison Population."

27. Government of Canada and the Province of British Columbia, "What Is a Hate Crime?"

28. Meiners, "Trouble with the *Child* in the Carceral State."

29. Snorton and Haritaworn, "Trans Necropolitics," 73.

30. In contrast, there has been no interruption of police violence against people of color, as evinced by the attention the Black Lives Matter movement has brought to the many Black people who have been murdered by police and security forces. See www.blacklivesmatter.com.

31. Lamble, "Queer Investments in Punitiveness," 151.

32. Slater, "Fire on the 57 Bus in Oakland."

33. Ibid.

34. I use "fat" not in a pejorative sense but in keeping with the way fat activists have reclaimed the term.
35. Freeman et al., *Health of Canada's Young People*, 167.
36. Quinn and Meiners, "From Anti-Bullying Laws," 157.
37. Berlowitz, Frye, and Jette, "Bullying and Zero-Tolerance Policies."
38. Lacharite and Marini, "Bullying Prevention and the Rights of Children," 313–314.
39. Fields et al., "Beyond Bullying."
40. Lacharite and Marini, "Bullying Prevention and the Rights of Children," 306–307.
41. See, for example, Berlowitz, Frye, and Jette, "Bullying and Zero-Tolerance Policies"; Gebhard, "Pipeline to Prison"; Hodgson, "Childhood of the Race."
42. Berlowitz, Frye, and Jette, "Bullying and Zero-Tolerance Policies," 3.
43. Quinn and Meiners, "From Anti-Bullying Laws and Gay Marriages," 158–159.
44. Hodgson, "Childhood of the Race," 41.
45. Meiners, "Ending the School-to-Prison Pipeline," 553.
46. Lacharite and Marini, "Bullying Prevention and the Rights of Children," 299.
47. Berlowitz, Frye, and Jette, "Bullying and Zero-Tolerance Policies," 13–14.
48. Quinn and Meiners, "From Anti-Bullying Laws," 161–163.
49. Meiners, "Trouble with the *Child* in the Carceral State," 132.
50. Quinn and Meiners, "From Anti-Bullying Laws," 168.
51. Butler, *Undoing Gender*, 32–33.
52. Siebers, *Disability Theory*, 73.
53. Kabeer, *Inclusive Citizenship*, 23, 21–22.
54. Lister et al., *Gendering Citizenship in Western Europe*, 9–10.
55. Arendt, *Origins of Totalitarianism*.
56. Canadian Civil Liberties Association, *Information Guide: LGBTQ Rights*.
57. N. Davis, "Drop in Teenage Suicide Attempts."
58. Manning, "Attached Advocacy and the Rights of the Trans Child," 590.
59. Dryden and McGregor, *In School*.

BIBLIOGRAPHY

Abramson, Alana. "North Carolina Governor Who Signed Bathroom Bill Says People Are 'Reluctant' to Hire Him." *Time*, March 15, 2017. www.time.com.

Ainsworth, Tiffany, and Jeffrey Spiegel. "Quality of Life of Individuals with and without Facial Feminization Surgery or Gender Reassignment Surgery." *Quality of Life Research* 19 (2010): 1019–1024.

Allen, Samantha Wright. "Court Ruling a Victory for Transgender Boy." *Prince George Citizen*, April 28, 2016. www.princegeorgecitizen.com.

American Civil Liberties Union. "This Court Decision in the Gavin Grimm Case Will Bring Tears to Your Eyes." April 10, 2017. www.aclu.org.

———. "What Is the School-to-Prison Pipeline?" 2013. www.aclu.org.

American Psychiatric Association. *Diagnostic and Statistical Manual.* 3rd ed. Washington, DC: American Psychiatric Association, 1980.

———*Diagnostic and Statistical Manual.* 5th ed. Washington, DC: American Psychiatric Association, 2013.

Appell, Annette. "The Pre-Political Child of Child-Centred Jurisprudence." In *The Children's Table: Childhood Studies and the Humanities*, edited by Anna Mae Duane, 19–37. Athens: University of Georgia Press, 2013.

Arendt, Hannah. *The Origins of Totalitarianism.* Orlando, FL: Harvest Books, 1973.

Banet-Weiser, Sarah. *The Most Beautiful Girl in the World: Beauty Pageants and National Identity.* Berkeley: University of California Press, 1999.

Bannerjee, Subhabrata. "Necrocapitalism." *Organization Studies* 29 (2008): 1541–1563.

BBC Sport. "Dutee Chand Cleared to Race as IAAF Suspends 'Gender Test' Rules." July 27, 2015. www.bbc.com.

———. "Dutee Chand: I Lost All My Honour in Landmark Gender Case." July 28, 2017. www.bbc.com.

Berkowitz, Dana, and Maura Ryan. "Bathrooms, Baseball, and Bra Shopping: Lesbian and Gay Parents Talk about Engendering Their Children." *Sociological Perspectives* 54, no. 3 (2011): 329–350.

Berlant, Lauren. "Slow Death (Sovereignty, Obesity, Lateral Agency)." *Critical Inquiry* 33, no. 4 (2007): 754–780.

Berlowitz, Marvin J., Rinda Frye, and Kelli M. Jette. "Bullying and Zero-Tolerance Policies: The School to Prison Pipeline." *Multicultural Learning and Teaching*, 2015, 1–19.

Birrell Susan, and Mary G. McDonald, eds. *Reading Sport: Critical Essays on Power and Representation.* Boston: Northeastern University Press, 2000.

Blum-Ross, Alicia. "What Does It Mean for Children to Have a 'Voice' in Research?" Connected Learning Research Network, August 18, 2016. http://clrn.dmlhub.net.

Brill, Stephanie, and Lisa Kenney. *The Transgender Teen: A Handbook for Families and Professionals Supporting Transgender and Non-binary Teens.* Jersey City, NJ: Cleis, 2016.

Brill, Stephanie, and Rachel Pepper. *The Transgender Child: A Handbook for Families and Professionals.* San Francisco: Cleis, 2008.

Broad, Kendal L. "The Gendered Unapologetic: Queer Resistance in Women's Sport." *Sociology of Sport Journal* 18 (2001): 181–203.

Brosnahan, Maureen. "Canada's Prison Population at All-Time High." CBC News, November 25 2013. www.cbc.ca.

Browne, Kath. "Genderism and the Bathroom Problem: (re)Materialising Sexed Sites, (re)Creating Sexed Bodies." *Gender, Place & Culture* 11, no. 3 (2004): 331–346.

Bryant, Karl. "Diagnosis and Medicalization." In *Sociology of Diagnosis*, edited by P. J. McCann and David J. Hutson, 33–57. Bingley, UK: Emerald, 2011.

———. "In Defense of Gay Children? 'Progay' Homophobia and the Production of Homonormativity." *Sexualities* 11, no. 4 (2008): 455–475.

———. "Making Gender Identity Disorder of Childhood: Historical Lessons for Contemporary Debates." *Sexuality Research and Social Policy* 3, no. 3 (2006): 23–29.

Bucar, Elizabeth, and Finn Enke. "Unlikely Sex Change Capitals of the World: Trinidad, United States, and Tehran, Iran, as Twin Yardsticks of Homonormative Liberalism." *Feminist Studies* 37, no. 2 (2011): 301–328.

Bull, Andy. "Caster Semenya Wins Olympic Gold but Faces More Scrutiny as IAAF Presses Case." *Guardian*, August 21, 2016. www.theguardian.com.

Bullough Vern L., and Bonnie Bullough. *Cross Dressing, Sex, and Gender.* Philadelphia: University of Pennsylvania Press, 1993.

Burke, Phyllis. *Gender Shock.* New York: Doubleday, 1990.

Burstyn, Varda. *The Rites of Men: Manhood, Politics and the Culture of Sport.* Toronto: University of Toronto Press, 1999.

Butler, Judith. *Frames of War: When Is Life Grievable?* London: Verso, 2009.

———. *Gender Trouble: Feminism and the Subversion of Identity.* New York: Routledge, 1990.

———. *Undoing Gender.* New York: Routledge, 2004.

Cahn, Susan K. *Coming on Strong: Gender and Sexuality in Twentieth-Century Women's Sport.* Cambridge, MA: Harvard University Press, 1995.

Canadian Centre for Ethics in Sport. *Sport in Transition: Making Sport in Canada More Responsible for Gender Inclusivity.* Ottawa: Canadian Centre for Ethics in Sport, 2012.

Canadian Civil Liberties Association. *Information Guide: LGBTQ Rights in Schools.* July 2014. http://ccla.org.

Canadian Press. "Human Rights Complaint Prompts New Gender Policy in Vancouver Catholic Schools." Canadian Broadcasting Corporation, July 16, 2014.

Canadian Teachers Federation. *Supporting Transgender and Transsexual Students in K–12 Schools: A Guide for Educators.* Ottawa: Canadian Teachers Federation, 2012.

Capehart, Jonathan. "Clinton's Geneva Accord: 'Gay Rights Are Human Rights.'" *Washington Post*, December 7, 2011. www.washingtonpost.com.

Carr, Grace. "Here's What the 2018 Olympic Gender Regulations Look Like." Daily Caller, July 3, 2017. http://dailycaller.com.

Carrington, Ben, and Ian McDonald. "Marxism, Cultural Studies and Sport: Mapping the Field." In *Marxism, Cultural Studies and Sport*, edited by Ben Carrington and Ian McDonald, 1–12. New York: Routledge, 2009.

Carter, Thomas. *The Quality of Home Runs: The Passion, Politics, and Language of Cuban Baseball.* Durham, NC: Duke University Press, 2008.

Castañeda, Claudia. "Childhood." *Transgender Studies Quarterly* 1, nos. 1–2 (2014): 59–61.

Cauterucci, Christina. "The Trans Boy Who Won the Texas Girls' Wrestling Title Exposes the Illogic of Anti-Trans Policy." *Slate*, February 27, 2017. www.slate.com.

Cavanagh, Sheila. *Queering Bathrooms: Gender, Sexuality, and a Hygienic Imagination.* Toronto: University of Toronto Press, 2010.

Cavanagh, Sheila, and Heather Sykes. "Transsexual Bodies at the Olympics: The International Olympic Committee's Policy on Transsexual Athletes at the 2004 Athens Summer Games." *Body and Society* 12 (2006): 75–102.

Chinn, Sarah E. "'I Was a Lesbian Child': Queer Thoughts about Childhood Studies." In *The Children's Table: Childhood Studies and the Humanities*, edited by Anna Mae Duane, 149–166. Athens: University of Georgia Press, 2013.

Cloutier, Danelle. "Transgender Girl's Human Rights Complaint against School Division in Winnipeg Resolved." CBC News, March 11, 2016. www.cbc.ca.

Cohen, Marilyn. *No Girls in the Clubhouse: The Exclusion of Women from Baseball.* Jefferson, NC: McFarland, 2009.

Collins, Patricia Hill. *Black Feminist Thought: Knowledge, Consciousness and Empowerment.* New York: Routledge. 1990.

———. *Black Sexual Politics: African Americans, Gender, and the New Racism.* New York: Routledge, 2005.

Collins, Tony. *Sport in Capitalist Society: A Short History.* New York: Routledge, 2013.

Connell, Raewyn W. *Gender: In World Perspective.* 2nd ed. Cambridge, UK: Polity, 2009.

Correctional Investigator. *Annual Report of the Office of the Correctional Investigator: 2014–2015.* Cat. No. PS100E-PDF. Ottawa: Government of Canada, 2015.

Coulthard, Glen Sean. *Red Skin, White Masks: Rejecting the Colonial Politics of Recognition.* Minneapolis: University of Minnesota Press, 2014.

Crenshaw, Kimberlé. *Fighting the Post–Affirmative Action War.* New York: Essence Communications, 1998.

Crissman, Halley P., Mitchell B. Berger, Louis F. Graham, and Vanessa K. Dalton. "Transgender Demographics: A Household Probability Sample of US Adults, 2014." *American Journal of Public Health* 107, no. 2 (2017): 213–215.

Davis, Heath Fogg. *Beyond Trans: Does Gender Matter?* New York: NYU Press, 2017.

Davis, Julie Hirschfield, and Matt Apuzzo. "US Directs Public Schools to Allow Transgender Access to Restrooms." *New York Times*, May 12, 2016. www.nytimes.com.

Davis, Nicola. "Drop in Teenage Suicide Attempts Linked to Legislation of Same-Sex Marriage." *Guardian*, February 20, 2017.

Denis, Claude. *We Are Not You: First Nations and Canadian Modernity.* Peterborough, ON: Broadview, 1997.

Douglas, Delia D. "Forget Me . . . Not: Marion Jones and the Politics of Punishment." *Journal of Sport and Social Issues* 32, no. 10 (2014): 3–22.

———. "Private Mark Graham, an Un/Known Soldier: Not Just Any Body Can Be a Citizen." *Gender, Place and Culture: A Journal of Feminist Geography* 22, no. 7 (2014): 1007–1022.

———. "The Wages of Whiteness: Confronting the Nature of Ivory Tower Racism and the Implications for Physical Education." *Sport, Education and Society* 18, no. 4 (2013): 453–474.

Douglas, Delia D., and Katherine M. Jamieson. "A Farewell to Remember: Interrogating the Nancy Lopez Farewell Tour." *Sociology of Sport Journal* 23, no. 2 (2006): 117–141.

Doull, Marion, Ryan J. Watson, Annie Smith, Yuko Homma, and Elizabeth Saewyc. "Are We Leveling the Playing Field? Trends and Disparities in Sports Participation among Sexual Minority Youth in Canada." *Journal of Sport and Health Science*, October 24, 2016. doi:10.1016/j.jshs.2016.10.006.

Dowling, Colette. *The Frailty Myth: Women Approaching Physical Equality.* New York: Random House, 2000.

Dreyfus, Hubert L., and Paul Rabinow. *Michel Foucault: Beyond Structuralism and Hermeneutics.* Brighton, UK: Harvester, 1982.

Dryden, Ken, and Roy McGregor. *In School: Our Kids, Our Teachers, Our Classrooms.* Toronto: McClelland and Stewart, 1995.

Duane, Anna Mae, ed. *The Children's Table: Childhood Studies and the Humanities.* Athens: University of Georgia Press, 2013.

Duggan, Lisa. *The Twilight of Equality: Neoliberalism, Cultural Politics, and the Attack on Democracy.* Boston: Beacon, 2004.

Dworkin, Shari L., and Faye Linda Wachs. *Body Panic: Gender, Health, and the Selling of Fitness.* New York: NYU Press, 2009.

Edwards-Leeper, Laura, and Norman P. Spack. "Psychological Evaluation and Medical Treatment of Transgender Youth in an Interdisciplinary 'Gender Management Service' (GEMS) in a Major Pediatric Center." *Journal of Homosexuality* 59, no. 3 (2012): 321–336.

Ehrensaft, Diane. *Gender Born, Gender Made: Raising Healthy Gender-Nonconforming Children.* New York: The Experiment, 2011.

Elliot, Patricia. *Debates in Transgender, Queer, and Feminist Theory: Contested Sites.* Farnham, UK: Ashgate, 2010.

"Family of Bella Burgos Ready to Go though Mediation over Human Rights Complaint." *Winnipeg Free Press*, April 15, 2014. www.winnipegfreepress.com.

Fausto-Sterling, Anne. *Sexing the Body: Gender Politics and the Construction of Sexuality*. New York: Basic Books, 2000.

Fields, Jessica, Laura Mamo, Jen Gilbert, and Nancy Lesko. "Beyond Bullying." *Contexts*, November 20, 2014.

Fitzpatrick, Cat. "Trans Activists, Don't Throw Mad People under the Bus!" *Feministing*, February 11, 2016. http://feministing.com.

Flasher, Jack. "Adultism." *Adolescence* 13, no. 51 (1978): 517–523.

Foucault, Michel. *The Birth of Biopolitics: Lectures at the Collège de France, 1978–79*. Basingstoke, UK: Palgrave Macmillan, 2008.

Fraser, Nancy. "Feminist Politics in the Age of Recognition: A Two-Dimensional Approach to Gender Justice." *Studies in Social Justice* 1, no. 1 (2007): 23–35.

Freeman, John G., Matthew King, and William Pickett, with Wendy Craig, Frank Elgar, Ian Jannsen, and Don Klinger. *The Health of Canada's Young People: A Mental Health Focus*. Ottawa: Public Health Agency of Canada, 2011.

Gebhard, Amanda. "Pipeline to Prison: How Schools Shape a Future of Incarceration for Indigenous Youth." *Briarpatch*, September 1, 2012. http://briarpatchmagazine.com.

Gender Spectrum. "Gender Inclusive Schools." Accessed August 23, 2015, www.genderspectrum.org.

Gill-Peterson, Julian. "The Technical Capacities of the Body: Assembling Race, Technology, and Transgender." *Transgender Studies Quarterly* 1, no. 3 (2014): 402–418.

Gilmore, Ruth Wilson. *Golden Gulag: Prisons, Surplus, Crisis and Opposition in Globalizing California*. Berkeley: University of California Press, 2007.

Giordano, Simona. "Lives in Chiaroscuro: Should We Suspend the Puberty of Children with Gender Identity Disorder?" *Journal of Medical Ethics* 34 (2008): 580–584.

Glenn, Evelyn Nakano. "Settler Colonialism as Structure: A Framework for Comparative Studies of U.S. Race and Gender Formation." *Sociology of Race and Ethnicity* 1, no. 1 (2015): 52–72.

GLSEN. *The 2015 National School Climate Survey: The Experiences of Lesbian, Gay, Bisexual, Transgender, and Queer Youth in Our Nation's Schools*. New York: GLSEN, 2015. www.glsen.org.

Goldberg, Alan B., and Joneil Adriano. "I'm a Girl: Understanding Transgender Children." ABC News, June 27, 2008. http://abcnews.go.ca.

Gosset, Che. "Silhouettes of Defiance: Memorializing Historical Sites of Queer and Transgender Resistance in an Age of Neoliberal Inclusivity." In *The Transgender Studies Reader 2*, edited by Susan Stryker and Aren Aizura, 580–590. New York: Routledge, 2013.

Government of British Columbia. "Change of Gender Designation on Birth Certificates." Accessed May 3, 2017, www2.gov.bc.ca.

Government of Canada. "Bill C-16: An Act to Amend the Canadian Human Rights Act and the Criminal Code." http://openparliament.ca.

Government of Canada, and the Province of British Columbia. "What Is a Hate Crime?" KnowHate. Accessed May 3, 2017, http://hatecrimebc.ca.

Government of Ontario, Ministry of Transportation. "New 'X' Gender Option Now Available on Ontario Driver's Licences." Ontario Newsroom, March 20, 2017. http://news.ontario.ca.

Grant, Jaime M., Lisa A. Mottet, Justin Tanis, with Jack Harrison, Jody L. Herman, and Mara Keisling. *Injustice at Every Turn: A Report of the National Transgender Discrimination Survey.* National Centre for Transgender Equality, 2011. www.thetaskforce.org.

Griffin, Pat, and Helen Carroll. *On the Team: Equal Opportunity for Transgender Student Athletes.* NCLR, Women's Sports Foundation, and It Takes a Team. 2010.

Grossman, Arnold H., and Anthony R. D'Augelli. "Transgender Youth and Life-Threatening Behaviors." *Suicide and Life-Threatening Behaviors* 37, no. 5 (2007): 527–537.

Gruneau, Richard. "There Will Never Be Another Gordie Howe." Unpublished discussion paper, 2014.

Grzanka, Patrick, and Emily Mann. "Queer Youth Suicide and the Psychopolitics of 'It Gets Better.'" *Sexualities* 17, no. 4 (2014): 369–393.

Halberstam, Jack. *Female Masculinity.* Durham, NC: Duke University Press, 1998.

———. *In a Queer Time and Place: Transgender Bodies, Subcultural Lives.* New York: NYU Press, 2005.

Hall, M. Anne. *The Girl and the Game.* Toronto: Broadview, 2002.

Haraway, Donna. *Modest_Witness@Second_Millenium.FemaleMan©Meets_Onco-Mouse™,* New York: Routledge, 1997.

———. *Simians, Cyborgs, and Women: The Reinvention of Nature.* New York: Routledge, 1991.

Haritaworn, Jin. "Loyal Repetitions of the Nation: Gay Assimilation and the 'War on Terror.'" *DarkMatter* 3 (2008). www.darkmatter101.org.

Haritaworn, Jin, Adi Kuntsman, and Silvia Posocco. Introduction to *Queer Necropolitics,* edited by Hin Haritaworn, Adi Kuntsman, and Silvia Posocco, 1–28. Abingdon, UK: Social Justice, 2014.

———, eds. *Queer Necropolitics.* Abingdon, UK: Social Justice, 2014.

Harper, Joanna. "Using Testosterone to Categorise Male and Female Athletes Isn't Perfect, but It's the Best Solution We Have." *Guardian,* July 3, 2017. www.theguardian.com.

Harris, Adrienne. *Gender as Soft Assembly.* Hillsdale, NJ: Analytic, 2005.

Hellen, Mark. "Transgender Children in Schools." *Liminalis,* 2009, 81–99.

Herman, Jody, Andrew R. Flores, Taylor N. T. Brown, Bianca D. M. Wilson, and Kerith J. Conron. "Age of Individuals Who Identify as Transgender in the United States." Williams Institute, University of California Los Angeles School of Law, 2017. http://williamsinstitute.law.ucla.edu.

Heywood, Leslie, and Shari L. Dworkin. *Built to Win: The Female Athlete as Cultural Icon.* Minneapolis: University of Minnesota Press, 2003.

Higgenbotham, Evelyn Brooks. "African American Women's History and the Metalanguage of Race." *Signs* 17, no. 2 (1992): 251–274.

Hochschild, Arlie. *The Managed Heart: Commercialization of Human Feeling*. Berkeley: University of California Press, 1983.

Hodgson, Lucia. "Childhood of the Race: A Critical Race Theory Intervention into Childhood Studies." In *The Children's Table: Childhood Studies and the Humanities*, edited by Anna Mae Duane, 38–51. Athens: University of Georgia Press, 2013.

Hoffman, Diane M. "Risky Investments: Parenting and the Production of the 'Resilient Child.'" *Health, Risk, and Society* 12, no. 4 (2010): 385–394.

Holman, Catherine White, and Joshua M. Goldberg. "Ethical, Legal, and Psychosocial Issues in Care of Transgender Adolescents." *International Journal of Transgenderism* 9, nos. 3–4 (2006): 95–110.

hooks, bell. *All about Love: New Visions*. New York: HarperCollins, 2000.

———. *Feminist Theory from Margin to Center*. Cambridge, MA: South End, 1984.

———. *Yearning: Race, Gender, and Cultural Politics*. New York: Routledge, 1990.

IOC Medical Commission. "Statement of the Stockholm Consensus on Sex Reassignment in Sports." October 28, 2003. www.olympic.org.

Joel, Daphna, Ricardo Tarrasch, Zohar Berman, Maya Mukamal, and Effi Ziv. "Queering Gender: Studying Gender Identity in 'Normative' Individuals." *Psychology & Sexuality* 5, no. 4 (2014): 291–321.

Jordan-Young, Rebecca. *Brain Storm: The Flaws in the Science of Sex Differences*. Cambridge, MA: Harvard University Press, 2010.

Kabeer, Naila. *Inclusive Citizenship: Meanings and Expressions*. London: Zed Books, 2005.

Kane, Emily W. *The Gender Trap: Parents and the Pitfalls of Raising Boys and Girls*. New York: NYU Press, 2012.

Kane, Mary Jo. "Resistance/Transformation of the Oppositional Binary: Exposing Sport as a Continuum." *Journal of Sport and Social Issues* 19 (1995): 191–218.

Kapoor, Dip, and Steven Jordan. "Introduction: International Perspectives on Education, PAR and Social Change." In *Education, Participatory Action Research, and Social Change*, edited by Dip Kapoor and Steven Jordan, 1–14. New York: Palgrave Macmillan, 2009.

Karkazis, Katrina, Rebecca Jordan-Young, Georgiann Davis, and Silvia Camporesi. "Out of Bounds? A Critique of the New Policies on Hyperandrogenism in Elite Female Athletes." *American Journal of Bioethics* 12, no. 7 (2012): 3–16.

Kirby, Sandra, and Judith Huebner. "Talking about Sex: Biology and the Social Interpretations of Sex in Sport." *Canadian Woman Studies* 21, no. 3 (2002): 36–43.

Klein, Augustus, and Sarit Golub. "Family Rejection as a Predictor of Suicide Attempts and Substance Misuse among Transgender and Gender-Nonconforming Adults." *LGBT Health* 3, no. 3 (2016): 193–199.

Klocker, Natascha. "An Example of 'Thin' Agency: Child Domestic Workers in Tanzania." In *Global Perspectives on Rural Childhood and Youth: Young Rural Lives*, edited by Ruth Panelli, Samantha Punch, and Elsbeth Robson, 83–94. New York: Routledge, 2007.

Kralik, Joellen. "'Bathroom Bill' Legislative Tracking." National Conference of State Legislatures, July 28, 2017. www.ncsl.org.

Krebs, Andreas. "Hockey and the Reproduction of Colonialism in Canada." In *Race and Sport in Canada: Intersecting Inequalities*, edited by Janelle Joseph, Simon Darnell, and Yuka Nakamura, 81–105. Toronto: Canadian Scholars Press, 2012.

Kumashiro, Kevin K. *Troubling Education: Queer Activism and Anti-Oppressive Pedagogy*. New York: Routledge, 2002.

———. *Troubling Intersections of Race and Sexuality: Queer Students of Color and Anti-Oppressive Education*. New York: Rowman and Littlefield, 2001.

Lacharite, Monique, and Zopito A. Marini. "Bullying Prevention and the Rights of Children: Psychological and Democratic Aspects." In *Children's Rights: Multidisciplinary Approaches to Participation and Protection*, edited by Tom O'Neill and Dawn Zinga, 297–324. Toronto: University of Toronto Press, 2008.

Lamble, Sarah. "Queer Investments in Punitiveness: Sexual Citizenship, Social Movements and the Expanding Carceral State." In *Queer Necropolitics*, edited by Jin Haritaworn, Adi Kuntsman, and Silvia Posocco, 151–171. Abingdon, UK: Social Justice, 2014.

LeGuin, Ursula K. *The Left Hand of Darkness*. New York: Ace Books, 1969.

Lemert, Charles. *Dark Thoughts: Race and the Eclipse of Society*. New York: Routledge, 2002.

Levin, Sam. "First US Person to Have 'Intersex' on Birth Certificate: 'There's Power in Knowing Who You Are.'" *Guardian*, January 11, 2017. www.theguardian.com.

LGBT Sports Foundation. "'All 50': The Transgender-Inclusive High School Sports and Activities Policy and Education Project." Accessed May 2016, www.transathlete.com.

Lister, Ruth. "Inclusive Citizenship: Realizing the Potential." *Citizenship Studies* 11, no. 1 (2007): 49–61.

Lister, Ruth, Fiona Williams, Anneli Anttonen, Jet Bussemaker, Ute Gerhard, Jacqueline Heinen, Stina Johansson, and Arnlaug Leira. *Gendering Citizenship in Western Europe: New Challenges for Citizenship Research in a Cross-National Context*. Bristol, UK: Policy, 2007.

Lopez, German. "Trump's Justice Department Just Rescinded a Memo Protecting Transgender Workers." *Vox*, October 5, 2017. www.vox.com.

Lorber, Judith. *Breaking the Bowls: Degendering and Feminist Change*. New York: Norton, 2005.

Lorde, Audre. *Sister Outsider: Essays and Speeches*. New York: Crossing, 1984.

Lorey, Isabell. *State of Insecurity: Government of the Precarious*. London: Verso, 2015.

Love, Adam. "Transgender Exclusion and Inclusion in Sport." In *Routledge Handbook of Sport, Gender and Sexuality*, edited by Jennifer Hargreaves and Eric Anderson, 376–383. New York: Routledge, 2014.

Lynch, Loretta E. "Attorney General Loretta E. Lynch Delivers Remarks at Press Conference Announcing Complaint against the State of North Carolina to Stop

Discrimination Against Transgender Individuals." Justice News, U.S. Department of Justice, May 9, 2016. www.justice.gov.

Macionis, John J., and Linda M. Gerber. *Sociology*. Toronto: Pearson, 2011.

Mackey, Eva. *The House of Difference: Cultural Politics and National Identity in Canada.* New York: Routledge, 1999.

Madigan, Lee, and Nancy C. Gamble. *The Second Rape: Society's Continual Betrayal of the Victim.* New York: Macmillan, 1991.

Manning, Kimberley Ens. "Attached Advocacy and the Rights of the Trans Child." *Canadian Journal of Political Science / Revue Canadienne de Science Politique* 50, no. 2 (2017): 579–595.

Manning, Kimberley, Cindy Holmes, Annie Pullen Sansfacon, Julia Temple Newhook, and Ann Travers. "Fighting for Trans* Kids: Academic Parent Activism in the 21st Century." *Studies in Social Justice* 9, no. 1 (2015): 118–135.

Marimow, Ann E. "Case of Virginia Transgender Teen Gavin Grimm Put Off by Appeals Court." *Washington Post*, August 2, 2017. www.washingtonpost.com.

Marten, James. "Childhood Studies and History: Catching a Culture in High Relief." In *The Children's Table: Childhood Studies and the Humanities*, edited by Anna Mae Duane, 52–53. Athens: University of Georgia Press, 2013.

Marx, Karl. "The Eighteenth Brumaire of Louis Bonaparte." In *The Marx-Engels Reader*, 2nd ed., edited by Robert C. Tucker, 594–617. New York: Norton, 1978.

Matthews, Sarah. "A Window on the 'New' Sociology of Childhood." *Sociology Compass* 1, no. 1 (2007): 322–334.

Mbembe, Achille. "Necropolitics." *Public Culture* 15, no. 1 (2003): 11–40.

McArdle, David. "Swallows and Amazons, or the Sporting Exception to the Gender Recognition Act." *Social and Legal Studies* 17, no. 1 (2008): 39–57.

McDonagh, Eileen, and Laura Pappano. *Playing with the Boys: Why Separate Is Not Equal in Sports*. New York: Oxford University Press, 2007.

McKittrick, Katherine, ed. *Sylvia Wynter: On Being Human as Praxis*. Durham, NC: Duke University Press, 2014.

Meadow, Tey. "Child." *Transgender Studies Quarterly* 1, nos. 1–2 (2014): 57–58.

Meiners, Erica. "Ending the School-to-Prison Pipeline / Building Abolition Futures." *Urban Review* 43 (September 2011): 547–565.

———. "Offending Children, Registering Sex." *Women's Studies Quarterly* 43, nos. 1–2 (2015): 246–263.

———. "Trouble with the *Child* in the Carceral State." *Social Justice* 41, no. 3 (2011): 120–144.

Menvielle, Edgardo. "A Comprehensive Program for Children with Gender Variant Behaviors and Gender Identity Disorders." *Journal of Homosexuality* 59, no. 3 (2012): 357–368.

Messner, Michael A. "Gender Ideologies, Youth Sports, and the Production of Soft Essentialism." *Sociology of Sport Journal* 28 (2011): 151–170.

———. *Power at Play: Sports and the Problem of Masculinity*. Boston: Beacon, 1995.

Messner, Michael A., Michele Dunbar, and Darnell Hunt. "The Televised Sports Manhood Formula." *Journal of Sport and Social Issues* 24, no. 4 (2000): 380–394.

Meyer, Elizabeth J. *Gender and Sexual Diversity in Schools*. New York: Springer, 2010.

Mills, C. Wright. *The Sociological Imagination*. New York: Oxford University Press, 1959.

Mills, Sarah. "Gender-Neutral Birth Certificate Fight Reaches Sask. Courts." 980AM CJME, July 10, 2017. www.cjme.com.

Molotch, Harvey, and Laura Nolen. *Toilet: Public Restrooms and the Politics of Sharing*. New York: NYU Press. 2010.

Morgensen, Scott. "Settler Homonationalism: Theorizing Settler Colonialism within Queer Modernities." *GLQ: A Journal of Lesbian and Gay Studies* 16, nos. 1–2 (2010): 105–131.

Namaste, Viviane. *Invisible Lives: The Erasure of Transsexual and Transgendered People*. Chicago: University of Chicago Press. 2000.

———. *Sex Change, Social Change: Reflections on Identity, Institutions and Imperialism*. Toronto: Women's Press, 2005.

Nestle, Joan. *Persistent Desire: A Femme-Butch Reader*. Boston: Alyson, 1992.

Noble, Bobby Jean. "'My Own Set of Keys': Meditations on Transgender, Scholarship, Belonging." *Feminist Studies* 37, no. 2 (2011): 254–268.

———. "Our Bodies Are Not Ourselves: Tranny Guys and the Racialized Class Politics of Incoherence." In *Transgender Studies Reader 2*, edited by Susan Stryker and Aren Aizura, 248–258. New York: Routledge, 2014.

———. *Sons of the Movement: FtMs Risking Incoherence on a Post-Queer Cultural Landscape*. Toronto: Women's Press. 2006.

Nordmarken, Sonny. "Microaggressions." *Transgender Studies Quarterly* 1, nos. 1–2 (2014): 129–134.

Nyong'o, Tavia. "The Unforgiveable Transgression of Being Caster Semenya." *Women and Performance: A Journal of Feminist Theory* 20, no. 1 (2010): 95–100.

OECD. *Equity and Quality in Education: Supporting Disadvantaged Students and Schools*. Paris: OECD, 2012. www.oecd-ilibrary.org.

Open Parliament. "Bill C-16." Accessed August 25, 2017, OpenParliament.ca.

Pascoe, C. J. *Dude, You're a Fag*. Berkeley: University of California Press, 2007.

Pieper, Lindsey P. *Sex Testing: Gender Policing in Women's Sports*. Urbana: University of Illinois Press, 2016.

Pierce, Chester M. "Psychiatric Problems of the Black Minority." In *American Handbook of Psychiatry*, 2nd ed., edited by Silvano Arieti, vol. 2, 512–523. New York: Basic Books, 1974.

Pronger, Brian. *The Arena of Masculinity: Sports, Homosexuality and the Meaning of Sex*. New York: St. Martin's, 1990.

Puar, Jasbir. "Homonationalism as Assemblage: Viral Travels, Affective Sexualities." *Jindal Global Law Review* 4, no. 2 (2013): 23–43.

———. "Q&A with Jasbir Puar." *DarkMatter*, May 2, 2008. www.darkmatter101.org.

———. "Rethinking Homonationalism." *Journal of Middle East Studies* 45 (2013): 336–339.

———. *Terrorist Assemblages: Homonationalism in Queer Times*. Durham, NC: Duke University Press. 2007.

Public Health Agency of Canada. *Questions and Answers: Gender Identity in Schools*. Ottawa: Public Health Agency of Canada, 2010.

Pyne, Jake. "Gender Independent Kids: A Paradigm Shift in Approaches to Gender Non-conforming Children." *Canadian Journal of Human Sexuality* 23, no. 1 (2014): 1–8.

———. "The Governance of Gender Non-conforming Children: A Dangerous Enclosure." *Annual Review of Critical Psychology* 11 (2014): 79–96.

Queer Voices. "California's Assembly Bill 1266 for Transgender Student Rights Signed by Governor Jerry Brown." *Huffington Post*, February 2, 2016. www.huffingtonpost.com.

Quinn, Therese, and Erica R. Meiners. "From Anti-Bullying Laws and Gay Marriages to Queer Worlds and Just Futures." *QED: A Journal in GLBTQ Worldmaking* 1 (2013): 149–175.

Razack, Sherene. *Casting Out: The Eviction of Muslims from Western Law and Politics*. Toronto: University of Toronto Press, 2008.

———. "Gendered Racial Violence and Spatialized Justice: The Murder of Pamela George." *Canadian Journal of Law and Society* 15, no. 2 (2000): 91–130.

Ricci, Talia. "Transgender Child Told You Can't Use Girls' Bathroom." *Global News*, October 3, 2014. http://globalnews.ca.

Ring, Jennifer. *Stolen Bases: Why American Girls Don't Play Baseball*. Urbana: University of Illinois Press, 2009.

Ring, Trudy. "Supreme Court to Hear Gavin Grimm Case: Huge Implications for Trans Students." *Advocate*, February 4, 2016. www.theadvocate.com.

Roberts, Andrea, Margaret Rosario, Heather Corliss, Karestan Koenen, and S. Bryn Austin. "Childhood Gender Nonconformity: A Risk Indicator for Childhood Abuse and Posttraumatic Stress in Youth." *Pediatrics* 129, no. 3 (2012): 410–417.

Sabo, Don. "The Myth of the Sexual Athlete." In *Reconstructing Gender: A Multicultural Anthology*, edited by Estelle Disch, 263–267. Boston: McGraw-Hill, 2003. Originally published 1994.

Saketopoulou, Avgi. "Minding the Gap: Intersections between Gender, Race, and Class in Work with Gender Variant Children." *International Journal of Relational Perspectives* 21, no. 2 (2011): 192–209.

Sax, Leonard. "How Common Is Intersex? A Response to Anne Fausto-Sterling." *Journal of Sex Research* 39, no. 3 (2002): 174–178.

Sedgwick, Eve. *Epistemology of the Closet*. Berkeley: University of California Press, 1990.

———. "How to Bring Your Kids Up Gay." *Social Text* 29 (1991): 18–27.

Serano, Julia. "Detransition, Desistance, and Disinformation: A Guide for Understanding Transgender Children Debates." *Medium*, August 2, 2016. www.medium.com.

Siebers, Tobin. *Disability Theory*. Ann Arbor: University of Michigan Press, 2008.

Simpson, Leanne. *Dancing on Our Turtle's Back: Stories of Nishnaabeg Re-creation, Resurgence and a New Emergence*. Winnipeg, MB: ARP Books.

Singal, Jesse. "How the Fight over Transgender Kids Got a Leading Sex Researcher Fired." *New York*, February 7, 2016. http://nymag.com.

Slater, Dashka. "The Fire on the 57 Bus in Oakland." *New York Times Magazine*, January 29, 2015. www.nytimes.com.

Snorton, Riley. "Trans-of-Color Roundtable Discussion." Trans* Studies Conference, Tucson, AZ, 2016.

Snorton, Riley, and Jin Haritaworn. "Trans Necropolitics: A Transnational Reflection on Violence, Death, and the Trans of Color Afterlife." In *The Transgender Studies Reader 2*, edited by Susan Stryker and A. Aizura, 66–76. New York: Routledge, 2013.

Spade, Dean. *Normal Life: Administrative Violence, Critical Trans Politics, and the Limits of Law*. Cambridge, MA: South End, 2011.

Stafford, Annika. "Is It Still a Boy? Hetero/Gender Normativity in Kindergarten." Ph.D. diss., University of British Columbia, Vancouver, 2013.

Stanley, Eric. "Gender Self-Determination." *Transgender Studies Quarterly* 1, nos. 1–2 (2014): 89–91.

Stanley, Eric, and Nat Smith, eds. *Captive Genders: Trans Embodiment and the Prison Industrial Complex*. Oakland, CA: AK, 2011.

Stern, Mark Joseph. "The HB2 'Repeal' Bill Is an Unmitigated Disaster for LGBTQ Rights and North Carolina." *Slate*, March 30, 2017. www.slate.com.

Stockton, Kathryn Bond. *The Queer Child: Or Growing Sideways in the 20th Century*. Durham, NC: Duke University Press, 2009.

Stout, David. "Transgender Teen Awarded $75,000 in School Restroom Lawsuit." *Time*, December 2, 2014. www.time.com.

Stryker, Susan. "Transgender History, Homonormativity, and Disciplinarity." *Radical History Review*, no. 100 (2008): 145–157.

Stryker, Susan, and Paisley Currah. "General Editors' Introduction: Decolonizing the Transgender Imaginary." *Transgender Studies Quarterly* 1, no. 1 (2014): 303–307.

Sullivan, Claire F. "Gender Verification and Gender Policies in Elite Sport: Eligibility and 'Fair Play.'" *Journal of Sport and Social Issues* 3, no. 5 (2011): 400–419.

Sykes, Heather. "Transsexual and Transgender Policies in Sport." *Women in Sport and Physical Activity Journal* 15, no. 1 (2006): 3–13.

Tannehill, Brynn. "The Truth about Transgender Suicide." *Huffington Post*, November 14, 2015. www.huffingtonpost.com.

Taylor, Catherine, and Tracey Peter. *Every Class in Every School: Final Report on the First National Climate Survey on Homophobia, Biphobia, and Transphobia in Canadian Schools*. Toronto: Egale Canada Human Rights Trust, 2011.

"Tearful Lynsey Sharp Says Rule Change Makes Racing Caster Semenya Difficult." *Guardian*, August 21, 2016. www.theguardian.com.

Teetzel, Sarah. "On Transgendered Athletes, Fairness and Doping: An International Challenge." *Sport in Society* 9, no. 2 (2006): 227–251.

Thobani, Sunera. "After UBC Ousted Arvind Gupta as President, It Made the University Whiter." Rabble.ca, March 4, 2016.

———. *Exalted Subjects: Studies in the Making of Race and Nation in Canada.* Toronto: University of Toronto Press, 2007.

Thomas, William I., and Dorothy Swaine Thomas. *The Child in America: Behavior Problems and Programs.* New York: Knopf, 1928.

Thorne, Barrie. *Gender Play: Girls and Boys in School.* New Brunswick, NJ: Rutgers University Press, 1993.

Tosh, Jemma. *Perverse Psychology: The Pathologization of Sexual Violence and Transgenderism.* London: Routledge, 2014.

TransAthlete.com. "High School Policies for Transgender Student Athletes." Accessed August 2017. www.transathlete.com.

———. "K–12 Policies." Accessed August 2017, www.transathlete.com.

Travers, Ann. "Queering Sport: Lesbian Softball Leagues and the Transgender Challenge." *International Review for the Sociology of Sport* 41, nos. 3–4 (2006): 431–446.

———. "The Sport Nexus and Gender Injustice." *Studies in Social Justice* 2, no. 1 (2008): 79–101.

———. "Thinking the Unthinkable: Imagining an 'Un-American,' Girl-Friendly, Women- and Trans-Inclusive Alternative for Baseball." *Journal of Sport and Social Issues* 37, no. 1 (2013): 78–96.

———. "Transgender and Gender-Nonconforming Kids and the Binary Requirements of Sport Participation in North America." In *Child's Play: Sport in Kids' Worlds,* edited by Michael A. Messner and Michela Musto, 179–201. New Brunswick, NJ: Rutgers University Press, 2016.

———. "Women's Ski Jumping, the 2010 Olympic Games, and the Deafening Silence of Sex Segregation, Whiteness, and Wealth." *Journal of Sport and Social Issues* 35, no. 2 (2011): 126–145.

Travers, Ann, and Jillian Deri. "Transgender Inclusion and the Changing Face of Lesbian Softball Leagues." *International Review for the Sociology of Sport* 46, no. 4 (2011): 488–507.

Underwood, Katie. "Ms. Chatelaine: Harriette Cunningham, Trans Rights Trailblazer." *Chatelaine,* December 23, 2015. www.chatelaine.com.

U.S. Department of Health and Human Services (HHS), Office of the Surgeon General and National Action Alliance for Suicide Prevention. *2012 National Strategy for Suicide Prevention: Goals and Objectives for Action.* Washington, DC: HHS, September 2012.

U.S. Transgender Law and Policy Institute. *Guidelines for Creating Policies for Transgender Children in Recreational Sports.* 2009.

Vancouver School Board. "ACB-R-1: Sexual Orientation and Gender Identities Policy." June 2014. www.vsb.bc.ca.

van Sterkenburg, Jacco, and Annelies Knoppers. "Dominant Discourses about Race/Ethnicity and Gender in Sport Practice and Performance." *International Review for the Sociology of Sport* 39, no. 3 (2004): 301–321.

Veale, Jamie, Elizabeth Saewyc, Helene Frohard-Dourlent, Sarah Dobson, Beth Clark, and the Canadian Trans Youth Health Survey Research Group. *Being Safe, Being Me: Results of the Canadian Trans Youth Health Survey*. Vancouver, BC: Stigma and Resilience among Vulnerable Youth Centre, School of Nursing, University of British Columbia, 2015.

Wall, John. "Childism: The Challenge of Childhood to Ethics and the Humanities." In *The Children's Table: Childhood Studies and the Humanities*, edited by Anna Mae Duane, 68–84. Athens: University of Georgia Press, 2013.

Wamsley, Laurel. "Oregon Adds a New Gender Option to Its Driver's Licenses: X." Oregon Public Broadcasting, June 16, 2017. www.opb.org.

Ward, Jane. "Gender Labor: Transmen, Femmes, and Collective Work of Transgression." *Sexualities* 13, no. 2 (2010): 236–254.

Watson, Amanda. "Accumulating Cares: Women, Whiteness, and the Affective Labor of Responsible Reproduction in Neoliberal Times." Ph.D. diss., Institute of Feminist and Gender Studies, Faculty of Social Sciences, University of Ottawa, 2016.

Weheliye, Alexander. *Habeas Viscus*. Durham, NC: Duke University Press, 2014.

Wente, Margaret. "Transgender Kids: Who Decides?" *Toronto Globe and Mail*, January 17, 2017. www.theglobeandmail.com.

Whitehead, Jaye Cee. *The Nuptial Deal: Same-Sex Marriage and Neo-Liberal Governance*. Chicago: University of Chicago Press, 2011.

Williams, Patricia J. *The Alchemy of Race and Rights*. Cambridge, MA: Harvard University Press, 1991.

Williams Institute, UCLA School of Law. "Incarceration Rate of LGB People Three Times the General Population." Accessed August 2017, http://williamsinstitute.law.ucla.edu.

Winters, Kelley. "The Proposed Gender Dysphoria Diagnosis in the DSM-5." *GID Reform Weblog*, June 7, 2011. http://gidreform.wordpress.com.

Witterick, Rogue. "Dancing in the Eye of the Storm: The Gift of Gender Diversity to Our Family." In *Chasing Rainbows: Exploring Gender Fluid Parenting Practices*, edited by Fiona J. Green and May Friedman, 21–42. Bradford, ON: Demeter, 2013.

Wong, Curtis M. "Texas Sportscaster Shreds Trans Phobes in Must-See Broadcast." *Huffington Post*, March 3, 2017. www.huffingtonpost.com.

Zeidler, Maryse, "Parent Fights to Omit Gender on B.C. Child's Birth Certificate." CBC News, June 30, 2017. www.cbc.ca.

INDEX

Note: participants are indexed under their pseudonyms

ABOUT THE AUTHOR

Ann Travers is Associate Professor in the Department of Sociology &
Anthropology at Simon Fraser University. They live in Vancouver with
their partner, three kids, and a dog named Thunder.

THE WILD HISTORY OF THE AMERICAN WEST

THE
AMAZING ERIE CANAL
AND *HOW* A *BIG DITCH*
OPENED UP THE *WEST*

Wim Coleman & Pat Perrin

30036009735554

MyReportLinks.com Books
an imprint of

 Enslow Publishers, Inc.

Box 398, 40 Industrial Road
Berkeley Heights, NJ 07922
USA

MyReportLinks.com Books, an imprint of Enslow Publishers, Inc. MyReportLinks®
is a registered trademark of Enslow Publishers, Inc.

Library of Congress Cataloging-in-Publication Data

Coleman, Wim.
  The amazing Erie Canal and how a big ditch opened up the West / Wim Coleman and Pat Perrin.
      p. cm. — (The wild history of the American West)
  Includes bibliographical references and index.
  ISBN 1-59845-017-4
  1. Erie Canal—History—Juvenile literature. 2. United States—Economic conditions—Juvenile
literature. I. Perrin, Pat. II. Title. III. Series.
  HE396.E6C65 2006
  386'.4809747—dc22

                                    2005029389

Printed in the United States of America

10 9 8 7 6 5 4 3 2 1

To Our Readers:
Through the purchase of this book, you and your library gain access to the Report Links that specifically
back up this book.
The Publisher will provide access to the Report Links that back up this book and will keep these Report
Links up to date on **www.myreportlinks.com** for five years from the book's first publication date.
We have done our best to make sure all Internet addresses in this book were active and appropriate when
we went to press. However, the author and the Publisher have no control over, and assume no liability
for, the material available on those Internet sites or on other Web sites they may link to.
The usage of the MyReportLinks.com Books Web site is subject to the terms and conditions stated on the
Usage Policy Statement on **www.myreportlinks.com.**
A password may be required to access the Report Links that back up this book. The password is found
on the bottom of page 4 of this book.
Any comments or suggestions can be sent by e-mail to comments@myreportlinks.com or to the address
on the back cover.

Photo Credits: AP/Wide World Photos, p. 108; Assumption College, p. 50; Chuck LaChiusa, p. 79;
© Corel Corporation, pp. 3 (painting), 10–11, 23; © Crowder Associates, p. 53; © 1996–2002 The
Peoples History Collection, p. 52; © 1997–2006 Annenberg Media, p. 81; © 1998 Archaeological
Institute of America, p. 27; © 2000 Evisum, Inc., p. 89; © 2000–05 by Frank E. Sadowski, Jr., p. 74;
© 2000–05 Museum of American Heritage, p. 36; © 2001 Monroe County (NY) Library System, p. 59;
© 2005 Educational Broadcasting Corporation, p. 21; © 2005 Harriet Beecher Stowe Center, p. 85;
© 2005 The Washington Post Company, p. 78; © 2006 ePodunk Inc., p. 18; Courtesy of the *Dictionary
of American Portraits*, © 1967, Dover Publications, Inc., pp. 25, 32, 72, 95, 100; Dr. James B. Calvert/
University of Denver, p. 12; Enslow Publishers, Inc., p. 5; Erie Canal Museum, p. 103; Hudson River
Maritime Museum, p. 37; Library of Congress, pp. 3; (Syracuse), 16, 31, 46–47, 63, 64, 67, 87, 91,
93, 97, 99; Medina Erie Canal Task Force, p. 112; MyReportLinks.com Books, p. 4; Nabataea.net,
p. 58; National Archives, p. 19; National Park Service, p. 110; New York State Archives, p. 71; New
York State Canals, p. 40; North Wind Picture Archives, pp. 54–55, 76, 82–83, 107; Photos.com, p. 38;
Preservation Coalition of Erie County, p. 105; The Manhattan Institute, p. 44; University of Illinois at
Urbana Champaign, p. 92; University of Rochester Department of History, pp. 14, 61; University of
Virginia, p. 45; Unknown Artist, p. 69; U.S. Army Center of Military History, p. 42; U.S. Department
of the Interior, p. 28.

Cover Photo: North Wind Pictures Archives

Cover Description: A canal boat towing a barge through the Erie Canal during the 1880s.

CONTENTS

MyReportLinks.com Books
Great Books, Great Links, Great for Research!

The Internet sites featured in this book can save you hours of research time. These Internet sites—we call them *"Report Links"*—are constantly changing, but we keep them up to date on our Web site.

When you see this "Approved Web Site" logo, you will know that we are directing you to a great Internet site that will help you with your research.

Give it a try! Type http://www.myreportlinks.com into your browser, click on the series title and enter the password, then click on the book title, and scroll down to the Report Links listed for this book.

The Report Links will bring you to great source documents, photographs, and illustrations. MyReportLinks.com Books save you time, feature Report Links that are kept up to date, and make report writing easier than ever! A complete listing of the Report Links can be found on pages 114–115 at the back of the book.

Please see "To Our Readers" on the copyright page for important information about this book, the MyReportLinks.com Web site, and the Report Links that back up this book.

Please enter **WEC1787** if asked for a password.

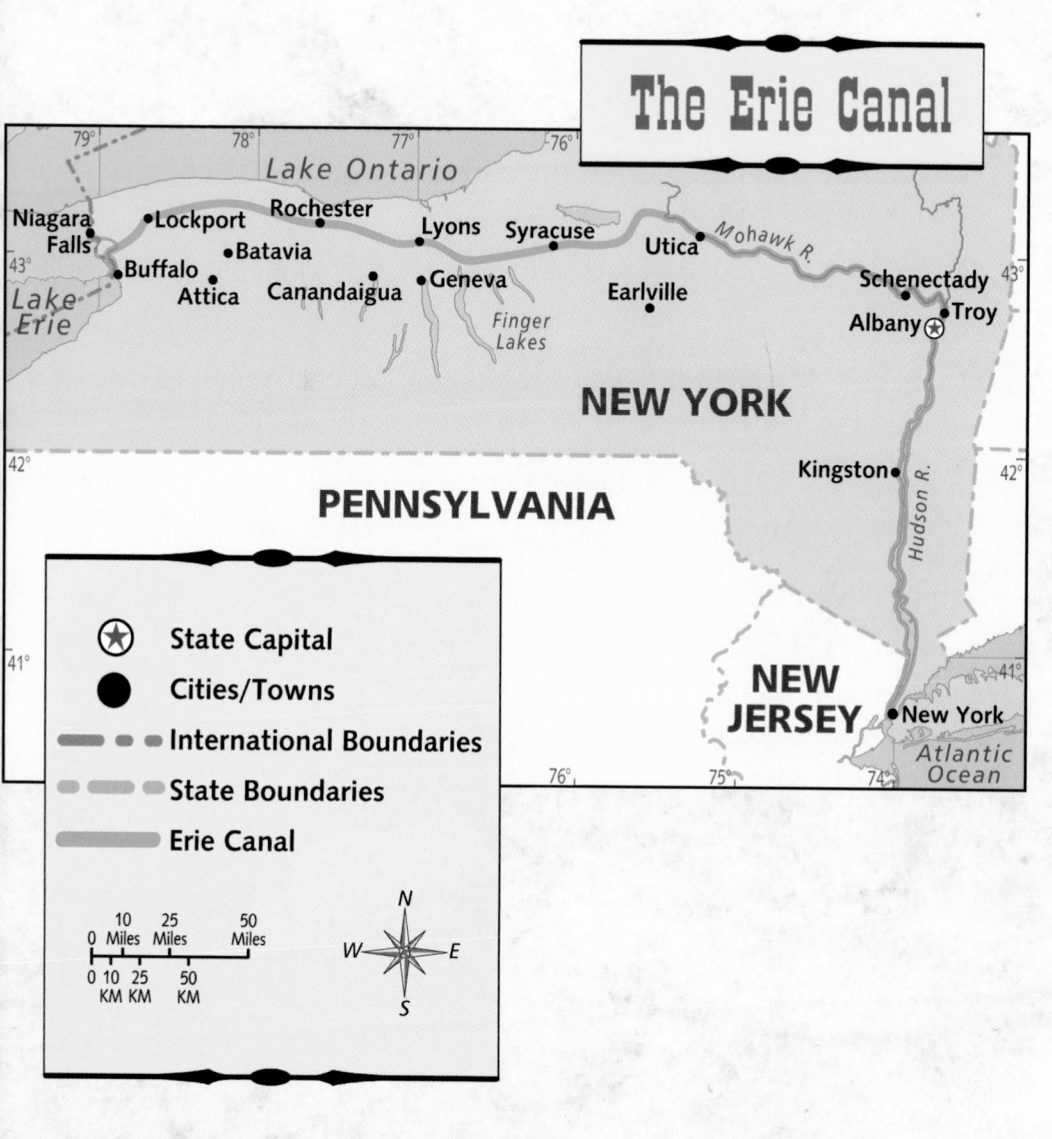

The Erie Canal

ERIE CANAL TIME LINE

▷ **1724**—Cadwallader Colden suggests a canal to link the Hudson River to Lake Erie.

▷ **1769**—Scotsman James Watt patents a practical steam engine in England.

▷ **1777**—New York politician Gouverneur Morris suggests building a canal in upstate New York.

▷ **1784**—Christopher Colles proposes improving the Mohawk River waterway.

▷ **1785**—George Washington holds a meeting at Mount Vernon to discuss a canal on the Potomac River.

▷ **1787**—Members of the U.S. Constitutional Convention see a demonstration of John Fitch's paddle-wheel steamboat on the Delaware River.

▷ **1791**—Elkanah Watson discusses the possibilities of digging a canal in New York with New York State Senator Philip Schuyler.

▷ **1792**—Western Inland Lock Navigation Company is incorporated to improve navigation between the Hudson River and the Great Lakes.

▷ **1797**—Robert Fulton writes to President George Washington about the possibilities of canals.

▷ **1807**—Robert Fulton puts his first American steamboat into service on the Hudson River.

—Jesse Hawley writes fourteen essays from prison, proposing and Erie Canal and describing how it could be built.

▷ **1808**—New York legislature hires engineer James Geddes to survey the route for the Erie Canal.

▷ **1810**—New York state appoints a Canal Commission to oversee the Erie Canal project.

▷ **1812**—The War of 1812 (1812–15) between Great Britain and the United States temporarily distracts attention from the Erie Canal Project.

▷ **1816**—New York legislature appoints five Canal Commissioners and funds the start of the Erie Canal.

▷ **1817**—De Witt Clinton is governor of New York, until 1823.

—*July 4:* Work on the Erie Canal begins.

—Canvass White studies canals in England.

▷ **1818**—Canvass White, back in New York, finds a suitable limestone for making waterproof cement.

▷ **1820**—John Jervis is put in charge of the canal's central section.

▷ **1823**—280 miles of canal between Albany and Rochester is opened to heavy traffic. Tolls help pay for finishing the canal.

▷ **1825**—De Witt Clinton again becomes governor of New York.

—*October:* The Erie Canal is completed with celebrations all along the waterway. The first fleet of canal boats travels from Buffalo to New York City.

▷ **1836**—The Erie Canal is enlarged.

▷ **1862**—The Erie Canal is again enlarged. Additional locks and a depth of seven feet allows larger boats and more traffic.

▷ **1882**—The Erie Canal stops charging tolls.

▷ **1905**—Steamboats are taking over the job of tow mules and horses.

—Travel by railroad is becoming more popular than canal travel.

—"Fifteen Years on the Erie Canal" written by Thomas S. Allen.

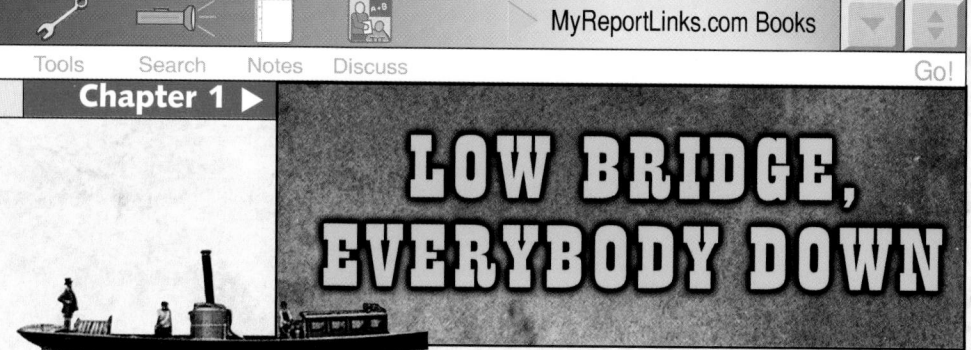

Chapter 1

LOW BRIDGE, EVERYBODY DOWN

"Bridge! Bridge!" cried the canal boat pilot.

But the Virginia schoolmaster was intent on his reading. He did not hear the warning.

With a dull "thunk," the man was knocked to the deck.

Author Nathaniel Hawthorne wrote that he "fully expected to see the treasures of the poor man's cranium [skull] scattered about the deck."[1] However, the schoolmaster got off with only a large bump and a few laughs from the other passengers. About the laughter, Hawthorne commented, "Oh, how pitiless are idle people!"

Hawthorne took a trip along the Erie Canal in 1832. At that point in his life, he was writing short stories and articles. He wrote about his travels in a series of "sketches" for popular magazines. Hawthorne later became famous for novels such as *The Scarlet Letter* and *The House of the Seven Gables*.

Like Hawthorne, many American writers took an interest in the Erie Canal. It was one of the great wonders of its time for those who imagined

it, created it, and rode along it.

America's Great Canal

Before automobiles and trains, land travel could be very difficult. Water travel was more convenient. That is why so many of the world's greatest cities are seaports or river ports.

Of course, rivers do not always go where people want to go. Even worse, rivers flow in one direction. Boats easily go downstream with the current. But before the invention of steam engines, going

This painting, by Edward Lamson Henry, is called "On the Erie Canal." It is a romanticized look at life in a canal town.

upstream was much harder. Sometimes it was impossible. Swift currents, rapids, waterfalls, rocks, and shallow areas can also make rivers hard to navigate.

In many places and times, people have built canals to help solve those problems. Canals are artificial waterways. They can improve rivers and streams and can connect existing waterways.

Canals were not a new idea when New Yorkers built the Erie Canal. Around 2200 B.C., the Babylonians dug a canal to connect the Euphrates and Tigris rivers. The ancient Egyptians built a canal to improve transportation on the Nile River. And they built another canal to connect the Nile with the Red Sea.

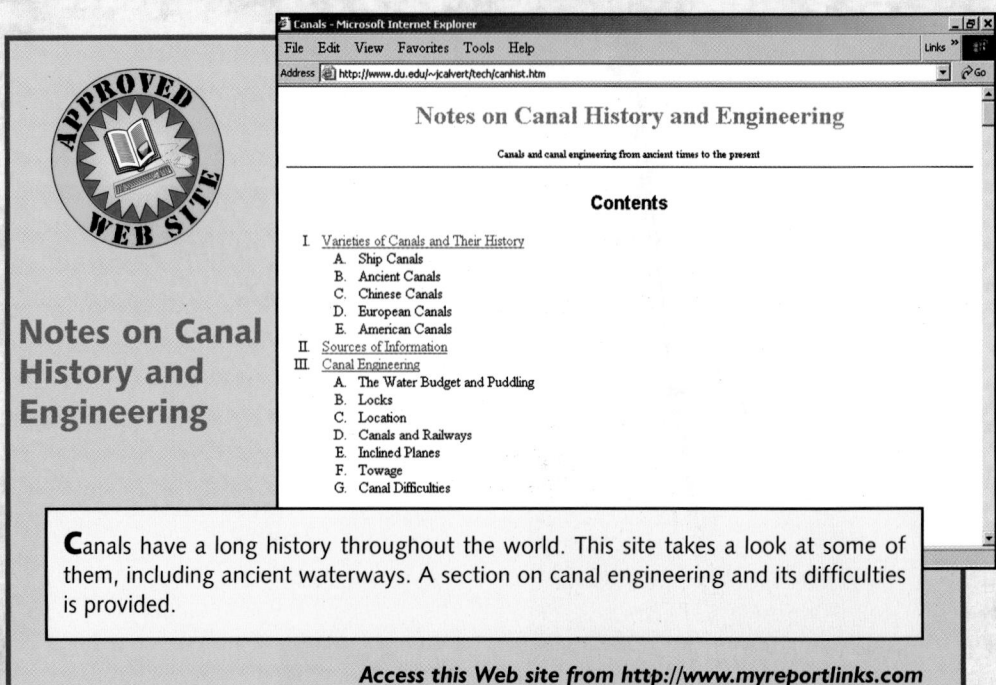

Notes on Canal History and Engineering

Canals have a long history throughout the world. This site takes a look at some of them, including ancient waterways. A section on canal engineering and its difficulties is provided.

Access this Web site from http://www.myreportlinks.com

By A.D. 610, the Chinese had developed a complicated system of canals. The Romans also built canals, and the Dutch and Italians had canal systems well before 1500.[2]

America's Erie Canal connects New York's Hudson River with Lake Erie. It was completed in 1825, although some sections were open before then. The canal is a long, wide ditch that passes right through towns, farms, and forests.

Every path that needed to cross the Erie Canal had to have a bridge. Some bridges were for wagon roads and others joined the streets of a town. Bridges also re-connected farmlands that had been divided by the canal. Early bridges were just high enough for a boat to pass under. They were not high enough for a person on the boat to remain standing.

Those Low Bridges

The Erie Canal's bridges caused constant problems. Passengers enjoying the view had to dive to the boat deck or return to their cabins when bridges appeared.[3] The schoolmaster that Hawthorne wrote about was more fortunate than some other canal boat passengers. Especially at night, those low bridges could be deadly. A few canal boat passengers did lose their lives because of them.

In 1836, a traveler named Thomas S. Woodcock wrote in his journal,

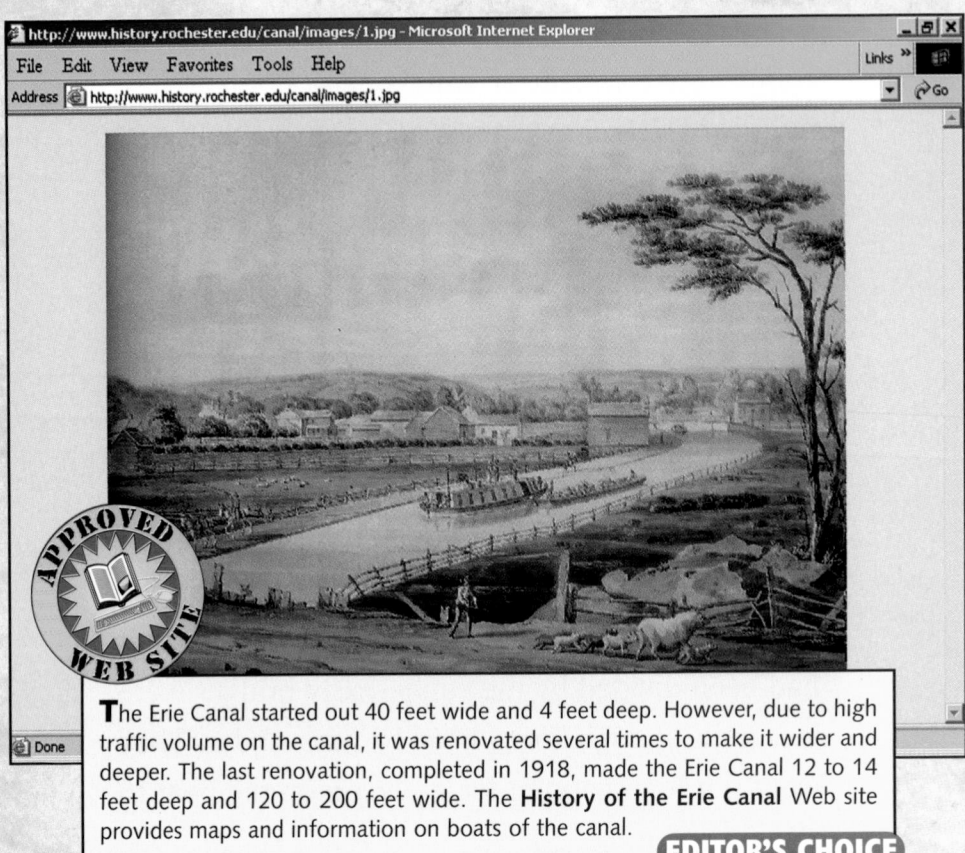

http://www.history.rochester.edu/canal/images/1.jpg - Microsoft Internet Explorer

File   Edit   View   Favorites   Tools   Help

Links

Address   http://www.history.rochester.edu/canal/images/1.jpg   Go

Done

The Erie Canal started out 40 feet wide and 4 feet deep. However, due to high traffic volume on the canal, it was renovated several times to make it wider and deeper. The last renovation, completed in 1918, made the Erie Canal 12 to 14 feet deep and 120 to 200 feet wide. The **History of the Erie Canal** Web site provides maps and information on boats of the canal.

EDITOR'S CHOICE

The Bridges on the Canal are very low, particularly the old ones. Indeed they are so low as to scarcely allow the baggage to clear, and in some cases actually rubbing against it. Every Bridge makes us bend double if seated on anything, and in many cases you have to lie on your back. The Man at the helm gives the word to the passengers: "Bridge," "very low Bridge," "the lowest in the Canal," as the case may be. Some serious accidents have happened for want of caution. A young English Woman met with her death a short time since, she having fallen asleep with her head upon a box, had her head crushed to pieces. Such things however do not often occur, and in general it affords amusement to the passengers.[4]

It was, indeed, fortunate that such terrible accidents were rare. One author who found the low bridges amusing was Caroline Gilman. She was the founder and editor of magazines for young readers and adults, and she became the most famous Southern female writer of her time. In 1838, Gilman described a trip on the Erie Canal in her book, *The Poetry of Travelling in the United States*.

> When it is possible to be on deck, canal navigation is pleasant enough. I do not object at all to the bobbing one's head down at the bridges—it is somewhat exciting. . . . When we are all prostrated [lying flat], I always peep about to see how comically everybody looks, and get up convulsed with laughter.[5]

The chorus of the most popular song about the Erie Canal also mentions those bridges:

> *Low bridge, everybody down!*
> *Low bridge, we must be getting near a town*
> *You can always tell your neighbor,*
> *You can always tell your pal,*
> *If he's ever navigated on the Erie Canal.*[6]

▶ Other Dangers

Nathaniel Hawthorne started his story of the canal in a romantic style. He compared the canal

Nathaniel Hawthorne was a well-known novelist and author of short stories. He wrote travel articles about the Erie Canal.

boat to stories of the Roman water god Neptune. "Behold us, then, fairly afloat, with three horses harnessed to our vessel, like the steeds of Neptune to a huge scallop-shell, in mythological pictures."[7]

Hawthorne was being humorous. He really found canal travel anything but grand and romantic. In his narrative of canal travel, Hawthorne mentioned a few other dangers that he saw:

> At the moment of changing horses, the tow-rope caught a Massachusetts farmer by the leg, and threw him down in a very indescribable posture, leaving a purple mark around his sturdy limb. A new passenger fell flat on his back, in attempting to step on deck, as the boat emerged from under a bridge. Another, in his Sunday clothes, as good luck would have it, being told to leap aboard from the bank, forthwith plunged up to his third waistcoat button in the canal, and was fished out in a very pitiable plight, not at all amended by our three rounds of applause.[8]

Wild Exaggerations

For most travelers, the canal trip was quiet, and even dull. The passengers sometimes sang to entertain themselves. "Low bridge, everybody down!" was one of the favorite songs.

Another popular song, called "The Raging Canal," was about imaginary dangers. It made the canal sound as rough as the open sea.

The Erie Canal:
A Journey
Through
History

The Erie Canal – A journey through history – ePodunk – Microsoft Internet Explorer

File   Edit   View   Favorites   Tools   Help   Links »

Address http://www.epodunk.com/routes/erie-canal/index.html   Go

PLACE SEARCH
Enter a community name:

State:
Alabama   ▼   Search

□ Include former names
Advanced search

The Erie Canal, built
across New York State
in the 1820s, opened
the Midwest to
development and
helped New York City
become a worldwide
trading center.

This journey through history
combines songs, historic
information, post cards,
panoramic photos, maps
and community profiles to
create a comprehensive

The Erie Canal
A JOURNEY THROUGH HISTORY

Take an online tour of the Erie Canal. Historic photographs, paintings, maps, postcards, canal songs, panoramas, and historic information are included in this very interesting and informative presentation.

EDITOR'S CHOICE

Access this Web site from http://www.myreportlinks.com

Come listen to my story, ye landsmen, one and all,
And I'll sing to you the dangers of that raging Canal;
For I am one of many who expects a watery grave,
For I've been at the mercies of the winds and the waves.

The song tells the story of a terrible storm. The songwriter reports that the tow horses disappeared under the raging waters and the canal boat got lost in the dark.

The Captain came on deck with a spy glass in his hand,
But the night was so dark he could not diskiver land;
He said to us with a faltering voice, while tears began
   to fall,
"Prepare to meet your death, my boys, this night on
   the canal."[9]

Due to the fact that the Erie Canal was just four feet deep and forty feet wide, the song was a wild exaggeration.

Mark Twain's Version

American author Mark Twain, originally known as Samuel Langhorne Clemens, also loved to exaggerate. Mark Twain's best-known books are

Mark Twain was a famous author who wrote about life in America, particularly in towns along the water. His birth name was Samuel Clemens.

The Adventures of Tom Sawyer and *Adventures of Huckleberry Finn*. Twain also wrote many newspaper articles, short stories, and poems about life in America.

Probably in response to "The Raging Canal," Twain wrote a canal poem of his own. Called "The Aged Pilot Man," it was published in Twain's book *Roughing It*.

> On the Erie Canal, it was,
> All on a summer's day,
> I sailed forth with my parents
> Far away to Albany.
>
> From out the clouds at noon that day
> There came a dreadful storm,
> That piled the billows high about,
> And filled us with alarm.

In Twain's poem, people on shore advise them to stop the boat and tie it up. But the boat pilot continues through the storm.

> Said Dollinger the pilot man,
> In noble words, but few,—
> "Fear not, but lean on Dollinger,
> And he will fetch you through."

The boat goes on, "the raging mules" tearing through wind and rain. The boat and its passengers are soon in danger "here upon the sea." People running along the shore watch the boat struggle through the storm.

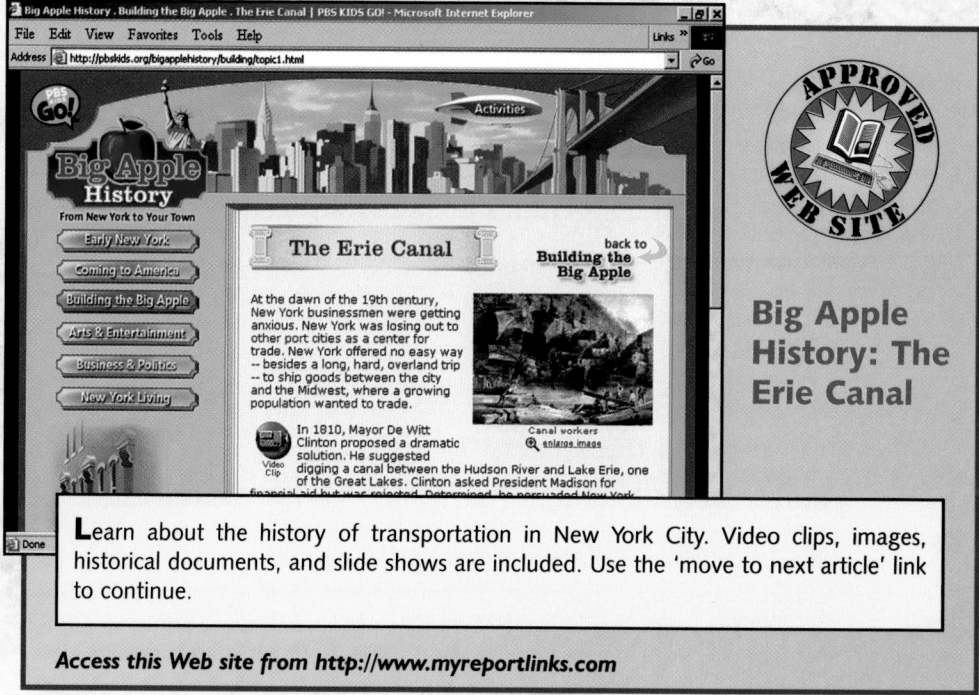

Big Apple History: The Erie Canal

Learn about the history of transportation in New York City. Video clips, images, historical documents, and slide shows are included. Use the 'move to next article' link to continue.

Access this Web site from http://www.myreportlinks.com

"Low bridge! low bridge!" all heads went down,
The laboring bark sped on;
A mill we passed, we passed church,
Hamlets, and fields of corn;
And all the world came out to see,
And chased along the shore

Crying, "Alas, alas, the sheeted rain,
The wind, the tempest's roar!
Alas, the gallant ship and crew,
Can nothing help them more?"

And from our deck sad eyes looked out
Across the stormy scene:
The tossing wake of billows aft,
The bending forests green,

The chickens sheltered under carts
In lee of barn the cows,
The skurrying swine with straw in mouth,
The wild spray from our bows![10]

At the end of Twain's poem, Dollinger the pilot man does get them safely through the storm.

The Canal's Pleasures

Some who traveled the Erie Canal simply enjoyed the trip and the scenery. In 1833, college student and traveler Jonathan Pearson noted the pleasures of the canal in his diary.

Every heart beats for joy at the noble scene. How pleasant too, to see the brilliant lamps of number-less boats passing and repassing upon the smooth unruffled surface of the Canal, to hear the song of the jolly boatman or driver-boy, to see the boats sweeping by freighted with the riches of the West."[11]

Author Frances Trollope moved to the United States from England in 1827. In her book *Domestic Manners of the Americans,* she criticized the culture as rude. She said that Americans did not even notice the natural beauties that surrounded them. Trollope showed her own appreciation of that beauty when she wrote about her travels along the canal.

The Erie Canal has cut through much solid rock, and we often passed between magnificent cliffs.

▲ *Edward Lamson Henry created this painting called "Waiting for the Ferry." Henry captures the idea that many who traveled along the Erie Canal enjoyed the trip and the scenery.*

The little falls of the Mohawk form a lovely scene; the rocks over which the river runs are most fantastic in form. The fall continues nearly a mile; and a beautiful village, called the Little Falls, overhangs it. As many locks occur at this point, we quitted the boat, that we might the better enjoy the scenery, which is one of the wildest description.[12]

American author Samuel Hopkins Adams was a journalist. Adams had grown up along the Erie Canal. In his *Grandfather Stories* he described what the canal meant to young boys. "Our juvenile ambitions centered upon the canal. Let others aspire to become locomotive engineers, Indian scouts, or baseball captains with whiskers; for us the grassy berm, the toiling mules and the smooth-gliding craft were the ultimate in ambition."[13]

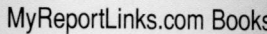

Chapter 2 ▶

WESTWARD BY WATER

Long before the Erie Canal was built, European explorers had searched for a water route across North America. Spanish and English ships sailed up and down both coasts looking for a way to cross between the Atlantic and the Pacific Oceans. This was called the search for the Northwest Passage. They found great rivers, but no route from coast to coast.

In the 1700s, English colonists began to dream of building a canal that would take them into the West.

▶ Erie Dreamers

In 1724, politician and royal official Cadwallader

Cadwallader Colden was a colonial administrator and philosopher who was fond of the natural beauty of upstate New York. He was the first to propose sailing boats from Albany to Lake Erie. Although, he thought it would be best to improve the Mohawk River to accomplish this feat.

Colden took an interest in waterways. Colden also had some expertise in the fields of science and surveying. He traveled northward, through the colony of New York and westward to the Mississippi River.

The Hudson River made a good route between New York City and Albany. Colden called it one of the New World's best waterways. Colden believed that boats could also travel westward from Albany to Lake Erie, and he recommended improving the Mohawk River for navigation. At that time, only a few people thought such a project was even possible to carry out.

Morris and Colles

In 1777, Gouverneur Morris, a New York politician and patriot, suggested building a canal in upstate New York. The American Revolution was underway, but Morris was certain that his country would free itself from British rule. After the war Morris wrote that "one tenth of the expense born by Britain in the last campaign, would enable ships to sail from London through Hudson's river into Lake Erie."[1]

About the same time, an Irish mathematician named Christopher Colles had a similar plan. Colles had worked on waterways in England and Ireland. After he immigrated to America, Colles suggested improving the Mohawk River to reach

the Great Lakes. Although he gained some support after the war, Colles was never able to raise enough money for his project.

After America won the Revolutionary War, several states did begin working on canals. One of those states was Virginia.

▶ George Washington's Canals

In Virginia, farmers who moved inland discovered fertile soil for growing tobacco. But they had to get their produce to Richmond, where it could be shipped to England. The oxcarts they used for carrying farm products moved very slowly on the poor roads and trails.

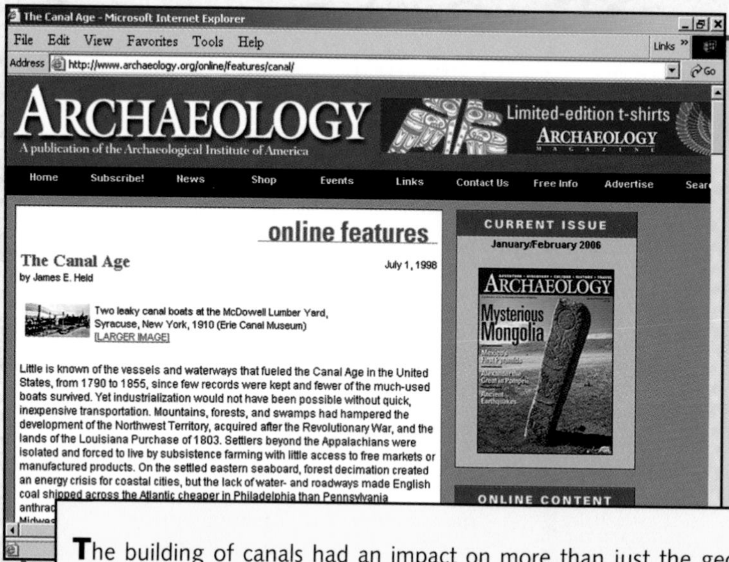

The Canal Age - Microsoft Internet Explorer

File   Edit   View   Favorites   Tools   Help   Links »

Address http://www.archaeology.org/online/features/canal/   Go

ARCHAEOLOGY
A publication of the Archaeological Institute of America

Limited-edition t-shirts
ARCHAEOLOGY
MAGAZINE

Home   Subscribe!   News   Shop   Events   Links   Contact Us   Free Info   Advertise   Search

online features

The Canal Age
by James E. Held

July 1, 1998

Two leaky canal boats at the McDowell Lumber Yard, Syracuse, New York, 1910 (Erie Canal Museum)
[LARGER IMAGE]

Little is known of the vessels and waterways that fueled the Canal Age in the United States, from 1790 to 1855, since few records were kept and fewer of the much-used boats survived. Yet industrialization would not have been possible without quick, inexpensive transportation. Mountains, forests, and swamps had hampered the development of the Northwest Territory, acquired after the Revolutionary War, and the lands of the Louisiana Purchase of 1803. Settlers beyond the Appalachians were isolated and forced to live by subsistence farming with little access to free markets or manufactured products. On the settled eastern seaboard, forest decimation created an energy crisis for coastal cities, but the lack of water- and roadways made English coal shipped across the Atlantic cheaper in Philadelphia than Pennsylvania anthrac...

CURRENT ISSUE
January/February 2006

ARCHAEOLOGY
Mysterious Mongolia

ONLINE CONTENT

APPROVED WEB SITE

The Canal Age

The building of canals had an impact on more than just the geography of an area. Information on canal construction, tunneling, and the legacy of canals is included.

Access this Web site from http://www.myreportlinks.com

Farmers also used rafts and shallow boats to send their goods along the James River. But the James had many shallow areas, rapids, and waterfalls, so the boats and rafts could not carry much weight.

Retired Revolutionary Army general and future president George Washington helped raise money to improve the James River. Workers blasted deeper channels in the river and built America's first canal system that included locks. Locks let boats move from one waterway to another that is at a higher or lower level.

Washington knew that good waterways would help trade. He also hoped that good waterways would help to hold the new country together.

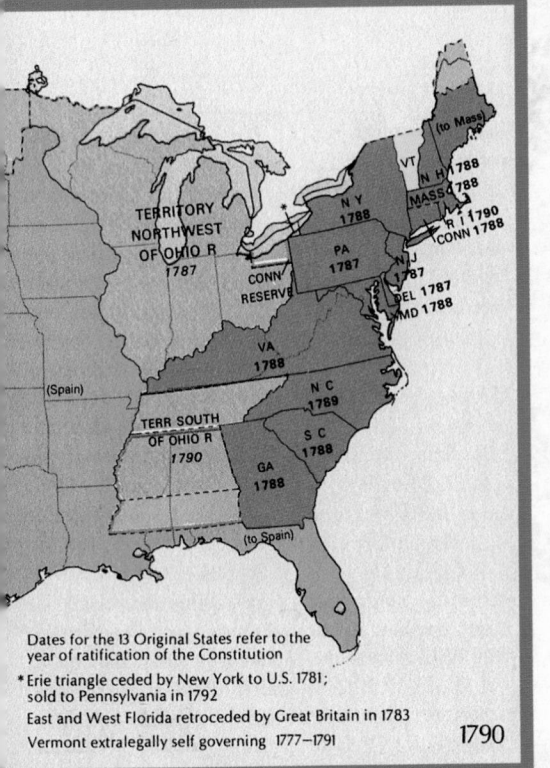

Dates for the 13 Original States refer to the year of ratification of the Constitution

* Erie triangle ceded by New York to U.S. 1781; sold to Pennsylvania in 1792

East and West Florida retroceded by Great Britain in 1783

Vermont extralegally self governing 1777–1791

1790

◁ This is a map of the United States that shows where the borders were in 1790. At this time, settlers were beginning to move into the region labeled "Territory Northwest of the Ohio River." The Erie Canal would bring goods back and forth from New York City to this area.

Beyond the Mountains

American settlers were moving farther westward, crossing the Appalachian Mountains into new territories. But once there, the settlers were on their own. The original thirteen states seemed very far away. In fact, at this time the "West" was considered to be anything west of the Ohio River.

National leaders were worried about those settlers. Off by themselves like that, might those Americans decide to become a separate country? Or might they decide to join another country such as Spain, France, or Great Britain? The British government still had a strong presence in North America. These settlers could simply attempt to join British Canada and become British subjects once again.

In 1785, George Washington wrote to Patrick Henry (then governor of Virginia), "The western settlers (I speak now from my own observations,) stand, as it were, upon a pivot. The touch of a feather would turn them any way."[2]

Washington thought that the Potomac River could be used for trade with the settlers west of the Appalachians. Surely that would help them feel like a part of the United States. But like the James, the Potomac was full of rocks, rapids, and waterfalls. To be useful, the Potomac River would have to be made into a canal.

Washington helped to raise money and to get the work started. Years later, the Potomac became a useful waterway, although it was never financially successful. Even so, the project did help to hold the country together.

From a River to a Constitution

In 1785, Washington held a meeting at his home, Mount Vernon, to discuss the Potomac River Canal. Leaders from Maryland and Virginia came to the meeting, but they did not limit their discussions to the river. They also talked about the new national government—especially about the lack of a strong national government.

In 1786, delegates from all thirteen states held a similar meeting in Annapolis, Maryland. Again, the delegates spoke of other problems besides waterways. By then, they were very concerned about the weakness of the original United States government. After the talks at Annapolis, the delegates called for a Federal Convention in Philadelphia.

The Federal Convention of 1787, also called the Constitutional Convention, completely reorganized our national government. The delegates wrote a new Constitution—the one we still have today (with some amendments added). Under the new Constitution, the United States would have a

Henry Mosler's painting "Washington Crossing the Delaware" shows George Washington before the Battle of Trenton. Washington was a supporter of building canals in America, although he focused on the possibility of canals near the James and Potomac rivers in Virginia.

president. As it turned out, the first president was George Washington.

In 1792, Washington had been United States president for three years. Virginia's Potomac River Canal project was going slowly. The focus of canal builders and engineers shifted from the rivers of Virginia to those of upstate New York.

The Waterways of New York

The Mohawk River was the closest thing to a water route between the upper Hudson River and the Great Lakes. The Mohawk had possibilities, but it also had problems.

Between Albany and the Mohawk River was a sixteen-mile portage. To portage means to haul a boat and its cargo across land. Along the Mohawk there would be other portages, varying in length from one to three miles.

The Mohawk River had about a hundred shallow areas.

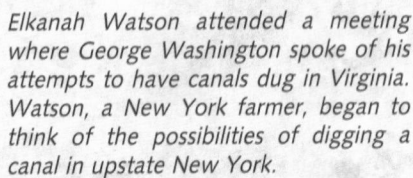

Elkanah Watson attended a meeting where George Washington spoke of his attempts to have canals dug in Virginia. Watson, a New York farmer, began to think of the possibilities of digging a canal in upstate New York.

Even worse, between the Mohawk and Lake Erie was 150 miles of rough territory that would have to be crossed by wagon.[3] All of those problems put strict limits on the kind of boat that could be used and the amount of cargo that could be carried along the Mohawk route.

In 1785, George Washington entertained many guests at his Virginia home, Mount Vernon. The Potomac River Canal was a popular topic in the conversations.[4] That started one guest, Elkanah Watson, thinking about the possibility of digging canals in other parts of the country.

▶ Elkanah Watson and the Mohawk Waterway

In 1788, Watson made a sightseeing trip along the Mohawk River Valley. He was impressed with the scenery, but he saw that the roads were terrible. Sooner or later, Watson thought, a canal must be built to travel between the Great Lakes and the Hudson River.

In 1791, Watson discussed the possibilities with New York State Senator Philip Schuyler. Since he had seen very good canals in England, Schuyler backed Watson's ideas. Influential members of the New York state government soon created a private company called the Western Inland Lock Navigation Company (WILNC) to improve navigation westward from Albany.

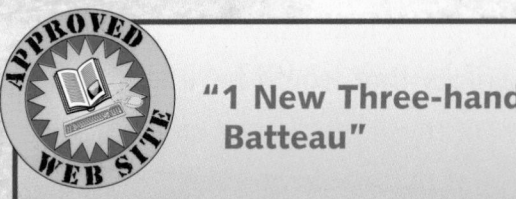

"1 New Three-handed Batteau"

Access this Web site from http://www.myreportlinks.com

This is a history of the Western Inland Lock Navigation Company and the part it played in the construction of the Erie Canal.

The WILNC built short canals around portages and dangerous rapids and dams to raise the water level in shallow areas. Within ten years, the WILNC had created a waterway from Schenectady, New York, to Oswego, New York, on Lake Ontario. Larger boats could now carry heavier loads farther westward than ever before, but the route to Oswego had its limitations.

Lake Ontario was still far from the lands in Ohio and along the Mississippi River that settlers and traders wanted to reach. The passage from Lake Ontario to Lake Erie was blocked by Niagara Falls, which meant a long and difficult portage to get from lake to lake. Even so, this remained the best water route to western New York until the Erie Canal was finished.

▶ Dusty Roads and Deep Mud

When Thomas Jefferson became president in 1801, the United States reached as far west as the Mississippi River. Even so, two-thirds of the population lived within fifty miles of the Atlantic Ocean.[5] Farther from the coast, it was harder to travel, buy goods, or sell goods. In most areas, it

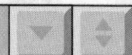

cost just as much to ship anything thirty miles inland as it did to ship the same thing all the way to England.[6]

At that time, American trade goods were being moved along natural rivers, across lakes, and on roads. To improve transportation to the West, several states built turnpike roads that charged tolls to users. These roads were very dusty in dry weather, and they turned to deep mud in wet weather. They were often blocked by fallen trees. Although such roads were very bad, they were cheaper to build than canals.[7]

▶ Steam Power

Meanwhile, a new technology was about to change water travel. Back in 1769, Scotsman James Watt patented a practical steam engine in England. Soon, several inventors were putting steam engines on boats.

American inventor John Fitch built several different kinds of steamboats. Some were pushed by water or air shot out of the engine. Others had paddles, paddle wheels, or propellers.[8] In 1787, members of the U.S. Constitutional Convention saw steam power in action. They watched a demonstration of Fitch's paddle-wheel steamboat on the Delaware River.

Another American inventor, Robert Fulton, spent several years in England and France. Fulton

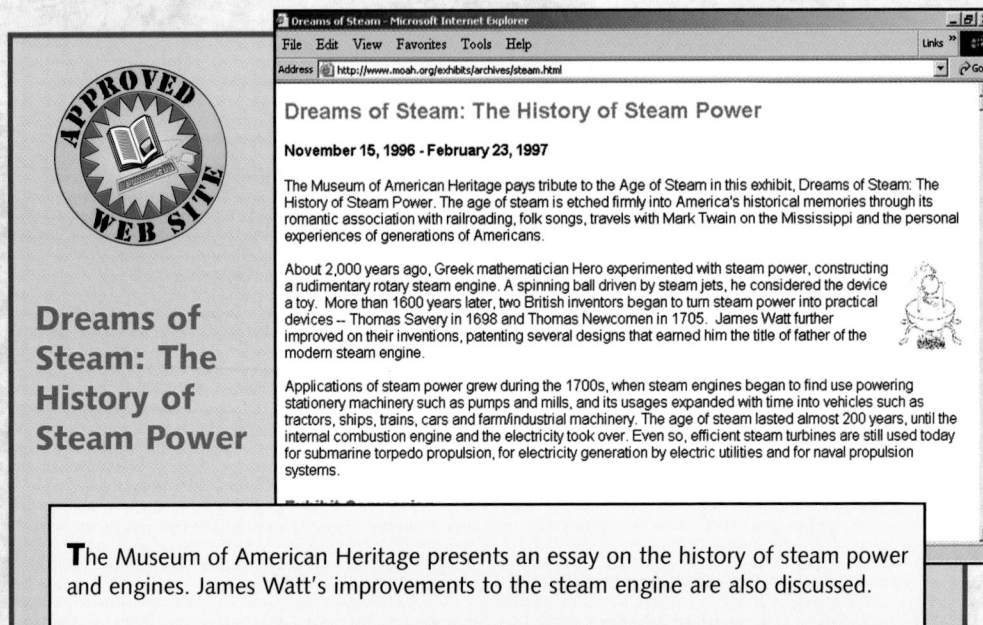

Dreams of Steam: The History of Steam Power

Dreams of Steam: The History of Steam Power

November 15, 1996 - February 23, 1997

The Museum of American Heritage pays tribute to the Age of Steam in this exhibit, Dreams of Steam: The History of Steam Power. The age of steam is etched firmly into America's historical memories through its romantic association with railroading, folk songs, travels with Mark Twain on the Mississippi and the personal experiences of generations of Americans.

About 2,000 years ago, Greek mathematician Hero experimented with steam power, constructing a rudimentary rotary steam engine. A spinning ball driven by steam jets, he considered the device a toy. More than 1600 years later, two British inventors began to turn steam power into practical devices -- Thomas Savery in 1698 and Thomas Newcomen in 1705. James Watt further improved on their inventions, patenting several designs that earned him the title of father of the modern steam engine.

Applications of steam power grew during the 1700s, when steam engines began to find use powering stationary machinery such as pumps and mills, and its usages expanded with time into vehicles such as tractors, ships, trains, cars and farm/industrial machinery. The age of steam lasted almost 200 years, until the internal combustion engine and the electricity took over. Even so, efficient steam turbines are still used today for submarine torpedo propulsion, for electricity generation by electric utilities and for naval propulsion systems.

The Museum of American Heritage presents an essay on the history of steam power and engines. James Watt's improvements to the steam engine are also discussed.

Access this Web site from http://www.myreportlinks.com

worked on canals and also developed mines, torpedoes, a submarine, and a steam-powered boat. In 1797, Fulton wrote a letter to President George Washington about the possibilities of canals. Fulton believed that small canals in Pennsylvania and New York could soon pay for themselves. He also figured that "in about twenty years the Canal would run into Lake Erie."[9]

▶ Fire on the Hudson

In 1806, Robert Fulton returned from Great Britain to the United States. In 1807, he put his first American steamboat into service on the Hudson River.

The *Clermont* had a large paddle wheel on each side, giving it real power to move against the river's current. The *Clermont* traveled the 150 miles upstream from New York City to Albany in thirty-two hours, a remarkable speed for the time.[10] Fulton wrote to a friend that he overtook many sailing sloops and schooners, "and parted with them as if they had been at anchor."[11]

Another of Robert Fulton's friends was Cadwallader Colden. He was the grandson of the Cadwallader Colden who had suggested improving the Mohawk River back in 1724. Colden wrote

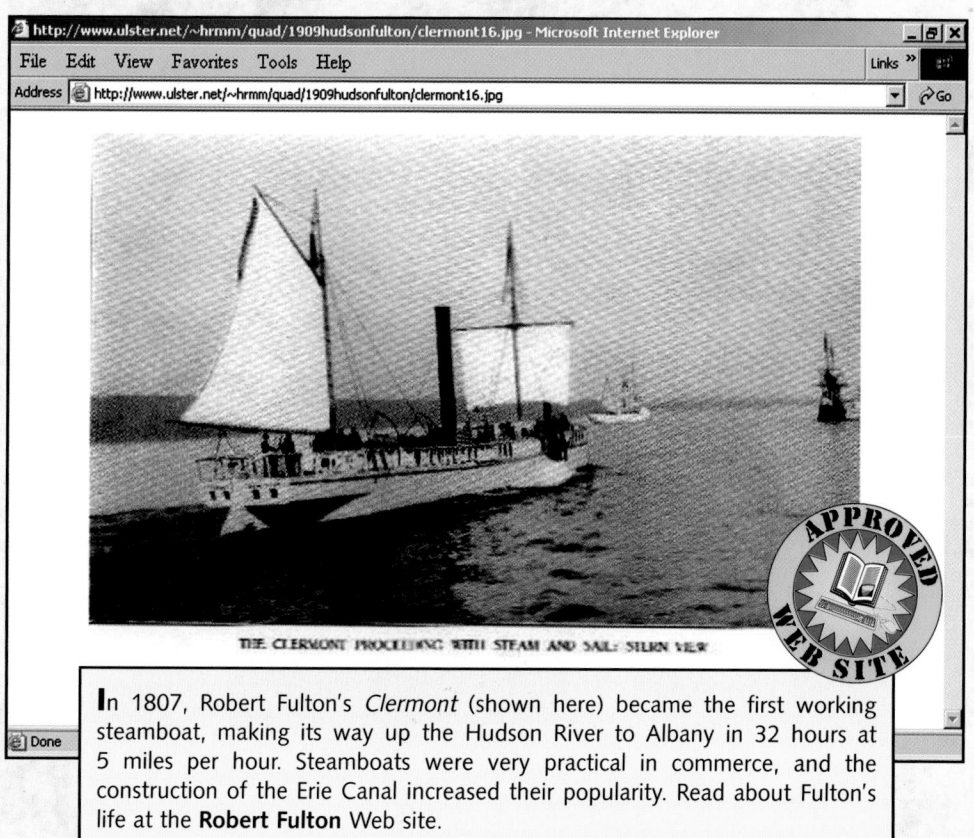

In 1807, Robert Fulton's *Clermont* (shown here) became the first working steamboat, making its way up the Hudson River to Albany in 32 hours at 5 miles per hour. Steamboats were very practical in commerce, and the construction of the Erie Canal increased their popularity. Read about Fulton's life at the **Robert Fulton** Web site.

a biography of Fulton, in which he described the steamboat in colorful terms.

The *Clermont* burned dry pine wood for fuel. Flames, smoke, and sparks rose in the air above the ships smokestack. According to Colden:

> This uncommon light first attracted the attention of the crews of other vessels. Notwithstanding the wind and tide were averse to its approach, they saw with astonishment that it was rapidly coming

A view of Lake Erie from the shores of Canada. The western end of the Erie Canal let out into Lake Erie at Buffalo, New York. From there, goods could be taken north to Canada or south to the Ohio Territory.

toward them; and when it came so near that the noise of the machinery and paddles was heard, the crews (if what was said in the newspapers of the time be true) in some instances shrank beneath their decks from the terrific sight, and left their vessels to go on shore; while others prostrated themselves, and besought Providence to protect them from the approach of the horrible monster which was marching on the tides, and lighting its path by the fires which it vomited."[12]

Steamboats greatly improved transportation on the Hudson River. In a few years, they would be in full-time service on the Mississippi River and other western waterways. Steamboats quickly became the most desirable way to travel and to ship goods.

▶ Essays From a Prison Cell

With the *Clermont* racing up and down the Hudson, connecting the river with Lake Erie began to interest more people than ever before. Gouverneur Morris was again talking about "tapping Lake Erie . . . and leading its waters in an artificial river, directly across the country to the Hudson River."[13]

A New York merchant named Jesse Hawley made a living shipping flour to New York City. But Hawley complained that the toll roads robbed him of his profits. Hawley's business failed, and he spent twenty months in debtors' prison.[14]

While he was in jail, Jesse Hawley decided to do something useful with his life. He believed that the country needed a canal between the Hudson River and Lake Erie, and he devoted himself to that cause. Even though Hawley had little education, he started writing essays about building a canal to Lake Erie. A newspaper published the essays under Hawley's pen name, Hercules. Some readers thought the essays were the ravings of a maniac. Others admired the detail that Hawley provided about how it might be done.

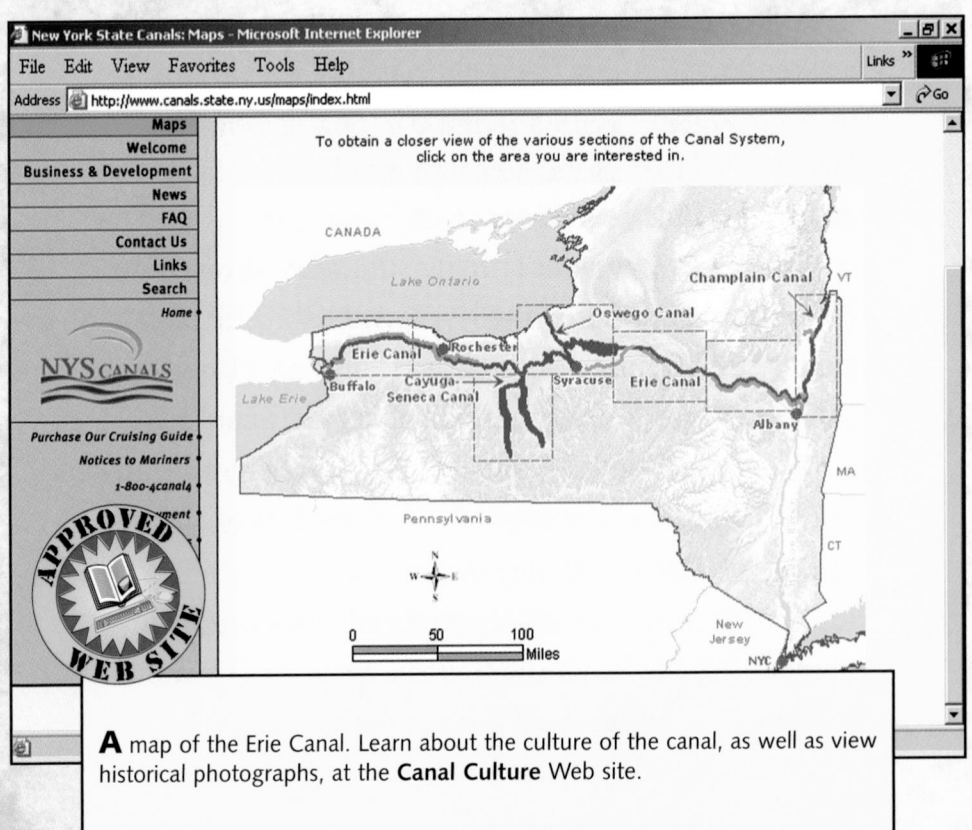

A map of the Erie Canal. Learn about the culture of the canal, as well as view historical photographs, at the **Canal Culture** Web site.

According to Peter L. Bernstein in *Wedding of the Waters,* "Jesse Hawley, bankrupt businessman and jailbird, accomplished more than anyone up to that point in provoking action to build an uninterrupted waterway across the State of New York. [His essays] attracted attention in the highest places. Later the essays would serve as a kind of guidebook . . ."[15]

Eyes On—and Off—an Erie Canal

In 1808, the New York legislature hired engineer James Geddes to survey the route for a canal. But the planners were not able to interest President Thomas Jefferson in making the canal a national project. Jefferson was still eager to complete Virginia's Potomac River Canal. An Erie Canal would be much longer and much more expensive. In 1809, Jefferson said, "you talk of making a canal of 350 miles through the wilderness—it is little short of madness to think of it at this day."[16]

In 1810, New York state appointed a board of wealthy and well-known men to oversee the development of the canal. The members of the Canal Commission included Gouverneur Morris and the mayor of New York City, De Witt Clinton. The following year, Robert Fulton joined the group. The commissioners tried to move ahead with plans for the canal, but soon everything was interrupted by the War of 1812.

Clinton and Morris made a trip to Washington in 1811, hoping to get support from President Madison for the Erie Canal project. But they could not attract any interest from either the president or from Congress. That was partly because of conflicts between other countries that the United States would not be able to avoid becoming involved in. The federal government was afraid to fund large projects like canals because it feared it would need the money to pay for armed forces to help protect the nation.

Wars were being waged between France and England for decades. This had disturbed America's efforts to build international trade. The British harassed United States ships. They even seized

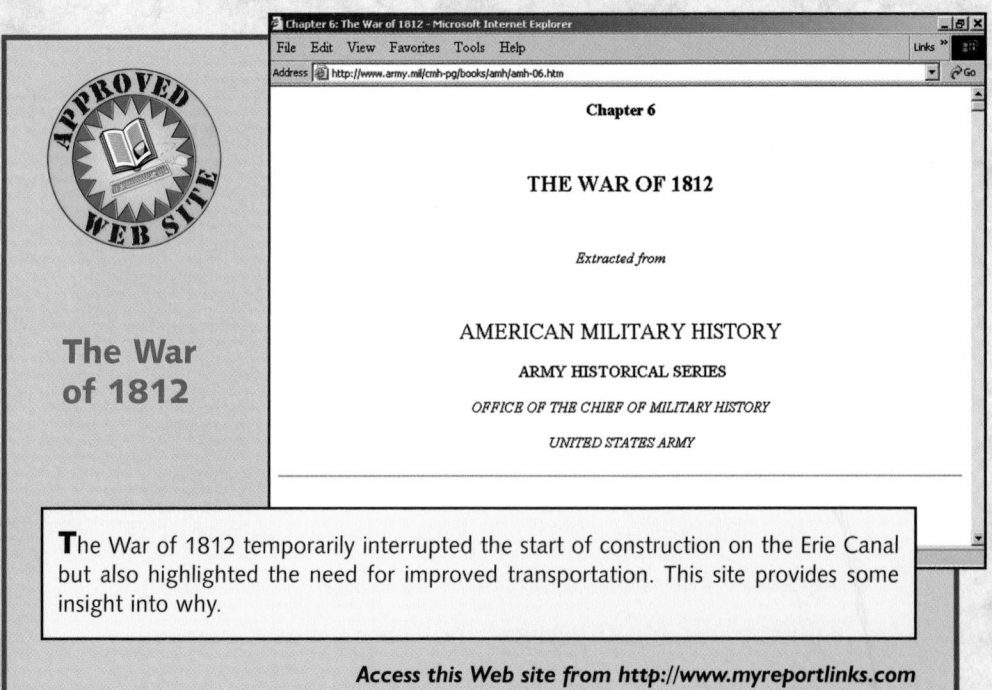

The War of 1812

Chapter 6: The War of 1812 - Microsoft Internet Explorer

File   Edit   View   Favorites   Tools   Help   Links »

Address http://www.army.mil/cmh-pg/books/amh/amh-06.htm   Go

Chapter 6

THE WAR OF 1812

Extracted from

AMERICAN MILITARY HISTORY

ARMY HISTORICAL SERIES

OFFICE OF THE CHIEF OF MILITARY HISTORY

UNITED STATES ARMY

The War of 1812 temporarily interrupted the start of construction on the Erie Canal but also highlighted the need for improved transportation. This site provides some insight into why.

Access this Web site from http://www.myreportlinks.com

sailors and forced them into the British Royal Navy. This was called impressment. In 1812, President Madison insisted that Congress must declare war on Great Britain. Congress did so in June.

The War of 1812 between Great Britain and the United States went on into 1815. Most of the fighting was in the north, especially in the region surrounding the Great Lakes. During the war, military supplies had to be moved from New York City to ports on Lake Ontario and Lake Erie. Moving supplies proved difficult, and that made it clearer to some New Yorkers that transportation needed to be improved in the Great Lakes region.

De Witt Clinton and the Canal

Clinton had been a U.S. senator from New York, mayor of New York City, a state senator, and lieutenant governor of the state. He held some of the jobs at the same time. He even ran a failed race for president of the United States. But Clinton would become best known for his support of the Erie Canal.

In 1816, President Madison again vetoed financial support for the canal.[17] If there was going to be an Erie Canal, New Yorkers were going to have to build it themselves. De Witt Clinton argued so strongly for the canal that even his political opponents finally voted for the project.[18] That same year, the New York legislature appointed

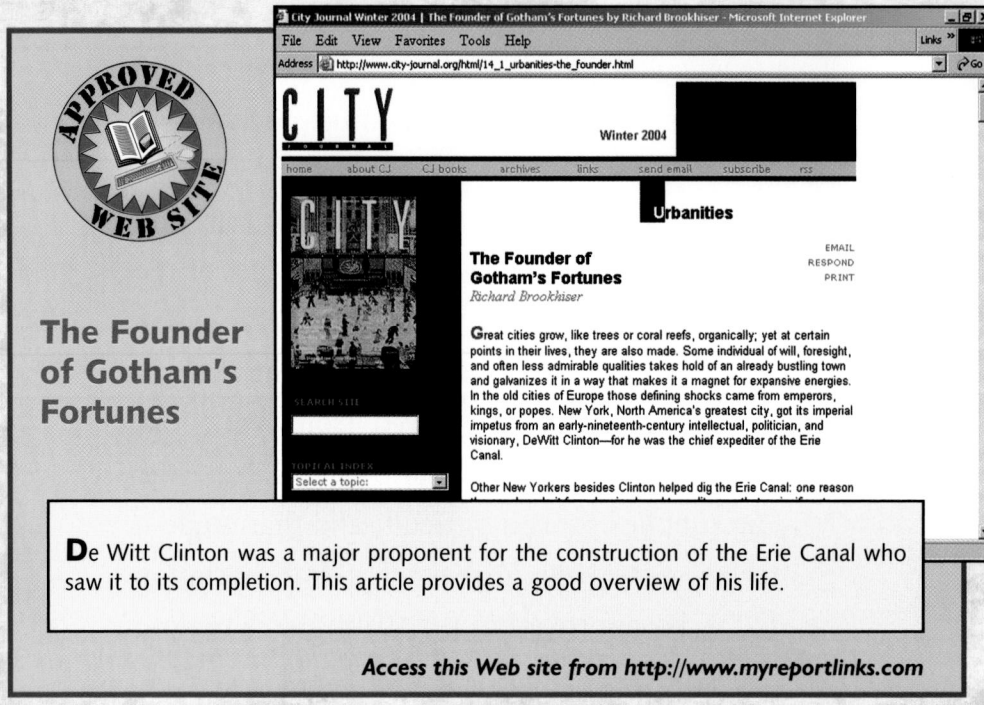

The Founder of Gotham's Fortunes

De Witt Clinton was a major proponent for the construction of the Erie Canal who saw it to its completion. This article provides a good overview of his life.

Access this Web site from http://www.myreportlinks.com

five commissioners and gave them funds to get started. Clinton was one of those new commissioners, and he secured the bulk of the funding from British investors.

Even while the Erie Canal was being built, many people would still laugh at the idea. Some politicians jeeringly called it Clinton's Big Ditch or Clinton's Folly. After all, the longest existing canal in the United States was ten times shorter than the canal that Clinton was proposing.

Chapter 3 ▶

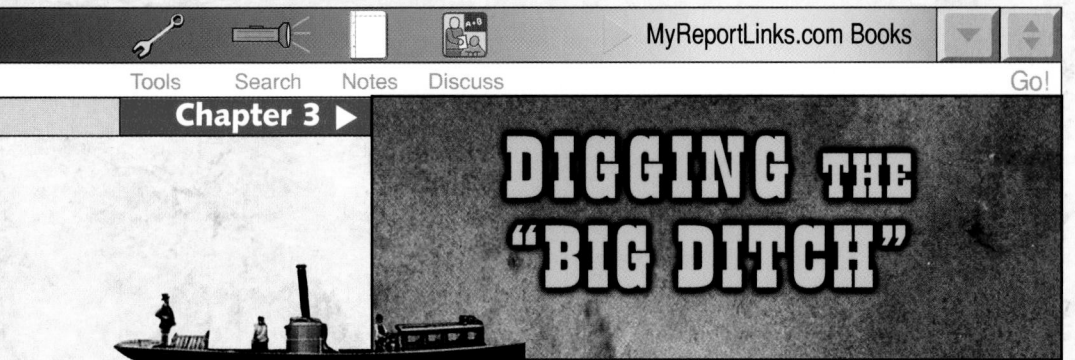

DIGGING THE "BIG DITCH"

On the morning of July 4, 1817, cannons boomed near the village of Rome, New York. Dignitaries made speeches, then a contractor dug the first shovelful of earth. After all the political and financial wrangling, after one hundred years of hopes and plans, work on the Erie Canal was beginning.

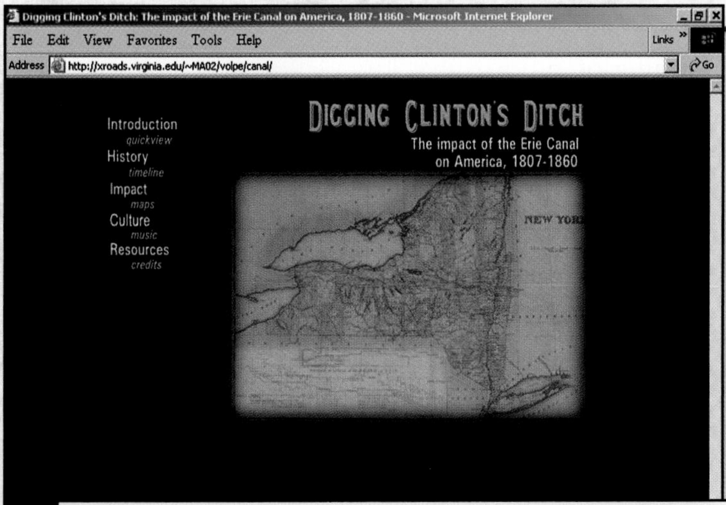
Digging Clinton's Ditch: The impact of the Erie Canal on America, 1807-1860 - Microsoft Internet Explorer
File Edit View Favorites Tools Help
Links
Address http://xroads.virginia.edu/~MA02/volpe/canal/
Go
DIGGING CLINTON'S DITCH
The impact of the Erie Canal on America, 1807-1860
Introduction
quickview
History
timeline
Impact
maps
Culture
music
Resources
credits
NEW YOR
Done

APPROVED WEB SITE

Digging Clinton's Ditch: The Impact of the Erie Canal on America, 1807–1860

Members of the University of Virginia have created a comprehensive Web site that provides good information on how the canal changed America. Maps, a time line, photographs, canal music, and an overview of its history are included.

Access this Web site from http://www.myreportlinks.com

▶ The Grand Project

When the digging of the Erie Canal got started, some canals were already in use in the United States. Most were less than 2 miles long, and the longest was only 28 miles.[1] That was because building a canal in the United States was usually a hard job.

European canals were built in populated areas and on level land. Workers were available, materials could be brought to the workers easily, and the canals were fairly simple. But in upper New York State, over three hundred miles of wilderness lay between the Hudson River at Albany and Lake Erie at Buffalo. The Erie Canal would have to cross over rivers and valleys, go through marshes and forests, and cut through rock. In many places, there were no roads on which to bring in supplies.

The ditch would finally be 363 miles long, 40 feet wide at the surface, 26 feet wide at the bottom, and 4 feet deep. It cost

Engineer Nathan Roberts designed the locks at Lockport. This was the steepest set of locks along the Erie Canal. This photo of what passengers on a canal boat would see as it headed into the locks was taken in 1970.

$7 million to build. The Erie Canal was a much larger and more difficult project than anyone had ever before attempted in America or in Europe.[2]

Planners and Designers

Surveyors and engineers chose the route and designed what was to be built. At that time, there were no professional American engineers with canal-building experience, but men with technical backgrounds applied their training to the new problems. They learned as they built, and by the time the canal was finished, they were experts.

The canal commissioners divided the job into three sections, and appointed the best men they could find to carry out the project. James Geddes was engineer on the western section, Benjamin Wright on the middle section, and Charles Broadhead on the eastern section. Wright and Geddes were not even trained as surveyors or engineers, but they proved very good at their jobs.[3]

A young veteran of the War of 1812 also joined the engineering team. His name was Canvass White, and he was eager to gain more information about canals in England. Beginning in 1817, White spent a year studying details of the English canals.

Another engineer, Nathan Roberts, designed the locks for the steepest and most difficult rise in the waterway. At a point near Lake Erie, boats had to get up or down a 60-foot change in the level of

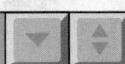

the canal. Roberts designed two sets of five locks each—one set for boats going up and the other for boats going down—to keep the traffic moving.

John Jervis started out as an axman working on the canal. He taught himself surveying at night and moved up to a job as a surveyor. In 1820, Jervis was put in charge of the canal's central section.[4]

The engineers staked out lines to show where the canal would go. First, axmen labored to cut brush and small trees out of the way. Then they cut and drove wooden stakes to mark the line. Then other workers, called targetmen, helped the surveyors measure changes in the level of the land. The engineers were paid at least a dollar a day, plus expenses. The targetmen received three dollars a week.[5]

Workers

The canal was built by hundreds of workers. This included quarrymen, stonecutters, masons, carpenters, loggers, bridge builders, farmers, teamsters, and general laborers. Many of these were hired locally for each section of the canal.

The canal commissioners decided to hire local people to work on each section of the canal. Those who lived nearby knew the territory, and they would take pride in the work. So the canal would be built in sections, some as short as one-quarter mile. Historian F. Daniel Larkin has pointed out

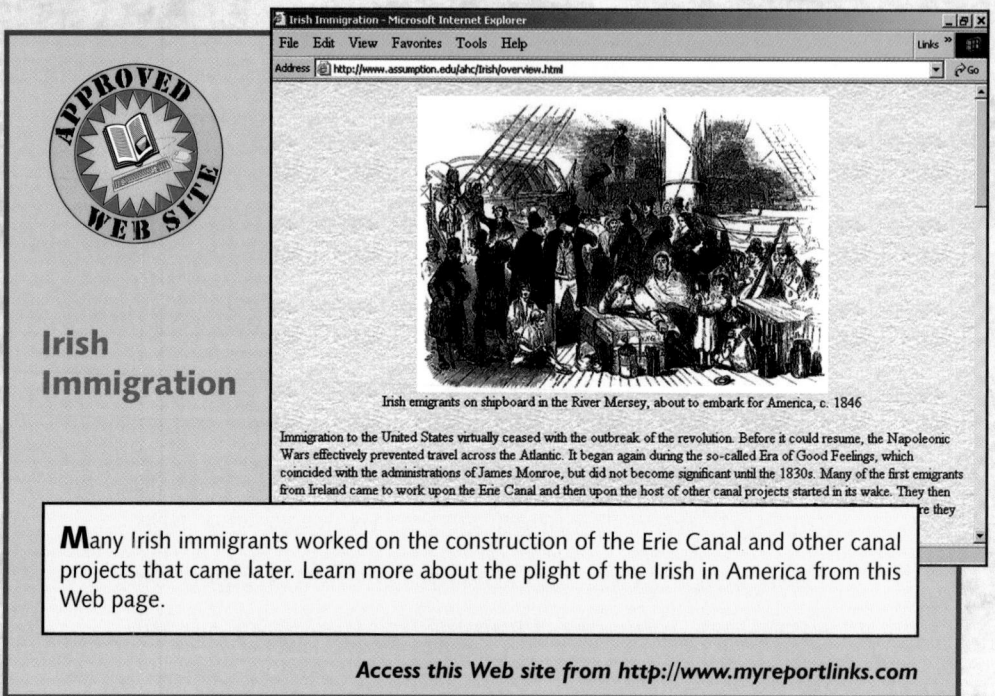

Irish
Immigration

Irish Immigration - Microsoft Internet Explorer

File   Edit   View   Favorites   Tools   Help

Address   http://www.assumption.edu/ahc/irish/overview.html

Irish emigrants on shipboard in the River Mersey, about to embark for America, c. 1846

Immigration to the United States virtually ceased with the outbreak of the revolution. Before it could resume, the Napoleonic Wars effectively prevented travel across the Atlantic. It began again during the so-called Era of Good Feelings, which coincided with the administrations of James Monroe, but did not become significant until the 1830s. Many of the first emigrants from Ireland came to work upon the Erie Canal and then upon the host of other canal projects started in its wake. They then

Many Irish immigrants worked on the construction of the Erie Canal and other canal projects that came later. Learn more about the plight of the Irish in America from this Web page.

Access this Web site from http://www.myreportlinks.com

that this allowed "as many people as possible to benefit from the project," and was "in keeping with the democratic reforms sweeping the country."[6] Some workers were freed slaves, and as time went on immigrants were added to the mix.

As the work progressed, more help was needed than was locally available. Irish laborers were brought in from New York City, and by the time the job was finished, one third of the work force was Irish.[7] For immigrants, the canal provided jobs.

Years later, one Irish laborer said that staying in America had worked out well for him and his family. In Ireland, he said, they had been landless and powerless. But here, "I have a fine farm of land now, which I own outright. No one can demand rent from me. My family and I can eat our fill of bread and meat, butter and milk any day we like throughout the year."[8]

But another immigrant wrote back to friends in Wales that both the passage to and life in the new land were expensive. "I beg all my old neighbors not to think of coming here," he warned.[9]

The workers were given sleeping quarters and sometimes food and drink. They lived in shanties that Carol Sheriff describes in *The Artificial River:* "By all accounts, workers were housed in these shanties like animals in barns; their very living conditions were dehumanizing."[10] Even so, it was the men who were doing the work who discovered ways to make the job faster and easier.

Clearing the Way

Many trees had to be removed from the path of the canal. The workers themselves invented machines to help get trees out of the way. Today, we do not even know their names, but their inventions certainly speeded up the work. For example, trees had to be cut down. These workmen might not have had a lot of schooling, but they knew that a little pressure applied in the right way could produce a much larger result.

The workmen attached a cable near the top of a tree they wanted to move. The other end of the

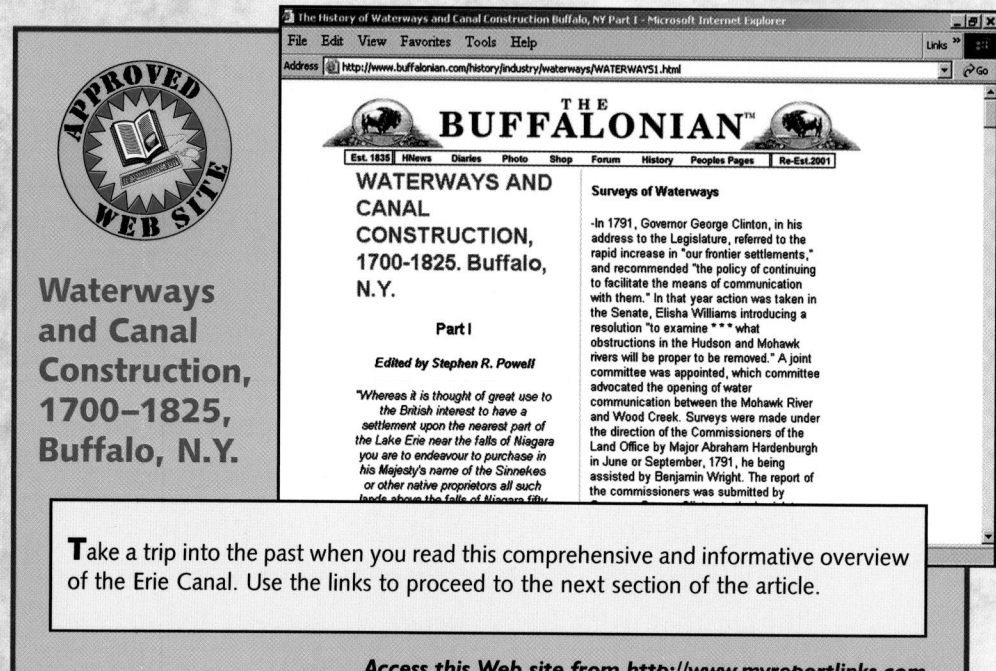

Waterways and Canal Construction, 1700–1825, Buffalo, N.Y.

Take a trip into the past when you read this comprehensive and informative overview of the Erie Canal. Use the links to proceed to the next section of the article.

Access this Web site from http://www.myreportlinks.com

line wound around a wheel. A single man could crank the wheel, which tightened the cable and pulled the tree over. The tree would either break or pull up by the roots. According to one historian, this machine did the work of one hundred swings of an ax.[11]

If a tree stump and roots were left in the ground, another invention took care of those. The huge stump removal device rested on two big wheels, each 16 feet in diameter. Between the two wheels was a thick 30-foot-long axle. Fastened to the center of the axle was another wheel, 14 feet in diameter, which did not touch the ground.

Workmen positioned the entire wheeled device over a stubborn stump. They blocked the big wheels, so the machine would stay in place. They wound a chain around the axle and fastened the chain to the stump. Then they wrapped a strong rope around the center wheel and attached it to a team of horses or oxen. The animals pulled the rope, which turned the center wheel and forced the axle to turn. That tightened the chain that was attached to the stump and popped the stump out of the ground.[12]

Digging the Ditch

At first, men with picks and shovels dug the big ditch by hand. They hauled the dirt away in

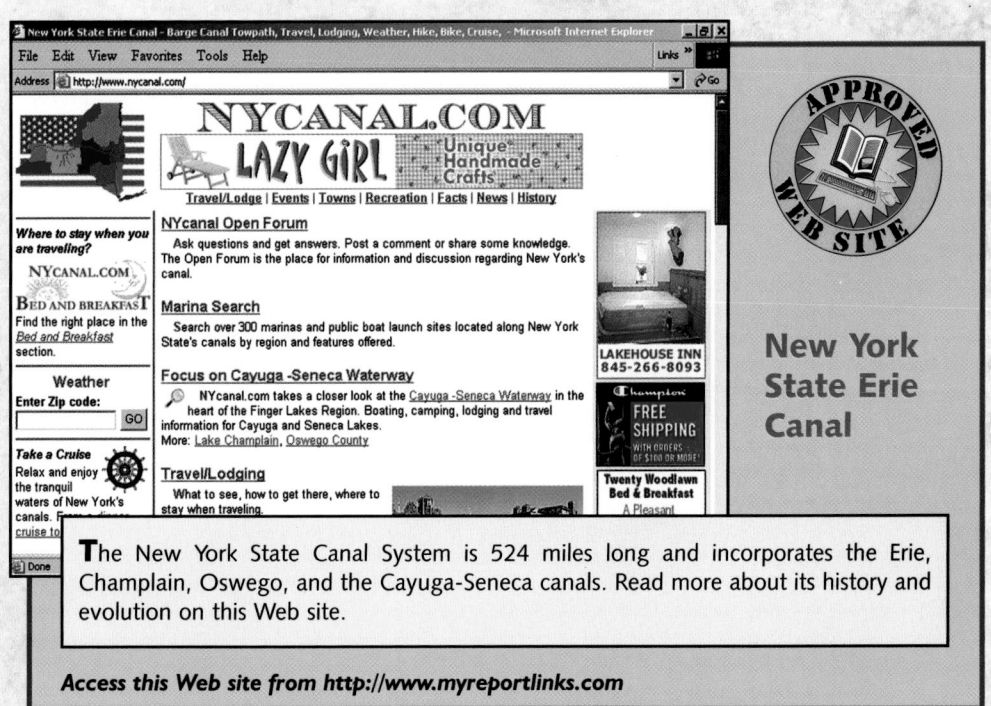

New York State Erie Canal

The New York State Canal System is 524 miles long and incorporates the Erie, Champlain, Oswego, and the Cayuga-Seneca canals. Read more about its history and evolution on this Web site.

Access this Web site from http://www.myreportlinks.com

wheelbarrows. Many tales were told of these immensely strong men that dug the canal. "Popular fancy turned the Irish immigrants who built the Big Ditch into epic fighters and drinkers."[13] But again, the workmen themselves came up with better ways to do the job.

Many of the workmen were local farmers who doubtless had experience with horse-drawn plows. The sharp, iron plows could slice open the earth much more easily than a man with a spade. Then the earth was much easier to remove. The workmen put to use a newly-invented plow known as the "slip scraper." This machine was

◁ *This is a sketch of how the town of West Troy, New York, looked along the Erie Canal in the late 1800s.*

a nineteenth-century version of what we would call a bulldozer.[14]

The workers used teams of horses pulling wagons to carry away the dirt much faster than wheelbarrows could. An added benefit was that the horses packed down the ground on the sides of the canal, making it more solid.[15]

As the workmen dug out the ditch, they built up the sides of the canal. On one side was a berm, or raised edge, to keep the water in. On the other side was a raised towpath, where teams of horses or mules would walk, pulling the canal boats along.

Blasting Through Rock

In some places, the ditch had to be cut through solid rock. The workmen had only black powder. Dynamite and nitroglycerine had not been invented yet. The workers had to drill holes in the rock by hand, place the powder, and set it off. Sometimes workers were injured or killed by the explosions.[16]

At Lockport, where Nathan Roberts's locks were built, the canal bed had to be blasted out of a mountainside. Called the "deep cut," it allowed the water to flow 30 feet below ground level. That seemed an amazing achievement to onlookers at the time.

Digging was held up by winter snows and by the runoff from melting snows. Heavy rains also

complicated the job. Even so, the work moved ahead during the summer of 1818. When it had to be stopped for winter, the commissioners were pleased with the progress. But they were still faced with one serious construction problem.

▶ Waterproof Cement

After the ditch for the locks was ready, workers lined it with stones. But how could they seal the spaces between the stones to prevent the canal from leaking? They soon found that the cement used for ordinary building was not waterproof.

Cement is a powder that is usually made from crushed, burned, and ground rock. Mixed with water, cement is the glue that holds concrete together. Concrete is a building material that also includes sand, clay, gravel, and other materials. Concrete can be used by itself (as in sidewalks) or to hold stones or bricks in place. For the locks of the Erie Canal, the concrete had to be both water-proof and very strong.

De Witt Clinton had read that the Romans had developed a cement to use under water, and he got some samples of it from Italy. The Roman cement worked, but it would be very expensive to import enough of it for the Erie Canal.

One of the engineers on the project, Canvass White, found a solution to the problem. He heard about an excellent type of limestone found about

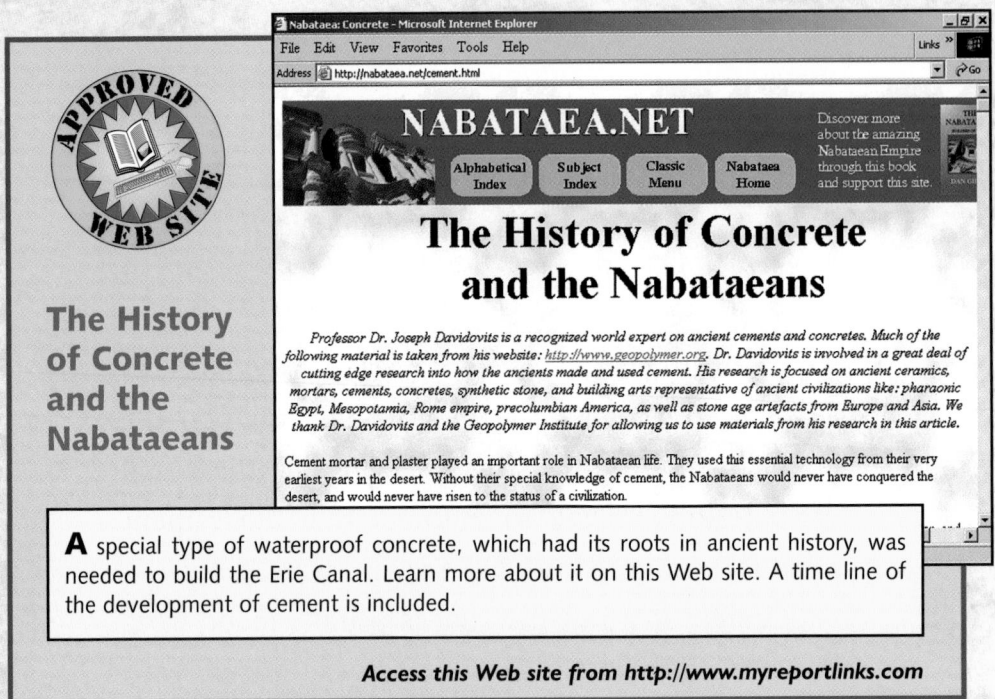

The History of Concrete and the Nabataeans

NABATAEA.NET

Discover more
about the amazing
Nabataean Empire
through this book
and support this site.

Alphabetical Index   Subject Index   Classic Menu   Nabataea Home

The History of Concrete and the Nabataeans

Professor Dr. Joseph Davidovits is a recognized world expert on ancient cements and concretes. Much of the following material is taken from his website: http://www.geopolymer.org. Dr. Davidovits is involved in a great deal of cutting edge research into how the ancients made and used cement. His research is focused on ancient ceramics, mortars, cements, concretes, synthetic stone, and building arts representative of ancient civilizations like: pharaonic Egypt, Mesopotamia, Rome empire, precolumbian America, as well as stone age artefacts from Europe and Asia. We thank Dr. Davidovits and the Geopolymer Institute for allowing us to use materials from his research in this article.

Cement mortar and plaster played an important role in Nabataean life. They used this essential technology from their very earliest years in the desert. Without their special knowledge of cement, the Nabataeans would never have conquered the desert, and would never have risen to the status of a civilization.

A special type of waterproof concrete, which had its roots in ancient history, was needed to build the Erie Canal. Learn more about it on this Web site. A time line of the development of cement is included.

Access this Web site from http://www.myreportlinks.com

twenty miles from Syracuse, New York, at a village called Chittenango. Limestone is a type of rock that can be used in building or ground into a powder for cement.

Canvass White and Benjamin Wright went to the village to check out the stone. A local scientist named Andrew Barto brought them a handful of wet, ground limestone. He mixed it with sand, formed it into a ball, and left it in a pail of water. The next morning they found that the ball had hardened.[17]

Soon a mill was set up at the village to manufacture cement at a reasonable price for the Erie

Canal project. It would be used in the waterway for locks, bridges, and aqueducts.

▶ Canal Locks

Building a canal on flat, empty land is basically a matter of digging a large ditch. But building a canal between two bodies of water that are at different heights above sea level is another matter. If water from one end flows downhill toward the other end, the canal then has a current. It is not an improvement over a natural river, and it can cause water problems at one end or the other.

🔲 http://www.rochester.lib.ny.us/rochimag/rochpublib/rpf/rpf01/rpf01901.jpg - Microsoft Internet Explorer   _ 🗗 ✕

File   Edit   View   Favorites   Tools   Help   Links »

Address 🗐 http://www.rochester.lib.ny.us/rochimag/rochpublib/rpf/rpf01/rpf01901.jpg   ▼ 🧷 Go

Since Lake Erie is 566 feet higher than the Hudson River, the Erie Canal must raise the boats at certain points along the route. This is done using locks, shown here. View documents and other photographs related to the Erie Canal at the **Rochester Images: The Erie Canal** Web site.

EDITOR'S CHOICE

One end of the Erie Canal would be much higher than the other end. Because of the valleys along the way, the difference between the lowest and highest points of the route was about 680 feet.[18] The difference in height between one end of the finished canal and the other would be about 575 feet.

Canal designers had to work out a series of level waterways for boats to travel, and a way to get those boats from one stretch of water to the next. Over the centuries, designers invented various kinds of locks for that job. For example, the famous Italian artist and inventor Leonardo da Vinci (1452–1519) drew plans for highly efficient canal locks.[19] The Erie Canal engineers and workmen had to build locks. Most of these were lift locks, to raise boats from one level of water to another.

A lift lock is an elevator for boats. When a boat floats into a lock, a gate closes behind it. Then water is let into or out of the lock, raising or lowering the boat. The boat can then float out of the lock into the next part of the waterway.[20]

Going Through the Locks

Jacob Abbott's book *Marco Paul's Travels on the Erie Canal* describes a young boy's journey on the canal in the 1840s. Abbott relates a story in which Paul's group comes upon a lock:

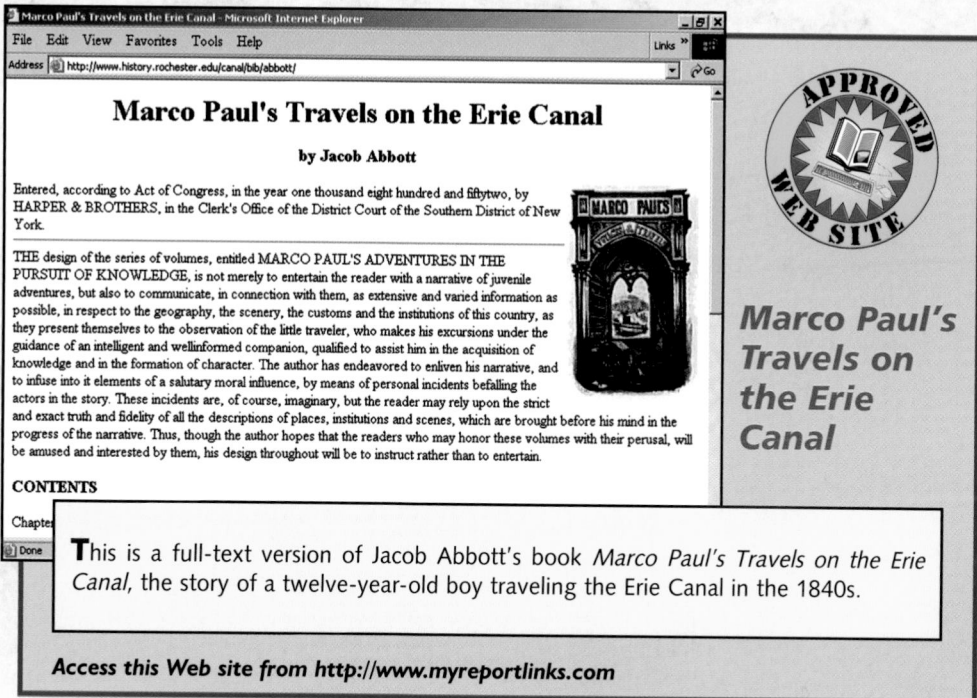

Marco Paul's Travels on the Erie Canal - Microsoft Internet Explorer

File   Edit   View   Favorites   Tools   Help   Links »

Address http://www.history.rochester.edu/canal/bib/abbott/   Go

Marco Paul's Travels on the Erie Canal

by Jacob Abbott

Entered, according to Act of Congress, in the year one thousand eight hundred and fiftytwo, by HARPER & BROTHERS, in the Clerk's Office of the District Court of the Southern District of New York.

THE design of the series of volumes, entitled MARCO PAUL'S ADVENTURES IN THE PURSUIT OF KNOWLEDGE, is not merely to entertain the reader with a narrative of juvenile adventures, but also to communicate, in connection with them, as extensive and varied information as possible, in respect to the geography, the scenery, the customs and the institutions of this country, as they present themselves to the observation of the little traveler, who makes his excursions under the guidance of an intelligent and wellinformed companion, qualified to assist him in the acquisition of knowledge and in the formation of character. The author has endeavored to enliven his narrative, and to infuse into it elements of a salutary moral influence, by means of personal incidents befalling the actors in the story. These incidents are, of course, imaginary, but the reader may rely upon the strict and exact truth and fidelity of all the descriptions of places, institutions and scenes, which are brought before his mind in the progress of the narrative. Thus, though the author hopes that the readers who may honor these volumes with their perusal, will be amused and interested by them, his design throughout will be to instruct rather than to entertain.

CONTENTS

Chapter

Marco Paul's Travels on the Erie Canal

This is a full-text version of Jacob Abbott's book *Marco Paul's Travels on the Erie Canal*, the story of a twelve-year-old boy traveling the Erie Canal in the 1840s.

Access this Web site from http://www.myreportlinks.com

"They saw that as the canal approached the lock, it suddenly narrowed and entered between two high walls of stone, so near each other that there was just room for the boat to go in. This was the lock, and at the farthest end of it were two great wooden gates, which closed the passage way, and Marco did not see how they were to get through."[21]

Marco Paul and the people on the canal boat with him had no reason to worry. On the other side of the gates, the Canal continued at a higher level than their canal boat was presently at. When the canal boat reached the lock, the horses that were pulling the boat stopped. A canal worker unhooked the ropes from the horses. When the boat was in place in the lock the ropes were attached to the horses once again.

Then, the gates would open allowing water to rush in from the other side of the canal. As the water filled the lock, it would raise the boat up with it. Soon, the boat would be level with the other side of the canal. Then, the gates at the other end swung open. The ropes that were attached to the horses, called the towline, were once again attached to the boat. Now, the horses could once again pull the boat with Marco and the rest of the passengers along the Erie Canal.

> After a short time the boat was raised quite high in the lock, and Forester and Marco found that the water was getting to be nearly as high in the lock as it was in the higher part of the canal above. When, at length, it was exactly at the same level, the man swung open the great gates, at the upper end, and then the towline was fastened to the boat again, and the packet was drawn along . . . and the boat glided away again on its voyage.[22]

▶ More Locks and Other Structures

In addition to lift locks, workers built dry dock locks. These were locks that contained no water. They were used for building and repairing boats. There were also special locks for weighing boats. Canal boats were charged tolls according to the type and weight of the cargo they carried. On the Erie Canal there were seven weigh locks used to

▲ *This tanker is about to leave Lock 11 on the Erie Canal. This photo was taken in October 1941.*

judge the tonnage of cargo. At the beginning of the season, the boat was weighed empty. Then on each trip it was weighed fully loaded. The difference between the two figures was the weight of the cargo which determined the amount of tolls that would be charged.

To be weighed, a boat would enter a special lock. In the earliest Erie Canal weigh locks, weight was judged by how much the water rose when the boat was in the lock. Later weigh locks could be drained to let the boat rest on a wooden cradle attached to a scale. After the boat was weighed, the lock again filled with water and the boat continued its trip.

Aqueducts were built so that the keelboats and animals pulling the boats could cross over rivers as they moved along the Erie Canal. This aqueduct crosses the Mohawk River in Rexford, New York.

Spillways along the canal let excess water run off and kept the canal depth at four feet. A spillway is a trench that allows water to flow over or around a lock. Reservoirs held an extra water supply, and culverts let small streams and drainage

water pass under the canal. A culvert is, in essence, an underground drain. At some towns laborers built canal basins and piers for docking the boats. But perhaps the most amazing-looking structures on the Erie Canal were the aqueducts.

Bridges for Boats

Since ancient times, aqueducts have been built to carry water to large cities. These can be simple troughs or pipes on hillsides, or they can be complicated raised channels. The ancient Romans were skilled at building aqueducts, and today we still build them to supply water to cities such as Los Angeles and New York.

Large streams crossed over the Erie Canal by aqueducts. And eighteen aqueducts allowed the canal to cross over rivers.[23] They would have to cross over the rivers by aqueduct, because otherwise they would float with the river in the wrong direction. Also, the mules pulling the barge or canal boat would be unable to cross the rivers without drowning. The canal, its towpath, and its boats would be raised on a series of stone arches. Canal boats floated along overhead, as if in the sky.

Chapter 4 ▶

CELEBRATIONS AND ADVENTURES

The Erie Canal was built in sections, and the completion of each part was cause for local celebrations. Townspeople held parades, parties, dances, and theatrical performances. They heard artillery salutes, speeches, prayers, and songs. They took to the water in festively decorated boats.

Each completed section of the canal was useful. In 1823, the 280 miles between Albany and

This is how the Erie Canal appeared in Syracuse, New York, around 1900. Syracuse was one of the cities that benefited greatly from the construction of the canal.

Rochester was finished. Boat traffic was soon heavy, and the tolls collected on that section helped pay for the rest of the canal.[1]

Putting parts of the canal into use changed the lives of those who lived nearby. Farms and towns that had been separated by rough country or difficult waterways were suddenly easy to visit. Trade improved, raising local living standards, and finer homes appeared in towns along the waterway.

Long before it was finished, the Erie Canal was one of the greatest wonders of its time. In 1820, a Canal Commission report expressed amazement at seeing "large boats drawn by horses, upon waters . . . through cultivated fields, forests, swamps, over ravines, creeks and morasses, and from one elevation to another . . ."[2]

Clinton Pushes On

Some people began to refer to the Erie project as "The Grand Canal," but others still considered it a folly, or foolish idea. Over the years, the opinions of politicians and the public about the canal—and about De Witt Clinton—changed many times.

Clinton was governor of New York from 1817, when the digging began, until 1823. Then, Clinton was defeated by opposing politicians and removed from his job as canal commissioner. But Clinton never gave up his support for the project. In a speech he gave in 1824, he described the exciting

▲ *This is an old print depicting New York Governor De Witt Clinton emptying water from Lake Erie into New York Harbor. This ceremony was the "wedding of the waters."*

future he believed the Erie Canal would help create:

> As a bond of union between the Atlantic and Western states, it may prevent the dismemberment of the American Empire. As an organ of communication between the Hudson, the Mississippi, the St. Lawrence, the Great Lakes of the north and west, and their tributary rivers, it will create the greatest inland trade ever witnessed. The most fertile and extensive regions of America will avail themselves of its facilities for a market. All their surplus productions, whether of the soil, the forest, the mines, or the water, their fabrics of art and their supplies of foreign commodities, will concentrate

in the city of New York, for transportation abroad or consumption at home. Agriculture, manufactures, commerce, trade, navigation, and the arts will receive a correspondent encouragement. The city will, in the course of time, become the granary of the world, the emporium of commerce, the seat of manufactures, the focus of great moneyed operations, and the concentrating point of vast disposable, and accumulating capita, which will stimulate, enliven, extend and reward the exertions of human labor and ingenuity, in all their processes and exhibitions. And before the revolution of a century, the whole island of Manhattan, covered with inhabitants and replenished with a dense population, will constitute one vast city.[3]

De Witt Clinton again became governor in 1825, the year that work on the Erie Canal was finished.

The Biggest Celebration of All

In October 1825, the Erie Canal was complete. New York State now had an excellent transportation route all the way from New York City to Lake Erie. The trip that had taken twenty days by horse and wagon would now take only nine days.

For New Yorkers, it was a satisfying personal victory. They had done the job that much of the rest of the nation had considered both impractical and impossible. And they had done it without help from the national government or from other states.

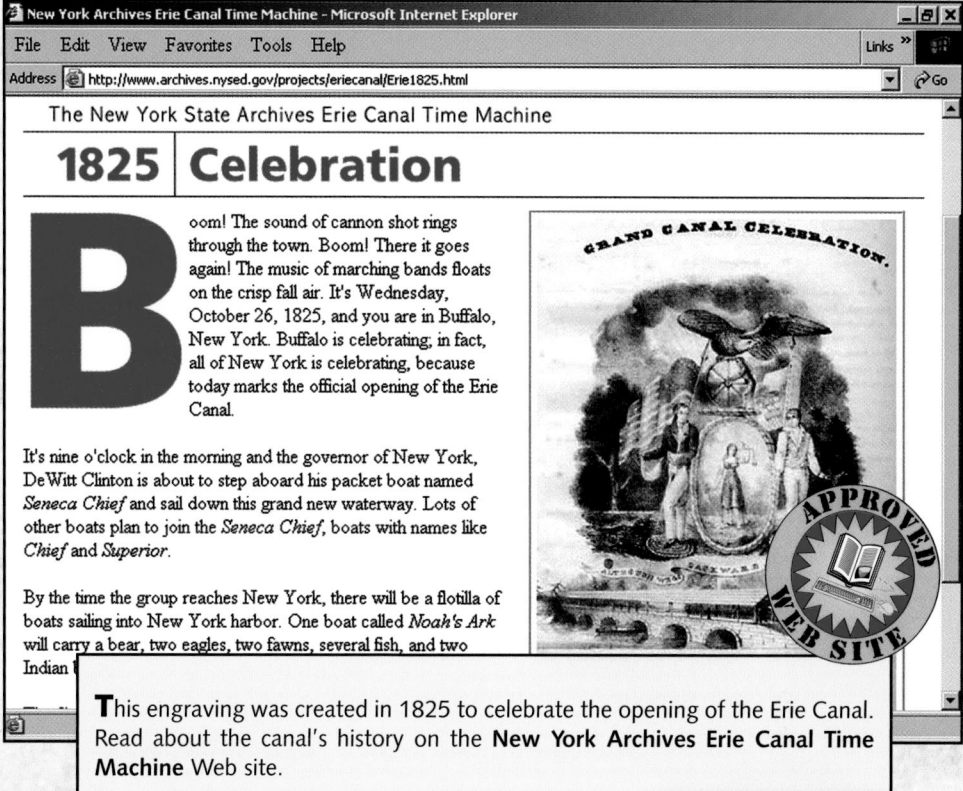

The New York State Archives Erie Canal Time Machine

1825 | Celebration

Boom! The sound of cannon shot rings through the town. Boom! There it goes again! The music of marching bands floats on the crisp fall air. It's Wednesday, October 26, 1825, and you are in Buffalo, New York. Buffalo is celebrating; in fact, all of New York is celebrating, because today marks the official opening of the Erie Canal.

It's nine o'clock in the morning and the governor of New York, De Witt Clinton is about to step aboard his packet boat named *Seneca Chief* and sail down this grand new waterway. Lots of other boats plan to join the *Seneca Chief*, boats with names like *Chief* and *Superior*.

By the time the group reaches New York, there will be a flotilla of boats sailing into New York harbor. One boat called *Noah's Ark* will carry a bear, two eagles, two fawns, several fish, and two Indian

This engraving was created in 1825 to celebrate the opening of the Erie Canal. Read about the canal's history on the **New York Archives Erie Canal Time Machine** Web site.

EDITOR'S CHOICE

On Wednesday, October 26, the big celebration began at nine o'clock in the morning in Buffalo, New York. Governor Clinton led a parade from the courthouse to the canal. Jesse Hawley—who, while in jail, had described how this job might be done—gave a speech. The party at Buffalo went on for days and included a grand ball.

▶ The First Fleet on the Canal

While Buffalo celebrated, De Witt Clinton and Lieutenant Governor James Tallmadge, Jr., got on board their canal boat, the *Seneca Chief.* They would stop for celebrations and speeches at twenty towns along the way.

Artillery and cannon fire announced that the first fleet of boats had entered the Erie Canal. Farther along the canal, another group of artillery-men heard the shots and fired off their own guns. All the way to New York City, a relay of gunfire passed the word along. Then the whole thing was repeated in reverse. Guns fired in sequence all the way back to Buffalo again.[4]

The *Seneca Chief,* pulled by four gray horses, was the first in an official fleet of five canal boats. Behind those, a line of more boats followed. All the boats, horses, and mules were gaily decorated for the occasion.

One canal boat, called *Noah's Ark,* was filled with "birds, beasts, and creeping things."[5] The ark carried a bear, two eagles, two fawns, some fish, and two American Indian boys in the dress of their nation. *Noah's Ark* was intended to show that the

De Witt Clinton was at one time a mayor of New York City, as well as the governor of New York State. He was the driving force behind the construction of the Erie Canal.

American wilderness had now been brought in touch with civilization.

There were speeches and celebrations at towns and cities all along the route. A week after leaving Buffalo, the canal boats reached Albany. As the *Seneca Chief* passed through the last Erie Canal lock and into the Hudson River, twenty-four cannon blasted a salute.

Important politicians from all over the state joined the Albany celebrations and contributed to the speeches. Six hundred guests were seated at tables in a huge tent. The evening's festivities included theatrical performances—one of which featured canal boats actually drawn across the stage by horses.[6]

At Albany, the canal boats were disconnected from their tow mules. Steamboats took over and towed the entire fleet the rest of the way to New York City.

The Wedding of the Waters

De Witt Clinton had come well prepared for the occasion. He brought with him several kegs of water from Lake Erie. These were beautifully made wooden kegs specifically for the celebration. With great ceremony, Clinton poured the waters from Lake Erie into the Atlantic Ocean. This ceremony was known as the "wedding of the waters."

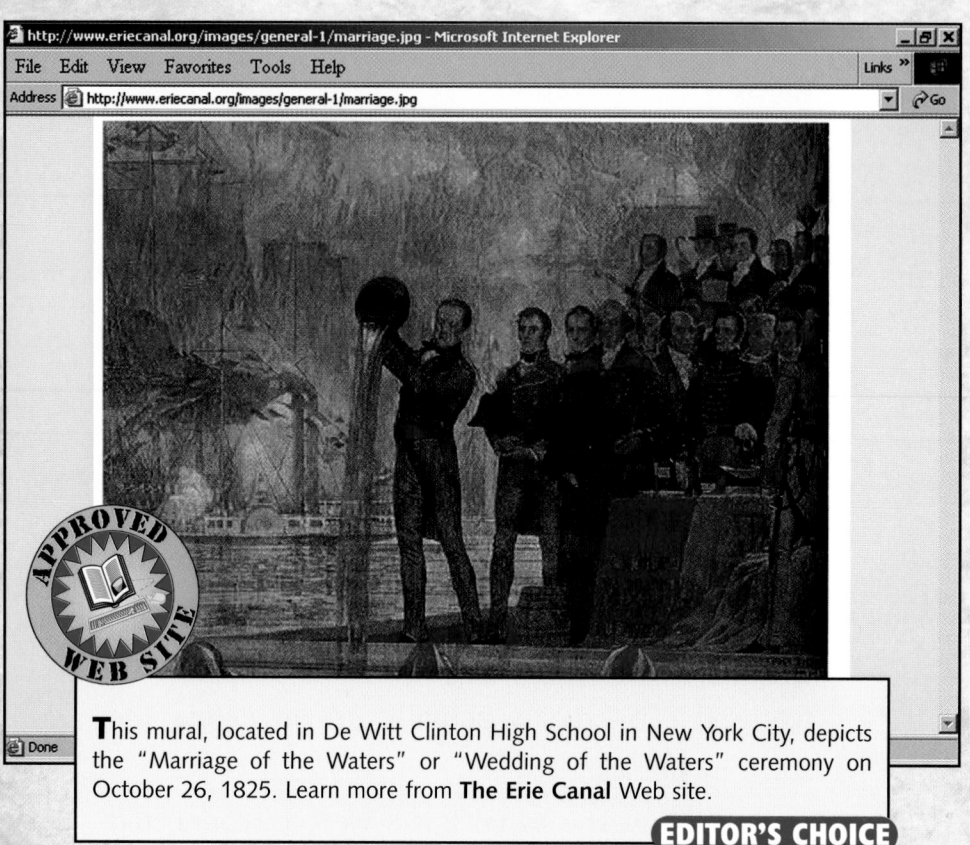

http://www.eriecanal.org/images/general-1/marriage.jpg - Microsoft Internet Explorer

File   Edit   View   Favorites   Tools   Help   Links »

Address 🔲 http://www.eriecanal.org/images/general-1/marriage.jpg   ▼ ⭕Go

Done

This mural, located in De Witt Clinton High School in New York City, depicts the "Marriage of the Waters" or "Wedding of the Waters" ceremony on October 26, 1825. Learn more from **The Erie Canal** Web site.

EDITOR'S CHOICE

Another dignitary had brought bottles of water from thirteen other rivers—the Amazon, Columbia, Danube, Gambia, Ganges, Indus, Mississippi, Nile, Orinoco, Rhine, Rio de la Plata, Seine, and Thames.

On November 23, the *Seneca Chief* traveled back up the river and through the canal to Lake Erie, carrying a keg of water from the Atlantic. The Atlantic water was poured in the lake, completing the ceremony known as "The Wedding of the Waters." The Erie Canal was officially open for business.

As the Erie Canal became a bustling water route, it created a new and different kind of world in upper New York State.

The Canawlers

Passenger or packet canal boat crews usually included a captain, a steward, two helmsmen who took turns steering, and two animal drivers who also took turns. Cargo boats might be owned and run by an entire family. Those who lived and worked on the canal boats were known as "canallers" or "canawlers." The word "canal" was often pronounced "canawl" in those days. They were transients, people who stayed in one place for only a short time.

Some canawlers were noisy people, known for their arguments and fist fights. More and more, permanent citizens complained about being called as jurors and witnesses in trials to settle these rowdy disputes.[7]

Jonathan Pearson was on a canal boat that was held up for two hours, waiting behind other boats to enter a lock. He wrote in his diary that part of the time "was uselessly spent by the gangs of a certain boat and raft in a wordy quarrel about their rights to enter the lock first." After a lot of threats and shouting, "the whole fuss ended with no other damage than the pushing of one of the raftsman off the boat and the fall of another into the canal which considerably cooled his ire. . . ."

This is a sketch of Buffalo Jack, a man who piloted keelboats on the Erie Canal in the 1800s.

Pearson added, "Such detestable occurrences are by no means seldom in every part of this canal."[8]

The canawlers developed their own culture, including music, folktales, and language. Some of their slang terms were:

hayburner—A mule

feeders—Channels to bring water into the canal

mudlarked—Grounded because of low water

shunpike—To avoid tolls by detouring around the toll booth

hoggee—Mule-driver

jigger-boss—Person who brought whisky to the workers

fog-gang—Workers who cleaned out the canal

foamer—A mug of ale

pritties—Boiled or baked potatoes

skimmagig—Buttermilk

fip—A coin worth about six cents

rhino-fat—Rich or well-off

hoodledasher—Several boats tied together and pulled by one team of animals[9]

Living on the Canal

Whole canawler families lived on their own cargo boats. They stabled their extra mules in a cabin on the boat's bow. Nathaniel Hawthorne described such a family:

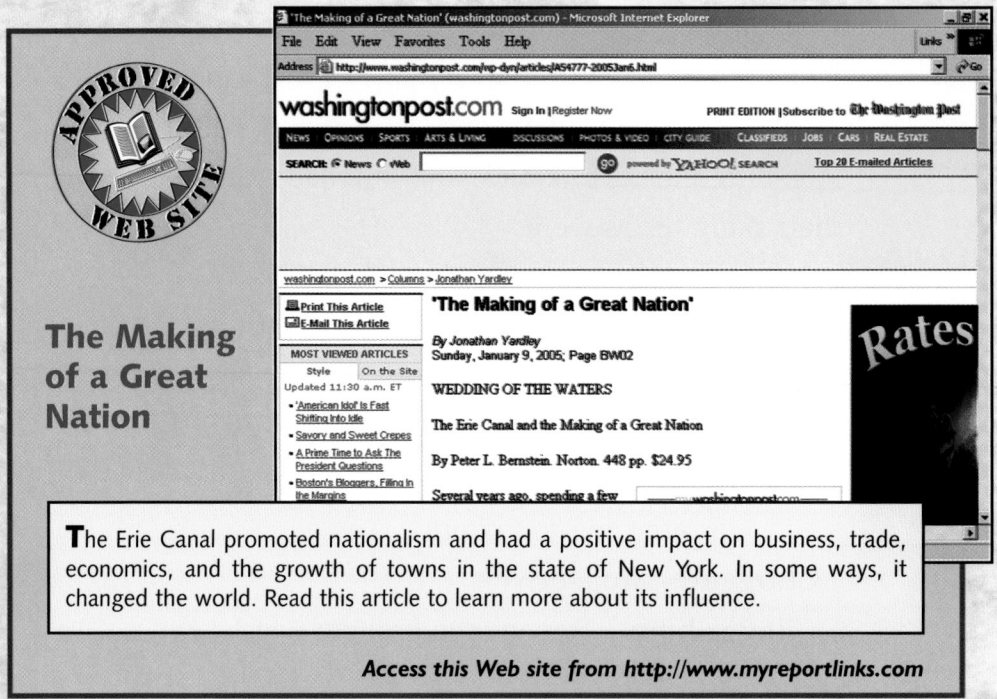

The Making of a Great Nation

The Erie Canal promoted nationalism and had a positive impact on business, trade, economics, and the growth of towns in the state of New York. In some ways, it changed the world. Read this article to learn more about its influence.

Access this Web site from http://www.myreportlinks.com

Sometimes we met a black and rusty-looking vessel, laden with lumber, salt from Syracuse, or Genesee flour, and shaped at both ends like a square-toed boot; as if it had two sterns, and were fated always to advance backward. On its deck would be a square hut, and a woman seen through the window at her household work, with a little tribe of children, who perhaps had been born in this strange dwelling and knew no other home. Thus, while the husband smoked his pipe at the helm, and the eldest son rode one of the horses, on went the family, travelling hundreds of miles in their own house, and carrying their fireside with them.[10]

Because the canawlers were transient, many of their children had little formal education. Some parents taught them the basics of reading, writing, and mathematics. And some canawler children went to school when the canal closed because of ice and snow.[11]

▷ Canal Towns

Along the banks of the canal, new businesses sprang up. General stores, blacksmiths, saloons, hotels, and boatyards served the canawlers. When these businesses clustered together, they created a little canal town.

The canal towns could be disorderly, especially when everyone took a Saturday night off to relax.

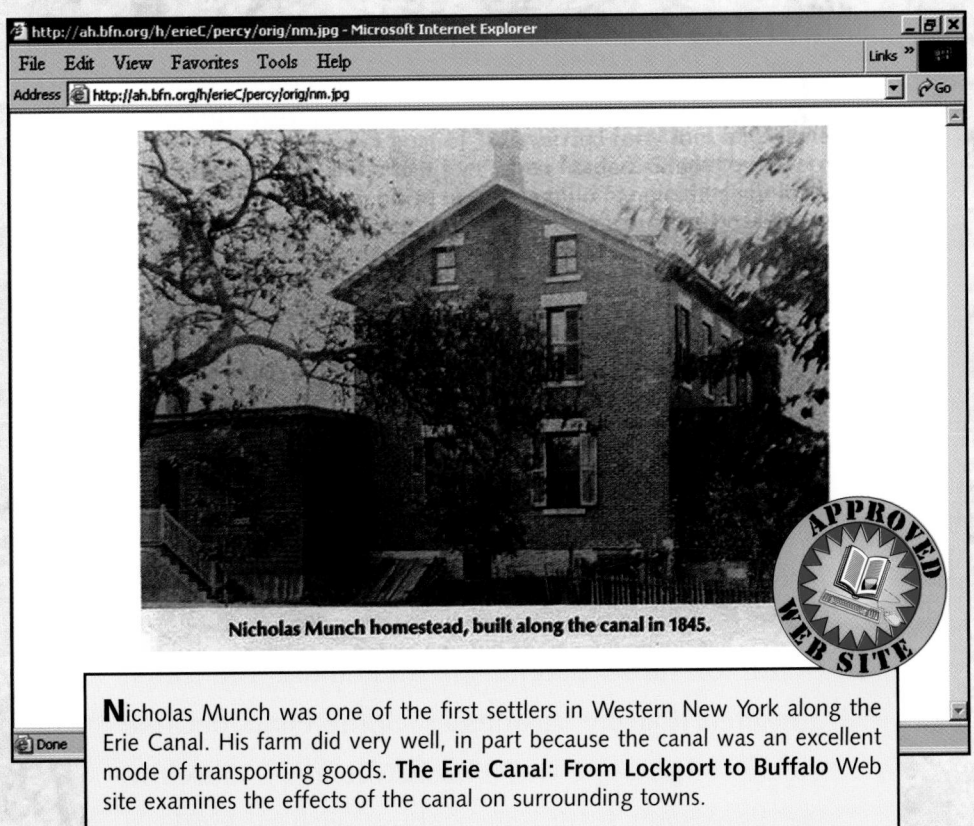

Nicholas Munch homestead, built along the canal in 1845.

Nicholas Munch was one of the first settlers in Western New York along the Erie Canal. His farm did very well, in part because the canal was an excellent mode of transporting goods. **The Erie Canal: From Lockport to Buffalo** Web site examines the effects of the canal on surrounding towns.

According to historian F. Daniel Larkin, "It was fairly common for someone to stagger out of a saloon, fall off a bridge, and drown in the canal on the way home."[12] Such things happened even though canal bridges were not very high and the water was just four feet deep.

Traveling on the Erie Canal

The canal was not only a waterway for shipping goods, it was also an inexpensive way for people to travel. Settlers who wanted to move west could go by canal. In their new homes, they received mail and goods promptly. And it was now much easier to go back east and visit relatives. On cheaper boats, settlers could camp out on deck while their trunks and furniture traveled inside.

Traveling preachers roamed the towns along the waterway, where many canawlers and towns-people listened eagerly to their sermons. The Erie Canal also became part of the Underground Railroad, a system of routes that helped escaped slaves find freedom in Canada.[13] And tourists flocked to the canal, both from America and from European nations. Many tourists traveled the canal on their way to see Niagara Falls.

All of these people on and about the canal attracted floating businesses. Some boats became grocery stores; one was a bookstore and a museum. Peddlers went from boat to boat with all kinds of

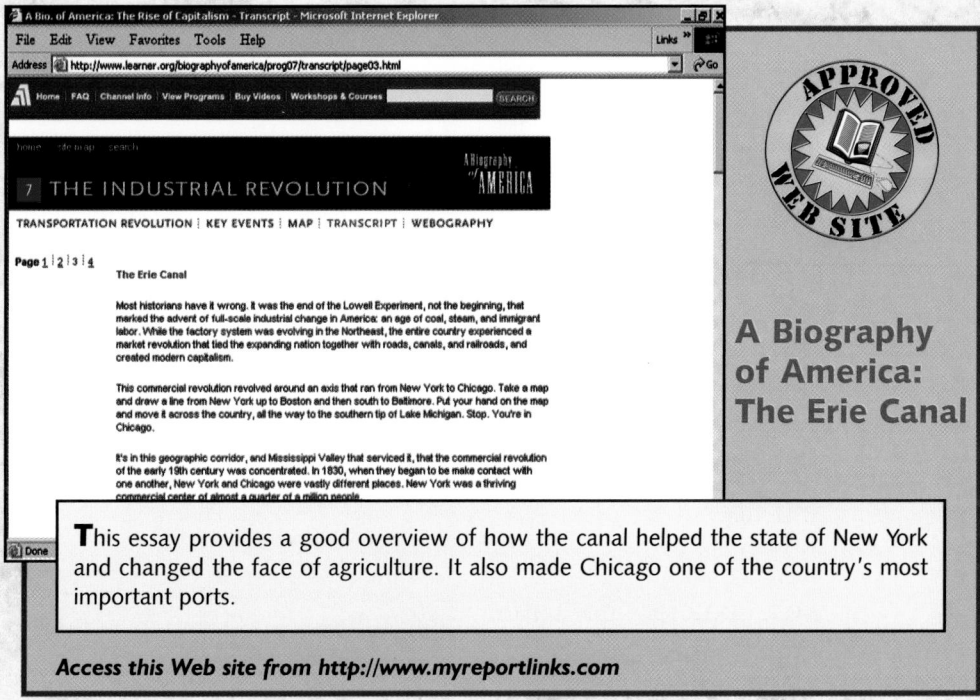

A Biography
of America:
The Erie Canal

This essay provides a good overview of how the canal helped the state of New York and changed the face of agriculture. It also made Chicago one of the country's most important ports.

Access this Web site from http://www.myreportlinks.com

wares. The dishonest among them sold fake reme-
dies or bought things with counterfeit bills.[14]

Whether rich or poor, all travelers on the canal
spent a lot of time waiting. They waited in port
while cargo was loaded, and they waited in line
at crowded locks. For recreation they sang songs,
gambled, and sometimes fought. They played
games and invented entertainments such as racing
caterpillars and frogs.[15]

▶ Packet Boat Travel

Passenger boats were called packet boats. For
wealthier travelers, packet boats were fitted out
as luxuriously as possible. Englishman Thomas

Woodcock recorded in his journal that "these Boats have three Horses, go at a quicker rate, and have the preference in going through the locks, carry no freight, are built extremely light, and have quite Genteel Men for their Captains, and use silver plate."[16]

Even if some boats were fancier, no canal boats were very large— at most seventy-eight feet long and about fifteen feet wide. Harriet Beecher Stowe traveled the Erie Canal early in her writing career. She would later become famous for *Uncle Tom's Cabin,* a novel about the injustices of slavery.

An artist's impression of how the Erie Canal appeared as it wound through the Mohawk River valley in the 1850s.

Stowe wrote that many travelers thought the space too small.

> "Mercy on us!" says one, after surveying the little room, about ten feet long and six high, "where are we all to sleep tonight?"
>
> Another replies, "Really, it's quite moderate for a canal boat: however, we can't tell till they have all come."
>
> "All! for mercy's sake, you don't say there are any more coming!" exclaim two or three in a breath; "they *can't* come; *there is not room!*"
>
> After this follows an indiscriminate raining down of all shapes, sizes, sexes, and ages—men, women, children, babies, and nurses. The state of feeling becomes perfectly desperate. Darkness gathers on all faces. "We shall be smothered! we shall be crowded to death! we *can't stay* here!" are heard faintly from one and another; and yet, though the boat grows no wider, the walls no higher, they do live, and do bear it . . .[17]

▶ The Changeable Cabin

It took some clever thinking to make a packet boat work for travelers who were used to expensive surroundings. One big central cabin was used for everything. The room was first set up as a sitting room, with comfortable furniture and reading materials. Sometimes musicians played to entertain the travelers.

At mealtime, the same central cabin was changed into a dining room, where elegant meals

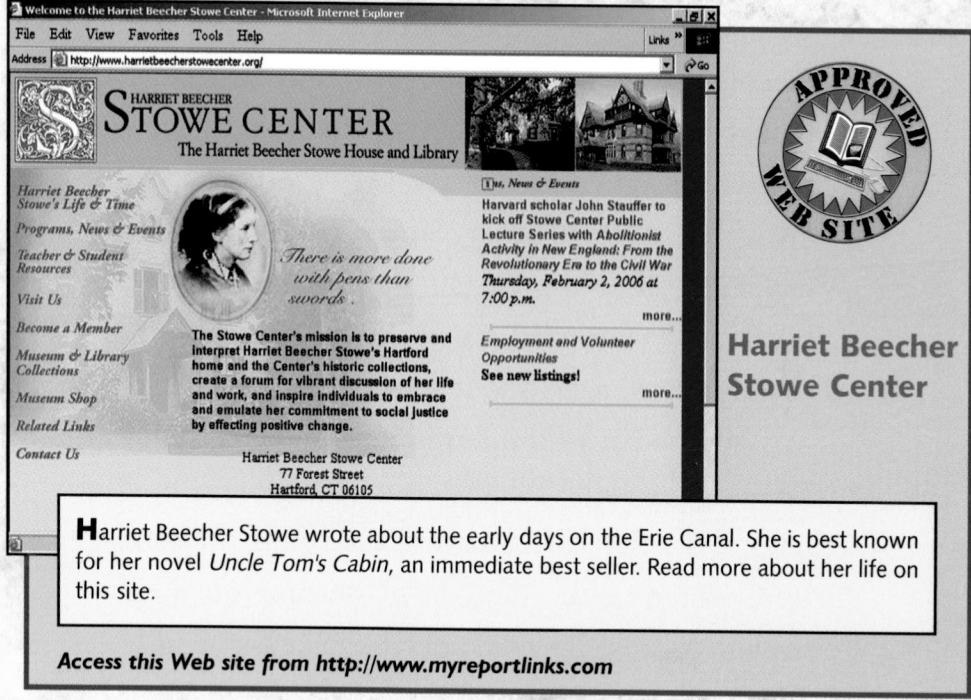

Welcome to the Harriet Beecher Stowe Center - Microsoft Internet Explorer

File Edit View Favorites Tools Help   Links »

Address http://www.harrietbeecherstowecenter.org/   Go

HARRIET BEECHER
STOWE CENTER
The Harriet Beecher Stowe House and Library

Harriet Beecher Stowe's Life & Time

Programs, News & Events

Teacher & Student Resources

Visit Us

Become a Member

Museum & Library Collections

Museum Shop

Related Links

Contact Us

There is more done with pens than swords.

The Stowe Center's mission is to preserve and interpret Harriet Beecher Stowe's Hartford home and the Center's historic collections, create a forum for vibrant discussion of her life and work, and inspire individuals to embrace and emulate her commitment to social justice by effecting positive change.

Harriet Beecher Stowe Center
77 Forest Street
Hartford, CT 06105

News & Events

Harvard scholar John Stauffer to kick off Stowe Center Public Lecture Series with Abolitionist Activity in New England: From the Revolutionary Era to the Civil War Thursday, February 2, 2006 at 7:00 p.m.

more...

Employment and Volunteer Opportunities
See new listings!

more...

APPROVED WEB SITE

Harriet Beecher Stowe Center

Harriet Beecher Stowe wrote about the early days on the Erie Canal. She is best known for her novel *Uncle Tom's Cabin,* an immediate best seller. Read more about her life on this site.

Access this Web site from http://www.myreportlinks.com

were served. Then at night, the space was changed into a sleeping area. These sleeping arrangements were so odd that some people traveled the canal just to experience them.[18]

A curtain was pulled across the width of the cabin. One end of the room was for men, the other for women. Bunk beds folded down from the walls, and the outer end of each bed was held up by cords attached to the ceiling. As Hawthorne described it, "The crimson curtain being let down between the ladies and gentlemen, the cabin became a bedchamber for twenty persons, who were laid on shelves, one above another."

▶ Bedtime

Sleeping was a problem for many travelers, though apparently not for others. There were always some who snored loudly and kept everybody else awake. Harriet Beecher Stowe described what happened after the curtain was pulled and the beds made. She said the walls were lined with small shelves, each about a foot wide. Each shelf was adorned with a mattress and some bedding. The shelves were hanging from the ceiling by a hook and a thin cord. Many of the young travelers were scared at the thought of sleeping on these shelves, because they did not look to be very sturdy. Some would exclaim, "What! sleep up there! I won't sleep on one of those top shelves, I know. The cords will certainly break."

Each of the women wished to sleep on the lowest shelf, but obviously not all of them would be able to. Some would be frightened if a heavy woman attempted to sleep on one of the higher shelves, fearing that the cord would snap. Then, someone would usually offer to change spots with her. Eventually, everyone would find a shelf and get to sleep. Stowe writes, "Tired and drowsy, you are just sinking into a doze, when bang! goes the boat against the sides of a lock; ropes scrape, men run and shout, and up fly the heads of all the top shelfites . . ."[19]

 *This is a photograph of an Erie Canal lock taken by photographer John Collier in 1941. The Erie Canal and its locks were enlarged multiple times after it initially opened in 1825.*

▶ Repairing and Rebuilding

The Erie Canal was an immediate success. In nine years time, the tolls that were collected more than paid back the cost of construction. Even so, problems naturally arose and things needed to be improved. Sometimes locks failed to work. During heavy rains, the canal sometimes overflowed its banks. If a canal bank collapsed, water—and occasionally boats—flowed out of the canal.

While repair crews worked, a hundred canal boats might be backed up, waiting to go forward again. And some repairs closed down the canal for as long as two weeks.[20]

Of course, the Erie Canal was completely held up in winter. When the water froze, the canal was shut down for as many as five months every year.[21] In the spring, melting snows flooded the canal, sometimes washing away waterfront piers and buildings.

In spite of such problems, traffic increased and the canal continued to make money. Between 1836 and 1862, the Erie Canal was enlarged to a depth of seven feet for bigger boats. Locks were also enlarged and in most locations, locks were built side-by-side to speed up travel in both directions.[22] In 1882, the canal stopped charging tolls. By then, value of the trade and travel alone had made the Erie Canal a worthwhile investment.

Chapter 5 ▶

SUPPORTERS AND BUILDERS

The identities of many who worked on the Erie Canal are unknown today. Even the names of those who designed some of the labor-saving machinery have been lost. This chapter provides brief biographical information on some of those whose contributions are well-documented.

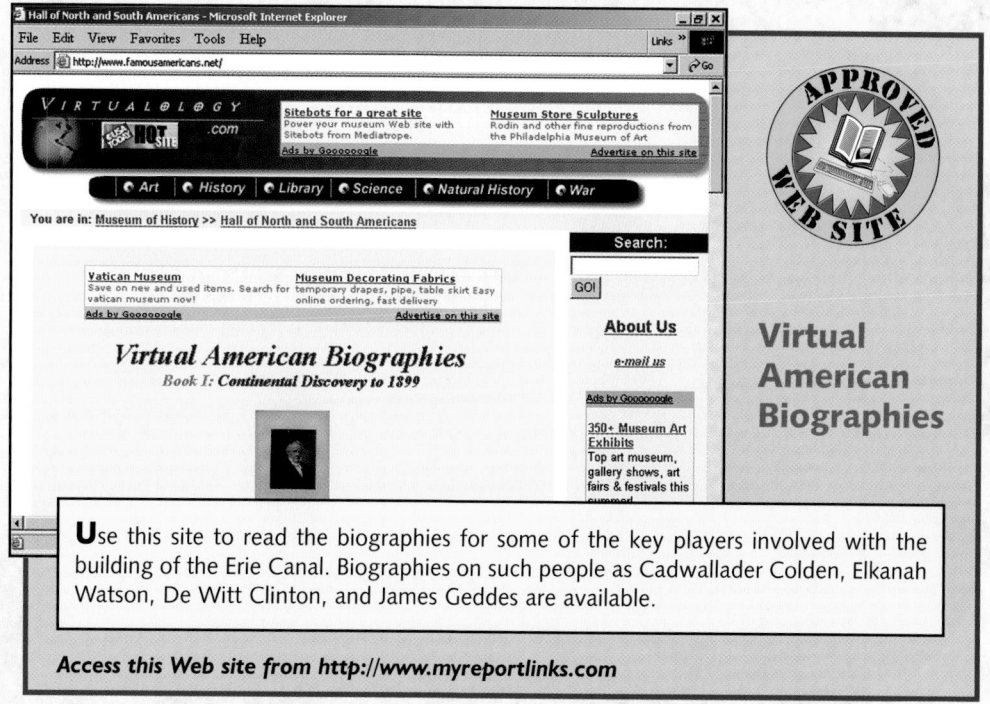

Virtual American Biographies

Use this site to read the biographies for some of the key players involved with the building of the Erie Canal. Biographies on such people as Cadwallader Colden, Elkanah Watson, De Witt Clinton, and James Geddes are available.

Access this Web site from http://www.myreportlinks.com

Charles Broadhead

Charles Broadhead (1772–1852) was born in New York. He took up surveying, and in 1816 he was one of the engineers in charge of surveys for the Erie Canal. Broadhead surveyed the eastern section of the canal, from where the Hudson River reached Albany, New York, to Rome, New York.

Cadwallader Colden

Cadwallader Colden (1688–1776) was a New York political leader, scholar, and scientist. He studied medicine in London and practiced it in Philadelphia. In 1720 he was appointed surveyor general of New York, and in 1761 he became lieutenant governor of New York. It was his initial idea to improve the Mohawk River that got others thinking about the prospect of a canal in upstate New York.

De Witt Clinton

De Witt Clinton (1769–1828) was born into a politically active New York family. Clinton served as a state legislator, United States senator, New York City mayor, and governor of New York. As a U.S. senator, he introduced the Twelfth Amendment to the Constitution. In 1812, Clinton ran unsuccessfully for president against James Madison. As a canal commissioner, Clinton was the driving force behind the development of the

▲ *This image, "The First Boat on the Erie Canal," by C. Y. Turner shows Turner's idea of what the first canal boat may have looked like. The first boat carried Governor De Witt Clinton and some guests.*

Erie Canal. He battled the New York State legislature to get the funding for the canal, and for the eight years of construction he worked tirelessly to keep it going.

When the canal was completed in 1825 Clinton was serving his third term as the governor of New York. On November 4, 1825, Clinton dedicated the Erie Canal in the ceremony known as the "wedding of the waters."

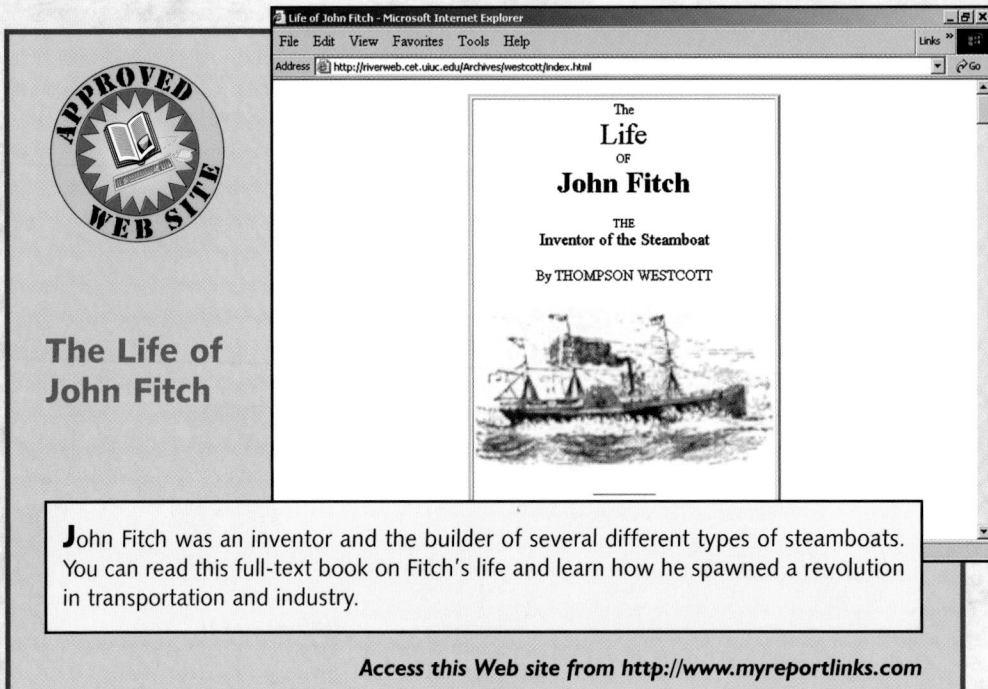

APPROVED WEB SITE

The Life of John Fitch

The Life of John Fitch

The Life OF John Fitch
THE Inventor of the Steamboat
By THOMPSON WESTCOTT

John Fitch was an inventor and the builder of several different types of steamboats. You can read this full-text book on Fitch's life and learn how he spawned a revolution in transportation and industry.

Access this Web site from http://www.myreportlinks.com

▶ Christopher Colles

Christopher Colles (1738–1821) was born in Ireland. He immigrated to America in the 1700s and lectured on technical subjects, including navigation by the use of canal locks. He was familiar with canals from having seen the Bridgewater Canal in Britain. Colles suggested a system of pipes to supply New York City with water. He lectured on gunnery and was an artillery instructor to the Continental Army when the American Revolution began. In 1777, Colles surveyed part of the Mohawk River. He was one of the first to suggest improvements on the waterways to connect

Lake Ontario with the Hudson River at Albany. He did this in a speech before the New York State legislature in 1784. Colles is also said to have built the first steam engine in the United States.

John Fitch

John Fitch (1743–98) was born in Connecticut. In 1785, he started work on his inventions for steam engines and steamboats. His 1776 partially successful trial run of a steamboat was followed by other designs. Some historians consider Fitch the inventor of the first American steamboat.

There would not have been any use for the Erie Canal without the invention of the steamboat. The steamboat made it

Robert Fulton designed the first steamboat that made it up the Hudson River. He was also a renowned painter.

possible for boats to bring passengers and goods upriver, against the current. Now goods could be shipped up the Hudson River from New York City to Albany. Once goods could get to Albany more easily there was now a need to ship them west, and a need for an Erie Canal.

Robert Fulton

Robert Fulton (1765–1815) was born in Pennsylvania. He was a man of many talents. Fulton became a gunsmith during the American Revolution, and then became a painter of landscapes and portraits. Fulton exhibited his paintings in England and France. While he was there, he became fascinated with canals and other new technologies. In 1797, he launched his steamboat, the *Clermont,* on New York's Hudson River. Although his was not the first steamboat, it was the first to become commercially successful. Fulton's designs also included a steam-powered warship.

James Geddes

James Geddes (1763–1838) was born in Pennsylvania. He worked on a farm and started a company for the manufacture of salt. Geddes had a limited education, but he saw the possibilities of a canal to connect Lake Erie and the Hudson River. In 1808, he was made one of the surveyors on the canal route. The portion of the route that he was responsible for engineering was the western section from Lake Erie to the Seneca River. Geddes became a judge in 1800, and also served as a member of the New York legislature, and a member of the United States Congress. In 1816, Geddes became engineer of the Erie Canal, and he later engineered other canals.

Jesse Hawley

Jesse Hawley (1773–1842) was a merchant and miller from the town of Geneva, New York, when he had a discussion with surveyor James Geddes. Hawley knew well the terrible state of roads in upper New York, so he grew very interested in the idea of building a canal from Lake Erie to the Hudson River. When his flour business went into heavy debt, Hawley was sent to debtor's prison for twenty months. In 1807, he proposed his idea for a canal

John Jervis learned to be an engineer while working on the Erie Canal. He then went on to design other canals and structures all over America.

across New York. During that time, Hawley wrote essays that helped to convince some important state leaders that such a canal was possible. Although many thought Hawley's idea was impractical, De Witt Clinton became a huge supporter.[1]

Thomas Jefferson

Thomas Jefferson (1743–1826) was a Virginia statesman and the author of the Declaration of Independence. He was the third president of the United States (1801–09). As president, Jefferson took an interest in exploration of the West. He organized the Lewis and Clark expedition across the Northwest and pushed through the Louisiana Purchase, doubling the size of the nation. He was also president when Geddes surveyed the land for a possible canal. Jefferson did not like the idea and would not consider making it a national project and giving it federal funding.

John Jervis

After leaving home at the age of twenty-two, John Jervis (1795–1895) worked as an axman on the canal while he taught himself engineering. During the winter layoffs and at other odd moments, Jervis taught himself surveying. He was eventually put in charge of the construction of the middle section of the canal, and then promoted to superintendent. He later built railroads, improved

Gouverneur Morris was an American patriot and revolutionary. He was heavily involved in the drafting of the U.S. Constitution and supported the Erie Canal project. In this painting by Augustus Tholey, there are four members of the Continental Congress. Left to right are John Adams, Gouverneur Morris, Alexander Hamilton, and Thomas Jefferson.

the Erie Canal in 1834, and engineered the New York City water supply system. He is regarded as America's leading consulting engineer during the antebellum period, which lasted from 1820 to 1860.[2] The city of Port Jervis, New York, was named in his honor.

Gouverneur Morris

Gouverneur Morris (1752–1816) was a New York and United States political leader. Born to a wealthy and influential family, Morris studied law, helped to draft the first New York State constitution, served in the Continental Congress, and was a member of the U.S. Constitutional Convention. He was a strong supporter of the Erie Canal, serving as chairman of the canal commission. Morris accompanied De Witt Clinton to Washington, D.C., in a failed attempt to drum up support for the canal from President James Madison.

James Madison

James Madison (1751–1836) was a Virginian, and the fourth president of the United States (1809–17). Madison was also the main author of the U.S. Constitution. Gouverneur Morris and De Witt Clinton appealed to Madison to give the Erie Canal project federal funding. Plans for the Erie Canal came to a momentary halt when Madison vetoed an act called the Bonus Bill that would have funded part of the cost of the canal's construction. One reason for this may have been the soaring national debt that built up while the United States was fighting the War of 1812.

Nathan Roberts

Nathan Roberts (1776–1852) was a self-educated engineer from New York State. He surveyed the route of the Erie Canal near Rome, New York, and served as engineer on several canal sections. At Mud Creek, between Lyons and Palmyra, New York, Roberts was responsible for changing the path of the canal from one side of the creek to the other. By doing this he shortened the canal by two and a half miles, making it easier to complete in that area.[3] In charge

Philip Schuyler was a Revolutionary War general and a senator from the state of New York. He backed Elkanah Watson's idea of digging a canal in New York near the Mohawk River. This portrait of Schuyler was painted by Alonzo Chappel.

of constructing the locks on a particularly difficult section at Lockport, he designed multiple locks that solved the problem. Roberts served as chief engineer on the Erie Canal from 1835 to 1841. He also worked on other canals and built the bridge across the Potomac River at Harpers Ferry.

Philip Schuyler

Philip Schuyler (1733–1804) was an American Revolutionary general, a New York State senator, a member of the Continental Congress (1775), and a United States senator. He also owned a lumber mill and maintained a farm in New York. Schuyler backed Elkanah Watson's idea for a canal in the Mohawk River Valley. This led to serious discussion about canals in upstate New York. The town of Schuylerville, New York, is named after the general.

Benjamin Wright

Benjamin Wright (1770–1842), like others who worked on the Erie Canal, became an

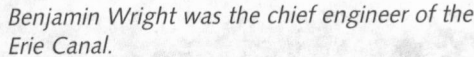

Benjamin Wright was the chief engineer of the Erie Canal.

engineer through "hands-on" experience. From a poor Connecticut family, Wright first became a country lawyer and a surveyor. He surveyed much of the route that the Erie Canal followed. He was made chief engineer on the Erie Canal, and the first boat on one section of the canal was named *Chief Engineer* in his honor. Wright worked on other canals and transportation projects, and is often referred to as the "Father of American Civil Engineering."

Canvass White

Canvass White (1790–1834) was born in New York. In 1817, he went to England to study the canals of that country. After his return, White worked as an engineer on the Erie Canal. He discovered and patented a waterproof cement that allowed the workers to construct locks that did not leak. White was chief engineer of many other canal projects.

Elkanah Watson

Elkanah Watson (1758–1842) was a merchant and a banker. He organized and promoted a number of agricultural societies and fairs and wrote pamphlets on agricultural topics. Watson was both a dreamer and a practical thinker. He contributed to improvement of agriculture and to the conception of projects such as the Erie Canal.

▶ George Washington

George Washington (1732–99) was active in colonial Virginia politics, the commander in chief of the Continental Army during the American Revolution, and the first president of the United States (1789–97). Washington, often called the Father of His Country, was a proponent of canals. He focused on building canals near the James and Potomac Rivers in Virginia. Washington, at one point, had also advocated building a passage between Lake Erie and the Ohio River. His discussion of canals led Elkanah Webster to push the idea of a canal in upstate New York.

Chapter 6 ▶

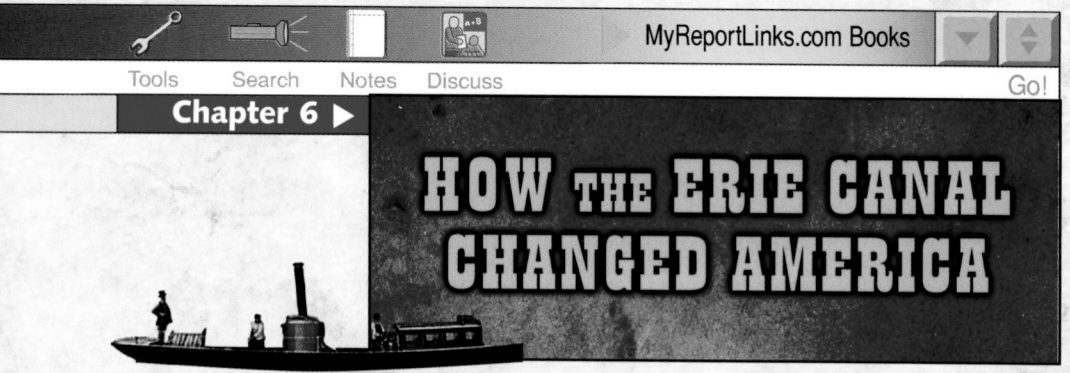

HOW THE ERIE CANAL CHANGED AMERICA

In his magazine stories about the Erie Canal, Nathaniel Hawthorne commented:

> Surely, the water of this canal must be the most fertilizing of all fluids; for it causes towns—with their masses of brick and stone, their churches and

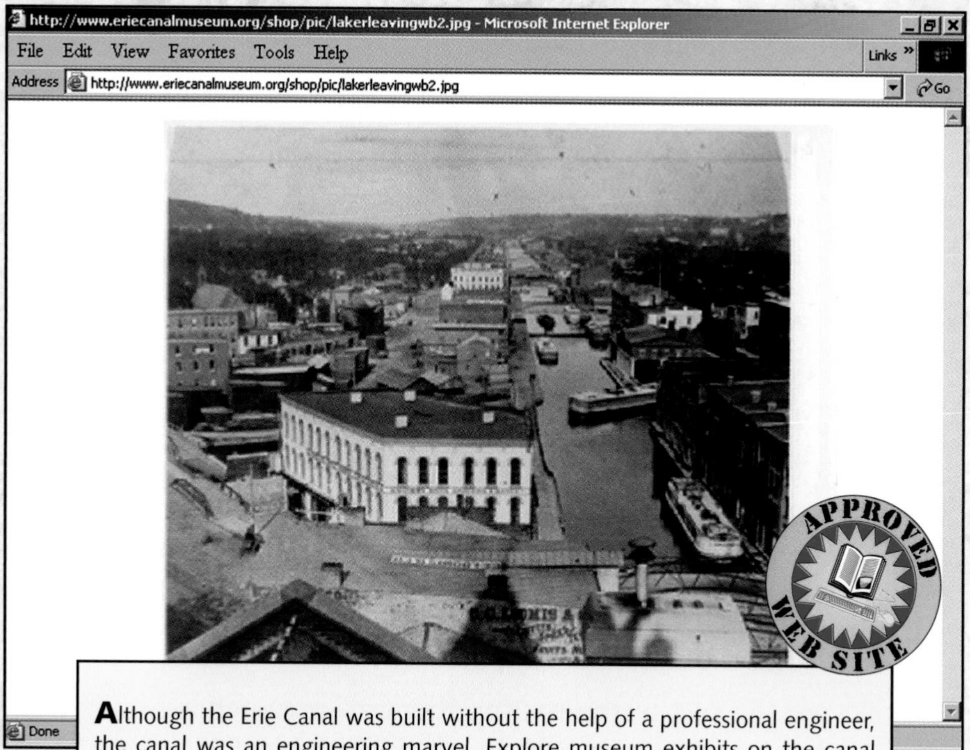
http://www.eriecanalmuseum.org/shop/pic/lakerleavingwb2.jpg - Microsoft Internet Explorer
File Edit View Favorites Tools Help
Links
Address http://www.eriecanalmuseum.org/shop/pic/lakerleavingwb2.jpg
Go
Done
APPROVED WEB SITE

Although the Erie Canal was built without the help of a professional engineer, the canal was an engineering marvel. Explore museum exhibits on the canal and more at the **Welcome to the Erie Canal Museum** Web site.

theatres, their business and hubbub, their luxury and refinement, their gay dames and polished citizens—to spring up, till, in time, the wondrous stream may flow between two continuous lines of buildings, through one thronged street, from Buffalo to Albany.[1]

Hawthorne was right—the Erie Canal did cause towns to spring up all along its route. It also gave new life to old towns. The population of Albany doubled; that of Buffalo and other cities more than doubled. In 1812, Buffalo had been just a trading post in the wilderness. By 1840, it had a population of 18,400.[2] Buffalo had become the gateway to the entire West.

In 1800, the major American ports were Boston, Philadelphia, and New Orleans. New York City, with the fourth-largest population in the country, was less important. A few years after the Erie Canal opened, New York City became the nation's major port and had the largest population.[3] New York was nicknamed the Empire State. The word "empire" means growth, progress, and financial power.

Speeding Up Trade

After the canal opened, the Midwest was connected to the rest of the nation. Farmers or merchants in the interior could easily get their goods to Eastern markets, and they could even send them to Europe.

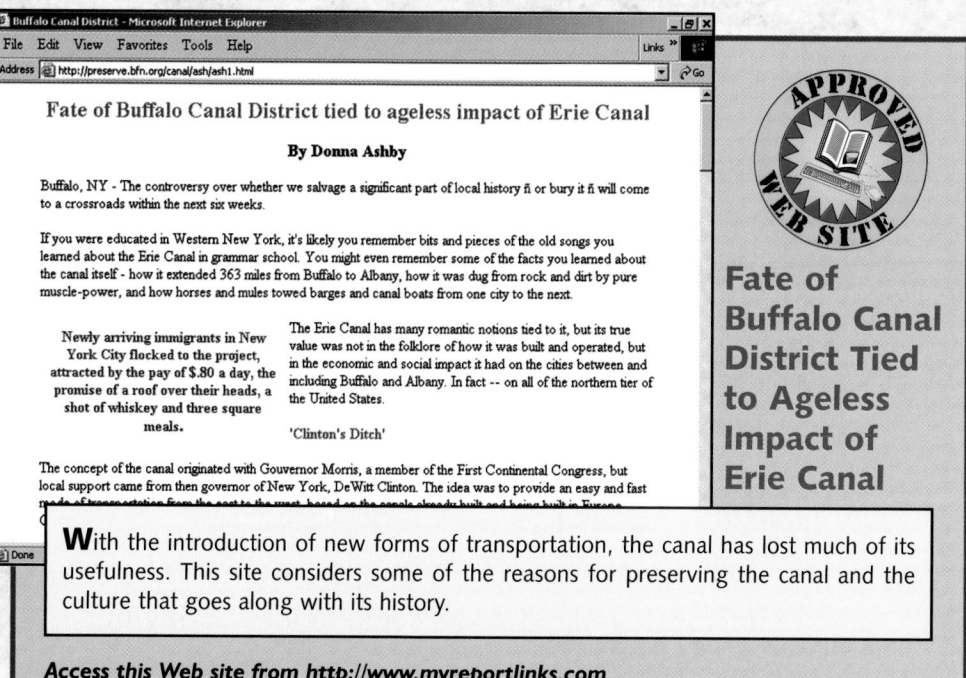

Fate of Buffalo Canal District tied to ageless impact of Erie Canal

By Donna Ashby

Buffalo, NY - The controversy over whether we salvage a significant part of local history fi or bury it fi will come to a crossroads within the next six weeks.

If you were educated in Western New York, it's likely you remember bits and pieces of the old songs you learned about the Erie Canal in grammar school. You might even remember some of the facts you learned about the canal itself - how it extended 363 miles from Buffalo to Albany, how it was dug from rock and dirt by pure muscle-power, and how horses and mules towed barges and canal boats from one city to the next.

Newly arriving immigrants in New York City flocked to the project, attracted by the pay of $.80 a day, the promise of a roof over their heads, a shot of whiskey and three square meals.

The Erie Canal has many romantic notions tied to it, but its true value was not in the folklore of how it was built and operated, but in the economic and social impact it had on the cities between and including Buffalo and Albany. In fact -- on all of the northern tier of the United States.

'Clinton's Ditch'

The concept of the canal originated with Gouvernor Morris, a member of the First Continental Congress, but local support came from then governor of New York, DeWitt Clinton. The idea was to provide an easy and fast

Fate of Buffalo Canal District Tied to Ageless Impact of Erie Canal

With the introduction of new forms of transportation, the canal has lost much of its usefulness. This site considers some of the reasons for preserving the canal and the culture that goes along with its history.

Access this Web site from http://www.myreportlinks.com

Before the canal was opened it took two weeks to ship grain from Buffalo to New York City, and shipping cost $100 a ton. On the canal, shipping goods was not only faster than ever before, it was much cheaper. By the 1830s, grain cost just $8 a ton and took only three-and-a-half days to ship.[4]

Wheat could be taken from Midwestern farms to mills farther east to be ground into flour. Rochester became known as the Flour City and would soon become an industrial center.[5]

Canal boats hauled agricultural produce to the East. They returned with finished goods for customers in the Midwest. By 1835, the canal was so

popular that it had to be widened from forty to
seventy feet and deepened from four to seven feet.

Changing Lifestyles

The once small and quiet towns along the waterway would never be the same. The long-time
inhabitants welcomed their new wealth but had
some difficulties adjusting to other changes. Some
of those who had come to help build the canal
stayed to live on its banks. Certain communities
took on a distinctly Irish flavor.

New Englanders and newly arrived European
immigrants created new communities, bringing
their own traditions with them. People from
foreign lands speaking various languages toured
through the towns and the countryside.

Perhaps some of the greatest changes were in
the lives of the canawlers themselves. Feeling tied
to no particular community, they experienced a sense
of freedom and independence that has frequently
been part of American folklore and legend. "The
brawling 'canawlers' with their mule-drawn
barges became a colorful part of American life."[6]

Samuel Hopkins Adams wrote a story called
"The Canal Wife" that reflected this pleasure in a
changed lifestyle. According to Adams's story,
Dorcas was the daughter of a judge. Her parents
were horrified when she decided to marry a canawler, but Dorcas was quite satisfied with her life.

▲ *An artist's rendition of grain boats being towed down the Hudson River to New York City after having come from the Erie Canal. This scene would have taken place in the 1870s.*

Land wives must go to market. My market comes to me. Before I am done with my morning survey, the farm children are paddling alongside in their homemade bateaux. They offer eggs, fowls, vegetables and fruits in season, milk, butter and maple syrup. . . .

Dinner is at eleven o'clock. The towpath hoggee has his carried out, hot, in a pail. After all is cleared away, I have several hours of leisure before supper. I may check the boat's manifest and reckon up our freightage, for I studied Mathematicks at the Academy. Or I may fetch out my . . . rocker and sit on the foredeck, as lady like as the squire's wife in her parlor . . .

Supper at five is soon out of the way. Again I have my leisure spell. Other boats may be moored near us for the night. Then there will be polite visits back and forth and the exchange of the news of the day, very excitable, lasting as late as nine o'clock. I go to bed, grateful for all my mercies and asking myself what other life could be so affording and pompous as that on the Grand Erie Canal.[7]

Moving Westward

The Erie Canal has been compared to a modern-day superhighway that sparked the first great migration of Americans to the Midwest and West.

▲ The success of the Erie Canal led to a surge of canal building throughout the United States. This is an image of the Ohio & Erie Canal, a canal that was built in Ohio and led to Lake Erie. This photo was taken at the Ohio Erie Canal Visitor Center in Valley View, Ohio.

Americans moved westward looking for a better life, to get away from overcrowding in Eastern cities, or just for the adventure of it.

Thousands of farm families passed through the canal on their way to the fertile lands farther west. In the 1830s, canal boat records often read, "Flour, wool, and hides eastbound, farmers westbound."[8] At Buffalo, the settlers took ships across Lake Erie to Cleveland, Toledo, or Detroit. Many continued westward by land to Michigan and Wisconsin, or crossed the Mississippi River and kept on going west.

When the Erie Canal was opened in 1825, the population of the West was about 2.5 million. By 1850, it was about 7.5 million—more than a quarter of the country's total population.[9]

Soon, canals were popping up all over the country. By 1840, there were 3,300 miles of canal in the United States. None of these waterways were as successful as the Erie Canal. The cost of construction was high and by the end of the 1830s the economy was not doing very well.[10]

Shaping the Civil War

When the Civil War loomed over the nation, it turned out to be important that so much westward migration had gone through the Erie Canal. Up until the canal was opened, most settlers in the Midwest were southerners who had come up the

Mississippi and Ohio rivers. Most of the settlers who came through the canal were New Yorkers and other Yankees. Soon, Northerners had the strongest influence on the Midwestern states and territories.[11]

Many Midwesterners had strong ties to the Northern states. They were participating in the North's industrial revolution. Most Midwesterners were anti-slavery and loyal to the Union.

The canal also provided the Northern states with agricultural products, so the Union was not dependent on the farms of the South.

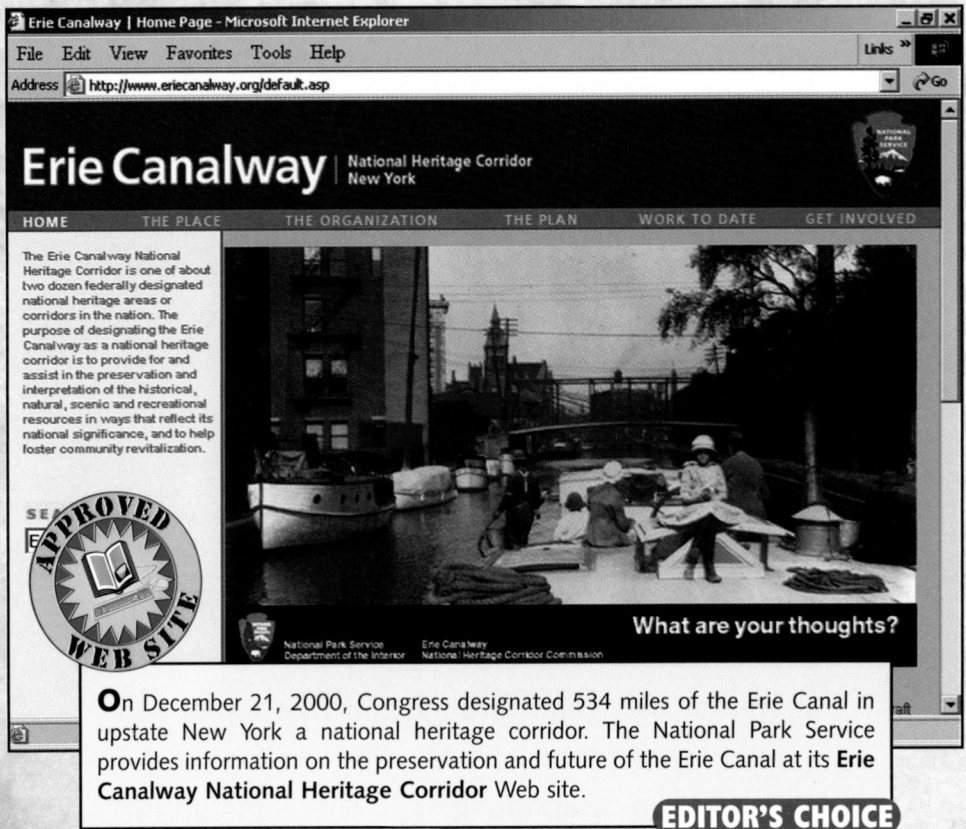

On December 21, 2000, Congress designated 534 miles of the Erie Canal in upstate New York a national heritage corridor. The National Park Service provides information on the preservation and future of the Erie Canal at its **Erie Canalway National Heritage Corridor** Web site.

EDITOR'S CHOICE

Progress and Change

The popular song "Low Bridge, Everybody Down," also called "Fifteen Years on the Erie Canal," was written by Thomas S. Allen in 1905. Allen was an early twentieth-century composer of popular songs. The song became famous for the mule named Sal.

Mules and horses had always moved boats along the Erie Canal, even though steamboats were used on the Hudson River and the Great Lakes. That was because the canal's walls were too delicate to withstand the waves and vibrations stirred up by a steam engine.

In the early twentieth century, the Erie Canal was widened and deepened again. Then steamboats could tow boats through the canal, itself. When Allen wrote his song, tow mules and horses were becoming obsolete. Their jobs were being taken over by steamboats. That is why Allen says that "We'd better look round for a job, old gal."

"Fifteen Years on the Erie Canal"

I've got an old mule and her name is Sal,
Fifteen years on the Erie Canal.
She's a good old worker and a good old pal,
Fifteen years on the Erie Canal.

We've hauled some barges in our day,
Filled with lumber, coal, and hay,
And every inch of the way I know
From Albany to Buffalo.

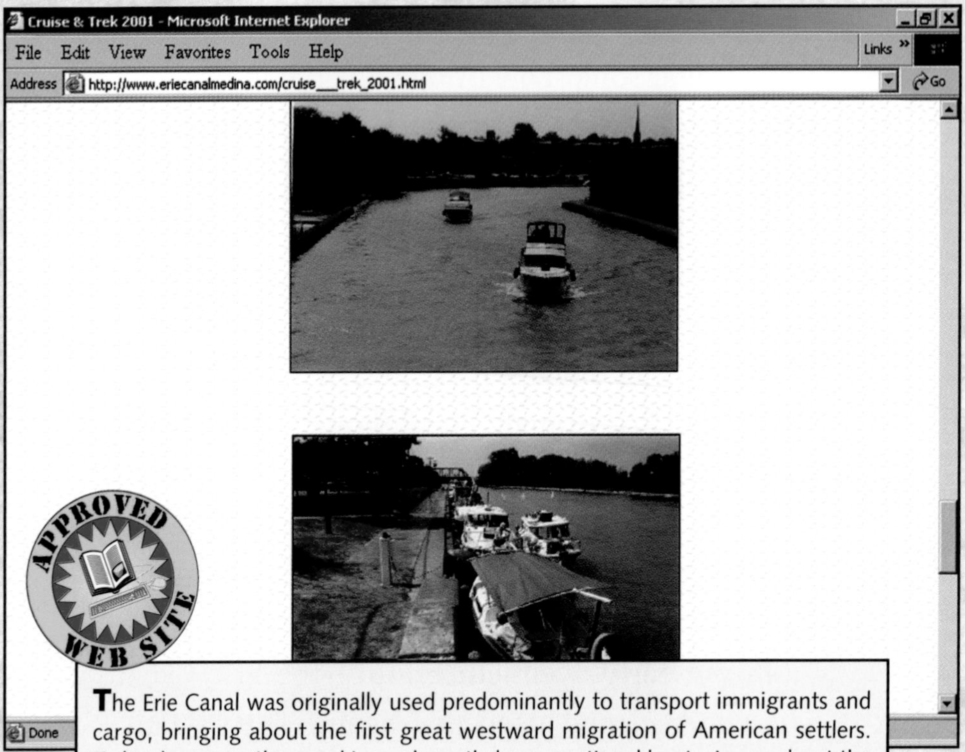
Cruise & Trek 2001 - Microsoft Internet Explorer
File Edit View Favorites Tools Help
Links
Address http://www.eriecanalmedina.com/cruise__trek_2001.html
Go
APPROVED WEB SITE
Done

The Erie Canal was originally used predominantly to transport immigrants and cargo, bringing about the first great westward migration of American settlers. Today, however, the canal is used mostly by recreational boats. Learn about the importance of Medina, New York, a canal town, in history at **The Erie Canal in Medina, NY** Web site.

(chorus)

Low bridge, everybody down!
Low bridge, we must be getting near a town
You can always tell your neighbor,
You can always tell your pal,
If he's ever navigated on the Erie Canal.

We'd better look round for a job, old gal,
Fifteen years on the Erie Canal.
You bet your life I wouldn't part with Sal,
Fifteen years on the Erie Canal,
Giddap there gal we're passed that lock,

We'll make Rome 'fore six o'clock,
So one more trip and then we'll go,
Right straight back to Buffalo.

(repeat chorus)[12]

American history is partly a story of change in transportation technology. Before the Erie Canal was built, Conestoga wagons carried farm produce from the West to Baltimore. The wagons returned westward with manufactured goods. But a wagon or stagecoach on a rough road could not compete with the speed and convenience of the canal. Eventually, canals and railroads drove Conestoga wagons out of business.

The Erie Canal was America's major commercial highway for about fifty years, until railroads became popular. Railroads were cheaper to build than canals. Trains could cross mountains, and they were faster than canal boats. Today, America's canals are mostly used for pleasure boating. How-ever, the great Midwestern Rivers such as the Ohio and Mississippi have been canalized. They are among the United States' most important transportation systems.

Even so, the Erie Canal was the technical marvel of its age, and remains one of the all-time greatest feats of American engineering.

Report Links

The Internet sites described below can be accessed at
http://www.myreportlinks.com

▶**The Erie Canal**
Editor's Choice This site is devoted to the appreciation and understanding of the Erie Canal.

▶**New York Archives Erie Canal Time Machine**
Editor's Choice Visit the New York Archives to learn about the Erie Canal.

▶**Erie Canalway National Heritage Corridor**
Editor's Choice Read about one of the nationally designated heritage areas.

▶**Rochester Images: The Erie Canal**
Editor's Choice A collection of historical photos and documents connected to the Erie Canal.

▶**The Erie Canal: A Journey Through History**
Editor's Choice This is a multimedia tour of the Erie Canal.

▶**History of the Erie Canal**
Editor's Choice The University of Rochester offers an historical overview of the Erie Canal.

▶**Big Apple History: The Erie Canal**
PBS presents this Erie Canal Web site for young people.

▶**A Biography of America: The Erie Canal**
This article looks at how a country was transformed when the Erie Canal was built.

▶**The Canal Age**
Archaeology Magazine presents an article on the history of American canals and tunnels.

▶**Canal Culture**
This is a brief history of the Erie Canal.

▶**Digging Clinton's Ditch: The Impact of the Erie Canal on America, 1807–1860**
This site looks at the importance of the Erie Canal to the state of New York and to the nation.

▶**Dreams of Steam: The History of Steam Power**
Learn about the power of steam from this site.

▶**The Erie Canal: From Lockport to Buffalo**
Read a history of the canal and view descriptive pictures.

▶**The Erie Canal in Medina, N.Y.**
This is a history of the canal town at Medina.

▶**Fate of Buffalo Canal District Tied to Ageless Impact of Erie Canal**
This Web site looks at the preservation of the canal.

Report Links

The Internet sites described below can be accessed at
http://www.myreportlinks.com

▶ **The Founder of Gotham's Fortunes**
Read about De Witt Clinton, one of the men responsible for making New York great.

▶ **Harriet Beecher Stowe Center**
This Center and its Web site are dedicated to the life and works of Harriet Beecher Stowe.

▶ **The History of Concrete and the Nabataeans**
Read this interesting history of concrete.

▶ **Irish Immigration**
This is a short article on Irish immigrants.

▶ **The Life of John Fitch**
Read about the life and times of John Fitch.

▶ **The Making of a Great Nation**
This article discusses the impact of the Erie Canal.

▶ *Marco Paul's Travels on the Erie Canal*
Become part of a fictional trip with accurate geographical descriptions and historical references.

▶ **New York State Erie Canal**
This site provides information about canals located in New York State.

▶ **Notes on Canal History and Engineering**
This is a history of canals from all over the world.

▶ **"1 New Three-handed Batteau"**
Read about the expedition of 1792 that changed the landscape of New York.

▶ **Robert Fulton**
The Hudson River Maritime Museum offers this essay.

▶ **Virtual American Biographies**
A collection of biographies of important Americans, including De Witt Clinton.

▶ **The War of 1812**
This is an overview of the War of 1812.

▶ **Waterways and Canal Construction, 1700–1825, Buffalo, N.Y.**
An excerpt from a book on the history of the canal.

▶ **Welcome to the Erie Canal Museum**
Visit the official Web site of the Erie Canal Museum.

aqueduct—A structure built to allow the waters of a canal to continue to flow over a river.

berm—A raised protective wall; a raised path at the edge of a canal.

canawler—Someone who lives and works on canal boats.

capita—The population of an area.

contractor—Person with a formal agreement, or contract, to do a specific job.

courier—Someone who delivers official documents, a messenger.

culvert—An underground or underwater drain.

delegate—Person chosen to represent another person or group.

dignitary—Person of high rank or position.

engineer—Someone trained in the design and construction of buildings and other building projects.

lock—A thruway in a canal with gates at either end that is used to raise or lower ships so that they can safely get from one stretch of water to another.

obsolete—No longer useful because replaced by something newer.

oscillate—To swing back and forth between two points.

packet boats—Canal boats for passengers.

pompous—Showy, impressive.

reservoir—A lake made by humans that is used for storing water.

sequence—Events that happen one after another in order.

shanties—Poorly built shacks.

simultaneously—At the same time.

slip scraper—A type of plow also known as a "scoop shovel." Horses would pull the plow, which removed the earth as it scraped along.

spillway—A passage that captures water as it spills over a structure such as a lock or a dam. This prevents the flooding of the land along the water.

surveyors—People with the training to measure land areas.

technology—The use of technical knowledge, tools, and skills.

transients—Those who stay in a place for only a short time.

version—An account from a particular point of view.

Chapter 1. Low Bridge, Everybody Down

1. Nathaniel Hawthorne, "The Canal Boat," *New-England Magazine,* No. 9, December, 1835, pp. 398–409. From Roger W. Hecht, *The Erie Canal Reader, 1790–1950* (Syracuse, New York: Syracuse University Press, 2003), pp. 77–85.

2. Peter L. Bernstein, *Wedding of the Waters; The Erie Canal and the Making of a Great Nation* (New York: W.W. Norton, 2005), p. 37.

3. Carol Sheriff, *The Artificial River: The Erie Canal and the Paradox of Progress, 1817–1862* (New York, Hill and Wang, 1996), p. 70.

4. "The Erie Canal: From the Journal of Thomas S. Woodcock, 1836," *Traveling the Erie Canal, 1836,* http://www.eyewitnesstohistory.com/eriecanal.htm> (September 8, 2005).

5. Caroline Gilman, "The Poetry of Travelling in the United States." From Roger W. Hecht, *The Erie Canal Reader, 1790–1950* (Syracuse, New York: Syracuse University Press, 2003), p. 87.

6. "Low Bridge Everybody Down (Fifteen Years on the Erie Canal)" as posted at <http://www.archives.nysed.gov/projects/eriecanal/ErieArchives/Archivelbwords.html> (September 8, 2005).

7. Nathaniel Hawthorne, "The Canal Boat." From Roger W. Hecht, *The Erie Canal Reader, 1790–1950* (Syracuse, New York: Syracuse University Press, 2003), p. 78.

8. Ibid., pp. 80–81.

9. "The Raging Canal." From Roger W. Hecht, *The Erie Canal Reader, 1790–1950* (Syracuse, New York: Syracuse University Press, 2003), pp. 112–113.

10. Mark Twain, "The Aged Pilot Man," from *Roughing It.* From Roger W. Hecht, *The Erie Canal Reader, 1790–1950* (Syracuse, New York: Syracuse University Press, 2003), pp. 112–113.

11. Jonathan Pearson, *Diary, July 25, 1833,* as posted at <http://www.eriecanal.org/UnionCollege/Recollections_and_Reflections.html> (September 8, 2005).

12. Frances Trollope, "Domestic Manners of the Americans." From Roger W. Hecht, *The Erie Canal Reader, 1790–1950* (Syracuse, New York: Syracuse University Press, 2003), p. 66.

13. Samuel Hopkins Adams, *Grandfather Stories,* as posted at "Reviewed by Suzanne S. Barnhill, November 28, 2000" <home.earthlink.net/~wordsintotype/GrandfatherStories .pdf>.

Chapter 2. Westward by Water

1. Peter L. Bernstein, *Wedding of the Waters; The Erie Canal and the Making of a Great Nation* (New York: W.W. Norton, 2005), p. 83.

2. Ibid., p. 62.

3. Carol Sheriff, *The Artificial River: The Erie Canal and the Paradox of Progress, 1817–1862* (New York, Hill and Wang, 1996), p.10.

4. Bernstein, p. 85.

5. "Circa 1803," *Lewis & Clark,* n.d., <http://www.pbs. org/lewisandclark/inside/circa.html> (September 8, 2005).

6. Sheriff, p. 15.

7. Ibid., p. 17.

8. "Inventors: John Fitch and Steamboats," <http:// inventors.about.com/library/inventors/bljohnfitch.htm> (September 8, 2005).

9. "Letter from Robert Fulton to President George Washington, February 5th, 1797" as posted at <http:// www.history.rochester.edu/canal/fulton/feb1797.htm> (September 8, 2005).

10. "Inventors: The History of Steamboats, John Fitch and Robert Fulton," <http://inventors.about.com/library/ inventors/blsteamship.htm> (September 8, 2005).

11. Robert H. Thurston, *Robert Fulton, His Life and Its Result—Part IV,* as posted at <http://inventors.about.com/ library/inventors/blfulton3.htm> (September 8, 2005).

12. Ibid.

13. Bernstein, p. 102.

14. Ibid., p. 104.

15. Ibid., p. 106.

16. Ibid., p. 124–125.

17. Ibid., p. 186.

18. Richard Hofstadter, William Miller, and Daniel Aaron, *The United States: The History of a Republic* (Englewood Cliffs, New Jersey, 1962), p. 199.

Chapter 3. Digging the "Big Ditch"

1. Carol Sheriff, *The Artificial River: The Erie Canal and the Paradox of Progress, 1817–1862* (New York, Hill and Wang, 1996), p. 17.

2. "Erie Canal—175th Anniversary: Monument of Progress" <http://www.eriecanal.org/UnionCollege/175th .html> (September 10, 2005).

3. Peter L. Bernstein, *Wedding of the Waters; The Erie Canal and the Making of a Great Nation* (New York: W.W. Norton, 2005), p. 192.

4. Ibid., p. 259.

5. F. Daniel Larkin, "Building the "Grand Canal," <http://www.archives.nysed.gov/projects/eriecanal/ ErieEssay/b.html> (September 10, 2005).

6. Ibid.

7. M. Paul Keesler, *Mohawk: Discovering the Valley of the Crystals,* "Chapter Ten—The Canals" <http://www .paulkeeslerbooks.com/ErieCanal.html> (September 10, 2005).

8. Carol Sheriff, *The Artificial River: The Erie Canal and the Paradox of Progress, 1817–1862* (New York, Hill and Wang, 1996), p. 41.

9. Ibid., p. 43.

10. Ibid., p. 42

11. Bernstein, p. 209.

12. Ibid., pp. 209–210. [Note: this book includes a good illustration of the stump-removal machine.]

13. John Bowman, et al., *American Folklore and Legend* (Pleasantville, N.Y.: The Reader's Digest Association, Inc., 1978), p. 138.

14. Richard C. Schmal, "Pioneer History," *Lowell Tribune,* June 29, 2004, p. 10, as posted at <http://www.lowellpl .lib.in.us/s2004jun.htm> (October 23, 2005).

15. Bernstein, pp. 210–211.

16. Sheriff, p. 44.

17. Bernstein, p. 213.

18. Sheriff, p. 30.

19. Bernstein, pp. 35–37.

20. [NOTE: There is a nice animation of locks for horse-drawn boats at http://www.eriecanal.org/locks.html]

21. Jacob Abbott, *Marco Paul's Travels on the Erie Canal,* "Chapter V. Canajoharie" (Harper & Brothers, 1852) as posted at <http://www.history.rochester.edu/canal/bib/ abbott/chapter5.htm> (September 10, 2005).

22. Ibid.

23. "Erie Canal" <http://www.canals.org/erie.htm> (September 10, 2005)

Chapter 4. Celebrations and Adventures

1. Richard Hofstadter, William Miller, and Daniel Aaron, *The United States: The History of a Republic* (Englewood Cliffs, New Jersey, 1962), p. 199.

2. Peter L. Bernstein, *Wedding of the Waters; The Erie Canal and the Making of a Great Nation* (New York: W.W. Norton, 2005), p. 261.

3. "Governor Dewitt Clinton's Dream" as posted at <http://www.canals.state.ny.us/cculture/history/finch/> (September 11, 2005).

4. Bernstein, pp. 311–312.

5. Carol Sheriff, *The Artificial River: The Erie Canal and the Paradox of Progress, 1817-1862* (New York, Hill and Wang, 1996), p. 34.

6. Bernstein, p. 316.

7. Sheriff, p. 74.

8. Jonathan Pearson, *The Diary of Jonathan Pearson,* "August 17, 1833," as posted at <http://www.eriecanal .org/UnionCollege/The_Pier.html> (September 11, 2005).

9. As posted at <http://www.ogdenny.com/Tour/ 2004/tour045.htm> (September 11, 2005).

10. Nathaniel Hawthorne, "The Canal Boat," *New-England Magazine,* No. 9, December, 1835, pp. 398–409. From Roger W. Hecht, *The Erie Canal Reader, 1790–1950* (Syracuse, New York: Syracuse University Press, 2003), pp. 77–85.

11. F. Daniel Larkin, "The Canallers," <http://www .archives.nysed.gov/projects/eriecanal/ErieEssay/c.html> (September 10, 2005).

12. Ibid.

13. Sheriff, p. 53.

14. Ibid.

15. "Canal Music," <http://xroads.virginia.edu/~MA02/ volpe/canal/music_body.html> (September 10, 2005).

16. "Traveling the Erie Canal, 1836" <http://www .eyewitnesstohistory.com/eriecanal.htm> (September 10, 2005).

17. Harriet Beecher Stowe, "The Canal Boat." From Roger W. Hecht, *The Erie Canal Reader, 1790–1950* (Syracuse, New York: Syracuse University Press, 2003), p. 98.

18. Sheriff, p. 60.

19. Harriet Beecher Stowe, "The Canal Boat." From Roger W. Hecht, *The Erie Canal Reader, 1790–1950* (Syracuse, New York: Syracuse University Press, 2003), p. 100.

20. Sheriff, p. 73.

21. Ibid., p. 75.

22. M. Paul Keesler, *Mohawk: Discovering the Valley of the Crystals,* "Chapter Ten—The Canals" <http://www .paulkeeslerbooks.com/ErieCanal.html> (September 10, 2005).

Chapter 5. Supporters and Builders

1. Crowder Associates, "New York State Canal's History," *NYCANAL.com,* 1997–2006, <http://www.nycanal .com/nycanalhistory.html> (February 2, 2006).

2. "John Bloomfield Jervis Papers,' *Jervis Public Library,* August 1999, <http://clrc.org/digital/jervis/jervisindex.htm> (February 2, 2006).

3. Noble E. Whitford, "Building the Erie," *History of the Canal System of the State of New York,* 1905, as reposted at <http://www.history.rochester.edu/canal/bib/whitford/1906/Chap02.html> (February 2, 2006).

Chapter 6. How the Erie Canal Changed America

1. Nathaniel Hawthorne, "The Canal Boat," *New-England Magazine,* No. 9, December, 1835, pp. 398–409. From Roger W. Hecht, *The Erie Canal Reader, 1790–1950* (Syracuse, New York: Syracuse University Press, 2003), pp. 77–85.

2. "State of New York Report on The Barge Canal, Legislative Document 1961," as posted on <http://www.bethpagecommunity.com/Schools/socialst/k5/eriedbq.htm> (September 11, 2005).

3. M. Paul Keesler, *Mohawk: Discovering the Valley of the Crystals,* "Chapter Ten—The Canals" <http://www.paulkeeslerbooks.com/ErieCanal.html> (September 10, 2005).

4. "In Love With Progress" http://www.pbs.org/wnet/historyofus/web04/segment3_p.html (September 10, 2005).

5. "Shaping the Age of Expansion." <http://xroads.virginia.edu/~MA02/volpe/canal/impact_body.html> (September 10, 2005).

6. Peter M. Chaitin, et. al, *Story of the Great American West* (Pleasantville, N.Y.: The Reader's Digest Association, Inc., 1977), p. 60.

7. Samuel Hopkins Adams, "The Canal Wife." From Roger W. Hecht, *The Erie Canal Reader, 1790–1950* (Syracuse, New York: Syracuse University Press, 2003), pp. 156–158.

8. "Beyond Massachusetts, Rhode Island, and Connecticut," excerpted from Ralph J. Crandall, *New England's Migration Fever: The Expansion of America* as posted at <http://www.usgennet.org/family/bliss/states/migrate.htm> (October 23, 2005).

9. Bernstein, p. 350.

10. Mary Beth Norton, et al., *A People & Nation: A History of the United States: Volume I: To 1877* (Boston: Houghton Mifflin Company, 1990), p. 246.

11. M. Paul Keesler, *Mohawk: Discovering the Valley of the Crystals,* "Chapter Ten—The Canals" <http://www .paulkeeslerbooks.com/ErieCanal.html> (September 10, 2005).

12. "Low Bridge Everybody Down (Fifteen Years on the Erie Canal)" as posted at <http://www.archives.nysed.gov/ projects/eriecanal/ErieArchives/Archivelbwords.html> (September 8, 2005).

Bial, Raymond. *The Canals*. New York: Benchmark Books, 2002.

Crompton, Samuel Willard. *Gouverneur Morris: Creating a Nation*. Berkeley Heights, N.J.: Enslow Publishers, Inc., 2004.

Levy, Janey. *The Erie Canal: A Primary Source History of the Canal That Changed America*. New York: Rosen Publishing Group, 2002.

Landau, Elaine. *Canals*. New York: Children's Press, 2001.

Mader, Jan. *Great Lakes*. New York: Scholastic, 2004.

Murray, Julie. *Erie Canal*. Edina, Minn. Abdo Publishing Co., 2005.

Myers, Anna. *Hoggee*. New York: Walker Books for Young Readers, 2004.

Santella, Andrew. *The Erie Canal*. Minneapolis, Minn.: Compass Point Books, 2005.

Stein R. Conrad. *The Erie Canal*. New York: Children's Press, 2004.

Ylvisaker, Anne. *Lake Erie*. Mankato, Minn.: Capstone Press, 2004.